THE ROSWELL ENCYCLOPEDIA

THE

ROSWELL

ENCYCLOPEDIA

Kevin D. Randle, Ph.D.

Quill
A HarperResource Book
An Imprint of HarperCollins*Publishers*

HarperCollins books may be purchased for educational, business, or sales
promotional use. For information please write: Special Markets Department,
HarperCollins Publishers Inc., 10 East 53rd Street, New York, NY 10022.

FIRST EDITION

Designed by Christine Weathersbee

Library of Congress Cataloging-in-Publication Data has been applied for.

ISBN 0-380-79853-0

00   01   02   03   04 ❖/   10   9   8   7   6   6   5   4   3   2

INTRODUCTION

Over the last decade there has been a great deal of information produced about the events outside of Roswell, New Mexico, during the summer of 1947. Some of it has been accurate, some of it has been inaccurate, some of it has been the invention of those seeking the spotlight or who desire to prove that what fell was something of an extraterrestrial nature, and some of it has been little more than wishful thinking. There have been writers who have believed that they had provided the evidence that what fell was alien, and there have been writers who believed they have provided evidence that what fell was terrestrial and mundane in nature. There has been a great deal of information discussed by both governmental sources and private citizens. There has been so much of it that only those who have spent a great deal of time and effort understand any of it. And so much of the data has been skewed that it is nearly impossible to wade through the mud and muck to come to any sort of intelligent conclusion about what really happened.

There is some agreement between the believers and the debunkers. Nearly everyone believes that Mack Brazel, a rancher living near Corona, drove into Roswell to report a field filled with metallic debris. Brazel, out on the range the day before, had found the debris. He told the sheriff, George Wilcox, about it and Wilcox, in turn, suggested that he inform the officers at Roswell Army Air Field (RAAF). Major Jesse Marcel Sr. took the phone call, arranged to meet with Brazel, and then followed him out to the ranch.

Marcel, the air intelligence officer, was accompanied by Captain Sheridan Cavitt, the chief counterintelligence officer at Roswell. Marcel later said that the field was filled with strange metallic material that wouldn't burn and wouldn't dent. He said that it covered an area about three-quarters of a mile by several hundred feet.

Cavitt at first denied that he had even been in Roswell, but later confirmed that he had gone out with Marcel. Cavitt said that he recognized the material as part of a balloon. He thought nothing about it at the time and certainly couldn't understand the interest it has generated in the last part of the twentieth century.

The U.S. Army did announce, on July 8, 1947, that they had "captured a flying saucer," but within hours had changed the story. According to Eighth Air Force headquarters in Fort Worth, Texas, the metallic debris was nothing stranger than parts of a radar reflector and a weather balloon, and that the officers in Roswell had overreacted to the stories of flying saucers that had been appearing in newspapers in the days preceding the discovery by Brazel.

The story stalled at that point. Reporters did not talk to any of the principals in the case. One reporter, J. Bond Johnson, took six pictures of the balloon and radar detector in the office of the commanding general of the Eighth Air Force. All the available evidence seemed to suggest that what Brazel had found and Marcel recovered was nothing more exciting than a balloon. It wasn't until Marcel was interviewed more than thirty-five years later that UFO researchers learned that what crashed was something other than a balloon.

The real question today is whether it is still possible to boil all that data down so that some sort of insight can be found hidden deep within it. If only basic information is provided, a "just the facts" type of presentation, might it be possible for those with a less than obsessive interest in the Roswell case to understand it without devoting a lifetime to the research?

That is the purpose here: Begin at a point that is beyond the

basics and provide the latest, and the best, of the Roswell information. Look at it from the point of view of the best information available, whether pro or con. Attempt to give that information without
a "spin" put on it. Ask the right questions so that the case can be
understood by those who have not devoted months, or years, to its
study.

Yes, I realize my own personal bias is going to show through,
but only when my intelligence is insulted by those arguing a point
of view. When evidence is presented that is obviously skewed, I can't
help but comment on it. When Captain (later Lieutenant Colonel)
Sheridan Cavitt, who traveled to the Brazel debris field with Major
(later Lieutenant Colonel in the Reserve) Jesse Marcel Sr. tells the
official Air Force investigator, Colonel Richard Weaver, that he
didn't pass any guards or roadblocks and that he wasn't sworn to
secrecy, it becomes necessary to point out that Cavitt's memories of
the event don't agree with those of his fellow soldiers. His statements are without corroboration, and there are several others who
tell a different tale about roadblocks and secrecy and who do corroborate one another.

For example, Lewis Rickett, Cavitt's second in command, who
said that he accompanied Cavitt out to the impact site on one of
the trips, talked, on audiotape, of going through MP roadblocks.
Jud Roberts, one of the owners of Roswell's radio station (KGFL),
said that he remembered military cars on the roads leading to the
crash site with MPs standing nearby to stop and control traffic. And
Roswell Air Field Provost Marshal Edwin Easley said that he was, in
fact, sworn to secrecy concerning these specific events. In this situation, who should be believed? The one man who originally said that
he wasn't even in Roswell at the time of the events, only to admit
later that he was, or those who haven't been caught in that sort of
misrepresentation?

It is also difficult to read the first Air Force Final Report on
Roswell, written in 1994, in which Colonel Weaver wrote that the
Air Force had made a good-faith effort to learn what they could

about the case, knowing that this isn't true. No, that is not a matter of opinion, but a matter of provable fact. In the text of the report, Weaver and his co-author James McAndrew quote from an affidavit written by Sallye Tadolini. They quote from the first paragraph, in which it sounds as if the strange metallic debris she handled is explainable as the remnants of a Project Mogul balloon array, the Air Force's proposed answer. They do not quote from the second paragraph in which it is obvious that the debris is not something that came from Mogul. It is clear from her description that the debris, whatever it was, was highly unusual. The debris, according to her affidavit, unfolds itself without a sign of a wrinkle or a crease.

Or why, in that first final report, Weaver and McAndrew quote from *The Roswell Events*, compiled by Fred Whiting of the Fund for UFO Research, proving that they have had access to the document, but do not attempt to discover exactly what Major Easley told me? They could read the transcript included in that report and learn that he told me repeatedly in that conversation that he had, in fact, been sworn to secrecy. This suggests that something unusual had fallen in Roswell and that military officers were sworn to secrecy, directly contradicting what Cavitt had said and the Air Force now claimed.

I could go on, but the Air Force report, and the Second Final Report, issued a couple of years later, are examined in the course of this work. It is difficult to report on those two documents and Air Force statements about them without editorial comment. They are, frankly, an insult to the intelligence of anyone who reads them. It is clear what the Air Force wanted to do, and it wasn't to make a good-faith effort as they claimed. It was to explain away the whole of the Roswell case without providing any solution for it.

In fact, I was curious about what instructions Weaver had received from his superiors and the Secretary of the Air Force when he was given the assignment to investigate Roswell. I believed then, and I believe now, that there would be interoffice memos, letters from the Secretary of the Air Force to Weaver, minutes of meetings in which the investigation was discussed, and a hundred other arenas that would leave documentation. My two Freedom of Information Act requests to the Office of the Secretary of the Air Force were sent back, as the law requires, telling me that all information had been sent to the Government Printing Office. This is, of course, absurd. There is no way that the documentation I wanted was sent to the Government Printing Office. The Government Printing Office is not an archive in which correspondence between Air Force personnel and the Secretary of the Air Force would be stored. The GPO is not a huge filing cabinet, but a printing office. The only documents they would retain would be those relating to the printing of the report, not the directives, orders, instructions, and minutes of meetings that lead up to the creation of the document.

That trouble is, of course, one of the reasons for this book to exist. The Air Force has weighed in with two long reports on Roswell, neither of which makes much sense, but they do throw out a lot of information, some of it relevant to the discussion. But there is another reason as well. Much of what we initially believed about the case has proven to be wrong. Further investigation by those interested has turned up new, and sometimes very disappointing, information.

Glenn Dennis, the Roswell mortician, seemed, in 1990, to provide an important key to the case. He talked of a nurse he had last seen in 1947 who had told him of alien bodies. It was a wonderful story that smacked of government duplicity in the disappearance of the nurse. They were hiding her so that we, the investigators, couldn't get the last little bit of information that we needed from a reluctant and important witness. We searched for her for five or six years but never found a trace. That new part of the story, including the results of the investigation, needs to be told now so that others aren't confused by the tales told by Dennis.

There are many other stories that aren't told here simply because there is nothing new to tell about them. Lydia Sleppy, a Roswell teletype operator, told Bill Moore and Stan Friedman, two of the earliest Roswell investigators, that she had been a secretary at one of the Roswell stations. She had been putting the story of the flying saucer crash over the teletype when the FBI interrupted her, telling her that she was not to finish. Nothing new can be added to that tale. She has told it several times and I spoke to her a number of years ago. The only new bit of information I learned was that she seemed to have compressed the events of two or three days into a single day. That information did not corrupt her tale, nor did it add anything of importance to the investigation.

Or take the story of the archaeologists provided by Mary Ann Gardner, a nurse who lives on the East Coast. She told of a dying cancer patient who had seen "little men" at the scene of a flying saucer crash in 1947. It seemed that Gardner's cancer patient was one of the missing archaeologists. There is no reason to disbelieve what she says about the tale or what she claims the cancer patient told her. On the other hand, nothing new has been learned about this small segment of the Roswell story. The name of the patient has eluded us, so we are unable to corroborate it. There is no reason to retell the story because it was told in its entirety the first time.

A note should now be made about the construction of this book and the entries themselves. Some entries are just information about specific people, events, and locations. I hoped that it would make the case clearer to those who are coming to it for the first time. I have tried, for example, to include reviews of the relevant Roswell books published in the last twenty years. These are, frankly, reviews written like all reviews and contain my opinions of those books. I have tried to be fair in my evaluations, but I doubt that many will be surprised by my opinions. I have attempted to support these opinions with facts.

Other reports are more essay than "encyclopedia" entries. They provide the relevant data on the specific aspects of the case and the supporting evidence about them. I have tried to avoid pejorative words and phrases, but once again, I do have some strong opinions about aspects of this case. While the intent was to provide the reader with the latest information as factually as possible, it is also true that my bias has sometimes colored my thinking.

There are entries provided in which I have made no commentary. For example, Kent Jeffrey, a Roswell skeptic, received a letter from three retired colonels who had at one time been members of the Air Force's Foreign Technology Division (FTD) at Wright-Patterson Air Force Base. FTD evolved from the Air Technical Intelligence Center (ATIC), where the Roswell crash materials may have been sent in 1947. The text of their letter is included here without any comment by me. We get their opinion of the reality of the situation at Wright-Patterson, and although there were comments I wanted to make, points that I thought needed clarification, I decided to allow the reader to form his or her own opinions about the validity of their letter.

What we have here can be seen as a book exploring the Roswell case from the perspective of the late 1990s. It contains the latest information about various aspects of the case and reveals where we all have gone astray in the past. It provides an insight into the backgrounds and the credibility of certain witnesses who have moved to the forefront of the Roswell case. It also provides some commentary on the investigators of the case, for in order to understand the history, it is necessary to understand the reporters of that history. The book allows the novice to understand all of this and provides the expert with the latest—and best—available information.

For those who want more information, UFO Crash at Roswell is as good a basic text as any. It provides the basis for understanding the Roswell case. The Truth About the UFO Crash at Roswell provides a great deal of updated information (as of 1994), but it has a major failing: It reports the Glenn Dennis story and the Jim Ragsdale story as if they are established fact. Today we see the holes in their reports, but in 1994 there was no good reason to reject these tales outright. They are interesting but badly flawed.

All three books, including the present one, provide a decade-long chronicle of the research into the Roswell UFO case. They provide a look at those who have attempted to exploit the interest in the case for personal gain and those who have attempted to contribute, in some fashion, to our understanding of what happened so long ago.

I believe, as I have for the last couple of years, that we now understand what happened outside of Roswell. I don't believe there will be any great new revelation in the future. We have now seen all the relevant facts and had all the important discussions. We will see a fine-tuning of the story as more precise information is uncovered.

It is fair to say that the data and information I have seen lead me to the conclusion that what fell near Roswell was of extraterrestrial origin. I base this not on the sensational stories told by those seeking the spotlight, but on little, subtle things I have discovered during my search. I mentioned Edwin Easley, the provost marshal. He was the man who would have been responsible for security at the site of the crash if there had been one. He told me that he couldn't talk about it because he had been sworn to secrecy and that he believed the craft was of extraterrestrial origin. He didn't say those things because he wanted to see his name in books and appear on television. He told me those things because he believed them to be true based on his own experiences in Roswell in 1947.

There are others who have made similar statements. Some of them were high-ranking officers in the 509th Bomb Group. Others were enlisted men who had some important knowledge. We have seen a great deal of information about the case published and reported in the last decade. Now it is time to evaluate that information and provide the best analysis available. And in this case, I have tried to arrange it so that the reader can provide his or her own evaluation of that information.

We must now weigh all of these statements, both military and civilian, and decide what we want to believe based on the evidence. This book, then, is an attempt to provide that evidence in an objective fashion. It is an attempt to supply the best of the latest information. It is not an attempt to change minds or argue the case. It is just the best information available.

N.B.: Cross-references to other entries in this book are indicated in *boldface italic* type.

Adair, Robin A. Robin A. Adair, the "wire chief," along with Jason Kellahin, a reporter, were dispatched from the Associated Press in Albuquerque to Roswell on July 8, 1947, to cover the breaking story of the flying disc crash. According to him, he was on an assignment in El Paso, Texas, when he received a call from AP headquarters in New York ordering him to Roswell. They told him to rent an airplane if he had to, but to get to Roswell as quickly as he could.

Adair landed at the Roswell municipal airport, but not before he had flown over one of the areas where it was alleged the crash had taken place. "We didn't do a bit of good by it," he said. "We couldn't get any [pictures] . . . even then the place was surrounded by policemen, FBI people. They wouldn't let us in within three-quarters of a mile of the place. We were afraid to go too low. Afraid they would shoot at us.

"We did take a plane up there but we couldn't land anywhere around it. We got as close as we could and we wanted to get lower but the indication [from the ground] was that they really didn't want [us] to." Later he said, "They [the military officers on the field] just waved . . . you couldn't tell if they were waving us off or just politely telling us to get the hell away from there."

From the air, Adair did get a good look at what was later deter-

1

mined to be the debris field. "We could make out a lot of stuff . . . looked like burnt places . . . you could tell that something had been there." The field was large and Adair said, "It was rather hard to line them up from the plane . . . I wanted to find out if they ran east to west or north to south."

Even though he was in an airplane, Adair could see the gouge and tracks on the ground. He said, "You couldn't see them too good from the air . . . apparently the way it cut into [the ground], whatever hit the ground wasn't wood or something soft. It looked like it was metal."

Adair didn't think that it had skipped as it hit the ground. It was his impression that it had come down flat. "Right straight down and right straight back up when it left. It took off the same damned way. It didn't skid off or slide off. It went straight up just like it came straight down."

Adair said that he saw two sites. "One of them wasn't very distinctive. The other was plainer."

After they landed in Roswell, Adair linked up with Jason Kellahin, the other AP reporter, a few minutes later. That evening, they went to the offices of the *Roswell Daily Record*. Adair set up his equipment to transmit photographs over the telephone lines from the newspaper office. According to Adair, "That sometimes runs into quite a little chore. Anyhow, got it done and got the picture moved."

Kellahin confirmed some of this, saying that "We went down to the *Roswell Daily Record* and I wrote a story and we sent it out on the AP wire . . . Adair developed his pictures and set up the wire photo equipment and sent it out."

The next morning, July 9, a new story was published, after Brigadier General Roger Ramey suggested the debris discovered was nothing more than a weather balloon. With the story suddenly dead, both Adair and Kellahin were ordered to return to their regular assignments.

See also ***Brazel, Bill; Brazel, Mack; Debris Field; Exon,***

Brigadier General Arthur; Gouge; Impact Site; Kellahin, Jason;
Roswell Daily Record

Air Force First Final Report on Roswell (1994) See *Report of Air Force Research Regarding the "Roswell Incident"*

Air Force Second Final Report on Roswell (1997) See **Roswell— Case Closed**

Air Intelligence Report No. 100-203-79 This report was officially entitled *Analysis of Flying Object Incidents in the U.S.,* dated 10 December 1948, originally classified as Top Secret, and apparently a joint effort between the Directorate of Intelligence of the Air Force and the Office of Naval Intelligence.

This was a report created to brief high-ranking officers on the unidentified-flying-object situation. It seems that the officers creating the document would have access to all the classified information needed to accurately assess the situation. They would be in a position tell their superiors everything they knew, or could discover, about UFOs, regardless of how highly classified that information might be. And, according to the thinking of many, if Roswell represented the crash of an alien spacecraft, it would be mentioned in this report. Because there was no mention of a crash in this report, many skeptics have suggested that this alone proves there was no flying saucer crash at Roswell.

The purpose of the study, according to the document itself, was "TO EXAMINE patterns of tactics of 'Flying Saucers' (hereinafter referred to as flying objects) and to develop conclusions as to the possibility of existence."

Under facts and discussions, the report said, "THE POSSIBIL-ITY [exists] that reported observations of flying objects over the U.S. were influenced by previous sightings of unidentified phenomena in Europe . . . and that the observers reporting such incidents may have been interested in obtaining personal publicity. . . .

However, these possibilities seem to be improbable when certain selected reports such as the one from U.S. Weather Bureau at Richmond are examined. During the observations of weather balloons at the Richmond Bureau, one well-trained observer has sighted strange metallic disks on three occasions and another observer has sighted a similar object on one occasion. . . . On all four occasions the weather balloon and the unidentified objects were in view through a theodolite [telescope]. . . ."

The report included an interesting paragraph about the origins of the objects. It said, "THE ORIGIN of the devices is not ascertainable. There are two reasonable possibilities: (1) The objects are domestic devices, and if so, their identification or origin can be established by a survey of the launchings of airborne devices . . . (2) Objects are foreign, and if so, it would seem most logical to consider that they are from a Soviet source . . ."

The conclusion drawn by the authors, at the bottom of page two and marked "Top Secret," was the following: "SINCE the Air Force is responsible for control of the air in the defense of the U.S., it is imperative that all other agencies cooperate in confirming or denying the possibility that these objects are of domestic origin. Otherwise, if it is firmly indicated that there is no domestic explanation, the objects are a threat and warrant more active efforts of identification and interception."

And, finally, the report said: "IT MUST be accepted that some type of flying objects have been observed, although their identification and origin are not discernible. In the interest of national defense it would be unwise to overlook the possibility that some of these objects are of foreign origin."

There is one fact that is important when reviewing this document. There are events left out of the Air Intelligence Report because, according to the officers, they did not have access to all areas of military secrecy. The authors admitted, subtly, that they did not have all the privileged information they needed. The report, by itself, does not prove that the Roswell UFO crash didn't happen, or that these officers were lying to their superiors if it did. They didn't know about Roswell, didn't have access to that highly restricted information, and therefore couldn't include it because they simply didn't know about it.

See also **The Real Roswell Crashed-Saucer Coverup**

Alamogordo Army Air Field/Holloman Air Force Base The Alamogordo Army Air Field began life on June 10, 1942, as the Alamogordo Bombing and Gunnery Range. It is located six miles west of Alamogordo, New Mexico, and about eighty-five miles north of El Paso, Texas.

On January 13, 1948, the name of the air field was changed to Holloman Air Force Base, in honor of Colonel George Vernon Holloman, an aviation instrument inventor and early experimenter with guided missiles. Holloman conducted the first instrument-only landing and was awarded the Distinguished Flying Cross for his effort. He was killed in March 1946 in an aircraft accident on Formosa.

During its existence so far, the base has played host to a large number of experiments, including the controversial Project Mogul, which is one of the explanations for the debris found by Mack Brazel. Holloman AFB is an active Air Force base.

See also *Project Mogul*

Alien Autopsy Early in 1995, rumors began to circulate about a piece of film that could prove that the UFO crash at Roswell in July 1947 was real. Philip Mantle of the British UFO Research Association (BUFORA) wrote to a number of UFO investigators who had been specializing in the Roswell crash retrieval, telling them that a film existed showing the autopsy of an alien creature. The alien's body had been recovered after an object had been discovered by military officers in the deserts of New Mexico. Mantle hoped to enlist the researchers' aid in authenticating the film and investigating the circumstances around its creation.

Ray Santilli, the man who owned the film and who had revealed its existence to a limited number of people, said he had been in the United States in 1994, searching for film footage of then-unknown Elvis Presley for a documentary he planned. In 1955, Bill Randle had produced a live rock and roll show in Cleveland that included Bill Haley and the Comets, Pat Boone, and Elvis. Santilli, apparently in search of this specific footage of Elvis, talked to the cameraman who owned the Presley footage and learned of the autopsy film at the same time.

The rumors, many of which were endorsed by Santilli at the time, suggested that the Army cameraman who had filmed the autopsy had somehow managed to keep some of the film. These were outtakes or reels that needed special processing, according to the cameraman, but somehow were never returned to Army control. It seemed to be a fairly cavalier way to handle material that should have been highly classified.

Kent Jeffrey, the man behind "The Roswell Initiative," a petition calling for the end to the secrecy about the Roswell crash, tried to learn more about the autopsy but early on seemed to have had little real luck. According to Jeffrey's information, Santilli had paid about a hundred thousand dollars for the film. The story circulated by Santilli at that time was that the cameraman had made a dupe of the original film so that the Army wouldn't know that some of it was missing. That was, of course, a different story than the film being outtakes.

There were other reports as well. First word was that there were fifteen rolls of film of about ten minutes each. That meant two hours and thirty minutes of film. There was a preliminary autopsy in a tent, more autopsy footage in a hospital operating room, film of the debris field with President Truman walking across it, and pictures of the craft as it was lifted onto a flatbed truck. All of the description sounded as if the film was spectacular and authentic.

Still more information and quite a few rumors were being circulated. In a letter from Philip Mantle in the spring of 1995, sent to various researchers, the cameraman's name was revealed as Jack Barnett. Apparently, according to some sources, Santilli had slipped up and inadvertently revealed the man's name. Searches began trying to locate any Barnett who had a connection to motion picture photography, whether through the military, old newsreel services, or Hollywood.

Several Jack Barnetts were found scattered around the United States, but none seemed to be the right man. Either they were too young or had no connection to photography or to the military. And Santilli began to hint that the Barnett name wasn't quite right. It was really Barrett, but he had allowed the wrong name to circulate as a cover for the real man.

The story of Barnett didn't end there. In the spring of 1999, rumors began to circulate that Barnett had died. To many, this meant that now his identity could be revealed because he was beyond the reach of government investigators and regulations. There was speculation that many of the questions would finally be answered. Within days, however, Bob Shell, editor of *Shutterbug* magazine, posted a message to various computer newsgroups that Barnett hadn't died. The shroud that had hidden his identity would remain in place.

Santilli eventually arranged for members of the media, representatives from television networks around the world, and UFO researchers to screen the film in early 1995. Kent Jeffrey, because of his regular job, could attend the screening. He would later provide a lengthy report on his impressions of that screening. In a special bulletin issued by the *International Roswell Initiative*, dated May 25, 1995, Jeffrey outlined his whole experience in a widely circulatad white paper at the showing of the film earlier that month. He wrote:

The film in question is presently in the possession of a company in London, Merlin Productions, owned by a Mr. Ray Santilli. On Friday, May 5, 1995, there was a special showing at the Museum of London. There were approximately one hundred people present . . . Despite the fact that the film is totally unauthenticated, it has received extensive publicity in Europe . . .

The actual showing of the film took place just after 1:00 P.M. in a small auditorium that is part of the Museum of London complex. A handout was distributed at the sign-in table consisting of a copy of the alleged MJ-12 briefing papers and a yellow cover sheet referencing the 1947 Roswell crash and the 509th Bomb Group (at Roswell Army Air Field). Merlin Productions was apparently very concerned about pictures being taken because everyone was physically searched (frisked) for cameras upon entering the auditorium. There was no speaker or announcement to formally welcome those present or to introduce the film. This seems somewhat bizarre and discourteous, as people had come from all over the world for this showing. Also conspicuously absent was a person on stage afterward to publicly answer questions pertaining to the film. . . .

At about 1:05 P.M., the lights dimmed and the film started rolling. Before the actual pictures began, a few short statements scrolled by on the screen with reference to the film having been "acquired from the cameraman who originally shot the footage" and to the copyright being "exclusively owned by Merlin Communications." Interestingly, one would think that if the film were genuine, the copyright would be "exclusively owned" by the United States government.

Also, contrary to what had been said previously about "10-minute reels," there was now a statement on the screen that the film was recorded on "three-minute" reels. . . .

The film opened abruptly with its single scene of a small operating or autopsy room with plain white walls and a table in the middle containing an unclad body lying face up. Two individuals in white anti-contamination suits, complete with hoods and narrow, rectangular glass face plates, were the only figures visible in the room. A third person, dressed in white hospital-type garb, was visible through a large glass partition, or window. Although he was outside the sealed room standing behind solid glass, he was wearing a surgical mask that covered his entire face. . . .

Jeffrey then described the procedures that were followed in the autopsy as the two doctors circled the body, cutting into it. It is clear that the cameraman was also in the room, circulating and trying to stay out of the way of the doctors. The film was black and white and the focus at times was inadequate.

Jeffrey wrote, "I would like to state up front and unequivocally that there is no (zero!!!) doubt in my mind that this film is a fraud."

In July 1995, more of the cameraman's story began to leak into the public arena. Obviously, the leaks were through Santilli and his organization, but they did provide a few clues. The cameraman, whether under the name of Barnett or anything else, now claimed to have photographed the first atomic test at Trinity Site. Here was something that could be independently verified.

It wasn't long before a list of names of those associated with the Manhattan Project as photographers was developed and circulated. There was no Jack Barnett on the short list. Santilli's cameraman seemed to indicate that he had been in charge, but the name of the man who was in charge was Berlyn Brixner.

John Kirby, a UFO researcher living in Portland, Oregon, wanted to pursue that lead. Using a CD-ROM telephone directory, he easily found a phone number for Brixner. Kirby was apparently the first researcher to call Brixner, a friendly eighty-four-year-old man who wanted to help. He provided Kirby with a list of the men he had worked with as photographers during the Manhattan

Project in the late stages of World War II. Again, Barnett, or Barrett, failed to appear on the list. Santilli had an answer for that. According to Santilli, his man been an Army cameraman who had been on one of the aircraft flying near Trinity Site to photograph the detonation from the air and had never been directly associated with the Manhattan Project. Because of that, he never had the opportunity to meet Brixner, according to Santilli, so it made sense that Brixner didn't know who he was.

All this was just one more area in which what Santilli had said originally didn't seem to fit with what could be established as fact historically. There were Army cameramen involved in the Manhattan Project, but the story told by Santilli's cameraman seemed to be at odds with historical fact. This, of course, caused many to conclude that the cameraman didn't exist.

The whole film of the autopsy, released by Santilli for broadcast by various television networks around the world, lasted just over twenty minutes. In addition, there were scenes of the metallic debris collected and displayed on tables in a single room. A lone figure is seen moving among it, lifting some of it, but he is photographed from the rear so that his identity, like that of those in the autopsy footage, is masked.

Before any of the specials could be aired, the *Sunday Times* in London published an article with the headline FILM THAT "PROVES" ALIENS VISITED EARTH IS A HOAX. The article, written by Maurice Chittenden, reported that "experts called in by Channel 4 [a British television network], which is due to screen the film as part of a documentary on August 28 [1995] have declared it bogus. A source close to the documentary said: 'We have had special effects guys look at it and they say it's a fake.' "

Chittenden continued, "Among the flaws found by the *Sunday Times* are: 'Security coding' on one film disappeared when its accuracy was challenged. A 'letter of authentication' from Kodak was signed by a salesman. President Truman, supposedly visible on the film, was not in New Mexico at the time. Symbols seen on particles of wreckage are totally different to those remembered by an eyewitness. 'Doctors'—performing a supposedly unique autopsy on an alien—remove black lenses from his eyes in a matter of seconds, as if they knew what to expect."

These points were, for the most part, the same that had been raised by UFO researchers during their attempts to verify the authenticity of the film. What was most troubling was not that there were problems, but that the revelation of those problems resulted in an alteration of the story. When evidence was presented that suggested the security markings, for example, were more appropriate to Hollywood, those markings disappeared. That in and of itself suggested the film was a hoax.

Santilli, however, maintained that the film was authentic. To prove it, he was going to allow some of the documentary producers an opportunity to meet with the cameraman. But the meeting never materialized. John Purdie, the producer of the Channel 4 documentary in Great Britain, did receive a phone call from a man who claimed to be the cameraman. They spoke for two minutes and almost no questions were answered.

During the last week of August 1995, some answers about the film would surface. The Channel 4 documentary aired on August 28, but there was nothing in it that hadn't been discussed on the Internet or in various UFO organizations in the weeks before. The most dramatic moments were those of Frank Kaufmann, a former military man who was assigned to the base at Roswell in July 1947 as a civilian employee. He provided his insights into the crash, told how he had participated in the retrieval, and provided an eyewitness account of what the bodies he saw looked like. According to Kaufmann, the alien in the film didn't match those he claimed to have seen himself.

Kodak came up again. In its September 1996 issue, *Fortean Times* reported, "The hint of conspiracy is underlined by Ray Santilli . . . Asked whether he still plans to accept Kodak's offer to analyze the film, he answers: 'With all due respect to Kodak, I simply do not trust an American corporation with lucrative defence contracts.' Way to go, Ray."

Small pieces of the film began to circulate in the spring of 1995, as the story began to leak. A short segment of leader, the opaque strip at the beginning of a movie, was provided for analysis. Kodak confirmed that a coding on it, a square and a triangle, suggested the film might be from 1947. The problem was that Kodak recycled the codes, so the film could have been manufactured in 1927 or 1967. Besides, there were no images on the leader, so it could have been a piece of film from anything or anywhere, not necessarily from the autopsy footage, and therefore proved nothing.

Santilli did provide a few people with small sections of film with some kind of image on them. Philip Mantle had three or four frames that contained a brightly lighted doorway, or what might have been a doorway, that might have been part of the autopsy footage. But Mantle told others that he had no footage with the alien or the interior of the autopsy room visible that would prove that it was part of the film—just that brightly lighted door that might have been part of the original autopsy footage, or might just be a few frames of another film used because the film was from the right era.

Bob Kiviat, producer of *Alien Autopsy: Fact or Fiction,* broadcast on Fox Television in the United States, was also given a small section of film. Again nothing that would identify it as having come from the actual autopsy footage could be seen. His original section of film was even shorter than that provided to Mantle.

Kodak insisted that they could provide fairly accurate dating, but they required several feet of film. They suggested that over the years film would shrink, and by measuring the distance between the sprockets, they could estimate the age. Chemical analysis, especially since the basic composition of film had changed after 1947, could provide additional clues. Kodak insisted that they receive, at a minimum, one frame with the alien visible on it. That way they would know that their analysis was not being wasted. That didn't happen, and from recent statements by Santilli, it appears that it will never happen.

After the British and American specials were aired, there was renewed interest, and Santilli's company began selling raw video-tapes of the autopsy footage for about fifty dollars each. It was claimed that additional footage not seen in the specials was on the video, but that was of the tent autopsy, which was so dark as to be nearly useless as evidence, more of the debris footage, and little else.

It should be noted here that originally Santilli had said there was over two hours of film showing the autopsy and related mater-ial. All the footage reviewed by various researchers, news reporters, and documentarians added up to little more than twenty minutes.

Other problems with the film began to surface. For example, it had been suggested early on that the film showed the autopsy of the body of a being recovered after the Roswell crash. Other informa-tion, including the alleged date of the autopsy and the date of the crash, did not follow the conventional wisdom of the Roswell case. Santilli and his friends, and the cameraman communicating through Santilli, were now suggesting that the crash and recovery had taken place more than a month earlier, in late May 1947.

Almost universally, UFO researchers, television producers and reporters, and anyone else interested in the film were demanding that the cameraman come forward. Without him to complete the chain of custody, the film was nearly useless. Couple this with the fact that Santilli, to that point, had refused to provide anything that would be of value in authenticating the film, and the arguments were all over nothing. The film was just an interesting aberration.

Santilli, through his various contacts, including the editor of *Shutterbug* magazine Bob Shell, finally offered the cameraman's alleged audiotaped statement. Shell, appearing on Cable Radio Network's September 2, 1995, edition of *UFOs Tonight!* hosted by Don Ecker, said that the transcript being circulated by him and Santilli was an exact transcript of the cameraman's statement. Under close questioning by Ecker, Shell said that he had heard the original tape and read or typed the transcript himself. At any rate, the transcript was an exact copy of what the cameraman had said. This discussion, recorded as a matter of course by Ecker, would become important to understanding more about the case.

During the conversation, Ecker said, "Somebody in the United Kingdom sent me allegedly the cameraman's statement, along with some facsimiles that were allegedly the film labels. Now, a number of weeks ago I read this entire statement verbatim on the air. And I think this is somewhat telling in itself. Now, this is purportedly this gentleman's actual statement. And I think it's very safe to say in this statement may be information he originally gave Ray Santilli, this is not the way an American former serviceman would ever describe himself. Have you . . ."

Shell interrupted and said, "What you have is probably the first version of that."

"Yeah," said Ecker. "And what I'm saying [is] this was passed off as his actual statement by Santilli, originally. And I think it's very safe to say that just ain't so, okay? It was passed off deceptively."

Shell responded by saying, "Well, yeah, but I think you have to understand what exactly happened. The cameraman made a taped statement. The tape was mailed to Santilli . . . Santilli had one of his secretaries transcribe it. The secretary is British."

"Okay."

Shell continued. "So quite a bit of British [terminology] got into the transcript . . . I have gone over and retranscribed it and posted it this week on CompuServe's library."

Ecker asked, "From the actual tape?"

"Yes."

"You have a copy of the tape?"

"Yes."

Later, Shell would deny that he had heard the actual tape or that he ever spoken to the cameraman. In other words, Shell, if he repaired the "transcript," did so without having heard the tape himself. It would mean that he was altering the transcript for no reason other than to remove the incriminating British colloqui-alisms from it.

Santilli, when questioned about the transcript, said, using the same excuse given by Shell, that the tape had been transcribed by a British secretary and she had changed the wording. It was a clumsy attempt to explain why common British terms were sprinkled through a statement allegedly made by an American. It also meant that Shell's claim of an exact transcript were false. He had been mis-taken when he said otherwise.

The cameraman claimed he remembered very clearly that he had received a call to go to White Sands. In the statement, in paren-theses, it says Roswell. But Roswell is not the same as White Sands. The missile range at White Sands was, and is, an Army facility, and it is nearly 150 miles from Roswell. If the cameraman was going to White Sands, why not fly him to the Alamogordo Army Air Field, now Holloman Air Force Base, less than twenty miles away? That part of the statement made no sense, unless it was an attempt to keep Roswell attached to the story for the commercial value of the Roswell name.

The cameraman, apparently casually, made a change in the sce-nario that is quite significant. He said, "I was ordered to a crash site just southwest of Socorro."

He was not content to drop that single bomb. He added others, explaining that he had been in St. Louis a few days earlier, where he claimed he had been filming tests of a new ramjet helicopter. He returned to Washington, D.C., where he was given his orders and then flew out of Andrews Army Air Field, on to Wright Field in Dayton, Ohio, and then on to the Roswell Army Air Field. From Roswell, he was driven overland to the crash site.

To anyone who has studied a map or the Roswell case, this makes absolutely no sense. Why fly a cameraman from Washington to Dayton, Ohio, and then on to Roswell? Even if they felt the need to land first in Ohio, the trip on to Roswell makes no sense. Why not fly into Kirtland Air Force Base in Albuquerque or directly into

Alamogordo? In 1947, there was no interstate highway system, but there was U.S. Highway 85. A trip from either base to Socorro was easy and quick. And even today a trip from Roswell to Socorro is long and difficult.

The statement by the cameraman did little to increase knowledge about Roswell. Once again there had been nothing that could be verified properly because there were no names attached to it. There were some researchers who did try to learn who would have been at both the Trinity Test in 1945 and at the "Little Henry" helicopter ramjet tests in St. Louis. No single name surfaced from both those events. In other words, there were two different groups of cameramen assigned.

In October 1995, Television France One (TF1) had finished their documentary about the autopsy film. They'd had access to material that had been unavailable to others as they put together their specials. For example, Nicolas Maillard of TF1 faxed a letter to the public relations department of McDonnell-Douglas (the corporate entity of the former McDonnell Aircraft Company), which confirmed that McDonnell had used their own employees for the photographic work concerning the Little Henry. Chester Turk shot the motion pictures and Bill Schmitt took the stills. No military personnel were used, though Santilli's cameraman had claimed to have been there, and his own statement suggested he was in the Army until 1952, or about five years after those tests had been made.

Although Santilli's promises to others, such as John Purdie of Channel 4 in the United Kingdom and Bob Kiviat of Fox in the United States, that they would be able to speak to the cameraman had not been fulfilled, he made a similar promise to those at TF1. The call, promised in early September 1995, never came. Santilli did agree to submit a list of questions to the cameraman. TF1 drew up the list, and on September 14, about three days after the list was submitted, TF1 received a fax from Santilli with the answers.

Two of the answers were of interest to researchers. TF1 asked,

"What tests of the ramjet 'Little Henry' did you film in St. Louis in May 1947?" The answer from the cameraman was, "The initial tests." This was a claim that was known to be false, given the information provided by McDonnell-Douglas several weeks earlier.

A second question that must have seemed somewhat irrelevant when asked but would become important later was, "Why didn't the Army use color film for such an event [filming the autopsy]?"

The answer was, "I was given instructions to leave immediately to film an aviation crash of a Russian spy plane. I did not have time to order either colour film stock or special camera equipment. I used standard issue film stock and a standard Bell and Howell."

Kent Jeffery wrote in *The MUFON Journal:* "Hypothetically, such an answer could explain why the cameraman didn't use color film at the initial crash scene. However, such an answer in no way explains why he didn't use color film for the autopsies—which he claims took place a month later in July [sic] in Fort Worth, Texas."

TF1, however, wasn't finished with their work. At the end of September 1995, Nicolas Maillard located Cleveland, Ohio, disc jockey Bill Randle, who was the real source of the early Elvis footage that supposedly started this whole episode. This is the footage that Santilli claimed had been sold to him by the cameraman who had also filmed the alien autopsy. According to Randle, the purchase of the Elvis film took place in his office on July 4, 1992, in the presence of Gary Shoefield.

That wasn't the end of it. According to Bill Randle, the footage Santilli bought was two short segments from two concerts held in Cleveland on July 20, 1955. The afternoon concert was at a Cleveland high school and the second at a Cleveland auditorium. The program featured the Four Lads, Bill Haley, Pat Boone, and the then-unknown Elvis Presley. Randle hired a freelance photographer to film the concerts. His named was Jack Barnett.

This provided the information needed to check out Jack Barnett and suggested that Santilli's first statement about the name was accurate. He was born of Russian parents on January 1, 1906, and died in 1967. He had been a newsreel cameraman during World War II, had been in on the Italian campaign, but had not been in the Army.

TF1 planned to confront Santilli with this information to gauge his reaction during a live interview on October 23, 1995, on the special hosted by Jacques Pradel. Once the interview with Bill Randle was played for Santilli, he said, "Well, firstly, I'm very pleased that you have found Bill Randle . . ."

Santilli then provided a new scenario for the discovery of the autopsy footage. Kent Jeffrey wrote in the *MUFON Journal* that "the person from whom he had purchased the Elvis footage was not really a military cameraman after all. He now claimed that he had met the real cameraman after he purchased the rights to the Elvis film from Bill Randle in Cleveland during the summer of 1992 (previously Santilli had given the year as 1993). Everyone, including the host, Jacques Pradel, seemed incredulous . . ."

In the August 28, 1995, Channel 4 documentary, Santilli now referred to the collector who had paid for the autopsy footage. He had said repeatedly that he, Santilli, did not have access to the film itself because the collector had it in a vault. It would be up to the collector to offer samples of the film for analysis. Santilli could do nothing to help researchers.

Through the efforts of the investigative team of TF1, however, the name of the collector was learned. Volker Spielberg was the man who supposedly owned the film. Coincidentally, Spielberg, like Santilli, is in the video distribution business.

During a live interview on TF1, Santilli, when pressed about providing the original film, said that it was out of his hands. TF1 then showed taped clips of Spielberg's business office, and the reporter said that TF1 had learned that Spielberg was not a film collector as claimed. Contrary to what Santilli had said about not knowing Spielberg personally, when questioned by others, TF1 learned of a confidential meeting in Hamburg, Germany, among Spielberg, Santilli, and one or two others. It was revealed that

Santilli and Spielberg are friends and business partners and have worked together on several occasions.

Michael Hesemann, who is working with, if not for, Santilli, has told many that the alien autopsy footage is from someone near Socorro, New Mexico. Hesemann has claimed that he has located the "real" crash site and is the only researcher to have done so. He has also claimed that the real date of this crash is May 31, 1947. Because this is not the Roswell case, Hesemann believes it explains the discrepancies between what researchers have learned about Roswell and the facts that have surfaced around the Santilli autopsy film.

The final and crushing blow for the alien autopsy came in July 1998. Philip Mantle, writing with Tim Matthews, alerted their colleagues in the UFO field that the tent footage was faked. They had found and interviewed one man who claimed to have worked on that segment of the autopsy footage.

According to Mantle, Matthews learned that the tent footage had been created by a British firm in Milton Keynes called A.R.K. Music Ltd. Those who put the tent footage together had experience with video and computer equipment. Mantle and Matthews name the names of those men involved.

In December 1998, the situation became even more complicated. Santilli, learning that Bob Kiviat, who had produced the original autopsy special in the United States for Fox, was now producing a second in which he would show that the tent footage was a fake. The spin began again.

According to Santilli, the tent footage is not part of the alien autopsy. According to Santilli, he has maintained this position all along and had warned Kiviat in 1995 about the tent footage. Santilli claimed that Kiviat was going to run a disclaimer about the tent footage, but in the end, Santilli claims he won and the tent footage was pulled from the broadcast. Of course, it is possible that it wasn't used because the footage was of such poor quality, dark to the point of being obscured, that it made no sense to broadcast it.

The tent footage was part of the material that Santilli had received from the cameraman but because it was so bad, he had asked a studio in Milton Keynes to do what they could to enhance the image. Sometime after he had received the enhanced image, he returned to the United States to show it to the cameraman. At that point, the cameraman said that he didn't remember photographing the tent footage or the style in which it had been filmed.

When Santilli returned to England, he learned that his friend and the owner of the studio had played a joke on him. They had been unable to retrieve anything from the film, so the studio owner had staged it as a joke. Santilli, then, in order to not compromise the importance of the "real" autopsy film, told all that the tent footage should not be used as part of the autopsy film.

But Santilli then went on to say some things that are extremely important. He said that Andy and Keith (one of the men who worked at the studio owned by Andy) were good friends of his. They didn't act out of malice but just to play a joke on their friend. This statement, however, shows that Santilli did know people who could fake the film and who had, in fact, faked some of it.

This is just one more aspect of the story that has collapsed, and the information about that collapse has proved to be accurate. Philip Mantle, to his credit, revealed what he had learned, and Santilli, after a fashion, confirmed it but said it wasn't relevant. Of course, the fact that some of the autopsy footage, as offered to various people, was faked is extremely relevant. The spin on it doesn't matter.

This is a story that smacked of hoax from the very beginning. This is a story that has no support. There is nothing other than an unidentified source and a piece of videotape of poor quality. Clearly, the only conclusion to be drawn is that this is just another of the hoaxes that have dotted the UFO landscape.

See also **Beyond Roswell;** *International Roswell Declaration; Jeffrey, Kent; Kaufmann, Frank; Majestic Twelve (MJ-12);* **Penthouse** *Alien Photograph*

Anderson, Gerald F. Gerald Anderson, who would become one of the most controversial of the new Roswell witnesses, emerged in February 1990 after he watched the *Unsolved Mysteries* report about the Roswell UFO crash and called the television show's toll-free number to offer his personal insights. Anderson told the telephone bank operator that he had been on the site of the UFO crash and that he had seen it all. According to Anderson, the show's producers had gotten their representation all wrong. Within weeks, he was telling his story to various UFO researchers, and anyone else who would listen.

Scene of the Plain of San Agustin crash according to Gerald Anderson. (*Courtesy of Kevin Randle*)

Anderson said he was only five years old in July 1947, but even so, he had a story that was surprisingly rich in specific detail. He told researchers he was surprised that anyone knew about the flying saucer crash in New Mexico. He believed that the military had been able to find and silence all the witnesses, including several members of the Anderson family.

According to the story told by Anderson:

> We came over a kind of small run . . . we were walk-
> ing down into this thing (arroyo) . . . not a real deep
> gully . . . There was an object and it wasn't stuck in the
> side of the gully, it was kind of impacted on a small
> slope.
>
> Of course, I'm a kid and this means nothing to me.
> Except I remember my dad grabbing me and saying,
> "Oh my God, let's get the hell out of here." And my
> cousin said, "Wait a minute. Look at this damn thing."
>
> They went over toward it. My dad told me [and my
> cousin Victor] . . . to stay right here. Don't move. He
> kept saying, "Well, it might be a bomb or something
> like that."
>
> When we [Anderson and Victor, age eight] got over
> there . . . they [creatures] were up underneath this thing.
> They weren't scattered around all over the area. This ves-
> sel was not torn open. The side was torn out of it and
> there was a lot of cables and junk like that . . . But there
> were four occupants. Three were on the ground under-
> neath the thing and one was sitting up next to it, like
> he was sunning himself. It was hot out there. We were
> there, probably about 11:30 in the morning . . . and this
> creature was alive . . . and this craft wasn't torn open . . .
> You couldn't see inside this thing.
>
> We hadn't been there more than a minute, two min-
> utes at the most and a group of people came up from the
> southwest . . . These people were from the University of
> Pennsylvania. They were doing something at some ruins.
> There were a bunch of old cliff-type ruins up on the rim.
> These people were from there . . . They worked with the
> university and I'm thinking Pennsylvania . . . they were
> like an archaeological research team. . . .

You know, as I recall, even as a child, I was aware that this person or this creature or whatever you want to call it, humanoid or whatever, was terrified of its fate. Every move that anybody made it was like it expected to be hit . . .

[I]t wasn't very long before the military types showed up . . . There was a captain . . . he had red hair. He was an asshole. He threatened everyone there with the most incredible things you could possibly believe . . . First off, he told my father if he repeated this he would see to it that he would spend his entire life in a military prison and he would never see his children again. He threatened me with if you ever opened your mouth you'll never see your parents again and this whole time, please understand this, I was . . . I was very aware of what the military was, of what machine guns were, and even as a child of six [sic] years old.

To make a long story short, they ran everybody off. Now, one thing they messed up on. Some of those people who came down from those diggings up there had pieces of the wreckage in their pockets. . . .

[The creature] had a slightly perceptible nose. I never saw a mouth. I don't know if he had one or not. I never really saw that. I think the thing that struck me the most were the eyes. The size of the eyes and the gentleness of those eyes. His head was . . . a child who has hydrocephalus . . . Have you ever seen that? It kind of reminds me of that. It was much larger than it should have been by my perspectives as a child. The person was much paler than we are. This could be shock. I don't know . . . he was very pale. I didn't see hair on his head.

He was wearing . . . all of them, all four of them, were wearing what appeared to be uniforms. They were small in stature. Their hands were the kind of hands you'd see on a violinist. They were almost effeminate . . . so they were long and slender, almost effeminate. . . .

He had bruising on his head like he'd been scraped. Like thrown against something. He didn't do much moving, but when he did, it appeared he was in pain.

The other three, that were on the ground. They looked like this other one had tried to help them. They were, like laying side by side. They were bandaged. I think this . . . some kind of bandage or rags or something, but it looked like they were injured, I can't recall . . . yeah, yeah, maybe there was blood.

When he was asked by the investigator if it was good red blood, Anderson responded, "It seems to me that it was. I'm trying to visualize . . . He had one side of his face, had been scraped, you know, like you'd . . . if you took a nosedive off a motorcycle into the rocks. Kind of like that. It was, it wasn't oozing blood. It was bloody, like a scrape. And it seems to me it was red.

"But this guy was very pale. His eyes, they were almost . . . I don't know how to explain this . . . they were oval-shaped and very, very big and very, very gentle. They were bluish. Not blue like blue in human eyes but blue like . . . sort of a milky blue. That would be a good way to describe it."

Anderson also provided a solid description of where the event took place and where the ship had crashed. He said that it was "not that far from Socorro . . . more northwest . . . there's, ah . . . looking at Socorro . . . do you know where the Very Large Array (National Radio Astronomy Observatory) is at . . . okay, if you're standing there looking to the west, looking at the Array . . . move approximately ten . . . five to ten degrees to the right north and you'll be looking over a ridge line and over a mountain there . . . Down on the other side of these Plains back there is where that thing landed."

Later he tried to make the location clearer by saying that they had driven down from Albuquerque on old Highway 85 (now Interstate 25) and that they turned off on a dirt road before they reached Socorro. He talked of back roads and of a child just wanting to get out of the car. They reached a point where they were coming back toward Magdalena and that was where the ship had crashed. He pointed out that when standing on the site, he could look across a basin toward South Baldy. It clearly established the crash site as north of Highway 60 and close to Magdalena. All of this information would become important as Anderson later tried to make his original story fit into the scenarios of the investigators with whom he was working.

There were, quite naturally, some problems with the Anderson report. One of them circled around Barney Barnett, who had told various friends and family that he had been to the crash site but had never mentioned that one of the aliens was alive when he arrived. And although Barnett mentioned archaeologists, he never said a word about a family with two small boys.

Anderson wasn't through with the interviews or providing data about the saucer crash. Here was the rarest of birds, a witness who claimed firsthand knowledge and who would talk to nearly everyone who asked questions. He provided a wide spoken and written record of his involvement, adding additional, and sometimes contradictory, details with each telling of the story.

In December 1990, Anderson gave an interview to the *Springfield* (Missouri) *News-Leader*. He claimed corroboration in the form of a family diary written at the time of the events in 1947. He told the reporter he had received it at his father's funeral several years earlier and that it would provide a written record about his experiences.

According to the diary, the Anderson family had arrived in New Mexico on July 4, 1947, and lived temporarily with Ted Anderson, an uncle. The next day, July 5, they left Albuquerque, driving down to the edge of the Plains of San Agustin to search for moss agate.

Although the diary says that the event took place near Magdalena, Anderson later claimed it was just a mile or so from Horse Springs on the western edge of the Plains. Horse Springs is about sixty miles from Magdalena.

It was during the rock-hunting trip that they discovered the alien ship and the bodies. According to Anderson, in this new version, three alien creatures were lying underneath the badly damaged craft, in the shade. Two weren't moving and the third was having trouble breathing. Now, according to Anderson, the fourth was sitting on the ground and wasn't hurt. It had apparently been trying to help its fellows.

A few minutes later six people arrived. These, according to Anderson, were five college students and their professor, Dr. Buskirk. According to Anderson, they had been working at some "cliff dwellings a few miles away." They had seen a meteor fall the night before and were out searching for it.

Just after the arrival of the archaeologists, according to Anderson, Barnett arrived. Barnett came from the southwest, over the top of the ridge. Following Barnett, so closely that Anderson wondered if Barnett hadn't led them in, was the military. Now it appeared like an invasion. The Army, using jeeps, trucks, and a staff car, drove onto the crash site. They had even blocked off a portion of the road so that airplanes could land on it.

On March 24, 1991, Anderson appeared on a radio program. Interviewed by Bob Oechsler on 21st Century Radio's *Hieronimus and Company,* Anderson reiterated the July 5 date and talked about the aliens and the arrival of the military. But there were some changes from what he'd said in February 1990 and what he was saying just over a year later.

Describing the alien eyes, for example, he said, "They were enormous . . . They were very black and very large. Almost oval-shaped."

And he was saying that it was as much as forty-five minutes before anyone else arrived on the scene. These were the archaeologists who, again according to Anderson, were from the University of

Pennsylvania. Again, he brought up the name of Dr. Buskirk, who was leading the archaeological team.

He said there were four aliens. "There were two that were obviously dead. One that was somewhere in between, obviously critically injured, and one that had no apparent injuries at all."

John Carpenter, MUFON Director of Abduction Research, in an attempt to salvage the Anderson story, attacked the earlier report of milky blue eye color in an article in the September 1991 issue of the *MUFON UFO Journal*. According to Carpenter, Anderson had not said milky blue as recorded on audiotape, but had actually said murky blue and thought the discrepancy was with the transcription of the tape. He wrote, "They [meaning Kevin Randle and Don Schmitt] also stated that he [Anderson] claims the aliens had 'big, milky-blue eyes'—which is in the transcript as well. But also in the transcript Gerald states, 'not blue like blue in human eyes . . .' "

But Carpenter doesn't finish the quote, which said, "not blue like blue in human eyes . . . sort of a milky blue." Since he had a copy of the transcript, he knew what it said.

Carpenter went one better on the eye color, claiming that Anderson had not said "milky blue" but had actually said "murky blue." This was a transparent attempt to cover the fact Anderson had significantly altered the eye color. Carpenter made this pronouncement without the benefit of having heard the tape of that interview.

Anderson said, during his very first interview with Randle, that he had been unable to see into the craft. There was a hole in the side with material that resembled wires hanging out of the hole.

Now Anderson was saying that there was a gash in the side that resembled the edge of the craft, looking as if another, similar craft had collided with it. That was the reason, according to Anderson, for the crash. And Anderson told Oechsler that he could see into the object. There was a double bulkhead with components set in arrays on it and some symbols of some kind visible.

Anderson talked originally about one being that had been

injured and three that had been killed. In his first interview, he pointed out that it looked as if it had been bounced off something inside the craft. "He had bruising on his head like he'd been scraped. He didn't do much moving, but when he did, it appeared that he was in pain. The other three, that were on the ground. They looked like this other one had tried to help them."

Anderson reversed himself on that point under questioning by others. Now he claimed that one was uninjured and that there was no blood. He described a clear fluid staining some of the uniforms.

Under hypnosis, performed by Carpenter, Anderson was able to remember more details about those long-ago events. He told researchers that he knew the MPs, he now remembered the military men were wearing armbands with MP on them, and he knew they were from Sandia because his uncle Ted recognized the nasty red-haired officer. Earlier Anderson said that his father had said the men were from White Sands because they wore a patch that was egg-shaped or oval, had white wings and some circles on it.

But the most damaging evidence added to Anderson's story is Dr. Buskirk. Anderson claimed his name was Adrian (or rather that was the name in the diary) and that he had been the leader of the archaeological expedition. Not content with providing a name, Anderson made an Identikit sketch of Buskirk.

In June 1991, Tom Carey, a MUFON State Section Director in Pennsylvania, located the only Dr. Buskirk in anthropology or archaeology. His name was Winfred and not Adrian, but he was the only Buskirk who had any sort of anthropological credentials.

Carey discovered that Buskirk had published a book on the western Apache in 1986 and wrote to the publisher, asking for a copy of the dust jacket. Using the photo on it and Anderson's Identikit sketch, Carey discovered that Winfred Buskirk was the man that Anderson had been describing.

When Buskirk was contacted in June 1991, he denied that he had been on the Plains of San Agustin during the summer of 1947. In fact, he had been on the Fort Apache Indian Reservation in

Arizona from late June until September. A July 4, 1947, photo that appeared in his book showed that he was on the reservation on that day. And Buskirk, who was working on his doctorate, confirmed that he had been on the reservation solidly from late June until he returned to Albuquerque in September.

In a letter, Buskirk wrote, "The ceremonial pictures in *The Western Apache* and the fairgrounds pictures were all taken around July 3–6 or 7. I was certainly too busy on the reservation to be engaged in any archaeological side-shows."

And although Anderson said the archaeologists were from the University of Pennsylvania and that Buskirk was the leader, Buskirk was, in fact, working out of the University of New Mexico. Another major discrepancy.

In February 1992, a meeting was held in Chicago, Illinois. Sponsored by the Fund for UFO Research and J. Allen Hynek Center for UFO Studies (CUFOS), its purpose was to examine the evidence of a crash on the Plains in general and the testimony of Gerald Anderson in particular. For two days, both the proponents and opponents debated the validity of the Anderson testimony and the lack of substantial, firsthand testimony to corroborate the events on the Plains. At the end of the meeting, both sides produced a report on their findings in *The Plains of San Agustin Controversy, July 1947.*

Carpenter was unable to attend, but did send an affidavit that was included in the report. Carpenter in his signed statement said, "He [Anderson] seemed to know very little about the UFO phenomenon . . . He never embellished or changed any aspects of his story . . . Nobody came forth with even a hint or slight suggestion that we should distrust or be cautious with regard to Gerald . . ."

The problem here was that although Carpenter claimed that "He seemed to know very little about the UFO phenomenon," Anderson clearly knew about the crash at Roswell and had read *The Roswell Incident* before he talked to anyone. During the first interview Randle conducted, Anderson began to talk knowledgeably about Erick von Daniken's *Gods from Outer Space* theories. More important, when he spoke to Stanton Friedman just twelve days later, he mentioned that *The Roswell Incident* had "knocked my socks off."

Although Carpenter claimed that "he [Anderson] never embellished or changed" his story, there were dozens of documented incidences of just that. None of the facts that Anderson provided had checked out. There has been a wealth of them and it has made the job of verification interesting, but there is no verification. Barnett told friends and family that he was the first on the scene. Anderson said that Barnett was the last. Barnett never mentioned seeing two small children there. Anderson originally said that the crash site was near Magdalena but then began claiming it was close to Horse Springs. The cliff dwellings where Anderson claimed the archaeologists were working that day simply don't exist. The archaeologists who were working the Plains deny that the crash happened. The vast majority of residents of Horse Springs say they heard nothing about the crash. Buskirk was from the University of New Mexico and not Pennsylvania, and he denies being in New Mexico in July 1947. Moss agate isn't found there. The patches of the soldiers are wrong. There are no firsthand witnesses to any of the activity. The dates don't track, and in fact, the diary Anderson submitted was written sometime after 1974, based on a forensic analysis of the ink.

Anderson pointed out that the nasty captain's name was Armstrong. Bill Brazel, son of the rancher who found the debris near Roswell, also mentioned a captain named Armstrong, but it doesn't seem to be the same man. Brazel's Armstrong was a nice, easygoing man while Anderson's was a mean, threatening officer. Don Berliner, who interviewed Brazel once in person, suggested that Brazel had mentioned that a black sergeant accompanied Armstrong, but Berliner is the only one to ever report this, including it in the book he wrote with Friedman. Brazel himself has denied it. In fact, on December 5, 1992, when Brazel was asked if he had ever told anyone that the sergeant was black, Brazel said, "It ain't right . . . To my recollection anyway, that's not right. In fact, I don't think there were any colored people in that whole contingent."

But all that suggested that the Anderson story might not be the whole truth. Researchers could argue the merits of it, but the smoking gun hadn't surfaced. There was nothing that proved Anderson was not telling the truth . . . until his telephone bill emerged.

On February 4, 1990, Anderson called Kevin Randle and told him the story of the crash. Randle taped the call and was surprised when Anderson began telling others that he had spoken to him, Randle, for only twenty-six minutes. Randle timed the tape, showing that the call lasted more than fifty minutes. Carpenter, responding to this discrepancy, wrote, "Check your tape player—maybe your tape player is running slowly."

Anderson, to prove that he was telling the truth, presented a copy of his phone bill showing a call to Randle lasting twenty-six minutes. Mark Rodeghier and George Eberhart, while preparing the exhibits for *The Plains of San Agustin Controversy, July 1947,* noticed that the typeface on the phone bill Anderson submitted exactly matched that on a letter he'd sent to Randle. That called the bill into question.

Becky Pim of Southwestern Bell confirmed that their records did not match that of the Anderson bill. She was sent a copy of the bill for comparison and she wrote, "This [a copy of the bill] appears to be a copy of our microfiche records. However, the length of the call and the amount [*sic*] is different."

That proved nothing except that Southwestern Bell's records did not agree with the bill supplied by Anderson. Then, on June 9, Pim sent a copy of the microfiche page from Southwestern Bell's records. It was clear that the bill Anderson had supplied was not a copy of the bill from Southwestern Bell. It was a forgery designed to corroborate his story. It did, however, corroborate Randle's version.

In September 1992, after the story of the faked phone bill was published in *The International UFO Reporter,* the publication of the Center for UFO Studies, presenting all the evidence, Anderson admitted the truth. He had forged the phone bill in an attempt to discredit Randle.

Friedman and Don Berliner, two advocates of the Anderson story, issued a belated and very brief statement several months later. In *The MUFON UFO Journal* for January 1993, they wrote, "[We] no longer have confidence in the testimony of Gerald Anderson . . . Anderson has admitted to falsifying a document, and so his testimony about finding wreckage of a crashed flying saucer near the Plains of San Augustin [*sic*] in western New Mexico and then being escorted out by the U.S. military, can no longer be seen as sufficiently reliable."

But that wasn't the end of the phone bill problems. During the Midwest Conference on UFO Research, held on September 19, 1992, Anderson asked Carpenter to arrange a meeting with a small group of UFO researchers so that he could present them with new documentation. After Anderson had presented some of the papers, according to Carpenter, "Gerald then apologized to Stan and myself for having constructed a fake phone bill statement toward the goal of 'making Kevin Randle look bad.' Originally, Randle had indicated that he and Gerald had had a long friendly conversation on February 4, 1990. Gerald claimed it was much shorter and not all that friendly."

Carpenter continued: "I finally was able to learn that Gerald had indeed had a friendly 54-minute phone call just as Randle had claimed . . . [A]t this meeting on September 19, he then produced a second 'original' bill—this one indicating a 28-minute phone call . . ."

Carpenter concluded by writing, "We now know four new things about Gerald Anderson: (1) He was capable of constructing a very clever fake phone bill. (2) He had admitted lying to us about that first phone bill. (3) He had just been caught lying to all of the gathered researchers about this 28-minute phone bill (which means he had just constructed another phony!), and (4) Gerald was now avoiding us—his main supporters . . . "

Now it seems that very few of those who did the original work on the Anderson story believe it to be true. Anderson provided too much information that couldn't be corroborated, told too many tales that seemed to contradict one another, and provided nothing in the way of evidence. Everything he knew could easily have come from what he had read or the sloppy investigative techniques of some of the researchers, who supplied "packets" of information before interviewing Anderson.

The Anderson tale is just one more example of the aberrations that dot the Roswell case. He was an opportunist who cashed in modestly on his imagined tale, took a few trips at the expense of researchers, and appeared on a number of television shows. But he provided nothing but confusion for the Roswell case.

See also *Alamogordo Army Air Field/Holloman Air Force Base; Anonymous Archaeologist; Archaeologists; Barnett, Barney; Brazel, Bill; Dennis, Glenn; Holden, Dr. W. Curry*

Anonymous Archaeologist On February 15, 1990, a man claiming to be one of the archaeologists who had allegedly been on the impact site called researcher Kevin Randle. The man refused to give his name because he was concerned with professional repercussions. He was convinced that if he told stories about crashed flying saucers and the dead flight crew, it would come back to haunt him in professional circles.

According to this source, they, meaning the archaeologists, had been surveying sites north of the Capitan Mountains in central New Mexico, searching for signs of pre-Columbian occupation and for sites that might have been used by the Spanish. They were driving cross-country when they came up over a rise and saw what to him looked like a crashed airplane without wings. He said that it looked more like a fat fuselage than anything else. There was no sign of a dome, portholes, or a hatch, and there were no markings of any kind on it anywhere.

As they approached the craft, he saw three bodies. The one closest to him was in the best condition. It was small, with a head larger than that of a similarly sized human. He said it had big eyes, though he did not describe them in terms that would match the descriptions given by those who claim alien abduction. He also mentioned seeing a mouth, but no sign of a nose. According to him, the creature was wearing a silvery flight suit and one arm was bent at a strange angle, as if it had been broken.

According to him, there were no military personnel on the scene, but they arrived quickly. All of them were armed with pistols, and some carried rifles. An officer ordered everyone away from the craft and then told them that what they had seen was a matter of national security. He said that the officer had stressed the national security aspect of the situation. He then took their names and asked where they were going to college. He told them all that if any of them ever talked, their government grants would disappear, there would be ramifications to the university, and they would find themselves in the unemployment line.

The archaeologist said they were then escorted from the site, and stressed that it was an escort rather than a simple instruction to leave. They were taken to the nearest road, little more than a dusty track, and told to drive to the east. They passed an Army car parked by the side of the road with two armed guards standing near it.

That was all he knew, and he refused to answer any questions. He said that he believed the information should be revealed and that was why he had called Randle. He wanted everyone to know that the story was true.

Many of those studying the Roswell case have suggested that such a story, while interesting, is virtually useless to the serious investigator. It is an anonymous story that fits, to some degree, the facts as they have been established. However, without some way of corroborating the tale, it is worthless.

However, sometime after this was first reported, more information was discovered. MUFON researcher Tom Carey, attempting to learn more about the archaeologists, decided that he wanted to identify the anonymous source. Carey believed that there could be only a finite number of men who could have been in New Mexico in 1947 and that by a careful review of the archaeological literature, he might be able to figure out who it was.

As he searched, he came across Dr. George Agogino, an archaeologist living in the Portales-Clovis area of New Mexico, who said that he had heard a similar story from a friend a number of years earlier. Carey read a copy of Randle's notes to Agogino, who said, "That's what he told me." It provided an interesting corroboration for what Randle had reported.

Agogino also said that the man had told others the same story over the years. Telephone calls to those others confirmed that the man had, in fact, been telling the tale for years. Suddenly the story told by the anonymous archaeologist wasn't as valueless as it had once seemed. Agogino supplied a name, and both Carey and Randle were able to figure out who the anonymous archaeologist was.

In the summer of 1994, Randle visited the anonymous archaeologist in his New Mexico office. Although asked specifically about the crash of the alien spacecraft, the man refused to confirm he was the anonymous archaeologist. He asked only, "Do I look old enough to be an archaeologist in 1947?"

The answer was obvious to Randle. While he wouldn't have been a fully trained archaeologist in 1947, he certainly could have been a student. Randle found it interesting that the man never answered the question but dodged around it, asking questions in return. In the end, and without an admission, there was only speculation that the anonymous archaeologist had been found. Until he admitted the truth, or more evidence was found, his identity was a best guess based on the testimony of others who had identified him for researchers.

See also *Anderson, Gerald F.; Archaeologists; Barnett, Barney*

Archaeologists It was Barney Barnett who introduced the concept of archaeologists into the Roswell crash case. Or rather, it was those repeating the Barnett story, since Barnett died before researchers began to investigate. It was Jean Maltais who said they were affiliated with the University of Pennsylvania. William L. Moore, in his 1985 paper about the status of his Roswell investigation, said that the link to the University of Pennsylvania had been confirmed. He offered nothing in the way of evidence that it had been confirmed, just that statement. With those bits of information, the stage was set for an area of investigation that would bear little fruit for more than a decade.

As the CUFOS-initiated Kevin Randle and Don Schmitt investigation began in 1989, there was no reason to assume that the Barnett testimony was in error in any fashion. Conventional wisdom accepted the Barnett story at face value, and the search for the archaeologists, potential firsthand witnesses to the craft and bodies, was launched. Following the well-mapped route, they began the task of learning who was working in the state of New Mexico in July 1947, with an emphasis on those working in the area of the Plains of San Agustin.

Records were available listing who was where and what was being done. The archaeological literature provided additional clues, and while some of the records available at the Museum of New Mexico and the Laboratory of Anthropology, both in Santa Fe, and the University of New Mexico in Albuquerque were incomplete, the articles contained acknowledgment sections of archaeological journals that often listed local help and amateurs who assisted on the projects. In other words, there was a paper trail that would lead back to the archaeologists if any had been involved.

The archaeologists who were working on or near the Plains in July have been identified and eliminated. All of them have denied knowledge of anything happening there. Their friends were located and questioned in the hope of a lead, but none developed. The only conclusion that could be drawn was that none of them had been involved.

Given the situation, it would be easy to decide that the story of archaeologists had somehow been created between what Barnett actually said and what those he spoke to heard. The Barnett end of the story was created from secondhand and thirdhand testimony, and it is possible that something had been misunderstood. Since no one can now interview Barnett, investigators were forced to speculate about his testimony.

Barnett wasn't the only lead to the archaeologists. After the *Unsolved Mysteries* broadcast of September 1989, Mary Ann Gardner came forward. She had been watching the program with her husband when she turned white and felt her stomach turn over. The story of the archaeologists was one that she'd heard about ten years earlier from a dying cancer patient.

The woman, whose name Gardner couldn't remember, had been alone in the hospital. Feeling sorry for her because she had no visitors, Gardner spent as much time as she could listening to the woman's stories. Several times the dying woman told about the crash of the ship and the little men she had seen.

According to Gardner, "Basically . . . they had stumbled upon a spaceship of some kind and . . . there were bodies on the ground. The Army showed up . . . and chased them away and . . . told them that if they ever told anything about it that the government could always find them."

Gardner couldn't get the woman to say much other than they had been "little people with big heads," and later she added, "large heads and large eyes." Gardner thought that the military officers had covered the bodies the way police covered accident victims.

Under questioning, Gardner remembered that the woman had used the word "spaceship." Gardner thought that one of the men had entered the ship. He didn't explore it too far and then "the military was everywhere, the Army people were everywhere."

The woman, according to Gardner, wasn't supposed to be there. They had been "looking for fossils. That's what she said. They were hunting rocks and looking for fossils . . . she went with a friend."

Gardner said that when she first heard the story, in 1976 or 1977, she thought it was the result of a drug-induced fantasy. The woman was on painkillers because of her cancer, but she told the story half a dozen times. It wasn't until the *Unsolved Mysteries* broadcast in 1989 that Gardner began to believe it.

Of course, there were things to be investigated. Gardner remembered which hospital it had been, and was able to provide a time frame for the event. It seemed simple enough to check the records at the hospital for the names of women who died of cancer during those years.

The hospital had been sold, but the hospital administrator said that if someone could get to Florida, the records would be available. But once that happened, there were a series of excuses as to why the records weren't available. Gardner was sure she would recognize the name if she heard it, but there was no way to learn it through the hospital.

The next best thing was to check the obituary pages of the local newspapers, but it was soon evident that the task was overwhelming. All deaths in the area, and many from the rest of the state, were listed. All hospitals were included. Without a little more information, or another way to limit the search parameters, the task was impossible.

These cases suggested that the Barnett data, that a group of civilian archaeologists had stumbled onto the crash site, were accurate. It was clear through research that the archaeologists had been neither on the Plains of San Agustin nor from the University of Pennsylvania, and that was about all that was known.

In fact, Tom Carey, remembering the statement made in 1985 by William Moore, author of *The Roswell Incident*, where he claimed that he, Moore, had confirmed the connection to the University of Pennsylvania, called Moore. Carey learned that Moore had spoken to an archaeologist at the university who, according to Moore, remembered the story. Moore identified him as Bernard Wailes, who was still at Penn. Carey called Wailes, who denied it was he, and said that he hadn't arrived in this country until the 1960s, and knew nothing about the UFO crash near Roswell. He didn't even remember meeting Moore.

The search then had to center on the area around the Brazel ranch and the areas north of Roswell. That was where something could be documented to have happened. It was the general area identified by the anonymous archaeologist, and it was about the only clue that was left.

Another possibility surfaced by the name of Cactus Jack. After the *Unsolved Mysteries* broadcast, Iris Foster called the toll-free telephone number, telling of an old pot hunter she knew only as Cactus Jack. He had told Foster that he had seen the "object which was round but not real big." He claimed to have seen four bodies and said they were small. Their blood, according to Cactus Jack, was like tar, thick and black, and stained the silver uniforms they wore.

Long lists of archaeologists and anthropologists have been located and interviewed. They included Joe Ben Wheat, Jesse Jennings, William Pearce, Art Jellinich, Ridgely Whitman, John Speth, Regge Wiseman, and so on and so on. It ranged from people who might have been involved to people who might have known who was involved.

For years it seemed that nothing concrete could be learned. Had it not been for Gardner and the unidentified archaeologist who called, who seemed to have some inside knowledge, it would be simple to ignore this aspect of the case. The long searches and the checks at universities all over United States had failed to find a clue. With few exceptions, all who were interviewed were friendly and interested. They wanted to help, but a point was reached where the names being given were the same ones already interviewed. There was nowhere to go.

Then Tom Carey received the big break. A new member of MUFON told him that her father, C. Bertram Schultz, had been telling the story of a crashed flying saucer for years. Although he wasn't an anthropologist, he was a vertebrate paleontologist. He had spent time in Roswell, and he had spoken to a group of archaeologists in Roswell who knew about the crash. And he saw the military cordon as he drove out of Roswell, speaking of guards on the western side of the highway. Since he didn't want to drive off to the west, he was curious but unconcerned.

The big question was, could Schultz remember the names of any of those archaeologists? According to him, W. Curry Holden was the leader of the group. Holden, at one time the chairman of the Department of History and Anthropology at Texas Tech in Lubbock, Texas, was ninety-six years old when he was discovered. Holden, when interviewed in 1992, said that he had been there. He could remember nothing specific about the event, other than that he had been there and had seen it all. Each time the question was asked during the short meeting, he confirmed that he had seen it all: that he had seen the crashed flying saucer, had seen the bodies of the alien flight crew killed in the crash, and had been escorted from the scene by the military officers.

Later, both his wife and daughter said that he was easily confused. Memories from his life were jumbled and reordered, and he had never mentioned to either one that he had been involved in a flying saucer crash. But Holden had been asked the question three separate times in three separate ways, giving him the opportunity to answer it differently, yet he always responded that he had been there.

Schultz was sure that Holden had been one of the primary archaeologists. Schultz mentioned that he had seen the cordon himself, and Schultz's daughter, when interviewed by Carey and Randle, confirmed that he had been to Roswell many times, particularly to a region south of Roswell.

Interestingly, records from Texas Tech did put Schultz and Holden together at the University of New Mexico for the 46th Annual Meeting of the American Anthropological Association on December 28 to 31, 1947. Holden attended the meeting and Schultz spoke about "The Lime Creek Sites: New Evidence of Early Man in Southwestern Nebraska."

Here were two major finds, archaeologists who had claimed to have knowledge of the events in Roswell, one firsthand and one who had both first- and secondhand information. But more important, both of them placed the site of the event in the Roswell area and not anywhere near the Plains of San Agustin.

The archaeologists had been found, but there weren't the revelations that had been expected. Holden, who died in April 1993, had been unable to share any additional data, and his age prevented a detailed questioning. Schultz, who could be interviewed, only related what he'd heard from Holden, and the little he'd seen himself.

The search for the archaeologists has nearly ended. Their leader, Dr. W. Curry Holden, has been identified, and he confirmed his involvement. Corroborating witnesses have been found and interviewed. The story of archaeologists on the impact site just north of Roswell is true. The details provided by them have been sketchy, but we now have a better understanding of what happened on that New Mexican desert in July 1947.

See also *Anonymous Archaeologist; Barnett, Barney; Cactus Jack; Holden, W. Curry*

ATIC Air Technical Intelligence Center. ATIC was the agency inside the U.S. Army Air Forces (later the United States Air Force) responsible for reverse engineering of captured enemy equipment and the gathering of intelligence about foreign capabilities. It is reported that the material recovered at Roswell was taken to ATIC facilities at Wright Field outside of Dayton, Ohio.

Kent Jeffrey, in his search to learn more about the Roswell case, managed, with the help of his father, a retired Air Force colonel, to interview three other retired colonels who had been assigned to ATIC at Wright-Patterson AFB at one time. Colonel Walter Klinikowski, FTD (Foreign Technology Division, ATIC's name in the 1960s) 1960–74, Deputy Director of Intelligence Collections, Director of Foreign Activities; Colonel Walter Vitunac,

Building 219, which housed the Foreign Technology Division in the late
1950s. (*Photo courtesy of USAF*)

ATIC and FTD 1957–62, Director of Intelligence Collections,
Director of Foreign Technology Programs, Director of Foreign
Activities; and Colonel George Weinbrenner, FTD 1968–74,
Commander of the Foreign Technology Division, produced a
signed statement on June 27, 1997.

> In view of recent worldwide media attention and
> apparent public misconception concerning the 1947
> Roswell Incident, we have chosen to issue a joint state-
> ment in an effort to help set the record straight on this
> most controversial matter. We are taking this step strictly
> out of a sense of responsibility to the truth, and are doing
> so of our own volition, without any pressure or encour-
> agement from the U.S. military or government.
>
> Over the past years, innumerable documentaries,
> books, television shows, and movies have conveyed the
> impression that the 1947 Roswell event is a matter of
> historical fact. Incredible-sounding but unsubstantiated

claims by alleged witnesses and participants have further exacerbated the situation. Consequently, according to recent opinion polls, the majority of Americans now believe in the reality of an event that never occurred— the crash of an alien spaceship northwest of Roswell, New Mexico, in July 1947, and its subsequent recovery and transportation by the U.S. military to Wright Patterson [*sic*] Air Force Base near Dayton, Ohio.

Wright Patterson [*sic*] is indeed where the Air Force technical and intelligence experts were, and still are, concentrated. It is where the recovered wreckage from a foreign craft of any kind with the potential of invading our skies, including an alien spaceship, would be taken and kept for technical analysis. Contrary to the Roswell legend, however, no such craft was taken to and stored at Wright Patterson [*sic*] Air Force Base. If such an event had occurred, as ranking officials of the Foreign Technology Division (FTD) at Wright Patterson, we would have known about it. During our collective tenure there, which spanned a period of 17 years— 1957 through 1974—there was no alien spaceship, and no secret hangar housing it—of that we give our word.

Going on record with such an unequivocal statement is not something we take lightly. As retired military officers, we would not dishonor ourselves, our military careers, our families, or our country by lying to the American people, especially about an issue of such great potential significance.

Any doubters should note that if an alien spaceship were actually being kept at Wright Patterson [*sic*] Air Force Base by the U.S. government, the administration in power could choose to declassify the matter at any time. With that uncertainty, public lying about such an issue, on top of all else, would be pure folly.

As is surely the opinion of the vast majority of Americans, both civilian and military, we are in total agreement that anything as important and profound as the knowledge of other intelligent life in the universe would be information that should not be suppressed or censored by any government. It would be information to which all humanity should be entitled.

See also *Jeffrey, Kent*

Atomic Blast *The Atomic Blast* was the base newspaper published by the 509th Bomb Group at Roswell. In July 1947, First Lieutenant Walter Haut was the editor, as part of his duties as the base public relations officer. The only mention of UFOs or flying disks was an article published about three weeks after the events at Roswell. It showed a picture of the Navy's "Flying Flapjack" and a suggestion that some of the flying saucers might be explained by the unconventional design of the aircraft.

See also *Flying Flapjack; Haut, Walter*

Balloon Bombs See *Japanese Balloon Bombs*

Barnett, Barney (1892–1969) The connection between the crash of an alien spacecraft near Roswell, New Mexico, and events on the Plains of San Agustin in July 1947 was drawn by Barney Barnett, a soil conservation engineer. Or rather, the connection was drawn by the original investigators talking to friends and relatives of Barnett.

During those early investigations, the only story of crashed craft and bodies came from Barney Barnett. Witnesses to the debris field, the area seventy-five miles northwest of Roswell, included Mack Brazel and Jesse Marcel Sr., and witnesses to the material picked up there included Brazel's neighbors and Marcel's fellow officers. There are literally dozens of people who saw and handled the debris, but it was only Barnett who talked of seeing a craft and the dead bodies of the alien flight crew.

Unfortunately, Barnett died before anyone had the opportunity to interview him. Investigators were forced to rely on the information as reported by Barnett's family and friends. Alice Knight, Vern Maltais, Harold Baca, and J. F. "Fleck" Danley all reported that Barnett had mentioned the story of the crashed alien ship to them. All of them spoke of Barnett in the highest terms, and all said that he was a reliable, fine man who was not given to practical jokes, nor was he one who told tall tales.

According to those friends, Barnett said that he had been driving through the desert when a flash of light caught his attention. He turned toward it and came upon a crashed disc-shaped object. Maltais said that Barnett told him that the craft was metallic, dull gray, and "pretty good sized." According to Maltais, Barnett thought it had burst open as it slammed into a low ridgeline. There was almost no wreckage scattered around the damaged ship. Barnett also said that he saw the flight crew. The beings were small, with pear-shaped heads, skinny arms and legs, and no hair. All wore metallic-like, form-fitting silver "flight suits" without buttons or zippers.

While on the site, Barnett said he was joined by a handful of archaeologists. They did not approach the craft or the bodies as he had. He'd gotten closest, standing over one of the bodies. Before they could do much more, the military arrived, warned them that what they had seen was classified top secret, and then escorted them from the site.

It is not clear if Barnett ever told anyone exactly where he'd seen the craft. Those he did speak to thought that he'd mentioned the Plains of San Agustin, west of Socorro, New Mexico, and about 125 miles from Corona and the debris field discovered by Mack Brazel.

That was where the story ended. Investigation failed to find a single firsthand witness to an event on the Plains. There were others, such as Robert Drake, who told of a trip into the Plains area in the summer of 1947. Drake, though he didn't see anything himself, did speak to a cowboy who told him of the crash of some kind of spacecraft somewhere out on the Plains.

Drake provided two other sources of information. According to him, students at Chaco Canyon, an archaeological site about a hundred miles north of the Plains, returned from a July Fourth holiday talking of a spacecraft crash. He also mentioned Roscoe Wilmeth, a documents clerk who worked at the Los Alamos National Laboratory who claimed that he'd seen a file that mentioned a crashed craft and alien bodies. Wilmeth told Drake that he wanted to travel to the "body" site. Drake, as well as others, interpreted that to mean he wanted to go to the Plains of San Agustin.

According to Drake, he had been making a preliminary survey of the Bat Cave on the southeastern edge of the Plains with Dr. Wesley Hurt, Dan McKnight, and Albert Dittert in July 1947. On the way back to Albuquerque, they stopped at a ranch. Drake, while searching for land snails, talked to a cowboy who told him of the crash. On the way back to Albuquerque, Drake, along with the others, discussed the story told by the old cowboy. Drake no longer remembers who that cowboy might have been.

But Hurt, McKnight, and Dittert, all interviewed by either Kevin Randle or Tom Carey, said they remembered nothing about such a conversation. In fact, Hurt said that he'd heard nothing about an alien spaceship crash on the Plains until researchers began to call him around 1980. Neither had McKnight or Dittert. Only Drake recalled the event. When questioned about it, Drake said that it hadn't been a topic of discussion on the way back to Albuquerque as he had originally said. Of course, no one had a clue as to who the anonymous cowboy who talked to Drake might be.

Carey, in his research, also located a number of students who had been at the Chaco Canyon site in July 1947. Flying saucers and crashed discs had not been discussed. Instead, they all had engaged in a cooling-off period. There had been an incident involving fireworks that had angered some of the students. That had been the topic of discussion.

When all the data about the Drake testimony are examined, it is clear that it fails to meet even the most lenient standards. Of all those interviewed, only Drake remembers the events he speaks of, even though others were involved. Those others fail to recall the events the way he does.

The other corroborating witness, Roscoe Wilmeth, was never interviewed. He died days before he returned from a vacation that would have allowed researchers to speak with him. His secondhand testimony doesn't corroborate an event on the Plains because he spoke of going to the body site, and it was others who made the assumption that he was talking of the Plains.

The archaeologists who have been located and can speak of the event firsthand have been located. Dr. W. Curry Holden was the leader of the expedition. According to the information supplied by Holden, it was north of Roswell, just to the west of Highway 285. Holden was clear that the site was close to Roswell and not over on the Plains.

It wasn't as if there hadn't been a search for archaeologists on the Plains. Several were identified as having worked on the Plains during the summer of 1947, although they might not have been there on the critical days at the beginning of the month. Herbert Dick, making a preliminary survey of the Bat Cave, arrived in the middle of July, and reported to various researchers that he knew nothing of a flying saucer crash. He knew many of the ranchers in the area and spoke to them frequently, but none of them mentioned any crash of a spacecraft.

Edward Danson, working with J. O. Brew on the Plains in 1947, wrote on August 20, 1991, that he had heard nothing about a crashed craft. In fact, Danson wrote that he didn't believe the story.

According to all the archaeologists who had spoken of the UFO crash, the impact site was between Roswell and the debris field found by Mack Brazel. It should also be noted that many of the neighbors of Brazel, as well as others in the Corona area, were aware that something was happening in July 1947. It was not a well-kept secret there.

By way of contrast, no firsthand sources were located who saw anything on the Plains. All the archaeologists who were there in the summer of 1947 said they had heard and seen nothing. The ranchers in the area, including Dave Farr, who owns the ranch where Gerald Anderson claimed the saucer crashed, say they had heard nothing about a crashed saucer until recently. The single exception was John Foard, who said that he knew nothing firsthand, but remembered someone, at some time, talking about a flying saucer crash. In other words, his information was secondhand at best.

With the elimination of Drake, Anderson, and the archaeologists, the only source for an event on the Plains was Barney Barnett. Then the Barnett story suffered a major setback.

Research by various investigators suggested that the crash happened on the night of July 4, and that the military recovered the craft and the bodies on July 5. It was a reconstruction based on eyewitness testimony and limited documentation. On those specific days it can be proven, by the diary kept by Ruth Barnett, that her husband was at home in Socorro.

What this means is that the story about Barnett, as related by others, does not track with the established facts. The diary takes Barnett out of the picture. What it doesn't do is explain how Barnett knew about the archaeologists. Clearly archaeologists were involved in the case. They weren't on the Plains, but they were involved.

This, however, is a minor point. There were articles about flying saucer crashes published in the newsmagazines in 1950. The stories related to Frank Scully's *Behind the Flying Saucers*. It's not known if this is the source of Barnett's tale, or if he actually saw something on the Plains in 1947. It could be the source of the contamination.

At this point no evidence has been found for an event on the Plains. The secondhand testimony used to support it has collapsed completely. The firsthand testimony that has been found was discovered to be nothing more than a hoax invented for publicity. The Barnett story, at one time the foundation for the Plains event and alien bodies found there, is gone. The whole Plains scenario fails to fit into the framework of the Roswell crash. Without better information, without firsthand corroboration, Barnett's story, as well as the whole Plains scenario, must be rejected.

Barnett, Ruth (1895–1977) Like her husband, Ruth Barnett died before the story of the flying saucer crash broke. She was never interviewed by the investigators, and her knowledge of the event was told through secondhand sources. Unlike her husband, she left a written record that could be critical in understanding what happened in 1947.

Either sometime late in 1946 or early in 1947, someone gave Ruth Barnett a daily reminder book. Throughout the year of 1947 she kept a diary of the daily events in her life. Most of the entries included what the weather had been, who they had seen, who had visited, and where Barney had been during the day. This information allowed for some deductions to be made.

The original story of Barney Barnett's involvement suggested that the object crashed on the night of July 2 and that Barnett found it late on the morning of July 3. The diary, however, tends to eliminate Barnett from the case if the dates are accurate. On July 3, the day that everyone thought Barnett found the saucer out on the Plains of San Agustin, he was in his office in Socorro. The diary, in fact, places Barnett in Socorro on every day of the first week of July with the exceptions of July 2 and July 8.

Given the chronology of the crash story, the July 2 date is a day too early. If Barnett was on the scene any time on July 2, it would have meant the event took place on the evening of July 1. There is no evidence to support that date anywhere in any of the various reports.

On July 5, the date that some researchers have suggested as the day the military recovered the main portion of the craft and the bodies near Roswell, Barnett was also in Socorro and not out in the desert. On that day, according to Ruth, Barnett was buying the glass for the windows of the house they were building. He was clearly in Socorro the whole day, which left no time for him to get out, far to the west, to find the crashed craft.

On July 8, the day that the story broke in the newspapers and when some believe the cleanup on the Brazel ranch began, the diary places Barnett in Pie Town, far to the west of Socorro, and even farther from the events taking place around Roswell. Barnett's area of responsibility centered on the Socorro area and to the west of town. He would have had no official business in the Roswell–Corona area on July 8.

The diary kept by Ruth Barnett tends to eliminate Barney Barnett as a participant in the events of early July 1947. There is simply no hint that he was on the scene of the crashed craft at any time in 1947.

See also *Barnett, Barney*

Barrowclough, Colonel Robert I. In July 1947, Robert Barrowclough was the executive officer of the 509th Bomb Group and was stationed in Roswell, New Mexico. Like the other members of Colonel William Blanchard's staff, he had served in World War II, eventually commanding a B-29 squadron on Tinian in the Marianas Islands in the Pacific Theater. He was awarded the Distinguished Flying Cross, the Bronze Star, the Air Medal, and the Asiatic and Pacific Medals.

During interviews with other members of the 509th Bomb Group, including Robert Porter, Barrowclough was identified as one of the pilots who had flown a special mission out of Roswell carrying the strange metallic debris. Porter had suggested that he had flown with Major Marcel on the July 8 trip to Fort Worth. Porter was of the opinion that Barrowclough had been the aircraft commander on that flight.

Of all the top officers at Roswell in 1947 interviewed by researchers, Barrowclough is the only one to suggest that nothing extraordinary happened there. In a June 15, 1997, handwritten note to Kent Jeffrey, Barrowclough noted, "Thank you for the copy of the *UFO Journal* on the Roswell myth. Maybe some of those crack pots will quit calling me up and say I'm covering up a deep gov't secret. You pretty well covered the subject." It was signed with his initials.

See also *Blanchard, General William H. (Butch); Easley, Major Edwin; Marcel Sr., Major Jesse; Saunders, Major Patrick*

Behind the Flying Saucers In 1950, Henry Holt and Company published Frank Scully's book about the alleged crash of three flying saucers in the desert Southwest. Scully, a Hollywood gossip columnist, reported that he had interviewed two men, Silas Newton (not to be confused with Fort Worth weather officer Irving Newton) and a mysterious "Dr. Gee," a government scientist. These men told Scully of a top secret project that revolved around the recovered flying saucers and the attempts to learn more about them.

Scully's book did very well and created a great deal of interest. If what he had written was true, then it was the biggest story of the last thousand years. One of Scully's sources, Newton, claimed that he had samples of the metal that was used in the creation of the flying saucers. Tests performed on them, at least according to Scully's sources, revealed metal that had extraordinary properties. The story reported by Scully was backed by Newton's metal, which was clearly created by a technology far advanced of the one on Earth.

Within two years, Newton and Dr. Gee, finally identified as a TV repairman named Leo GeBaur, were exposed as con men. They had no inside knowledge of the UFO field, had nothing to do with the recovery of alien spacecraft, and had been spinning tales. The exposé by reporter J. P. Cahn was so well done and so convincing that any story of a UFO crash was rejected out of hand by serious UFO researchers from that point on.

Scully's book, rather than convincing people of the reality of the UFO phenomenon, had the opposite effect. It marked a watershed of gullibility, one that no one wanted to repeat. Scully was indirectly responsible for the failure by UFO researchers to investigate any tale of a UFO crash at all. It meant that when the first suggestions that something had crashed at Roswell were being discovered, the majority of those in the UFO community rejected them without a second glance.

Beyond Roswell This book, by Michael Hesemann and Philip Mantle, is an outgrowth of Mantle's and Hesemann's involvement in the alien autopsy film and the interest in the Roswell UFO case. Hesemann traveled throughout New Mexico and has claimed that he is the only researcher to ever find the scene of the crash that is the basis for the Santilli film. Both Hesemann and Mantel were at one point convinced that the Santilli film was real, and the book is about their search for evidence, but also about the Roswell case.

Unfortunately, events have overtaken this book. The Santilli autopsy film is now believed by many to be a hoax. Philip Mantle reported in 1998 that he had spoken to a man at a computer art company who claimed to have been a participant in part of the hoax. Only Hesemann remains a true believer.

To make matters worse for the book, there are too many errors in it for it to be taken seriously. Many of the errors are the result of information that has since been proven to be inaccurate. For example, the authors use Jim Ragsdale and Glenn Dennis as sources of information. What this means, simply, is that the mistakes are not all generated by sloppy reporting but also from a lack of better information, which has emerged since the book's publication.

It is clear from their work that they want to believe in the Roswell case. They accept nearly everything as accurate and report little of the negative information. This renders their book of little use to the serious student because all this information has been reported elsewhere. The only new information they brought to the table was that from the Santilli autopsy, and that information has no value.

Both authors are European—Mantle is English and Hesemann is German. Both have extensive backgrounds in UFO research, and both have published other UFO-related books. Hesemann is a cultural anthropologist and a historian. Since 1984 he has edited a large-circulation magazine in Europe. Mantle has a regular day job and until recently was the Director of Investigations for the British UFO Research Association (BUFORA) in Great Britain.

See also *Alien Autopsy*

Colonel William "Butch" Blanchard.
(*Photo courtesy of Walter Haut*)

Blanchard, General William H. (Butch) (1916–1966) William Blanchard was born in Boston, Massachusetts, and graduated from the United States Military Academy at West Point in June 1938. From there he went into flight training at Randolph Field, Texas, and on to advanced training at Kelly Field, Texas.

During World War II he served in a number of positions. In 1943, he was selected for duty with the first B-29 bomber wing being formed outside Salina, Kansas. In 1944, he was deputy commander of the 58th Bomb Wing and flew the first B-29 into China to begin his participation in the strategic bombing of Japan. He was later the commander of the 40th Bomb Group (B-29) and eventually became the operations officer for the 21st Bomber Command in the Marianas. There he planned and flew low-level fire raids against Japanese targets. At the end of the war, he was ordered to prepare and supervise the detailed operations for the atomic bombing of Hiroshima in 1945.

After the war, he was appointed commander of the 509th Bomb Group, at the time the only nuclear strike force in the world. He was involved in "Operation Crossroads," the atomic tests at Bikini in 1946.

In 1947, as the commander of the 509th, he was responsible for the press release that claimed his unit had found remnants of a flying saucer outside of Roswell, New Mexico. Within hours, his announcement had been superseded by another from higher headquarters suggesting that the debris was from a weather balloon and radar reflector.

In 1948, he was assigned to Eighth Air Force Headquarters as the director of operations. There he helped direct the atomic training for air crews of the B-36. In 1952, he was promoted to brigadier general and was appointed the director of operations for the Strategic Air Command.

As a major general in 1957, Blanchard assumed command of SAC's Seventh Air Division in England. Three years later he returned to SAC Headquarters as the Director of Operations. In October 1961, he was appointed the Inspector General of the Air Force and promoted to lieutenant general.

In February 1965, Blanchard was appointed Vice Chief of Staff of the Air Force and promoted to general. On May 31, 1966, while on duty at the Pentagon, Blanchard suffered a heart attack and died.

Blanchard rarely, if ever, mentioned the events of July 1947. In the days that followed, he suggested during a regularly scheduled staff meeting that they had made a bad mistake. Others who knew him well, but were not at the meeting, said that he never mentioned the events at Roswell. In recent years, a few people have suggested that Blanchard had confided cryptic admissions to them, but none of those alleged statements can be verified.

Colonel William "Butch" Blanchard (*left*) greets Brigadier General Roger Ramey (*right*). (*Photo courtesy of Walter Haut*)

Bodies Over the years, stories were told of alien bodies at Wright Field, and it was believed that they were those recovered outside Roswell. Len Stringfield, in his research, located a number of witnesses to the presence of alien bodies on the Wright-Patterson Air Force Base complex.

One of the people whose report found its way to Stringfield was a woman named Norma Gardner, a one-time employee at Wright-Patterson. In 1959, she retired for health reasons. She hinted to friends that she knew more about the "flying saucer" situation than the government was comfortable with her knowing. Given a top security clearance, she had the chore of logging in all UFO-related material, which included parts of the interior of a craft that had been brought to the base in the past. Everything had been photographed, tagged, and labeled, and all the documents had to be filed by someone. Norma Gardner was that someone.

Hanger 84, where the bodies were allegedly stored overnight. (*Photo courtesy of Kevin Randle*)

At one point, she saw two bodies as they were moved from one location to another. The bodies had been preserved in some kind of chemical solution. She said that they were small, four or five feet tall, with large heads and slanted eyes, and obviously were not human. In the course of her duties, she also typed the autopsy reports on them.

Her story, told years earlier, had been ignored by most researchers. Without corroboration, there was no reason to accept Gardner's tale. But now, with the reports from Roswell, there was that corroboration. Melvin Brown and Thomas Gonzales, among others, confirmed that bodies were found near Roswell. Each story, coming from independent sources, helped to confirm, to some extent, the next.

Gardner is not the lone source on the bodies and their location. Others have hinted of inside knowledge over the years. Again, according to Stringfield, he was told by a man that he had attended a high-level secret conference at Wright-Patterson and saw, in an underground facility, a body in deep-freeze preservation.

The source described the body as having long arms positioned at its side. It was about four feet tall, and the skin on the face appeared smooth and gray. The eyes were open, and there was no hair visible.

It wasn't much, and without a name and further confirmation, it was almost useless, but it did address the question of the location of the dead. It also suggested that the bodies had not been buried or burned, but were being preserved.

Truman Weaver, a former Air Force major, provided some additional confirmation. He showed researchers a letter from a friend who claimed to have worked across the alley from the building where the bodies were kept. The source claimed that on some days a strong odor drifted across the alley, and when he asked about it, he was told that it was embalming fluid.

A strong odor of formaldehyde drifting on a breeze at Wright-Patterson isn't enough to even suggest alien bodies or that those bodies were there. The source went on, however, explaining that his boss, a man named McAdams, showed him an interim report that confirmed the rumors of the bodies and the captured craft.

It was another piece of the puzzle that provided a little confirmation. The McAdams report is, unfortunately, secondhand, but a few of the details mesh with those of other, firsthand accounts and lend some support to these cases.

Another source, an electrician, was employed by General Electric and accepted a job at Wright-Patterson. He was taken into an icy room that had a strange, offensive odor. There were a number of cases in the room that had electrical connections and air ducts hooked to them. The source managed to sneak a look at one of the cases. Inside, resting on a marble slab, was a body that wasn't human.

The source, once he finished the job at Wright-Patterson, returned home. He told his family of the pungent odor in the cold room. The source's daughter said that she remembered her father's clothes having a strong odor of ammonia on them.

The problem is that none of those stories directly connect the events at Roswell with the bodies seen at Wright-Patterson. John Timmerman, a researcher on the board of directors of the J. Allen Hynek Center for UFO Studies in Chicago, may have provided some of that connecting material.

Timmerman has a traveling UFO exhibit that he sets up in malls, schools, and shopping centers. Along with the displays of photos and other material, Timmerman has a small cassette recorder, and he asks those who stop by to share any of their UFO experiences with him.

On January 13, 1990, he had a brief interview with a man who refused to give his name. The man said that he knew something about the bodies recovered at Roswell in 1947. He said that he knew the victims of the crash had been taken to Wright Field. The source said that the bodies were not from this planet. He had worked with a doctor who had been involved with the medical research on the dead.

That evidence, by itself, is nearly worthless. An unnamed source talking about the bodies at Wright-Patterson provides nothing that can be verified. But when joined with the other reports where firsthand witnesses have told what they saw, it becomes convincing, or at the very least interesting. It is important because the source said that the bodies were from the Roswell crash and that they were taken to Wright Field. It completes the chain of evidence.

Helen Wachter was a nursing student at a school in Dayton, Ohio, in the summer of 1947. According to her, she was visiting a friend when the friend's husband returned from Wright Field in an agitated state. He dragged his wife into the bedroom and told her, in a voice that could be easily overheard, that something of a top-secret nature had happened at the base. Bodies of alien creatures had arrived, four of them. He had been one of the guards posted when the plane had come in with them.

That was all that was said about it: Four bodies had come into the base during the summer of 1947—another suggestion that the bodies recovered at Roswell went to Ohio.

The problem with the stories is that none of the people telling them, other than Norma Gardner, had much to do with the bodies. They saw them in connection with other duties and didn't have the opportunity to examine them. Or they saw them under less than ideal conditions. One source had to look through the glass top of a freezer that had frost on it. But even with those problems, they were able to describe, sometimes in detail, what they had seen.

Stringfield, who has interviewed one man who claimed to be a pathologist involved in the autopsy of one of the bodies, said, "The head is large, very large by human proportions. There is no hair, hair follicles. There are no earlobes. These is no nose as we have as humans. The mouth is just a slit, an orifice that goes in approximately one inch, (is) membranous, which leads to no digestive tract or eliminatory system. There were no striated muscles. There was atria, or a heart, a pumping station so to speak for the colorless liquid which was, in a sense, blood."

Another witness who was at the crash site and saw the bodies provided a description that fit with that published by Stringfield in one of his Crash/Retrieval Status Reports. According to both those at Roswell in 1947 and Stringfield, the bodies were between three and a half and four and a half feet tall and weighed about forty pounds.

The eyes were large and almond-shaped (or teardrop-shaped, according to our witness), without pupils and under a heavy brow-ridge. The eyes appeared to be slightly slanted, giving the face an Asian look. They were set deep and were wide apart, without eye-lids.

The torso was small and thin. The arms were long and thin, too, reaching down to the knee. The length from the shoulder to the elbow was shorter than the length from the elbow to the wrist. The hands had four digits and no opposable thumb. Two fingers appeared longer than the others. This is consistent with the account given by the nurse at Roswell.

The skin, as everyone who ever saw the bodies pointed out, was not green. It was a pinkish-gray, though Melvin Brown thought it was more yellowish. The skin was tough and leathery. Under mag-nification, it had a mesh-like structure.

One of the few people who claimed to have seen the bodies at Roswell is Frank Kaufmann. Some have suggested that his tale is the invention of an opportunist, but there are some clues that suggest Kaufmann might be exactly who he claims to be. Kaufmann has said that he was on the impact site and that he had an opportunity to see the bodies. He has provided for various researchers a descrip-tion that matches, generally, that provided by others. The major dif-ference is the size. Kaufmann has suggested that the bodies were as tall as five or five-and-a-half feet, which means they were just slightly shorter than the average American adult male.

Kaufmann's description of the facial features matches, generally, that given by others. He said that the head was only slightly larger than a human head and that the eyes were only slightly larger. The eyes did have pupils, so he wasn't describing the black orbs so com-mon in tales of alien abduction, which conflicts with what a few have claimed. He said they were slender and lightweight.

Although Kaufmann is one of the few from Roswell to have spoken of alien bodies, he is not alone. Edwin Easley, the Roswell provost marshal, was reluctant to talk of alien beings, but just before he died, when asked about them he said to family and friends, "Oh, the creatures." Granted, the statement is cryptic, but it is also interesting given Easley's desire to help in the investigation and live up to the oath he took in 1947.

The anonymous archaeologist also claimed to have seen bodies. His description, that they were small, with a head larger than that of a similarly sized human, matches, for the most part, the descriptions provided by others. It is, however, a description that was provided by a firsthand source near Roswell.

These firsthand sources at Roswell had no opportunity to see any internal structures. Stringfield's source said there were no teeth and no apparent reproductive organs. Stringfield's doctor provided one of the most comprehensive descriptions of the bodies. He had the opportunity to work on them, but most of the other firsthand sources did not.

There are others who have firsthand knowledge, but who did not see the bodies personally. Through their work with the military, they saw files containing notes about the crashes and photographs of the debris field, impact sites, and the bodies themselves.

One of those is a man who worked at NORAD in Colorado Springs in the 1970s. In the course of computerizing some of the files, he came across one labeled, "USAAF (United States Army Air Forces) Early Automation." The file dealt with the recovery of several small bodies and included black-and-white photographs of them. The man said the bodies were small, no more than four or five feet tall, with oversized heads.

There have been a few additional hints about the location of the bodies. Although it seems that they eventually made their way to Wright Field, they may not have been taken there directly. One man, who asked that his name not be used because of his current job, who was at Walker Air Force Base in Roswell in 1960, said that

discussions at the base sometimes revolved around the events of
thirteen years earlier. There was a great deal of speculation about the
reality of the crash. Because the man had a Top Secret crypto clearance, which meant that he had access to a wide variety of sensitive
documents, he decided to check the old files. Crypto message traffic
was filed away and not supposed to be destroyed. By going through
the traffic for July 1947, he hoped to find verification of the story.

There were only two messages. One referred to the crash but
didn't have anything more specific. A check by him showed that it
wasn't a conventional crash because there was nothing that related
to a conventional craft. Without the other, routine follow-up traffic, the conclusion was that the event mentioned in the message was
something extraordinary.

The other message was more specific, mentioning the craft
and the bodies. There was no question that this document referred
to the crash of an alien spacecraft. According to that message, some
of the wreckage and some of the bodies were taken to Andrews Air
Force Base. That was the first time that Andrews had surfaced in
relation to the bodies.

The man reported to his friends that the story of the crash was
true. Within hours, the man was transferred from his position there
and found himself a telephone operator. No one ever explained why
he was suddenly transferred from a position of importance to one
that was relatively unimportant. The lieutenant who made the
transfer never suggested it was punishment—it was for the good of
the service.

Brigadier General Arthur Exon also had heard about the bodies
supposedly shipped to Wright Field in 1947. He added the twist
that one of them was sent on to Denver, where the Army had the
mortuary service in 1947. Exon made it clear that this was secondhand information. His theory was that one of the bodies was used
for experimentation so that those at Wright Field would be able to
use the best methods to preserve the remaining bodies.

What is interesting is that there have been those who have seen the bodies since the crash took place. Many of those stories are secondhand, simply because the witnesses themselves have died. But others, a crucial handful, are told by the men and women who saw the bodies themselves, seven men who saw the creatures from another world and have described what they saw.

All this leads to one conclusion: There were bodies of some kind recovered in New Mexico. They were removed from the crash sites, packed in ice in Roswell, and flown out. At least one crate containing some of the bodies was taken to Fort Worth. Later that crate and bodies arrived at Wright Field. They may not have gone directly to Wright Field, but the information is that they all eventually made it there. And once there, they were examined, at least one was autopsied, and all were frozen for study as the techniques for genetic tracking, cellular mapping, and biological explanation were improved.

See also *Anonymous Archaeologist; Easley, Major Edwin; Exon, Brigadier General Arthur; Kaufmann, Frank; Stringfield, Leonard H.*

Brazel, Bill The first thing that Bill Brazel said to UFO researchers Kevin Randle and Don Schmitt on February 19, 1989, was, "I don't really know what I could tell you guys."

Brazel then said, "My dad found this thing and told me a little bit about it. Not much, because the Air Force asked him to take an oath that he wouldn't tell anybody in detail about it. And my dad was such a guy that he went to his grave and he *never* told anybody."

Brazel said that he had found a few little bits and pieces later on. It was just a few scraps. He said that his father told him there was tin foil and some wood, and some of the wood had Japanese or Chinese figures.

Brazel Junior himself said that he found eight to twelve small fragments of material in the field during the months after the crash had taken place. He said that he found "something on the order of balsa wood and something on the order of heavy gauge monofilament fishing line and a little piece of . . . it wasn't really aluminum foil and it wasn't really lead foil but it was on that order. A piece about the size of my fingers with jagged edges."

Brazel described the debris he found in detail. Although he said that the most numerous pieces he found looked like wood, it was not wood. He noted that they were like balsa wood. One piece was about six inches long and would flex a little under pressure. But it was much tougher than balsa wood. Brazel said that he couldn't break it and couldn't cut it with his pocket knife. This was the knife, according to Brazel, that he had used in the past to cut barbed wire, yet he couldn't even get a shaving from the wood. He had wanted to see if it contained the "layering" or grain found in normal wood.

Bill Brazel in cowboy hat. (*Photo courtesy of Kevin Randle*)

He also found some "wire-like" material that he said reminded him of monofilament fishing line but had the properties of fiber optics. Brazel noticed that a light at one end could be seen at the other end.

The most interesting debris he found was the foil. He said it was a jagged piece that was so strong he couldn't tear it. He didn't try to cut or burn it. He said, "It was about the gauge of lead foil. Thicker than tin foil. It was pliable. Real pliable. I would bend it over and crease it . . . It would flatten out and it was just as smooth as ever. Not a crinkle or anything in it."

Although he said he had found eight, ten, or twelve pieces of the material over a couple of months, he found only those three kinds of debris. He had showed them to his father, who said that it looked like some of the "contraption" he had found in the pasture.

Brazel also said he had seen a gouge down across the pasture where the debris had been found. He said it was about five hundred feet long, about ten feet at its widest, and only a foot to eighteen inches deep. Not far under the soil is a layer of very tough shale. Brazel said that the gouge took about two years to grass over.

The debris that Brazel had found would have proved that his story was true. The lead foil, even on a very elementary level, would have demonstrated a technology that still does not exist. There is no tough foil that when rolled into a ball will unfold itself without a sign of a crease or fold. Brazel, however, did not have the samples of the material. The military, according to him, had retrieved them.

Sometime after the events, Brazel believes about two years later, he was in Corona and the talk turned to the object his father had found. Brazel mentioned that he had found a few scraps, just pieces and fragments of it. "And lo and behold, here comes the military."

An officer and three enlisted men, all in uniform, visited him at the ranch. Brazel said, "I still am not really sure, but I'm almost positive that the officer in charge, his name was Armstrong. A real nice guy. And he had a sergeant with him that was real nice. And I think there were two other enlisted men. They came out to the ranch and they was talking to me and they said, 'We understand your father found this weather balloon,' and I said, 'Yeah.' And they said, 'We understand that you found some bits and pieces of it.'"

Brazel said that he had a cigar box full. They asked if he had examined it at all. Brazel said, "Well enough to know that I don't know what it is."

The officer, according to Brazel, said that they would like to take the material with them. When Brazel hesitated, the officer smiled and according to Brazel said, "Your father turned the rest of it over to us. You know he's under oath not to tell anyone."

Brazel just smiled at the man and then, according to Brazel, it was clear that he wasn't going to leave without the debris. Brazel said that they didn't confiscate it. They just put it to him in such a way that he should give it to them and they would leave. Brazel said, "It's kind of like when I was in the Navy. We want volunteers. We want you, you and you. I said, 'Okay, you can have the stuff. I have no use for it.'"

Another segment of Brazel's story would become important later. It was the way he became involved in the first place. According to him, he was living in Albuquerque in July 1947. He was aware that his father was living at the ranch house about twenty miles from Corona and that the rest of the family was living in Tularosa near Alamogordo. While reading the morning newspaper, he noticed the story that concerned his father. He realized that his father would need help at the ranch. Brazel said, "So I proceeded out to the ranch. I think it was two or three days before my dad showed up."

This corroborated the reports that Mack Brazel had been in Roswell for a number of days before he returned. Bessie Brazel Schrieber, a daughter, during interviews conducted in the mid-1990s, would suggest that she had been at the ranch when the events took place, that she and her father had picked up all the pieces, and that her father had not been in Roswell for several days. This discrepancy would become important to the factions arguing over the truth of the Roswell events.

See also *Brazel, Mack; Debris Field; Strickland, Marian*

Brazel, Mack (1899–1963) If Mack Brazel hadn't been in his field on the morning of July 5, 1947, the story might never have reached the public. The strange metallic debris that was scattered over one of his pastures southeast of Corona, New Mexico, might never have been discussed. Had it not been for Mack Brazel, the entire story of the crash near Roswell might have remained a military secret.

Brazel heard a loud crashing sound late on the evening of July 4. It came during an electrical storm that raced across Lincoln County, New Mexico, but it did not sound like thunder. It was strange enough that other ranchers would later remember it. Early the next morning, as Brazel and a young neighbor boy, Dee Proctor, rode the range, they discovered the source of that crash. A field south of the ranch headquarters was filled with metallic debris. It extended from near the top of a small arroyo up another hill, and disappeared on the reverse side. There was quite a bit of debris. Some of it was shiny, but most looked like dull metal. There were big chunks and little pieces. The material was so densely packed that the sheep refused to cross it.

A closer examination produced no clear evidence of an aircraft accident. There was no indication of passengers in whatever had crashed. The debris was so thin and so light that it stirred in the wind, but it was so strong that most pieces wouldn't flex. Brazel couldn't cut it with his knife and he couldn't burn it with matches.

Taking some of the smaller samples with him, Brazel headed off to see his nearest neighbors, Floyd and Loretta Proctor, Dee's parents, who lived about ten miles from the ranch headquarters and twenty from the debris field. When Brazel showed his neighbors a sliver of the material, they were as puzzled by it as he was. Loretta Proctor later said she "didn't know what the stuff was." Floyd tried to whittle on it but couldn't make a mark. Brazel held a match up to it to show that not only wouldn't it burn, it wouldn't even blacken.

Brazel suggested they drive down to look at the debris field, but the Proctors, busy with their own ranch, declined. Today Loretta says, "We should have gone, but gas and tires were expensive then. We had our own chores and it would have been twenty miles . . ."

Brazel didn't know what to do about the material, which was causing him practical problems. Because the sheep wouldn't cross the field, Brazel had to drive them the long way around to get them to water. Somebody, possibly whoever was responsible for it, was going to have to clean up the mess. He was too busy to take time to do it. And there was so much of it that it would take days for him to complete the task.

The next day, July 6, Brazel drove to Roswell to see the Chaves County sheriff, George A. Wilcox. Wilcox let one of the deputies handle Brazel at first. According to Jay Tulk, son-in-law of the sheriff, Brazel was an old cowboy in old clothes and scuffed boots. But when Brazel showed a small piece of the debris to Wilcox, the sheriff suggested that he call the local air base.

Before that call was made, Frank Joyce, an announcer and reporter for Roswell radio station KGFL, phoned looking for anything new. Wilcox put Brazel on the line and Joyce, while he was changing records and running the control board, interviewed Brazel over the phone. Today, Joyce is specific about what Brazel said, saying that his story told on Sunday was significantly different from that told by Brazel later, on Tuesday, July 9.

Major Jesse A. Marcel was eating lunch in the officer's club when, as he would recall, "I got a call from the sheriff from Roswell and he wanted to talk to me. He said, 'There's a man here and he told me something weird.' . . . I said, 'Well, I'm all ears,' and he said . . . he found something on his ranch that crashed, either the day before or a few days before, and he doesn't know what it is."

Marcel drove immediately to the sheriff's office, questioned Brazel, and then returned to the base. Because Brazel had described a field filled with debris, Marcel realized he would have to make a trip to the ranch. And he would need some help.

Marcel and a plainclothes counterintelligence officer later identified as Captain Sheridan Cavitt departed in separate cars, with

Brazel in the lead. According to Marcel, "He [Cavitt] drove a jeep carryall. I drove my staff car . . . We took off cross country behind this pickup truck this rancher [Brazel] had. He didn't follow any roads going out there. We got to his place about dusk. It was too late to do anything so we spent the night there in that little shack." They spent the night at the Hines house just three or four miles north of the debris field.

Early the next morning, July 7, Brazel took the two military officers out to the crash site. Brazel, in preparation to lead the military men to the debris field, had saddled two horses, but Marcel had never ridden a horse. Marcel said, "You two ride the horses . . . so they took off . . . we went up there."

After watching the two officers for a short time, Brazel rode off to complete his duties. Marcel and Cavitt spent the day examining the field, walking the perimeters of it and then picking up the debris.

In Roswell, Joyce told KGFL owner Walt Whitmore about Brazel's strange claims. Intrigued, Whitmore decided to pursue the story. He drove out to the Brazel ranch, picked him up, and returned to Roswell. George "Jud" Roberts, minority owner of the radio station, later said, "They hid him out at Whit's [Walt Whitmore Sr.] house. Kept him there over night."

They made a wire recording about Brazel's find but it was too late to air it that night. According to the "Radio Log—KGFL—1400" as published in the *Roswell Daily Record*, KGFL signed off at 10 P.M. on July 7. The interview would never be aired and was destroyed on direct orders of both the Federal Communications Commission and part of the New Mexico congressional delegation. Roberts later said, "We were told that we would have twenty-four hours to find something else to do because we would no longer be in the radio business."

On the evening of July 8, military officers escorted Brazel into downtown Roswell to talk to reporters at the offices of the *Roswell Daily Record*. Two reporters from Albuquerque, Jason Kellahin and

R. A. Adair, had brought a portable wire photo transmitter with them so they could transmit pictures over the telephone lines. AP in New York had ordered them to Roswell to obtain and transmit pictures of Brazel and Sheriff Wilcox.

Brazel told some reporters that he had found the debris on June 14, while on the ranch with his wife, his daughter Bessie, and his son Vernon. In that interview, published in the July 9 edition of the *Daily Record* and picked up by the wire services, Brazel now claimed that the debris was smokey gray rubber and that it was confined to an area about two hundred yards in diameter. While no words were visible, there were letters on part of it, along with a little scotch tape and some tape with flowers on it. Although no strings or wires were fastened to it, a few eyelets in the paper indicated that an attachment might have been used.

The new story ended with Brazel saying he had found weather observation devices on two other occasions but that this object didn't resemble those. "I am sure what I found was not any weather observation balloon," he said.

Of course, there was another article in the July 9 *Roswell Daily Record* in which it is suggested that the debris had been "found several days ago." That is more consistent with the information developed through other sources.

The military escort officers, reported *Daily Record* editor Paul McEvoy, then led Brazel out of the newspaper offices. While they were walking toward the car, two of Brazel's neighbors, Floyd Proctor and Lyman Strickland, happened to pass by. Both were surprised that Brazel didn't say a word to them. Proctor said later that the military was keeping Brazel on a very short leash.

Brazel got into the car and was taken to radio station KGFL, where he went inside alone. According to Frank Joyce, Brazel stood against the wall and told the cover story the Army had given him: The strange object was a balloon.

Joyce bluntly told Brazel that he knew the story wasn't true. He listened to it and then pointed out it was not the same story that Brazel had told a couple of days earlier, before the "Army had gotten to him." Specifically, Brazel had said nothing about his family being with him, and he had described a debris field considerably larger than two hundred yards in diameter.

Joyce said that Brazel stuck with the new story, however, while growing more agitated. Finally he said, "It'll go hard on me." Presumably he had been warned of the consequences if he said anything else.

Three weeks later, speaking to neighbors Lyman and Marian Strickland, Brazel complained bitterly about his treatment. He said he had been refused permission even to call home, to Tularosa where the family lived, to tell his wife where he was.

Before long, the military knew everything, including that Dee had been with Brazel and that he had friends who had been to the site. Within days military personnel visited the boys who had taken some samples home, demanding that the material be turned over immediately. The officers obtained all the pieces that had been taken from the field.

Brazel remained in custody in Roswell for approximately eight days. After his return to the ranch, he would say little about what had happened to him in Roswell. Some of his neighbors reported that he now talked about finding a weather balloon.

Privately, to his family and his closest friends, Brazel told a slightly different story, all the while remembering the security oath the Army had insisted he take. Bill Brazel said, "My dad found this thing and told me a little bit about it. Not much, because the Air Force asked him to take an oath that he wouldn't tell anybody in detail about it. And my dad was such a guy that he went to his grave and he *never* told anybody."

All Mack Brazel would say was that whatever it was, it wasn't any type of balloon. He told his son Bill that he was better off not knowing a thing about it. By the time Brazel returned to the ranch, all signs of the debris were gone. The military had packed the wreckage into trucks and taken it away.

Months later, while riding the range, Brazel spotted a piece of the debris in a sinkhole. He pointed it out to Tommy Tyree, but neither man climbed down to retrieve it. At that time it seemed to be more trouble than it was worth.

Cactus Jack After seeing the *Unsolved Mysteries* program detailing the Roswell UFO crash story, Iris Foster wrote to researchers, telling them about Cactus Jack. He was an old-time prospector and Indian artifact hunter who made a marginal living in the desert Southwest. According to Foster, he told her in 1971 that he had been there when the spaceship crashed. The story was intriguing because he was apparently telling it nearly twenty years before the Roswell case became well known.

According to Foster, Cactus Jack told her that he had seen the "object which was round, but not real big." He said he saw four bodies and said that they were small. Their blood, according to Jack, was like tar, thick and black, and it stained their silvery uniforms.

Foster was sure of the time frame because it was when she owned a cafe and Cactus Jack came in frequently. According to Foster, he had been injured in a fire in the mid-1980s, but she wasn't sure what happened to him after that. She thought he was dead but just didn't know.

Tom Carey, fascinated by any of the stories that touched on archaeology or anthropology, wanted to find Cactus Jack. He knew that Kevin Randle had been to Taos, the last known home of Cactus Jack, had searched the newspaper files for a mention of the

story about the fire, and had failed to learn anything. To Randle the
search for Cactus Jack was a side issue, but Carey wanted to learn
more about it.

Although he didn't have much luck at first, Carey finally was
able to learn that Cactus Jack had died and managed to obtain a
copy of his last driver's license. He also found the article in the Taos
newspaper confirming that Cactus Jack had been injured in a fire,
just as Foster had said. There was a picture of Jack in the hospital
with his head wrapped in bandages.

But, more important, Carey was able to locate some of Jack's
old friends. They, too, had heard the story of the crashed UFO.
Although it doesn't prove that Cactus Jack had seen what he
claimed, it did prove that he had been telling the tale for quite a
number of years, certainly before there had been any real publicity
about the Roswell case.

Carey, writing in the *International UFO Reporter*, concluded
that the tale, based on anecdotal testimony, was still consistent.
There were claims of letters written by Cactus Jack that could at
least document when he had been telling the tale. Although such
letters wouldn't prove that there had been a UFO crash, they could
demonstrate that Jack had been telling his tales before the Roswell
case had received widespread publicity. Those letters would provide
a nice bit of corroboration, but, unfortunately, they haven't surfaced.

Circleville, Ohio The recovery of a weather balloon and rawin
radar target in early July 1947, near Circleville, is important to
understanding the Roswell case because of the close parallels to it.
Sherman Campbell, a farmer, found the remains of a balloon and
radar target about July 1, 1947. He recognized it for what it was
immediately, but believed that the shiny aluminum radar reflector,
if high in the atmosphere and spinning, might look disk-shaped.
He gathered up the material quickly and took it to the local sheriff.

The sheriff recognized it for what it was and called the local newspaper. Pictures of Jean Campbell, Campbell's daughter (though identified in some of the newspapers as his wife), holding the rawin target were printed. It was offered as an explanation for some of the "flying disc" reports that were being made throughout the country.

The balloon and radar reflector were on display in the window of the local newspaper for a number of weeks. When the interest died, the balloon was returned to Campbell. In the 1990s, Jean Campbell Romero told investigators that the balloon had remained in the barn for several years but she no longer knew where it might be.

The case is interesting to Roswell investigators because here was a farmer, as ignorant of weather balloons and radar reflectors as those in New Mexico, who, when confronted with what was apparently the same sort of debris, identified it immediately. He took it to the local sheriff, who also identified it immediately, and they took it to the local newspaper, where the reporters identified it immediately. This suggests that weather balloons carrying rawin targets were not so unusual that they would not be identified for what they were.

The difference in Roswell was that no one could identify the same kind of debris, according to the officers at Fort Worth. Later, the Air Force would imply that the debris found in New Mexico was from a Project Mogul balloon array train and that might have fooled the people. The problem is that Mogul was nothing more than a cluster of weather balloons and a series of rawin targets. Although there were more of them in the Mogul array, they should have been as easily identifiable as a single balloon and target. There would be nothing to fool anyone into believing that the Mogul array was anything other than terrestrial balloons.

The Circleville report provides an interesting parallel to the Roswell case. It demonstrates that anyone, even those unfamiliar with weather balloons and rawin radar targets, should have been able to identify them.

Corso, Lieutenant Colonel Philip J. (1915–1998) Philip Corso burst on the Roswell UFO scene in the summer of 1997 with the publication of his book, *The Day After Roswell*. It was Corso's story of his involvement with the flying saucer crash at Roswell, first as an officer at Fort Riley, Kansas; later, as a staff officer in the Pentagon and the Eisenhower White House; and finally on the staff of Lieutenant General Arthur Trudeau. Corso claimed that he had been responsible, under orders from Trudeau, for leaking bits of alien technology to American industry for duplication and replication.

According to Corso's military records, he was born on May 22, 1915, entered the Army on February 23, 1942, and remained on active duty until February 28, 1963, when he retired. He saw service in the European Theater during World War II, rising to the rank of major. His assignments at that time were with Intelligence, and he was an interpreter in Italy. In 1947, he returned to the United States and was assigned to Fort Riley, Kansas, in April 1947, where he remained until 1950.

It was at Fort Riley that Corso was introduced, according to him, to the alien crash at Roswell. Corso was an above average bowler and because of his skill was invited to participate on the Fort Riley team by Master Sergeant Bill Brown. Corso was surprised because enlisted men weren't supposed to fraternize with officers, but apparently Corso's skill was such that the master sergeant took a chance and breached military protocol.

The friendship that developed between Corso and the master sergeant, whom he now called by the nickname Brownie, would play an important role in what happened on the evening of July 6, 1947, after the arrival of a "secret" convoy. Corso was assigned as the post duty officer, in charge of security and, as he described it, the "human firewall between emergency and disaster." As he walked his post, checking the security, he failed to find Sergeant Brown where he was supposed to be. Instead, Brown was in the doorway of the veterinary clinic. There was something inside that Corso just had to see.

Forget for the moment that Brown would have had no reason to enter the building unless there was some sort of a disturbance inside, or that the secret convoy of five "deuce and half" (two-and-a-half-ton trucks) with its accompanying "low boy" side-by-side trailers would have been guarded by the men who brought them to Fort Riley. Forget also that the best evidence suggests that the material from the crash was shipped by air to its various destinations. Corso, in his firsthand account, claimed that it all stopped at Fort Riley, and that the Military Police assigned to it as guards were all armed. These guards, once the material was secured in the veterinary clinic, apparently abandoned their posts to leave the guarding of the crates to the local soldiers.

Those local soldiers, being curious men, began to search the material from the top secret convoy. What they found so upset them that they risked the wrath of the post duty officer by telling him that there was something he had to see. Brown told Corso that he had to take a look at what the convoy was transporting. Corso warned Brown that he wasn't supposed to be there and had better leave. Brown said that he would watch the door.

Inside the building, Corso found the crates but hesitated to pry open any of them. He searched among them until he found one that had apparently already been opened, because the nails were loose. He opened that crate and then looked down inside. In a glass tube containing a blue fluid, floating, suspended, was what Corso thought at first was a small child. Then he knew it wasn't a child, but a human-looking creature with "bizarre-looking four-fingered hands . . . thin legs and feet, and an oversized incandescent light-bulb-shaped head . . ."

Rifling through the crate, Corso found an Army Intelligence document detailing that the creature was from a craft that had crashed outside of Roswell. It appeared to manifest the remains to, first, the Air Materiel Command at Wright Field, and then to Walter Reed Hospital for what Corso believed would be an autopsy. Realizing that he was not supposed to have read the document, seen the creature, opened the crate, or penetrated the security around the cargo, Corso put everything back and hurried outside. He told Brown that he had seen nothing and that he was to tell no one.

That wasn't, of course, Corso's last brush with the Roswell case. It was, however, more than a decade before he again saw anything dealing with Roswell. Instead he had a number of military assignments, moving him to Washington, D.C., and then to Fort Bliss, Texas. At Bliss he was trained in anti-aircraft artillery, then assigned as an inspector of training and then as battalion commander for several weeks before he was reassigned to Europe. While at Bliss, according to Corso, he was assigned as the commander of the White Sands Missile Range. At least, that is what he told reporters in the summer of 1997.

In Germany in 1957, he was a commander of a Nike battalion. In March 1959, he became the Special Assistant to the Chief of Staff at the Seventh Army Headquarters. In May 1959, he became an Inspector General at Seventh Army HQ, and continued in that assignment for about a year. In 1960, he returned to the United States. In 1961, he was assigned as a staff officer to the Plans Division in Washington, D.C., and then as a staff officer to the Army's Foreign Technology Division until April 1961, when he became the Chief of Foreign Technology. Three months later, he was reassigned as a staff officer at Plans, and just over a year later he retired.

It was during the tour in 1961 that he became involved once again with the Roswell case. According to an affidavit prepared by Peter Gersten, "In 1961, I [Corso] came into possession of what I refer to as the 'Roswell File.' This file contained field reports, medical autopsy reports and technological debris from the crash of an extraterrestrial vehicle in Roswell, New Mexico in 1947."

Corso's job in 1961 was to parcel the debris into American industry hands for research and development. The idea was to suggest to various companies that the small artifact or metal had come from an unknown source. The expertise of the scientists at the companies was supposed to unlock the secrets of the debris. This led, according to Corso, to the creation of the transistor, night vision equipment, fiber optics, lasers, microwave ovens, and a host of other recent developments.

All of this was outlined in Corso's book, which became news in July 1997. He appeared on NBC's *Dateline* for an exclusive interview. About a week later he appeared in Roswell for a press conference, a lecture, and a book signing. For three weeks in August, his book appeared on the *New York Times* bestseller list.

Corso was the highest-ranking officer to write a book about Roswell and to make public claims about the case. According to him, he had been a member of the NSC, had worked inside Eisenhower's White House, and had served with the Army's Foreign Technology Division. If he could be believed, then here was the truth about the Roswell crash. Finally, a witness with impressive credentials had gone on the record.

The stories told by Corso to friends and family are even more impressive than those detailed in his book. In a proposed chapter that was edited out of his book, Corso claimed that in 1957 he had taken command of missiles at Red Canyon, where he trained specialists in the management of sophisticated radar and range-finding equipment. It was here that Corso saw a series of radar contacts showing objects that could outperform the best Air Force interceptors.

Corso, according to the details of the missing chapter, had been told to report all unidentifiable sightings and then finally was told to forget them. He also claimed that at "times of intense UFO activity during his tenure as commander . . . he is ordered to turn his targeting radars completely off because, he believes, the craft themselves are in danger from our missiles as well as from our high-energy radars."

There is also a hint that Corso, if not a member of MJ-12, the committee allegedly created in 1947 to study the Roswell UFO crash, was fully aware of its existence. In a somewhat ambiguous statement in his book proposal, Corso "also recounts the continuing reports of UFO activity that passed through Eisenhower's White House, when the author was on assignment there to the staff of MJ-12."

Naturally Corso's claims were subjected to intense scrutiny. Problems with his book began to arise almost immediately. For example, Corso had claimed to be a member of the NSC in the Eisenhower White House. Herbert L. Pankratz, an archivist at the Eisenhower Library, reported that Corso was not a member of the National Security Council or its ancillary agency, known as the Operations Coordinating Board.

Corso, in his book, told of how he had intimidated the CIA director of covert operations after Corso learned the CIA was following him. He told Frank "Wiesner" that he was going to start carrying a gun and that if he ever spotted a CIA agent following him, they would find the agent's body with bullet holes in the head. Corso then noted that Wiesner was found dead in his London hotel room in 1961. Wiesner had killed himself by hanging.

The problem is that most of the facts used by Corso to support this story, from the claim that he had charged into the Langley headquarters of the CIA to the facts surrounding the death of Frank Wisner (note correct spelling), are wrong. Corso couldn't have charged into the Langley headquarters because it wasn't open when Corso supposedly entered the building. Corso couldn't have driven to Wisner's office as he claimed because in April 1961, Wisner was, in fact, assigned to the CIA's London office. Wisner did eventually commit suicide, but it was with a shotgun, at the family farm, and on October 29, 1965.

What may be the most telling of the events surrounding the publication of Corso's book is the foreword by Senator Strom Thurmond. Here seems to be an endorsement for Corso's book from a man who has served in the U.S. Senate longer than almost anyone. When the book was published, Thurmond objected, claiming that the foreword he had written had been for a different book. The publisher, Simon and Schuster, issued an apology and pulled the foreword from future printings of the book.

Corso tried to explain it away, saying that Thurmond's staff had written the foreword and that "the old man knew it," and that they hadn't really known the nature of the book. The whole flap, according to Corso, was a misunderstanding about the nature of the book and who actually authored the foreword. As a matter of courtesy, given the controversy, Simon and Schuster decided to pull the foreword.

Karl Pflock, who had been around Washington, D.C., in various capacities, decided to look into the matter himself, believing that his friends and sources inside the Beltway would give him a unique perspective on the matter. Pflock, it turned out, knew the senator's press secretary, and learned that "Yes, it's true the foreword was drafted by one of the senator's staff . . . It was done at the senator's direction on the understanding he had from Corso that it was to be for Corso's memoirs, for which he and his staff were supplied an outline, a document which made no mention of UFOs." Pflock added, "I know of my own certain knowledge the senator was and is mad as hell about the cheap trick that Corso pulled on him . . ."

Pflock continued, pointing out that Deputy General Counsel Eric Raymond demanded, "Recall all copies of the first printing— failing that, remove all dust jackets with the senator's name on them; stop using any reference to the foreword by the senator in promoting the book; do not use the foreword in any subsequent printings of the book; issue a statement acknowledging the truth, 'to establish for the public record' that the senator 'had no intention or desire to write the foreword to *The Day After Roswell*,' a 'project I completely disavow.'"

The apology issued by Simon and Schuster was not as bland as Corso had characterized it but was, in fact, damning in its wording. It was clear that Thurmond did not know the nature of the book and that the outline he had read was for a completely different book. The publisher did remove the foreword from all subsequent editions of the book.

This might seem as if it is an argument over trivia, but it does speak to the general attitude of Corso in constructing his book. If he was willing to mislead a U.S. senator, one whom Corso considered a friend, why believe that he wouldn't want to mislead the rest of the country? The evidence is that he played fast and loose with the truth.

For example, it was Corso who said that he had been the commander at the White Sands Missile Range, but a check of the range's Website revealed that with two exceptions, the range had been commanded by a general officer. The first exception was Colonel Turner, who had been the first commander, and the second was when a full colonel took over temporarily when the commanding general died. Corso's name did not surface as a commander.

However, as noted, his records indicated that he had been a battalion commander at Fort Bliss in El Paso, Texas. The two organizations, Fort Bliss and White Sands Missile Range, share some facilities. So it might be said Corso was *a* commander at White Sands, but not *the* commander. Clearly Corso was inflating his record when speaking to members of the press.

During those same press conferences, Corso made other statements that were quite revealing. He mentioned the Philadelphia Experiment, a hoax that began in 1956 when a man claimed he had witnessed, during World War II, Navy efforts to teleport a destroyer. The story is an admitted hoax, but Corso began telling reporters about the event, claiming that he had read the top secret files about it.

Research into Corso's claims showed that they were firmly grounded in the UFO community. Corso had read and reviewed everything that had been printed, published on the Internet, or shown in television documentaries over the last five or six years. There was nothing new in Corso's book, except for his claim that he had seen one of the bodies at Fort Riley and that he was the conduit for the alien technology to American industry. For evidence, he offered nothing more than his claim that it happened and documentation that had nothing to do with his claims.

In fact, when Corso came into conflict with other witnesses or information that was contrary to his point of view, he retreated. He was quick to suggest that his information might not have been the best. In other cases, it seemed to have been the worst. The caption over a photograph in his book read, "Lt. Col. Corso was never able to confirm the veracity of the following purported UFO surveillance photos which were in Army Intelligence files as support for material for the R&D project to harvest the Roswell alien technology for military purposes."

The first of the pictures is of a well-known hoax. The photographer, Guy B. Marquand Jr., told various UFO researchers, as well as the editors of *Look,* that he was sorry, but it was a hoax. He had been young and foolish and thought it a great joke. It would seem that if Corso was on the inside, he would have been aware that this particular UFO photograph was faked.

Given the information available, given the mistakes in Corso's book, and given his inflation of his own importance during his military career, it seems that the logical conclusion is that Corso's claims are of little value. They added nothing to what was already known, and certainly have detracted from the whole of the Roswell case. When his claims break apart, those who know little about Roswell become convinced that the whole case is built on structures similar to those built by Corso.

Crash Sites Over the last decade, there have been a multiplicity of crash sites identified for the Roswell events. First is the Debris Field found by Mack Brazel and visited by Major Jesse Marcel, Sheridan Cavitt, and others. Nearly everyone, skeptic, debunker, and true believer, has accepted that something was found on the Debris Field. It is the identity of that debris that is in dispute.

Second is the site on the Plains of San Agustin, identified through the secondhand testimony of Barney Barnett. Barnett had suggested to his boss, "Fleck" Danley, that the crash had taken place to the west of Socorro, in the high country around the Plains of San Agustin. There has been no reliable firsthand testimony to corroborate this site. Gerald Anderson, who surfaced after the *Unsolved Mysteries* broadcast in early 1990, seemed to be that corroboration. His story, however, broke apart under objective investigation.

For a period, these were the only two sites that had been identified. However, beginning in the mid-1980s, information was developed suggesting a third location not far from the Debris Field. The information, for the most part, came from the Eisenhower briefing document that was a portion of the MJ-12 film sent to Jaime Shandera. It suggested that "On 07 July, 1947, a secret operation was begun to assure recovery of the wreckage of this object for scientific study. During the course of this operation, aerial reconnaissance discovered that four small human-like beings had ejected from the craft at some point before it exploded. They had fallen to Earth about two miles east of the wreckage site."

In both Roswell and Corona, there were people who suggested that this site was south of a pair of windmills, in a rocky valley that could not be seen from the Debris Field. The problem here was that the MJ-12 briefing document was eventually discredited, and there were no firsthand witnesses who could supply definitive information.

Kevin Randle and Don Schmitt, in their book *The Truth About the UFO Crash at Roswell*, proposed another location for the "Impact Site." Based on testimony they had uncovered, they believed that the craft had come to rest against a rocky cliff about twenty or thirty miles north of Roswell, just off Highway 285. Although the location of the site was partially based on information from Jim Ragsdale, whose testimony was later discredited, there were others who provided the exact location, including Frank Kaufmann. Other witnesses, using detailed maps, corroborated what Kaufmann had said.

Ranch owner Hub Corn, at first disturbed that researchers were crossing his land, eventually became interested in the UFO crash site. He erected a sign offering escorted tours to the location and then put up a marker at the alleged site. He created a minor tourist attraction that now includes two large rocky obelisks, a marked pathway, and a small flag where the craft is supposed to have come to a rest.

The International UFO Museum and Research Center provided another location for the crash. According to Hub Corn, the museum had tried to arrange for a joint venture to develop the site on his property. When that failed, they found another crash site based solely on the testimony of Jim Ragsdale. According to this version, Ragsdale had not been in the desert north of Roswell, but had been northwest of town at a place known as Pine Lodge. According to the new Ragsdale story, this was where he had been when he watched the object flash overhead and smash into a huge rock after damaging several large trees.

While Ragsdale insisted that this was the "true" site, others disagreed with him. Longtime residents of the area, including the relatives of those who had owned Pine Lodge, said that nothing had happened in the area. Those who had lived around Pine Lodge in the summer of 1947 were quite clear in their statements: They had seen or heard nothing that could have been either the crash or the military retrieval operation.

Yet another site was developed from the *Alien Autopsy* film. Originally claimed to be part of the Roswell events, it evolved into a separate crash that had taken place a month earlier and near Socorro. According to the cameraman, who had said that he as well as others were flown into Roswell, they were eventually taken by truck and jeep into the Socorro area. This is where he saw and photographed the remains of the alien craft. He was vague as to the exact location. Once again there was no firsthand testimony that anything had crashed near Socorro in the time frame mentioned.

Don Schmitt, not content with the Impact Site north of Roswell, suggested that the real Impact Site, while in the general area originally identified, is in reality south of there. He has developed new sources that have given him this information about the crash.

Just recently, there has been talk of another crash site to the east of Roswell. Some have suggested that it is in the Bottomless Lake area, a state park about fifteen or twenty miles from Roswell. As has happened in the past, it is based on rumor and speculation, with little or no testimony to corroborate it.

Day After Roswell, The The book authored by Philip J. Corso and William J. Birnes in which Corso claims to have seen an alien creature recovered by military authorities and that alien technology was back-engineered by American scientists to produce many devices used today.

See also ***Corso, Lieutenant Colonel Philip J.***

Debris There have been a number of people who claimed to have seen strange metallic debris that came from the alleged alien spacecraft. Those descriptions have agreed, in large part, but, more important, they tend to rule out many of the mundane explanations offered by skeptics. To accept some of those explanations, it becomes necessary to reject out of hand the descriptions offered by both civilian observers and military officers.

Major Jesse A. Marcel Sr. told researchers, "I'd never seen anything like that. I didn't know what we were picking up." Later he said that some of the debris was as thin as newsprint, feather light, but so strong they couldn't dent it or burn it. He described foil-like material, I-beams, and ". . . other stuff there that looked very much like parchment that didn't burn."

Marcel was so impressed by what he had seen that he stopped at his house on the way back to the base. He wanted his wife and son to see the debris. When Jesse Marcel Jr. saw the strange material, he asked his father what it was. Marcel Sr. replied, "It's a flying saucer."

Marcel Jr. said that he saw some foil material that was thicker than lead foil and much stronger. He mentioned the I-beams, which seemed to be made out of layered foil and embossed with writing. Marcel Jr. described the writing as "Purple. Strange. Never saw anything like it."

Mack Brazel, who originally found the debris field, was not interviewed in person by UFO investigators, but his son Bill Brazel was. In the months after the crash, Brazel searched for pieces of the debris. He found, according to him, ". . . oh, not over a dozen and I'd say eight. There were three items involved. Something on the order of balsa wood and something on the order of heavy gauge monofilament fishing line and a little piece of . . . it wasn't really aluminum foil and it wasn't lead foil."

Brazel said the wood-like piece would flex a little. "I couldn't break it and I couldn't whittle it with my pocketknife . . . The only reason I noticed the tin foil was that I picked this stuff up and put it in my chaps pocket . . . when I took it out and put it in the box it started unfolding itself and flattened out . . . I would fold it or crease it and lay it down and watch it. It was kind of weird."

Brazel showed that small piece of foil to others. Sallye Tadolini was the daughter of Marian Strickland, one of Brazel's neighbors in 1947. Brazel showed her the foil and she has the impression that it was dull in color, maybe gray, and that it was a small piece. Brazel, according to her, balled it up in his hand and then opened his hand, letting it return to its original shape. She thought it was stiff, like aluminum foil, but that it did not seem metallic.

Others around the Brazel ranch, such as Loretta Proctor, saw a small "sliver" of the debris. It was a pencil-size piece that couldn't be cut with a knife or burned with a match. Proctor said that it looked like plastic but that she "didn't know what the stuff was."

Tommy Tyree, who was hired as a ranch hand after the events

of July 1947, said that he was riding with Brazel late that summer when they spotted a piece of debris floating on top of the water in a sinkhole. Brazel told him it was a piece of the debris from the crash, something light enough to float on top of the water.

Military men picked up the debris for shipment from Roswell to various labs around the country. Robert Smith, an NCO with the 1st Air Transport Unit stationed at Roswell, told how he, along with a number of other men, loaded three or four aircraft with crates. All them were large, and many of them felt as if they were empty. Smith wasn't sure what was in them, but did say the loading took place under armed guard away from the main part of the ramp area at the airfield.

Smith did learn what was in the crates. According to Smith, "We were talking about what was in the crates and so forth and he [another of the sergeants] said, 'Oh, do you remember the story about the UFO?' . . . We thought he was joking, but he let us feel a piece and stuck it back in his pocket."

Like all the others, Smith said, "It was just a little piece of metal or foil or whatever it was . . . It was foil-like, but it was a little stiffer than foil . . . being a sheet metal man, that intrigued me, being that you could crumble it up and it would flatten back out again without any wrinkles showing up in it."

Pappy Henderson, one of the pilots who flew debris out of Roswell, told a couple of friends about the debris. More important, he apparently was in possession of a piece for a number of years. He showed it to a close friend, John Kromschroeder, who had an interest in metallurgy. Kromschroeder said that he had never seen anything like it.

The metal, according to Kromschroeder, was gray and resembled aluminum but was harder and stiffer. He couldn't bend it but had to be careful because the edges were sharp. He said that based on its fracturing, it didn't seem to have a crystalline structure. It hadn't been torn.

Kromschroeder said Henderson told him that the metal was

part of the lighter material lining the interior of the craft. Krom-schroeder said that when properly energized, it produced perfect illumination. It cast a soft light with no shadows.

That piece of debris apparently came from Major Ellis Boldra. Boldra subjected the sample to a number of tests. It was thin, incredibly strong, and dissipated heat in some matter. Boldra used an acetylene torch on the material, but it didn't melt and barely got warm. It didn't glow when heated, and once the flame was removed, it could be handled in seconds.

Boldra tried to cut it with a variety of tools and failed. No one remembers if he tried to drill through it. One of Boldra's friends said that it wasn't any type of metal that he could identify.

Boldra and Kromschroeder weren't the only ones to describe the debris as incredibly strong. Lewis Rickett, the noncommis-sioned officer in charge (NCOIC) of the counterintelligence office at Roswell, had an opportunity to see some of the debris still on the impact site. By the time Rickett arrived, on July 8, the vast majority of the debris had been collected, but there were still some pieces scattered around.

As Rickett walked the field with Captain Sheridan Cavitt, he wanted to know if it was "hot." He was told that there was no evi-dence of radioactivity.

Rickett found one piece that was about two feet square and crouched to pick it up. It was slightly curved, but the only way he could tell that was to place it on something that was flat. He then locked it against his knee and used his arm to try to bend it. According to Rickett, it was very thin and very lightweight.

Rickett said the metal wasn't plastic and didn't feel like plastic, but he had never seen a piece of metal that thin that couldn't be bent.

There were three types of debris consistently described by the witnesses. First, by far the most common, was the foil that was thicker than normal aluminum foil, more like a lead foil. But unlike either of those, this foil, when folded or wadded into a ball, would unfold itself with no sign of a crease. Among the witnesses to the foil are Bill Brazel, Frankie Rowe, Robert Smith, and Sally Tatalini.

Second, Bill Brazel talked of the lightweight material that reminded him of balsa wood but was so strong that it couldn't be cut. Loretta Proctor handled something with similar properties. Rickett, Marcel, Easley, Boldra, Kromschroeder, and W. E. Lounsbury talked of lightweight material "as thin as newsprint" that couldn't be bent or marked.

Finally, there were the wire-like pieces that Bill Brazel described as flexible. He said that he could shine a light in one end and it would come out the other no matter how he twisted the wire around. This sounds suspiciously like fiber optics.

These are the eyewitnesses who saw or handled the debris found on either the debris field or the Corn ranch impact site. Dozens of people saw the material and describe it in the same terms over and over. These remains are not the stuff of balloons, experimental aircraft, or rockets. If, for example, the lead gauge foil could be made into something stronger, and it was Jesse Marcel's opinion that it was used to make the I-beams, then it could be used in the manufacture of automobiles. The next fender bender could be resolved by the drivers backing up and letting the metal return to its former shape.

The point is that no such material exists today. There are, after a fashion, molecules with a memory, but nothing that can be twisted out of shape and then return when the pressure is released.

The question becomes, who was making material with such strange properties in 1947? Why isn't there a hint of that material anywhere today?

Debris Field The best evidence available suggests that Mack Brazel found a field filled with strange metallic debris on the morning of July 5. The material was spread over a large area which, according to various witnesses, the sheep refused to cross. This area was on the Foster ranch, about twenty miles southeast of the small New

Mexico town of Corona. Others such as Jesse Marcel Sr. would suggest that the debris was scattered over an area of about three-quarters of a mile long and a few hundred feet wide. Bill Brazel Jr. and Bud Payne would mention a gouge through the center of it.

Debris Field as described by eyewitnesses. Its appearance was re-created for the Showtime movie *Roswell*. (*Photo courtesy of Kevin Randle*)

Debris, Fiftieth Anniversary In one of the more controversial aspects of the fiftieth anniversary celebration held in Roswell in 1997, it was announced that a bit of debris recovered by a soldier who had been among those on the cleanup contingent had been analyzed. Here at last was the physical evidence that everyone had demanded. Paul Davids, one of the executive producers of the Showtime original movie *Roswell*, told media representatives and UFO researchers that they had found the evidence to prove that the Roswell craft was extraterrestrial.

Davids told some researchers that the chain of custody had been preserved and that the debris had been analyzed at some of the top universities in the country. The information was solid, documented, and persuasive. In a pseudo press conference and public lecture, Davids took center stage and provided what seemed to be proof of the extraterrestrial nature of the Roswell crash.

When Davids finished, he introduced Dr. Russel VernonClark, a chemist employed by the University of California, San Diego. VernonClark, using a variety of slides and the results of his laboratory analysis, told reporters at the fiftieth anniversary that it was impossible for the metallic sample, something that had clearly been manufactured, to have come from Earth. Because it was a manufactured object and because the isotopic ratios of the elements of the sample were not those of Earth-based manufacture, this was proof that the sample came from another planet.

Although Davids had promised that the chain of custody had been preserved, the name of the man who owned the sample was not revealed. According to the story, the man's grandfather, whose name had been checked against the *RAAF Yearbook,* had slipped the sample into his pocket in 1947. Unfortunately for Davids and the media representatives, those who knew the name of the man refused to reveal it, as had been promised. The chain of custody, at least in the eyes of the media and many of the assembled researchers, had not been preserved.

Although VernonClark was employed at the University of California in San Diego and had taught classes there, his analysis of the metal was not endorsed by the university. None of the other university analyses nor the names of those universities were revealed. VernonClark's claims were left out there by themselves. Then, to make it worse, other scientists contacted suggested that Vernon-Clark's claim that the material was extraterrestrial because of its unusual characteristics was flawed. Metal with strange isotopic ratios could be purchased from the Department of Energy's Oak Ridge National Laboratory. A University of Kentucky chemist, Rob Toreki, told reporters that all that was needed to make the "extraterrestrial" material with its unusual isotopic ratios was some of the Oak Ridge samples and a chemistry lab.

In September 1997, VernonClark suggested that his report might have been premature and that he had been under pressure from those who held the sample to make the announcement. He acknowledged that the sample could have come from the Earth, but said that it was the isotopic ratios that were not naturally occurring on Earth that had influenced his report. He also said that he should have refused to participate in the lecture–press conference in Roswell and that he should have been more careful about what he said.

What is interesting, however, is that since that first burst of information about the sample, nothing new has been reported. The list of other universities that had allegedly corroborated the work has not been released, the names of the man who picked up the sample and the man who owns it have not been released, and no further analysis has been performed, or rather, none has been reported. This sample, which was supposed to break the Roswell UFO debate wide open, slipped into oblivion, as have so many other such claims. As it stands now, the sample can be called interesting, it can be called manufactured, but it can't be called extraterrestrial.

Dennis, Glenn Glenn Dennis was the man who first connected bodies of alien creatures to the base in Roswell. Although claiming to be reluctant to talk to reporters and television crews, he has always eventually submitted to their requests. Since he began to speak publicly in 1990, he has told the same basic story he tells today.

It all began, according to Dennis, a mortician by trade, when he received a number of phone calls from the base mortuary officer asking questions about bodies and small coffins. Later, because the mortuary also ran an ambulance service, he had to take an injured airman out to the base hospital. While there, he claims he saw strange metallic wreckage in the backs of a number of ambulances. He didn't think much of that because in aircraft accidents, wreckage was sometimes transported in the ambulances.

Inside the hospital, he noticed there was a great deal of unusual activity. He ignored most of it, instead thinking he would look for a nurse he knew and buy her a Coke. She saw him first, in the hospital hallway, and told him to get out before he got himself into deep trouble. But then, according to Dennis, a nasty officer saw him and asked what he was doing there. Dennis was being escorted from the hospital when another, red-haired officer ordered him held right there. The red-haired officer wanted some words with Dennis.

The only building of the original base hospital still standing. (*Photo courtesy of Kevin Randle*)

According to the tale told by Dennis, this officer was accompanied by a black NCO and both had bad attitudes. Dennis was told that there had been no aircraft accidents, in case that was what he thought, there had been nothing interesting happening at the hospital, and he, Dennis, would return to the city. He would tell no one what he saw, or what he thought he saw, or what he heard. If he mentioned it, they would be picking his bones out of the sand.

Dennis left the base puzzled, but a day or so later he spoke to the nurse, whom he later identified as Naomi Self. He met her at the officers club, where she told him the tale of a preliminary autopsy of little creatures from another star system. She told him not to tell a soul about the event and within days she was transferred off the base, apparently sent to England. Dennis received a note from her, telling him her address in England. The letter he wrote to her came back marked DECEASED. She had been killed in an aircraft accident, according to the other nurses at the base.

There were some ways to verify the story. One of the first was to check the yearbook produced in 1947. It contained the names and photographs of the majority of the people assigned to the base that year. According to Walter Haut, who put the yearbook together, 10 to 20 percent of the people failed to appear in the book, so when there was no picture of a Naomi Self, that wasn't particularly significant.

Don Berliner searched *Stars and Stripes,* a newspaper printed for the military personnel overseas. It contains military news, and if a group of Army nurses had been killed in an aircraft accident, as Dennis had said, it would have been reported there. It was not. A similar review of the *New York Times* from July 1947 to the mid-1950s did not reveal a crash that killed Army nurses.

Researchers, with the help of a police officers, credit bureaus, and CD-ROM telephone directories, were able to identify five women named Naomi Self. None of them were the right women. Dennis had also said she had a brother named William who had been a Marine Corps master sergeant in 1947. Again, researchers located more than 250 men with that name. None of them provided a clue about the nurse in Roswell.

A number of the former members of the medical team at Roswell in 1947 have been located. A nurse, Rosemary Brown, for example, said that she had no memory of a nurse who had been with the unit for a short period, as described by Dennis, or of a nurse named Naomi. A doctor said that he remembered very little of the staff at Roswell because it was so long ago. Still another man

who had been on the medical staff denied that there had been a
Naomi Self, or any sort of preliminary autopsy, at the base hospital.

In fact, there is no documentation for the existence of a nurse at
Roswell named Naomi Self. An Arizona researcher, V. G. Golubic,
undertook the search for the nurse thinking that he could find
something. Golubic has become the expert on the medical staff at
Roswell in July 1947. He has identified about eighteen women who
were assigned to the base as nurses, both military and civilian, in the
correct time frame, nurses who were not part of the yearbook or the
base telephone directory but whose names did surface in various
documents recovered through Freedom of Information Act
requests, interviews, and other sources.

Golubic has spoken to another nurse (other than Rosemary
Brown) who was at Roswell in 1947, and she has no memory of
Naomi Self. According to Golubic, he has found no trace of her,
except for confirmation provided by David Wagnon, who was an
enlisted technician in 1947. Golubic has spoken to Wagnon a number of times about it. He also points out that he has spoken to

Ballard's Funeral Home in Roswell. (*Photo courtesy of Kevin Randle*)

twenty to twenty-five members of the medical team at Roswell, and Naomi just doesn't surface, other than with Wagnon.

Golubic received the morning reports, which would document those assigned to the base in July 1947. He was able, after four or five attempts, to obtain the morning reports from October 1, 1946 through December 31, 1947, for Squadron M of the 509th Bomb Group. Naomi Self did not appear on those documents anywhere. Had she signed into the unit, signed out from it, been sent on temporary duty, been released from active service, or have had her status changed in any number of ways, her name should have surfaced in the morning reports. It did not.

As this information developed, Dennis began changing his story. He had not provided researchers with the real name of his nurse. He had given information that was close, but her real name was Naomi Maria Selff. Had that been right, researchers should have turned up something in one of the documents. If anyone had found a Naomi Selff, it would have been noticed because it is so close, but even with the new name, there was no documentation.

Dennis told another researcher that her real name was Naomi Sipes. Of course, had the name Naomi Sipes appeared anywhere, that would have been noticed as well. With the unusual first name and a last name that began with an "S," it is certainly close enough. But again, even with the new name, there was no documentation.

But the tale doesn't end there. When it was pointed out that no documentation, no corroboration, nothing verified the existence of the nurse, Dennis changed the tale once again. He had not supplied anyone with the right name. In fact, the last name didn't even begin with an "S." He was changing the tale as he was confronted with all the evidence, and such changes do not bode well for the credibility of the tale.

Glenn Dennis, who had once been considered one of the important witnesses, now seems to be another who was just out to grab the spotlight. There is little that can be said except that nothing has been found to confirm that his nurse exists or existed. And when challenged on these points, he began to change the tale. In a police investigation, such changes signal the end of the story. It means, simply, that the Glenn Dennis story, no matter how thrilling, exciting, or entertaining it might be, no longer has any supporting evidence.

DuBose, Brigadier General Thomas J. According to a statement signed in front of a state of Florida notary public, Thomas J. DuBose in July 1947 was the Chief of Staff of the Eighth Air Force, serving under Brigadier General Roger M. Ramey. During an interview conducted in August 1990, DuBose said that he had received a telephone call from Major General Clements McMullen, the Deputy Commander of the Strategic Air Command in Washington, D.C., on Sunday, July 6, 1947, who asked about the events that had occurred outside of Roswell. DuBose, in turn, called Colonel William Blanchard, commander of the 509th Bomb Group, and ordered him to send the material, in a sealed container, to him at Fort Worth.

A plane carrying some of the debris was dispatched from Roswell. DuBose asked the base commander, Colonel Al Clark, to take the material from Fort Worth to Washington, D.C., and deliver it to McMullen. DuBose then called McMullen, who told DuBose that he, McMullen, would send the material on to Benjamin Chidlaw at Wright Field. DuBose identified Chidlaw as the commanding general of the Air Materiel Command, but in reality, Nathan F. Twining was the commander in July 1947.

DuBose also identified the material photographed in Ramey's office as part of a weather balloon. DuBose said that the weather balloon explanation was a cover story designed to divert the attention of the press.

In interviews conducted in the early 1990s and videotaped for inclusion in the Fund for UFO Research's video library, DuBose elaborated. He added that McMullen ordered Ramey to cover up the whole thing. "They," meaning those at a higher command level, wanted to "put out the fire" as quickly as they could.

Speaking of the orders he received from McMullen, DuBose said, "He [McMullen] called me and said that I was . . . there was talk of some elements that had been found on the ground outside Roswell, New Mexico . . . that the debris or elements were to be placed in a suitable container and Blanchard was to see that they were delivered . . . they were placed in a suitable container and Al Clark, the base commander at Carswell [Fort Worth Army Air Field], would pick them up and hand-deliver them to McMullen in Washington. Nobody, and I must stress this, no one was to discuss with their wives, me with Ramey, with anyone. The matter as far as we're concerned was closed as of that moment."

DuBose then called Blanchard and "told him that there is this material his S-2 [Marcel] found in the desert and I said this is to be put in a suitable container by this major and you are to see that it is sealed, put in your little command aircraft, and flown by a proper courier [meaning an officer or NCO who is cleared to carry classified material], flown to Carswell and delivered to Al Clark, who will then deliver it to McMullen."

Because it was hot that day, DuBose waited in his office until he was told that the aircraft from Roswell was in the traffic pattern. Once he had the word, he drove out onto the ramp and waited for the airplane to land. He couldn't remember whether it was a B-25 or a B-26, but did say he knew it wasn't a B-29. McMullen would not have approved of using one of the bombers in that way.

As the plane rolled to a stop, Colonel Alan Clark walked over and received the bag from the Roswell crew. DuBose said, "Clark took the package and got into the B-26 [or B-25, the Fort Worth plane standing by] through the belly of it . . . he handed it to somebody . . . it was one of those things you tied to your wrist and he handed it to somebody and climbed in there. And that's the last I saw of it. In a couple . . . three hours it was delivered to McMullen and that's the last I heard of it."

DuBose wasn't sure of what happened to the debris after it got to Washington because McMullen had told him not to talk about it. But he did say, "McMullen said to me, or someone . . . what we're going to do with this is send it out to Wright Field and have it analyzed. That's a capability they didn't have at Andrews [the base in Washington where Clark and the flight landed]."

According to DuBose, there were no guards on the flight from Roswell and none on the Fort Worth aircraft. He also said that he never had the opportunity to see the debris. "I only saw the container and the container was a plastic bag that I would say weighed fifteen to twenty pounds. It was sealed . . . lead seal around the top . . . The only way to get into it was to cut it."

That, according to DuBose, was the only package. He made it clear that the debris in the bag was different from the debris that would later be displayed in Ramey's office two days later. The only flight with debris that DuBose knew about was the one made on Sunday, July 6. There would be other flights, but by that time, everything would be highly classified. In fact, DuBose said that "McMullen told me you are not to discuss this and this is a point at which this is more than top secret, beyond that . . . This is the highest priority and you will say nothing. That was the end of it."

Easley, Major (later Colonel) Edwin In July 1947, Edwin Easley was the provost marshal at the Roswell Army Air Field, which meant he was responsible for security and police functions. Asked during a first conversation if he was the right man, meaning had he been the provost marshal in July 1947 at Roswell, he said he was. When asked specifically about the UFO crash, he said, "I can't talk about it."

There are those in the UFO community who insist that Easley suggested the topic was classified because he didn't want to talk about it. Skeptics have suggested the quickest way to get rid of UFO investigators was to say that the events were classified and couldn't be discussed. In reality, the quickest way would have been to suggest that nothing was known about the crash.

Easley said repeatedly during that telephone interview that he had been sworn to secrecy. He couldn't talk about these events. Not that the events didn't happen, not that it was all invention, delusion, and imagination, but that he was sworn to secrecy. He couldn't talk about it.

In February 1991, Easley was interviewed once again. During that conversation, Easley provided the details of the case that he could. For example, he said that Mack Brazel had been held at the guest house on the base. Mack Brazel had told friends and family

that he had been in jail, put
there by the military. Easley's
statement seemed to corroborate that story, though being
held in the guest house is not
exactly the same as being in
jail. The question that springs
to mind, of course, is why
Mack Brazel would be held
by military authorities if there
wasn't some truth to this story.

But the most important
aspect of that conversation
with Easley was the end of it.
Here was a man who clearly
knew something about the
details of the Roswell case. He

Major Edwin Easley. (*Photo courtesy of
Walter Haut*)

had been sworn to secrecy, according to what he had repeatedly
said himself. He didn't want to talk about it, and his answers were
often short and sometimes cryptic. For example, asked if he
thought UFO researchers were following the right path, he asked,
"What do you mean?" The reply was that it was believed the craft
found had been of extraterrestrial origin.

He said, "Let me put it this way. That's not the wrong path."

Here is a man who retired from the military as a full colonel. In
1947 he was a major and in charge of the military police at the
Roswell Army Air Field. He went from Roswell to a long career in
the Air Force. He certainly wasn't the type of individual to invent
such a tale. In fact, had he not been sought out and interviewed, his
role in the Roswell events would never have been known. He didn't
come forward to find his place in the spotlight. His testimony
about the craft being extraterrestrial is extremely important.

But there is additional corroborative testimony for Easley. Joe
Stefula, a researcher living in New Jersey, tracked down another of

the officers who had been assigned to the MP company at Roswell in July 1947. The man told Stefula that Major Easley had told him to go out to the crash site. He said, "The military police had guards there."

Stefula also learned from the former military officer that he had been told he was not to talk about what he had seen in the field. According to Stefula, Easley reminded the officer that they were not to discuss anything about the crash incident. That officer remained quiet, not even telling his wife about those events, until Stefula called him.

So Easley's testimony, especially that from February 1991, is extremely important to understanding the nature of the Roswell case. Had the object found been of mundane configuration, had it merely been an aircraft of some new design or even a weather balloon that had been launched as part of a top secret project, Easley would have known. He wouldn't have been sworn to secrecy, and he certainly wouldn't have said that it was something extraterrestrial in origin.

Edwards, Frank (1908–1967) Frank Edwards might have been the first to mention in a public forum that he believed the Roswell crash was of an extraterrestrial spacecraft and not a weather balloon as suggested by Army and Air Force officers. During a question-and-answer session after a lecture in the late 1950s, Edwards was asked if a flying saucer had ever crashed. He then sketched, briefly, the details of the Roswell case.

In 1965, he reported on it in his book, *Flying Saucers—Serious Business,* a title he took from a real military memo. Edwards wrote: "There are such difficult cases as the rancher near Roswell, New Mexico, who phoned the Sheriff that a blazing disc-shaped object had passed over his house at low altitude and had crashed and burned on a hillside within view of his house. The Sheriff called the military; the military came on the double quick. Newsmen were not permitted into the area. A week later, however, the government released a photograph of a service man holding up a box kite with an aluminum disc about the size of a large pie pan dangling from the bottom of a kite. This, the official report explained, was a device borne aloft on the kite and used to test radar gear by bouncing signals off the pie pan. And this, we were told, was the sort of thing that had so excited the rancher. We were NOT told, however, how the alleged kite caught fire—nor why the military cordoned off the area while they inspected the wreckage of a burned-out box kite with a non-inflammable pie pan tied to it."

While the report was essentially correct in a gross sense, the details were nearly all wrong. But the point is that Edwards had exposed the Roswell case to a wide audience in 1966, when the book was published. Nearly everyone ignored the case because of the lack of detail, other than a location in the then small and anonymous town of Roswell.

Frank Edwards died in 1967.

Exon, Brigadier General Arthur (1916–) General Exon surfaced in 1990 as a witness to some of the events surrounding the crash of the craft near Roswell in 1947. Exon, a lieutenant colonel in 1947, was an Army Air Force officer assigned to Wright Field. He was there when the crash debris and the bodies arrived at that base. Though he now claims no firsthand knowledge of those events and says that he was, in fact, speculating about them when Kevin Randle and Don Schmitt interviewed him beginning in May 1990, the situation as described by Exon then was considerably different from what he claims today.

It is clear from the various published documents and histories of the Air Force that Exon rose to the rank of brigadier general and that he at one time commanded the sprawling Wright-Patterson Air Force Base complex. He joined the Army in 1942, and flew 135 combat missions in Africa and Europe before his aircraft was damaged and he was forced to bail out. He spent about fourteen months as a prisoner of war.

After he returned to the United States, Exon was first assigned to a two-year course at what became the Air Force Institute of Technology. Exon held various procurement assignments, including Deputy for Procurement and Production and Deputy Chief of Staff for Materiel.

Exon was, because of his assignments and his locations during those assignments, in a position to see and hear things about flying saucers. These he reported during the initial interviews with him, drawing on his memories of the situation and what he had seen himself. During these interviews, Exon kept referring to a group of high-ranking officials, both governmental and military, who controlled access to all the data about the Roswell crash in particular and UFOs in general. He never heard an official name for the group, referring to them simply as "The Unholy Thirteen."

As the information about the Roswell UFO crash came to light, various conclusions were drawn by researchers. Everyone agreed that if the crash had happened, there would have been a research project designed to exploit the find. Men at the top level of the government would have been informed and would have been appointed to oversee the study of the recovered craft. There is no question that the events at Roswell would have precipitated such a response.

In the early 1980s, it seemed that documents confirming this speculation had been discovered. These papers, labeled MJ-12, suggested that a government study had been initiated after the crash outside Roswell. No one provided a provenance for the documents, and without that, good research technique demanded that they be treated as fakes.

As these data were reported by Randle and Schmitt, there were challenges to the validity of it. Some suggested that they had misquoted Exon, or that they had misunderstood what Exon was saying. Then Exon himself began to suggest that he had been speculating about the situation and that he didn't know anything firsthand.

Of course, by listening to the tapes of the interviews and reading the letter that Exon sent to Randle on November 21, 1991, it is clear that most of what he told them was not speculation. It was information that he acquired because of who he was and where he was and what he had seen himself. The areas of speculation were quite small.

Exon told Randle, for example, that he had been at Wright Field when they heard the material found at Roswell was being brought in. He said that he knew it was coming in. He said that the bodies had been brought to Wright Field and that he believed that one of those bodies had been sent to Lowry Army Air Field because the Army's mortuary service was based there. Obviously they were sent there for study and to learn the best way to preserve the tissues.

During the interview conducted on May 19, 1990, Randle asked Exon, "You've heard the rumors about the little bodies and all that stuff, haven't you?"

Exon responded, "Well, yes, I have. In fact, I know people that were in photographing some of the residue from the New Mexico affair near Roswell."

Exon then said, "As a result of that, I know they saw the one sighting and then where . . . a good bit of the information came down. There was another location where it was where apparently the main body of the spacecraft was . . . where they did say there were bodies there . . . I've got special information but it may be more rumor than fact about what happened to those bodies, although they were all found apparently outside the craft itself but were in fairly good condition. In other words, they weren't broken up a lot."

Exon said that he heard, from those he knew at Wright Field, that the rumored bodies and the "residue" from New Mexico were being brought to the base. It was clear from what he said that he did not personally see the bodies, but had heard of them from those who had. He spoke of his special knowledge, suggested it might be rumor, but then described the discovery of the bodies in a serious light based on what his friends, who were firsthand witnesses, had told him.

Talking of the bodies and whether they were taken to Wright-Patterson, he said, "Well, that's my information. But one of them was that it went to the mortuary outfit . . . I think at that time it was in Denver, where these people were being identified. But the strongest information was that they were brought into Wright-Pat. But, whatever happened to the metal residue, I imagine it's still in the . . . someplace."

Exon continued, "But back in that '47 time period, everybody was, it happened and why wasn't there more information and who kept the lid on it. Well, *I know* [emphasis added] that at the time the sightings happened it went to General Ramey [Commander of the Eighth Air Force], who is now deceased, who was at Carswell Air Force Base [Fort Worth Army Air Field in July 1947], and he along with the people out at Roswell decided to change the story while they got their act together and got the information into the Pentagon and into the President."

There is no speculation here. Exon was telling researchers what he knew from his conversations with the people directly involved. Notice that there was no hint of speculation anywhere, but that Exon, in fact, uses the term "I know" instead of anything suggesting that he was guessing based on who he was and what he had heard through the grapevine.

"Of course President Truman and General Spaatz [then commander of the Army Air Forces], the Secretary of Defense [Forrestal], who has now passed away, and other people who were close to them were the ones who made up the key investigative teams in relation to the released information. One of my officers who did some research who worked for me at Wright-Patterson, who had done some research on this as part of his school came up with a deal that there was great concern at that time and there was fear that people would panic if the sketchy information that they had such as what was it and where did it come from and what was their mission and so on and so on got out. So they decided to make it a national cover-up . . . *I did know* [emphasis added] that their numbers one and two people were at the top of the staff including the Secretary of Defense and the Chief of Staff and the intelligence circle including the President, I don't know whether anybody outside the President's office, I never hear of any elected officials."

He then qualified the statements, saying, "This is stuff I've heard from '47 on to the present time, really. About why wasn't it . . . about who was responsible and it was no problem to find out who was in those positions in '47 and '48 and I just happen to remember them because the Air Force was being formed and I was in the Pentagon and worked around a lot between the Pentagon and the field so I knew these people."

Although he speculated about the location of the metal, meaning he believed that it was still at Wright-Patterson in 1990 when the interviews took place, he did know what happened once it had arrived at the base in 1947. He said, "I think it was there because there was quite a bit of effort to take it to the labs and try to analyze it chemically and metallurg[icall]y and everything else involved in trying to find out what the material was because some of it was very flimsy and was tougher than hell and other was almost like foil but strong. It had them pretty puzzled so I know people were investigating trying to find out what it was. And it wouldn't surprise me if some of the material wasn't still around. Certainly the reports."

So Exon was aware of the various laboratory tests that were conducted. It is not necessary for him to have witnessed the tests to know what had transpired during them. Exon might not have seen the tests, but reported exactly what he had heard from those who had.

In fact, the only area of speculation was whether the material was still around Wright-Patterson somewhere. And if the material itself couldn't be located, then the reports and analysis of the debris would be available. That was reasonable speculation by Exon considering who he was and what he had already admitted to knowing.

Exon then began to speak of the alien bodies. Randle mentioned the bodies to Exon, saying that he knew the bodies from

Roswell had been taken to Wright-Patterson. Exon answered that he knew it, too, and then added, "Well, I don't know that."

Exon then said, "People I have known were involved in it and they're the ones that told me they [the bodies] got to Wright-Patterson. But what I've been trying to do is try to imagine what could have been done with them scientifically from a storage standpoint for further investigation. It's one thing to kind of have an autopsy and another thing to keep them. I know there were facilities available that could have done that, but I don't believe they were at Wright-Patterson."

In other words, Exon's speculation wasn't about the bodies arriving at Wright-Patterson, or even the fact that bodies were recovered. Instead, he was speculating on the tests that could be conducted on them when they arrived at Wright-Patterson and where they could have been stored once the preliminary research had been completed.

His knowledge of the Roswell events went far beyond what he had been told by those he trusted. Again, in the last few months, Exon has suggested to some researchers, or more accurately it has been reported by those researchers, that the situation isn't exactly as has been reported. He supposedly told some investigators that he had flown over many areas in the desert Southwest, and as he had, he had speculated about the location of the crash.

But this reading of the situation simply isn't the case. On June 18, 1990, Schmitt had the opportunity to visit Exon at his home. Schmitt was able to record most of the conversation, though he had trouble with his recorder and a gardener who decided that it was time to mow the lawn. Schmitt also made notes to back up the tape.

Again, Exon explained about the oversight committee that controlled access to the information about the crash. Exon was telling Schmitt what he knew, based on his position as the base commander at Wright-Patterson.

Schmitt asked, "Was there any name for the operation?"

Exon answered, "Well, I . . . no, I don't recall that there was. Our contact was a man, a telephone number. He'd call and he's set the airplane up. I just knew there was an investigative team. There probably was a name but I . . ."

There was a slight break in the tape and then Exon said, ". . . Stuart Symington, who was Secretary of Defense [actually he was Under Secretary of War for Air in July 1947], Joe [actually Carl] Spaatz [Chief of the Army Air Forces] . . . all these guys at the top of the government. They were the ones who knew the most about Roswell, New Mexico. They were involved in what to do about the residue from that . . . those two findings."

Schmitt said, "You say those two."

Exon answered, "Probably part of the same accident but two distinct sites. One, assuming that the thing, as I understand it, as I remember flying the area later, that the damage to the vehicle seemed to be coming from the southeast and northwest but it could have been going in the opposite direction but it doesn't seem likely. So that farther northwest pieces found on the ranch, those pieces were mostly metal . . ."

Exon described the debris that had been found, saying, ". . . couldn't be easily ripped or changed . . . you could change it. You could wad it up, you could change the shape, but it was still there and . . . there were other parts of it that were very thin but awfully strong and couldn't be dented with heavy hammers and stuff like that . . . which at that time were causing some people concern . . . again, say it was a shape of some kind you could grab this end and bend it but it would come right back. It was flexible to a degree."

Since Exon began claiming that he had flown over many possible sites and was only speculating, a letter he sent Randle on November 24, 1991, becomes important. At that time he had been accused of misquoting Exon. After Randle supplied a copy of his taped interviews, a copy of the book, and other data, he asked in what area Exon believed he had been misquoted.

He wrote back, "I'm sorry that a portion of my interview has caused you trouble. I will acknowledge that the 'quick' quote does have me saying that my flights later, much later, verified [*sic*] the direction of possible flight of the object. I remember auto tracks leading to pivital [*sic*] sites and obvious gouges in terrain."

In 1998, Exon was interviewed again in an attempt to clarify some of the confusion that had grown up around Exon's statements about the crash site. Now, instead of suggesting that there were multiple sites and multiple locations, Exon again talked of two distinct sites. He spoke of them as if he had known, in 1947, what he was seeing. He knew that these were the locations where the metallic debris and the craft and bodies had been recovered. He said that there had been discussion in the aircraft about the Roswell crash. The idea that Exon's testimony was "speculation" is an obvious attempt to reduce the critical information to unimportance. Audiotapes of that interview also exist.

What becomes clear upon reviewing the tapes, the 1991 letter, and the new interview is that Exon was not speculating about these events and activities, as some now suggest. There is nothing in the statements he made or in the letter he wrote that suggests that he wasn't discussing what he knew from either firsthand observation or communication with those who were directly involved. The speculations revolved around what happened after the debris or bodies had arrived at Wright-Patterson, not about the recovery of the craft, material, or bodies. In fact, he wasn't even speculating about some of the testing. He said that he received the information about the tests from technicians who had actually conducted the tests and whom he personally knew.

There are some areas in which Exon's statements could be corroborated. Exon mentioned that the bodies had been taken to Wright Field. There have been many who said the same thing. Frank Kaufmann said that he had been on one of the aircraft that eventually flew into Wright-Patterson.

Exon said that the material, the metallic debris, was flown on to

Wright Field. Pappy Henderson, a pilot with the 1st Air Transport Unit at Roswell, said that he was one of the pilots who flew the debris to Wright Field.

Exon described the debris in the same terms used by a dozen other witnesses, including Bill Brazel, son of the rancher who found the debris field, Major Jesse A. Marcel, Master Sergeant Lewis S. Rickett, Sergeant Robert Smith, Frankie Rowe, Sallye Tadolini, and Loretta Proctor. There is no indication that Exon was personally acquainted with any of these people, though it is clear that he was aware of the Roswell case before we interviewed him.

Exon's somewhat vague description of the location of the impact site agrees with what has been suggested over the last several years. Originally, it was believed that the debris field found by Mack Brazel was related to claims of an impact site near the Plains of San Agustin. The original theory was that the craft had come apart over the Brazel ranch and fallen to the ground some 150 miles to the west, near Magdalena, New Mexico. When Randle first interviewed Exon in 1990, no one was questioning this scenario. In other words, if Exon was relying on previously published material and the conventional wisdom, then he would have made similar claims. But Exon was telling of what he knew from his experiences at Wright Field. In fact, looking back to his statement about two distinct sites, there is another clue about the validity of the statements made by Exon. He said, "So the farther northwest pieces found on the ranch, those were mostly metal."

He was speaking of flying over the two sites, and if he had followed the conventional wisdom, if he had followed the scenario developed in the late 1970s, then Exon's statement should have read, "So the farther east pieces found on the ranch . . ."

Clearly Exon was not speculating, nor was he drawing on what he might have read elsewhere. He was describing a situation he had witnessed firsthand. And as the investigation continued, drawing on the testimonies supplied by Frank Kaufmann, Edwin Easley, Lewis Rickett, W. Curry Holden, and Thomas Gonzales and the secondhand information from Frankie Rowe and Barbara Dugger, it is obvious that Exon's claim that the impact site was to the southeast of the Brazel ranch was correct. This suggests an inside and intimate knowledge of the events near Roswell. Exon was not relating what he believed to be the truth, or speculating about what he believed to be the truth, but was describing the situation as he had lived it in 1947. The statements are on tape and the words are clear.

The question to be asked, then, is if Exon was speaking candidly, and if the information is accurate, then why now the claim that he was speculating? The answer is threefold.

First, it seems that the change in Exon's attitude was precipitated by outside events. Exon provided many facts that he should have kept to himself. He was caught off guard by the first interviews, speaking of events that were more than forty years old. He assumed that the information was no longer classified and no longer important. Because of that, he spoke freely of events when he should have kept silent.

Second, some of the controversy around Exon's statements was the result of the politics inside the UFO community. If Exon was telling the truth about the development of an oversight committee to control the debris, craft, and bodies, and if his information was accurate, then clearly the MJ-12 documents were fraudulent. The wrong people were named on the oversight committee. Because of that, proponents of MJ-12 claimed that Exon had been misquoted. They didn't want any information that suggested MJ-12 was fraudulent to be accepted. Rather than suggest where Exon was wrong, they attacked the accuracy of the quotes, ignoring the fact that the statements were recorded on audiotape.

Finally, and most telling, is the information given to Schmitt near the end of his interview with Exon. Schmitt said, "We still have witnesses involved with Roswell that tell us they are sworn to secrecy or at least that's still their perception . . . they will go to their graves honoring their commitments."

Exon then said something that becomes important when all is considered. He said, "I'd do the same thing. You'd just be hazed and hassled by everybody who was trying to reconstruct the thing . . ."

Exon, now being "hazed and hassled" and probably having been reprimanded by someone inside the Air Force, is trying to subtly "rewrite" history. He is claiming that his statements were speculations, and there are those who dismiss his statements as speculations. This simply isn't the case. Exon might not like it, but his words are on tape and taken in context. He let quite a bit of information out of the bag, probably not realizing what he was doing. It is clear from what he said and from the corroboration that has been found that Exon knows the truth.

F-95A See **XF-95A.**
  See also *Flying Wing*

FBI Telex (July 8, 1947) The FBI office in Dallas, after interviewing a number of people in the area, sent a message to the director of the FBI and to the Special Agent in Charge (SAC) of the office in Cincinnati, explaining what had been learned locally about the "Flying Disc, Information Concerning." That report said:

> Major Curtan [in reality Major Kirton, an intelligence officer at 8th Air Force Headquarters in Fort Worth], Headquarters Eighth Air Force, telephonically advised this office that an object purporting to be a flying disc was recovered near Roswell, New Mexico, this date. The disc is hexagonal in shape and was suspended from a balloon by a cable, which ballon [*sic*] was approximately twenty feet in diameter. Major Curtan further advised that the object found resembles a high altitude weather balloon with a radar reflector but that telephonic conversation between their office and Wright Field had not borne out this belief. Disc and balloon being transported to Wright Field by special plane for

examination. Information provided this office because of national interest in this case and fact that National Broadcasting Company, Associated Press, and others attempting to break story of location of disc today. Major Curtan advised would request Wright Field to advise Cincinnati office results of examination. No further investigation being conducted.

According to newspaper accounts, General Ramey canceled the special flight and no other FBI documents have been located concerning the Roswell events specifically. However, it should be noted that the facts outlined in this document do not agree with the events in Texas. More important, this message seems to be saying that the balloon explanation being offered does not agree with the facts as known by the FBI at that time.

Flight No. 4 First, it must be remembered that the Air Force claimed that Project Mogul Balloon Launch No. Four, made on June 4, 1947, is responsible for the debris found by Mack Brazel. They imply in their 1994 final report that these Mogul balloon arrays were something special, unusual, and highly classified. There was even a hint that polyethylene was used in some of the launches and that this might account for the failure of the rancher, the sheriff, and even the officers of the 509th to recognize it. However, the records show that the first of the polyethylene balloon was not launched until July 3, 1947, and therefore couldn't have been the material found on the Brazel ranch.

Balloon Launch No. 4, according to the diary kept by Dr. Albert Crary, the project leader, was made of a cluster of regular neoprene meteorological balloons. It did contain a "sonobuoy" or microphone, but no "official" record was kept because no data of scientific importance were recovered. Charles Moore, project engineer, told researchers that he believed they had lost track of Launch No. 4 near Arabela, New Mexico, which is twenty or thirty miles south of the Brazel ranch site. Unfortunately, there is no documentation to support this claim.

The other important point, though the Air Force certainly doesn't make it clear, is that there was nothing special about the weather balloons or array in Launch No. 4. There was nothing on it that would fool anyone. They were standard balloons, about 15 feet in diameter, made of neoprene. Attempts to cut them or burn them would have been successful. And surely someone in Roswell, if not Jesse Marcel himself, would have recognized the material as having come from a neoprene weather balloon.

The Air Force also implies that the reason there was a cover-up in 1947 was to protect the classified Project Mogul. While the project itself was highly classified, the balloons, rawin radar targets, and other equipment used in it were not. There was little of intelligence value to be recovered by Soviet or other foreign agents if they knew that balloon clusters and long arrays were being launched from the Alamogordo Army Air Field.

In fact, there was so little of importance attached to the launch of the balloons that a story about them was published in the *Alamogordo News* on July 10, 1947. If Soviet agents were interested in Mogul and balloon launches, that article provided more than enough clues for them. There are photos of the balloon clusters, but more important, Watson Laboratories and some of the men involved in Mogul are identified by the newspaper.

Had what Brazel found been nothing more than a Project Mogul balloon, there would have been no reason for the elaborate events that took place to hide it. When other Mogul balloons were found in the days following, those balloons were reported to military authorities and no elaborate cover story was developed. More important, had the debris been from Project Mogul, Brazel would have recognized it as such and disposed of it without having to consult the local sheriff or the military at the Roswell base—that is, if there was no tag found on the debris to suggest a reward would be paid for the recovery.

If it was only a weather balloon, as Cavitt and the Air Force now claim, why didn't he, Cavitt, mention it to anyone, saving the 509th from the embarrassment of announcing they had a flying saucer, only to have that statement challenged by the officers at Eighth Air Force? Cavitt told some investigators that he was never involved in any balloon recoveries.

Project Mogul, although highly classified, does nothing to explain the events on the Brazel ranch. There is too much testimony from too many firsthand witnesses. When all the data are examined, it is obvious that Project Mogul Flight No. 4 is inadequate as an explanation.

Flight No. 9 The United States Air Force, on September 8, 1994, announced that they had reviewed their records and determined that the debris found by Mack Brazel on his ranch northwest of Roswell was the remains of a balloon and array train from Project Mogul. At that time, the Air Force reported that they suspected it was balloon Flight No. 4. Karl Pflock, in his report *Roswell in Perspective*, published by the Fund for UFO Research, agreed that it was a Project Mogul balloon, but selected Flight No. 9.

Pflock wrote, "No information is available for the next numbered launch, Flight 9, which is missing from all Mogul documentation I have gathered to date. Both [C. B.] Moore and [Colonel A. C.] Trakowski have told me they recall nothing about it. However, Moore remembers several flights were 'classified out' of the NYU Project 93 reports and reports on subsequent balloon programs in which he was involved. It appears that Flight 9 was one of those."

The documents for Flight 9, however, have been found. They weren't "classified out," because nothing of scientific importance was learned by the flight. It was overlooked because it was useless. Moore located the diary of Dr. Albert Crary, currently the only written record for the missing balloon launches. Using it, Moore was able to recall what happened to balloon Flight No. 9.

A little additional data might be helpful here. The early-morning July 3, 1947, launch of the V-2 rocket from the White Sands Proving Ground was postponed for some reason, but the Mogul balloons were launched prior to the postponement. The data gathered by that flight, No. 8, were considered to be of scientific value and were mentioned in official records.

The V-2 launch was rescheduled for 7:30 P.M. that evening, but there was an accident on the pad, injuring several people, some seriously. Newspapers around the country carried the report of the accident. Because of the accident, the rocket launch was canceled. According to Crary's diary, "At the last minute before the balloon went up, V2 was called off . . . account [sic] accident at White Sands." Newspaper reports and statements by the commander at White Sands have corroborated this.

Crary wrote of the second attempted launch on July 3, "Sent up cluster balloons with dummy load." That is all that he says about it, and this is apparently the only written record of it. C. B. Moore added to the detail, reporting that the balloons were stripped of their equipment, but the project engineers couldn't put the helium back into the bottles. These were not the new polyethylene balloons used for the morning launch, but regular neoprene rubber. Helium leaked slowly from them. Because of that, they released the balloons.

There is additional evidence that eliminates Flight No. 9 completely. One of the graduate students assigned to the project took photographs of that flight. The pictures show the balloons but no array train. Without an array train, there were no radar targets to scatter metallic debris, and with no capability to scatter metallic debris, Flight No. 9 is eliminated as a culprit once and for all.

Flying Disk In June 1947, soon after Kenneth Arnold made the first public flying saucer report, the term "flying disk" was often used to describe the objects seen. At first, "flying disk" and "flying saucer" were used interchangably, but over the years, "flying saucer" became the preferred term. "Flying disk" fell into disfavor and was rarely used. When Captain Edward Ruppelt created the term "unidentified flying object," that is, UFO, it became the term preferred by the Air Force, researchers, the media, and the general public.

Flying Flapjack Designated as the XF-5-U-1, this was an experimental Navy propeller-driven aircraft that had a very unconventional shape. The project was eventually abandoned, especially with the development of jet-powered aircraft. Records suggest that it flew only near Bridgeport, Connecticut, though it has been offered as the explanation of several UFO sightings.

Flying Wing The history of the development of the Flying Wing, an aircraft that is little more than a wing, is not one of the so-called black projects. While certain information and some specific developments by Northrop Aircraft, as well as by others interested in "tailless aircraft," might have been considered proprietary in 1947, the whole of the project was out in the open where the public could easily watch the evolution of the aircraft. It is interesting that interest in a flying wing remained high, even after it became clear that there was no advantage to the flying wing design and that it was unstable.

Although the Germans are often given the credit for developing the concept of a flying wing, it seems that a British military officer, John William Dunne, first tested a flying wing–type aircraft in 1908. In 1911, one of Dunne's "tailless" designs crossed the English Channel. The Dunne aircraft designs were viewed as too radical by most engineers, and offered too few advantages to shape early commercial aircraft development.

Dunne's work apparently influenced John K. Northrop, who became interested in the design in 1923 while still an engineer at the Douglas Aircraft Company. But Douglas Aircraft was not interested, and it would be more than ten years before Northrop would have a chance to pursue his dream.

Flying wing designs, however, were popular for a time in the

1920s. Various designers and engineers—including Northrop, Rene Arnoux, Georges Madon, and Charles Fauvel in France, B. I. Cheranovsky in the Soviet Union, Alexander Soldenhoff in Switzerland, G. T. R. Hill in Great Britain, and Alexander Lippisch in Germany—all experimented with flying wing aircraft.

In Germany, the Horten brothers began their activities in Bonn around 1930. F. J. Berger, it seems, became interested in the idea of a tailless aircraft and joined the Horten brothers in 1931. Berger had a history of interest in sailplanes and had gained knowledge in their modification and construction. Although he had a basic knowledge of technical aspects, he was not an engineer and was forced to join with more technically oriented people.

Riemar Horten, an Oberleutnant (First Lieutenant) in the Luftwaffe (German Air Force), was convinced that the most efficient aircraft would be all wing. There were no vertical stabilizing or control surfaces on Horten-designed aircraft. The Horten brothers designed and built a number of aircraft prior to World War II. Just before the surrender of the Nazis in 1945, the American and British armies captured Berger and the drawings, photographs, models, and documents relating to the Horten designs. All the information about the Horten designs was published in the restricted access document (*restricted* being the lowest level of classification, equivalent to the present *confidential*) "German Flying Wings Designed by Horten Brothers" by N. LeBlanc, an Air Corps captain. It was prepared on January 10, 1946, released on July 5, 1946, and issued at the headquarters, Air Materiel Command at Wright Field.

Northrop, who in August 1939 became the president and chief engineer of Northrop Aircraft, continued to be fascinated by the flying wing design. Although the purpose of his corporation was to develop and manufacture military aircraft, in less than a year, Northrop had the N-1M, a flying wing, ready for testing. It interested high-ranking officers of the Army Air Corps, and they wanted it developed fully. They changed the designation to XB-35 and told Northrop they wanted it as a long-range bomber.

In September 1941, the U.S. Army Air Forces (redesignated from the Air Corps in June) approved the proposal submitted by Northrop and purchased the engineering data, test models, and evaluation reports of the N-1M. In other words, the Army was paying the research and development costs of the flying wing. They also purchased the N-9M, a one-third-scale flying mockup of the B-35. The contracts anticipated that the costs of development would rise significantly before the delivery date of November 1943, and provisions were established to meet those costs.

A second contract was signed at the end of 1942, calling for the construction and testing of thirteen XB-35s, now designated YB-35. They also contracted for three additional N-9Ms. These were built of welded steel tubes and covered with wood. It looked like the larger YB-35 but contained two rather than four engines.

The first flight of an N-9 took place on December 27, 1942, and nearly every flight after that was shortened by a mechanical failure of one kind or another. On its forty-fifth flight, on May 19, 1943, the N-9 crashed, killing the pilot.

Testing of a second N-9 began and was also plagued by mechanical problems. Although the AAF was disappointed in the results, they ordered two hundred YB-35s in a contract signed in June 1943, with the delivery of the first flying wing to be by June 1945 (which would be a month after the war ended in Europe and three months before it ended in the Pacific).

Testing continued throughout the war. Even with the peace treaties signed and the war over, and the pressure to produce a long-range heavy bomber significantly reduced, Northrop continued to test its flying wing aircraft. The last test flight of the N-9 took place in 1946. It was replaced by a full-scale YB-35, which first flew on June 25, 1946, from Muroc Army Air Field (later Edwards Air Force Base). On September 11, 1946, the YB-35, suffering gear box and propeller control problems, was grounded. A full-scale flying program would not resume until February 1948. There was a series of test flights made on June 26, 1947, but the aircraft didn't leave Southern California, and only one aircraft was involved in the testing.

Two weeks after Kenneth Arnold reported nine crescent-shaped objects in Washington State, officers, ranchers, and newspaper and radio reporters, among others, claimed that something strange had crashed in southeastern New Mexico near the Army airfield there. Speculation by some researchers suggests that it was one of the Northrop flying wings. Obviously, based on the history, it couldn't have been a smaller wooden N-9M mockup because those were no longer flying. Besides, according to "A Synopsis of Flying Wing Development 1908–1953," written by Richard P. Hallion, only one of the N-9s crashed, and that was in 1943. If the flying wing was the culprit in the Arnold sighting, it would have had to be the larger YB-35. Of course, those had been grounded months earlier.

On July 10, the *Chicago Daily News* reported that they had asked Army officers at Muroc Army Air Field if the flying wing could account for the flying disk reports. Lieutenant Robert Jones, the public relations officer at Muroc, said, "None of our flying wings has been in the air recently." Although he refused to provide much in the way of additional information, he did say, "We have just two." That would eliminate the possibility that the YB-35 had been responsible for the debris found by Mack Brazel.

The YB-49, the jet-powered version of the flying wing, made its first flight on October 21, 1947. While gear box problems plagued the propeller version, such problems didn't infect the jet version. But the first flight date, October 21, 1947, takes it out of the picture. There is no evidence that it was flying prior to that, and that effectively eliminates it. It also means that none of the various versions of the Flying Wing could have scattered the debris.

Friedman, Stanton T. (1934–) Stanton Friedman has described himself as an itinerant nuclear physicist, moving from job to job and canceled program to canceled program. While working for General Electric between 1956 and 1959, he read Edward Ruppelt's book, *The Report on Unidentified Flying Objects*. According to Friedman, that book sparked his interest in the topic. Later, as he moved from job to job, Friedman read Frank Edwards's *Flying Saucers—Serious Business*. When he finished that book, he contacted Edwards to see what he could do to make the public more aware of the phenomenon.

Edwards suggested that Friedman contact one of the Pittsburgh radio stations, where he, Friedman, lived at the time. Eventually he did a talk show about flying saucers and one of the technicians asked him to speak to her book review club about Edwards's book. That was his first UFO-oriented lecture.

In the 1980s, after Friedman had divorced his first wife, and with the money to fund various nuclear research programs drying up, Friedman began to write and lecture to larger and more diverse groups about UFOs. He remarried and moved to Canada. There he began working on the commissioning of the Point Lepareu nuclear power plant, and when that ended, he began to study food irradiation, seed stimulation with radiation, and the like for a local company. Since 1982, Friedman has mixed his technical work with his UFO research.

In the late 1970s, he began detailed research into the crash of a craft outside of Roswell. Working with William L. Moore, whose first book was about the "Philadelphia Experiment," Friedman interviewed about ninety people who claimed to have some knowledge of the Roswell UFO crash. That work culminated in *The Roswell Incident*, written by Moore and Charles Berlitz. Friedman contributed research to the project. With aviation writer Don Berliner, Friedman wrote and published his own book on the case, *Crash at Corona*.

In the mid-1980s, Friedman became interested in the MJ-12 documents, which referred to the Roswell crash. Friedman received a $16,000 grant from the Fund for UFO Research to study the

papers and search for corroboration for them. He published a
report about that research. Later he wrote a book about the documents called *Top Secret/Majic*. He has continued to defend the documents as being authentic, believing them to provide valuable clues
about the U.S. government's continuing UFO interest, which he
has labeled "the Cosmic Watergate."

GAO Roswell Report In what has been described as little more than a poor high school book report, the Government Accounting Office, the investigative arm of Congress, reported what they had found after eighteen months of studying the Roswell UFO crash. The study, begun when New Mexico congressman Steven Schiff asked for an investigation, found little in the way of evidence that the Air Force or other agencies of the government had acted improperly in 1947. The report does mention the Air Force conclusion that what fell near Roswell was a Project Mogul balloon, but offers nothing in the way of support for that conclusion. It merely states that conclusion with no commentary whatsoever.

The GAO was unable to uncover any government records that related to the Roswell case except two, both of which were already well known in the UFO community. These were an FBI telex dated July 8, 1947, and an entry from the 509th Bomb Group's unit history for July 1947. Because of this failure to locate other relevant documents, the GAO offered no conclusion as to the source of the debris discovered by Mack Brazel.

The one fact that some Ufologists have found interesting is that the GAO reported that some records, specifically the outgoing message traffic from Roswell from October 1946 through December 1949, had been destroyed in the 1950s. According to the report, the "document disposition form did not properly indicate the authority under which the disposal action was taken."

The message traffic would have been helpful because it would have contained the messages from Colonel Blanchard of the 509th to Eighth Air Force headquarters and General Ramey in Fort Worth. While that message traffic might have provided clues about what was going on around Roswell, the fact that the messages have been destroyed might have been part of routine housekeeping. The Chief Archivist at the Records Center said that many records from that era seem to have been improperly destroyed.

What is interesting in the GAO investigation is the lack of an attempt to find the messages received by Fort Worth and Washington, D.C., at the time. While the outgoing messages from Roswell might be gone, it is possible that the incoming messages (from Roswell to Eighth Air Force or SAC headquarters) were not searched.

The GAO did query other agencies about the possibility of documents concerning the Roswell case but received nothing of interest from them, with one exception. The CIA response said that they had searched their databases using the key words "Roswell, New Mexico" and "Project Mogul." Their databases found no matches. It would seem that the CIA database would have contained references to Mogul if only because Mogul was designed in 1947 to provide data on the possibility of Soviet nuclear testing. In other words, the mission of Mogul was intelligence-gathering, which explained the top secret classification.

The GAO provided little in the way of answers about the Roswell case. It did fuel the cover-up controversy with its revelation that a large group of documents had been improperly destroyed. It found nothing new about the case. It was an exercise in futility simply because it added nothing to the knowledge of the Roswell events.

Goldwater, Senator Barry (1909–1998) Former senator and former Air Force major general Barry Goldwater had been involved in the Roswell case almost from the very beginning. Or rather, he was involved in tales of alien spacecraft and hidden bodies at Wright-Patterson Air Force Base for a number of years. He was the one who brought this to the attention of many who had never heard of it.

Goldwater had become interested in UFOs about the time Kenneth Arnold made his sighting. Hearing the rumor that there was a "blue room" at Wright-Patterson Air Force Base that contained exhibits relating to the retrieval operation, and that such a room might provide clues about the nature of the UFO phenomenon, he asked General Curtis LeMay for permission to see it. According to the story as told by Goldwater, LeMay told him, "Not only no, but hell no, and if you ask again, I'll have you court-martialed."

It is a wonderful tale that corroborates what many UFO researchers would love to believe. It confirms the existence of the material at Wright-Patterson that relates to UFOs. It suggests a reality to UFOs and offers corroboration of a cover-up. However, given the fact that information is often "spun," there is a distinct possibility that what Senator Goldwater actually said might have been different and might not have related to Roswell, or to the recovery of alien craft and technology.

Fortunately, this was something of interest to a large number of people. When Larry King did his Area 51 special from the deserts of Nevada, there was a short taped interview with Senator Goldwater. He said that he had heard about a "landing" and that there was a room where they kept all the "secret stuff." It was Senator Goldwater himself who tied the exchange with General LeMay to UFOs and material that had been recovered.

If that isn't enough, there is another piece of evidence that ties his beliefs to the Roswell case. In a letter dated July 26, 1994, and sent to Kent Jeffrey, Senator Goldwater wrote, "Roswell has long been a point of great interest to me, since the first UFOs turned up . . . Butch Blanchard was a very close friend of mine. I worked with him in the Air Force . . . There is not much we can do about

getting the things about Roswell that you would like. I tried dili-
gently to get them from General LeMay, and the only cussing out he
ever gave me, was when I very vociferously asked him for information."

It would seem that the information is very specific. Goldwater,
a man of high integrity, a man respected by his peers and colleagues,
said that there was something to the Roswell case. No, it is not the
"smoking gun" from the president, with his hands on a stack of
newly declassified documents, but it is something. Here was a man
who, if he knew nothing about the topic, would have said as much.
He did not.

Goldwater, in fact, left a number of letters that suggested that
there was something housed at Wright-Patterson. Goldwater wrote
to Salomo Amon, telling him, "The subject of UFOs is one that has
interested me for some long time . . . I made an effort to find out
what was in the building at Wright-Patterson Air Force Base where
the information is stored that has been collected by the Air Force,
and I was understandably denied this request. It is still classified
above Top Secret."

In a letter sent to UFO researcher William Steinman, Goldwater wrote: "I have never gained access to the so-called Blue Room
at Wright Patterson, so I have no idea what is in it. I have no idea
who controls the flow of need-to-know because, frankly, I was told
in such an emphatic way that it was none of my business that I've
never tried to make it my business since."

Once again, the evidence has eluded UFO researchers. Senator
Goldwater suggested that there is something real to the story but
that even someone of his elevated status was unable to learn the
truth. Not that there was no truth to learn, that Roswell or the
UFO crash was a hoax, but that he was not allowed to see the truth.

Senator Goldwater knew there was something to this case. Had
there been a more mundane answer, he would have had it.

Gonzales, Thomas John Price of the UFO Enigma Museum was the first to interview Thomas Gonzales, a member of the 509th Bomb Group in 1947. Unlike so many others who had told a tale of involvement in the retrieval operation, Gonzales's picture does appear in the Yearbook created in 1947. If nothing else, it confirms that Gonzales was stationed in Roswell in 1947.

Gonzales told researchers, including Don Ecker of *UFO* magazine, that he, although a member of the transportation squadron, had been one of those sent out on guard duty. During the guard duty, he had the chance to see both the craft and the alien bodies. Once the guard duty was over, within days, Gonzales was transferred overseas, which caused a hardship for his wife and children.

Ecker interviewed a number of the Gonzales children, asking if they had heard the Roswell story while growing up. All of them said that their father had been telling it for years, but no one understood the significance of it.

Gonzales, not an articulate man, had trouble describing the alien creatures, but he did carve representations of them. Ecker, who had seen the carvings, as well as drawings made of the bodies by other alleged eyewitnesses, suggested that they all looked alike. There was no glaring inconsistency between what Gonzales had produced and the descriptions offered by those others.

Skeptics have rejected Gonzales's story simply because he was in the transportation squadron rather than in one of the MP units or the intelligence section. They believe that Gonzales would not have had the opportunity to be a member of the guard, but given the situation, it wouldn't be surprising if the need for soldiers to reinforce the various cordons that had been thrown up had been drawn from the supply of soldiers available. Nearly everyone who has been in the Army remembers "recruiting" parties swinging through the barracks, day rooms, PX, or snack bars, searching for soldiers who could be "volunteered" for a special assignment, a work detail, or to fill out a KP roster. In other words, if there was a shortage of MPs, other soldiers would be drafted to stand guard.

The tale told by Gonzales is, like so many others, a frustrating one. There are no written records that can confirm that he was involved in a recovery, though they do confirm that he was in Roswell in July 1947 and that he was transferred shortly thereafter. The family relates that he had been telling the story for years, but again, no one wrote anything down, so it can't be confirmed. In the end, Gonzales is among those who claim to have been involved in 1947, but can offer nothing as proof.

The Gouge It was Bill Brazel Jr. who first suggested there had been a gouge in the debris field found by his father in 1947. Brazel said it was about five hundred yards long and about ten feet at its widest. He said that it took two years to grass back over. There is no visible sign of it today.

Later there was other talk about a gouge, and it would seem that if the ground, especially that in the high desert northwest of Roswell, had been gouged, it would suggest something large enough and heavy enough to do it. Charles Moore, of Project Mogul fame, said that if there was a gouge in the terrain, then Mogul was not the answer. The balloons in the array train and the equipment attached were not heavy enough to gouge the terrain.

But according to those claiming Project Mogul balloons as the answer, the fifty-year-old memories of Bill Brazel were just not sufficient to reject Mogul. If there was a gouge, then others would have mentioned it.

Well, the truth is, they have. The first is former judge Bud Payne, who escorted some researchers to the debris field in the early 1990s. Payne pointed to the same areas that Bill Brazel had indicated, telling of a gouge on the ground.

Brigadier General Arthur Exon had the opportunity to fly over the Roswell sites sometime after the crash. He talked of gouges in the terrain, as well as tire marks from the recovery vehicles.

Not long ago Tom Carey had the opportunity to talk to Exon again. The general confirmed two sites, the debris field near Corona and a second site much closer to Roswell where the craft had been recovered. He talked of a gouge in the terrain, again confirming what Bill Brazel had told others several years earlier.

More important is what this means to the only explanation that has been offered by the Air Force and the skeptics for the Roswell UFO crash. A balloon, no matter how long the array train, will not drag equipment across the hard New Mexico ground, creating a gouge the size of that reported by so many witnesses. Remember, Charles Moore himself said that if the gouge existed, as reported, then the balloon explanation was inadequate.

There are a number of witnesses who said they saw the gouge and provided a fairly complete description of it. There are written and recorded statements from those who saw it.

This does not mean that what crashed was of extraterrestrial origin. It means only that every mundane explanation offered over the last decade has been eliminated. The Air Force said it wasn't an experimental airplane, a rocket or missile from White Sands, or any other aircraft. They came up with their Project Mogul balloon arrays. But the testimony they have ignored, the testimony of a gouge in the terrain, has eliminated that answer.

Hall, L. M. L. M. Hall served first at the Roswell Army Air Field with the military police, and upon his discharge in 1946 became a Roswell city policeman. He rose to chief of police and later served on the city council.

Hall had little to do with the Roswell events in July 1947. He did remember, however, that one day in July, he visited with Glenn Dennis at Ballard's Funeral Home on South Main Street. According to Hall, Dennis said, "I got a funny call from the base. They wanted to know if we had several baby caskets." He started laughing and said, "I asked them, 'What for?' and they said they wanted to bury [or ship] those aliens." Hall thought it was a joke and, according to him, didn't bite. Dennis never mentioned it again to Hall.

Haut, Walter Haut was a first lieutenant assigned to the Roswell Army Air Field in July 1947. He had trained during World War II as both a navigator and a bombardier. He served in the Pacific during the war and later, in 1946, participated in Operation Crossroads, the atomic tests at Bikini. He had been assigned to the 509th Bomb Group on temporary duty for the atomic tests, but that duty was expanded into a permanent assignment.

According to Haut, about 9:30 on the morning of July 8, 1947, he received a call from Colonel William Blanchard, who told Haut

they had found a flying saucer, or parts from one. Blanchard said the wreckage came from a ranch northwest of Roswell and that the base intelligence officer, Major Marcel, was going to escort the material on to Fort Worth.
Blanchard wanted Haut to write a press release explaining the situation and then take it to the local media. According to Haut, it was about noon or a little after when he made the rounds to radio stations KGFL and KSWS and then on to the *Roswell Daily Record* and the *Morning Dispatch.*

The *Daily Record* published the account in the afternoon edition, but the next day announced that the debris had been identified as a weather balloon. In another story in the same edition, Mack Brazel was interviewed, giving a description of the debris that sounded

Walter Haut. (*Photo courtesy of Kevin Randle*)

suspiciously like that of a weather balloon. Brazel also said, however, that what he had found that time didn't look like any of the other balloons he had seen.

At the same time, other newspapers, some of which identified Haut as Warren Haight, suggested that he had received blistering telephone calls from the Pentagon and other top military officials rebuking him for the press release. Haut maintains that he received no such telephone calls and said, "A first lieutenant getting telephone calls from Washington? Had it happened, I would have remembered it."

The press release did not affect his military career. Haut had

applied for a regular Army commission and received it. He was promoted to captain. In early 1948, he received orders that would have
transferred him to another military base. Haut had established a
home in Roswell, his first child having been born there, and the
family had no desire to leave. Haut resigned from the service in
early 1948.

Hatch (N.M.) Debris It was in the January 28, 1993, issue of the
Hatch Courier that it was reported that a strange piece of metallic
debris had been found the previous summer. According to the story,
written by *Courier* reporter and editor Gene Ballinger, members of
the family who had found the metal had been unable to cut it, burn
it, or bend it. Ballinger noted that it was found near Horse Springs,
where a UFO was reported to have crashed in which "three beings
were found, one still living, one dead and one dying."

Unfortunately, Ballinger did not have the names of the family
members, nor did he have any other details, other than those supplied by a source who, Ballinger said, had been reliable in the past.
He hoped to hear more about the find in the days following the
newspaper report.

Once the story of the "Hatch Enigma" was reported in *The
International UFO Reporter,* nothing new was learned. The family
was never identified, the metal was never submitted for scientific
and objective analysis, and no additional information was reported.
This appears to be another of the many dead ends that dot the recovered debris landscape.

Henderson, Sappho (Henderson, Oliver Wendell [Pappy]) Sappho
Henderson was the wife of Oliver Wendell (Pappy) Henderson, a pilot
in the 1st Air Transport Unit located at Roswell in July 1947.
Henderson had a top secret clearance and was, according to Sappho,
used for a variety of special and important assignments.

According to her, in 1980 or 1981 her husband began to talk of
a special flight he had made out of Roswell. He showed her a news-

paper article that he had found in the grocery store and told her to
read the article. It concerned the crash of an alien spacecraft and the
recovery of the bodies of the flight crew.

Henderson told her, "I want you to read this article because it's
a true story. I'm the pilot who flew the wreckage of the UFO to
Dayton, Ohio. I guess now that they're putting it in the paper, I can
tell you about this. I wanted to tell you for years."

Unfortunately, Pappy Henderson died before any UFO
researchers spoke to him. He did, however, mention the crash and
the flight to both family and former crew members. It was a story
that he told a number of times before his death.

Holden, Dr. William Curry (1896–1993) W. Curry Holden,
according to the biography contained in the Southwest Collections
at Texas Tech University, was born in Coolidge, Texas, on July 19,
1896. He attended Rotan High School and then taught for a year
or two at a rural school in Fisher County, Texas. He entered the
armed forces in 1918, but a year or so later, after separation from
the military, was the principal of the Rotan High School for the
1919–1920 session.

In 1920, he enrolled at the University of Texas and was graduated in June 1923. He was an instructor at a junior college in
Abilene, Texas, but continued his education, receiving his M.A. in
1924, and eventually his doctorate in history.

Holden ran many of his archaeological site studies on a shoe-
string and conducted his first fieldwork in 1929 in the Panhandle
area of Texas. In 1930, Holden excavated a site near Pecos, New
Mexico. His field trips alternated between sites in central Mexico
and the Arrowhead Ruin near Pecos. He was also involved in exca-
vation of caves in West Texas and worked other sites in east-central
New Mexico.

Interestingly, his work in archaeology, as well as his ethno-
graphic and ethnohistorical research, provided him with information to write both nonfiction works and novels. His *Hill of the*

Rooster (1956) was called by Yaqui Indian leaders one of the best portrayals of the Yaqui. He published a number of nonfiction works detailing the history of West Texas. Holden ended his long and distinguished career as the chairman of the Department of History and Anthropology at Texas Tech and as Professor Emeritus of History.

Holden was married twice and had one daughter, Jane Holden, whom he described as "the professional," meaning that she was the anthropologist and archaeologist while he was a historian.

Holden was ninety-six years old when researchers first learned that he had been involved in the events of July 1947. Because of his advanced age, arrangements were made to interview him as quickly as possible. On November 21, 1992, Holden gave Kevin Randle the only statement on the subject that he ever made.

Although Holden was elderly when interviewed, he seemed to be in good health, living at home. He was a tall, thin man who looked to be frail, but who still moved easily. Because of the circumstances, Randle had only thirty minutes or so to speak with him. Given the situation, and Holden's relative good health, Randle planned to speak with him again. This was just a preliminary interview conducted to verify his participation in the events near Roswell in 1947. Unfortunately, it was not recorded.

In the course of an investigation, it is best not to provide any information to the subject of an interview prior to that interview. That prevents contamination and means that the information retrieved is pure. With Holden it was necessary only to mention an interest in an event outside Roswell in 1947 and let Holden fill in the details about the crash and the retrieval.

Holden said, "I was there. I saw it all, but it was so long ago."

Holden seemed to have a firm grasp on the reality of the situation. He went on to confirm that the crash site had been just north of Roswell, off the main highway leading out of town, but he had no recollection of the exact location. He wouldn't have been able to find it on a map, other than to provide a very general location west of the highway and north of the town.

Holden didn't provide a good description of the craft, suggesting only that it wasn't a flying saucer in the classic sense of the word. It was more rounded toward the front. He never got too close to it, seeing it from fifty or sixty yards. He, and those with him, thought it was some kind of government experiment and didn't want to intrude. Later, during their interrogation at the Roswell Army Air Field (RAAF), they learned that the government had nothing to do with it, and that it was, in fact, something made on another world.

Holden confirmed that there had been bodies, but again, he was vague about it. He thought they were smaller than humans, but he remembered very little about them.

Randle said that he had supplied no hints as to what was wanted from Holden. Randle tried to ask the questions in a very nondirect way, waiting for Holden to introduce a concept before exploring it. Holden, for example, mentioned those killed in the crash and Randle then asked if he remembered what they looked like. When Holden said something about a crumpled craft, Randle asked what it looked like.

But Randle had to be careful with the questions because he didn't want it to sound like an interrogation. And Randle didn't want Holden to anticipate him. Randle asked Holden three different times if he had been there, even phrasing one of the questions negatively, in case Holden was picking up verbal clues. Holden told him each time, "I was there."

What Holden had done, under the careful and gentle questioning, was to corroborate the information received from other sources, including Frank Kaufmann.

Before Randle left, he asked if it would be all right to contact Holden again. Both he and his wife said that it would be fine, though he had trouble on the telephone because of poor hearing. Mrs. Holden, however, mentioned quietly that her husband, though in good physical health, was elderly and was easily confused. His mind was no longer as sharp as it had once been. She had never heard the flying saucer story from him and thought that he was mistaken.

This was the second Mrs. Holden, though she was his wife in 1947. According to her, she accompanied him on all the expeditions and did the record-keeping and the cooking. He did make some short trips that she didn't. These were daylong or two-daylong affairs exploring West Texas and southeastern New Mexico. She also said that she didn't believe that he had been involved in the Roswell events, despite his statements to the contrary.

Holden's daughter, Dr. Jane Kelly, echoed the claim. She said that he had never mentioned a thing about the crash or the bodies to her. She was sure he would have, had it actually happened. She also said that he sometimes jumbled his memories, coming up with a new sequence that he was positive was right, even when documentation from others showed he was mistaken.

All of Holden's records were donated to the Southwestern Collections, which is part of the library on the Texas Tech University campus. It seemed like an easy task to check his research diaries for the appropriate dates and find out exactly where he was on the critical weekend in 1947.

Holden, however, didn't keep chronological diaries. Instead, he kept diaries on specific topics. In other words, to search for the important information, the investigator had to know what he had been working on and then search that specific diary. The task seemed nearly impossible. However, when the archivists at the library learned of the specific time frame of interest, they mentioned that Holden's banking records, his income tax returns, and various boxes of university and related correspondence were available. Clues might be obtained in those records.

According to the documents, Holden wrote a check to the Lubbock Rotary Club on July 3. He made a bank deposit on July 9. Both these documents clearly indicate that he was in Lubbock on those two days. In addition, Holden was invited to a wedding on the evening of July 8. There is nothing in the record to show whether or not he attended.

The *Bulletin of the Texas Technological College* (now Texas Tech

University), *Division of Graduate Studies* revealed that during the summer session 1947, Holden taught a seminar for three semester hours. The catalog shows that it was a graduate seminar in history.

The catalog also revealed that Holden taught classes in Field and Museum Technique and in Southwestern Archaeology in the anthropology division of the Department of History and Anthropology during the spring session 1947. In other words, there is nothing conclusive in the catalog, especially when it is remembered that the events in Roswell took place over a three-day weekend and that Roswell is less than two hundred miles from Lubbock.

Nothing in the records revealed where Holden was on the critical weekend. He could easily have made the trip to Roswell with a few of his students for any number of reasons. There were a number of archaeological sites in eastern New Mexico that Holden had investigated on several separate occasions. He could have been in New Mexico, or he could have been in Lubbock.

There is currently no way to corroborate Holden's story. He did, however, speak to colleagues about the events. Dr. Charles Bertrand Schultz, a vertebrate paleontologist from the University of Nebraska, had originally provided the clue that led to Holden.

According to Schultz, interviewed a number of times, including one videotaped session in May 1993, he had heard the story from those involved shortly after it happened. Schultz was in Roswell, according to him, on the critical weekend, but saw nothing of the crashed ship or the bodies. However, when leaving Roswell and driving north along Highway 285, Schultz said that he had seen the military men who were part of the cordon. They were all to the west of the highway, and since Schultz had no desire to drive in that direction, it didn't bother him.

Later, from Holden, he heard the rest of the story, including information about the crash, the craft, and the bodies. Schultz, in the years that followed, shared the story with family members, including daughters Donna Wilcox and Tranda Schultz. Both have said their father told them of the flying saucer crash while they were growing up.

Records at the University of Nebraska, including the field research notes, fail to establish where Schultz was on the July 4, 1947, weekend. Later in the week, Schultz was at an early man site called Lime Creek in southwestern Nebraska. He worked the site with Dr. W. D. Frankforter. Frankforter, according to Tom Carey, has corroborated Schultz's report of the crashed saucer. He, too, heard it long ago and was aware of Holden's involvement.

Documentation from the Holden collection at Texas Tech confirmed that Holden and Schultz were together in December 1947. At the forty-sixth annual meeting of the American Anthropological Association held at the University of New Mexico in Albuquerque, Schultz presented a paper on the Lime Creek site. Although Holden didn't present a paper there, he was one of those who attended the conference.

Holden provided the answers to some of the questions. Although Randle had planned to interview Dr. Holden again, to formulate a list of questions and carefully ask them, all on audiotape, that didn't happen. Dr. W. Curry Holden passed away on April 21, 1993, in Lubbock.

Hoover Note There is very little in the way of official documentation for the believers that some kind of alien craft crashed outside of Roswell in July 1947. Declassified documents, coming from a variety of governmental and military sources in recent years, have suggested that no crash took place because the men responsible for the creation of those documents were the very ones who would have been responsible for the retrieval and study of such a craft. For example, in a letter dated September 24, 1947, Lieutenant General Nathan F. Twining, commanding officer of the Air Materiel Command, lamented the lack of crash recovered debris that would provide some definitive answers about the flying saucers.

Conversely, there is a document, again found through FOIA

and with a provenance that is unquestioned, that suggests some kind of crash did take place. On July 10, 1947, an FBI memo was created by D. M. Ladd for E. G. Fitch. It was in response to an Army Air Forces request from General Schulgen for assistance by the FBI "in locating and questioning individuals who first sighted the so-called flying discs. . . ." This was, in essence, a request by the Army Air Forces for FBI assistance in investigating the backgrounds of those who sighted and reported flying saucers. On July 15, Clyde Tolson, the number two man in the FBI at that time, endorsed the memo, writing, "I think we should do this."

Under that endorsement was a second, this one by J. Edgar Hoover, at that time the director of the FBI. It is undated and reads, "I would do it but before agreeing to it we must insist upon full access to discs recovered. For instance in the La. case the Army grabbed it and would not let us have it for cursory examination."

The question that develops concerns the "La" notation. In the handwritten version, it can also be interpreted to say "SW" or "gov" or "Sov" or "2a." In other words, Hoover's handwriting on this is so poor that it can't be determined clearly what the two letters are or if they are even both letters.

There is now a solution. On July 24, 1947, in another document recovered through FOIA, D. M. Ladd has provided a typewritten version of the Hoover endorsement. According to that document, Ladd interpreted the two letters as "La." That would seem to end the discussion of what the letters are. Surely, if there was a question about the letters, Ladd would have asked someone at FBI headquarters to clarify them for him. Had Ladd's interpretation of those letters been inaccurate, they would have been corrected by someone at FBI headquarters. Here, at last, is a document that answers one of the questions. The letters are "La."

The next question concerns to what "discs recovered" this note refers. The debunkers have suggested a hoax from Shreveport, Louisiana, as the culprit. According to the information contained in the official Air Force investigation of UFOs, Project Blue Book, the

Headquarters, Air Training Command, the office of the AC of S, A-2 [Assistant Chief of Staff, Air Intelligence] Barksdale Field, Louisiana, had received a report that a "Flying Disc [had been] Found in Shreveport, Louisiana [on] 7 July 1947."

What this means is that there is a case that seems to fit the basic description provided by Hoover. It concerns a disc recovered and it is in La., that is, Louisiana.

What might be the critical point in this discussion is the notes in the Project Blue Book file. While the FBI made a background investigation of the witnesses in Shreveport and concluded that the story was a hoax, it is clear that it was not given access to the disc found in Shreveport. The last line of the FBI report—". . . they took the disc in their possession"—indicates that the Army Air Forces had taken the disc before the FBI agents had had a chance to examine it.

There is nothing in the Project Blue Book file, or in any of the other documentation available, that excludes Shreveport as the case to which Hoover referred. The facts all seem to match. Roswell is eliminated here because of the "La." notation. There simply is no way to stretch "La." into something that relates to Roswell. What Hoover would have written, given what we know now, is "in the NM case." Of course, that is not what he did.

Impact Site The area designated as the impact site, based on the testimony of a number of alleged eyewitnesses including Frank Kaufmann, Edwin Easley, W. Curry Holden, and Dr. C. Bertrand Schultz, is north of Roswell. The impact site is where the craft and the bodies were allegedly found. Although there are other locations where it was claimed the craft came to rest, the designation "Impact Site"

The Impact Site on the Corn ranch. (*Photo courtesy of Kevin Randle*)

refers specifically to the location north of Roswell just off Highway 285. The turnoff is now marked by a sign erected by owner Hub Corn. Tours can be arranged, although there is a charge for them.

See also *McKnight Affidavit*

International Roswell Declaration In 1995, in discussions with UFO researchers in Germany, including Joachim Koch, Kent Jeffrey created what has come to be known as the International Roswell Declaration. It has been described as a grassroots movement that originally focused on the Roswell case in particular and UFOs in general.

According to the declaration, it was "part of a worldwide effort to end U.S. Government secrecy surrounding the 1947 Roswell incident. It contains an appeal to the Administration for an Executive Order to declassify any U.S. Government information regarding the existence of UFOs or extraterrestrial intelligence."

The declaration itself was a single sheet that asked for a signature and contained a date when it was to be sent either to the Center for UFO Studies or to the Mutual UFO Network. At the top was a plea to "Please Copy and Circulate." The body of the document said:

> Forty-seven years ago an incident occurred in the southwestern desert of the United States that could have significant implications for all mankind. It involved the recovery by the U.S. Military of material alleged to be of extraterrestrial origin. The event was announced by the U.S. Military on July 8, 1947, through a press release that was carried by newspapers throughout the country. It was subsequently denied by what is now believed to be a cover story claiming the material was nothing more than a weather balloon. It has remained veiled in government secrecy ever since.
>
> The press release announcing the unusual event was

issued by the Commander of the 509th Bomb Group at Roswell Army Air Field, Colonel William Blanchard, who later went on to become a four-star general and Vice Chief of Staff of the United States Air Force. That the weather balloon story was a coverup has been confirmed by individuals directly involved, including the late General Thomas DuBose who took the telephone call from Washington, D.C., ordering the coverup. Numerous other credible military and civilian witnesses have testified that the original press release was correct and that the Roswell Wreckage was of extraterrestrial origin. One such individual was Major Jesse Marcel, the Intelligence Officer of the 509th Bomb Group and one of the first military officers at the scene.

On January 12, 1994, United States Congressman Steven Schiff of Albuquerque, New Mexico, announced to the press that he had been stonewalled by the Defense Department when requesting information regarding the 1947 Roswell event on behalf of constituents and witnesses. Indicating that he was seeking further investigation into the matter, Congressman Schiff called the Defense Department's lack of response "astounding" and concluded it was apparently "another government coverup."

History has shown that unsubstantiated official assurances or denials by government are often meaningless. Nevertheless, there is a logical and straightforward way to ensure that the truth about Roswell will emerge: *an Executive Order declassifying any information regarding the existence of UFOs or extraterrestrial intelligence.* Because this is a unique issue of universal concern, such action would be appropriate and warranted. To provide assurance for all potential witnesses, it would be need to be clearly stated and written into law. Such a measure is essentially what presidential candidate Jimmy Carter promised and then failed to deliver to the American people eighteen years ago in 1976.

If, as is officially claimed, no information on Roswell, UFOs, or extraterrestrial intelligence is being withheld, an Executive Order declassifying it would be a mere formality, as there would be nothing to disclose. The Order would, however, have the positive effect of setting the record straight once and for all. Years of controversy and suspicion would be ended, both in the eyes of the United States' own citizens and in the eyes of the world.

If, on the other hand, the Roswell witnesses are telling the truth and information on extraterrestrial intelligence does exist, it is not something to which a privileged few in the United States Government should have exclusive rights. It is knowledge of profound importance to which all people throughout the world should have an inalienable right. Its release would unquestionably be universally acknowledged as an historic act of honesty and goodwill.

The plan eventually evolved into one that would end in the delivery of some twenty thousand declarations to the White House in time for the fiftieth anniversary celebration of Roswell. The declarations came from around the world and were collected by Jeffrey.

But Jeffrey's attitude was changing. His own investigations were leading him in another direction. He was disappointed by the quality of some of the so-called eyewitnesses. He was in communication with those pursuing specific aspects of the case, such as Vic Golubic, whose search for Glenn Dennis's missing nurse was succeeding, but not in the way expected. This, plus the release of formally classified documents that seemed to prove that no UFO crash had taken place, convinced Jeffrey that nothing extraordinary happened at Roswell.

To those who felt betrayed by him, Jeffrey wrote:

There are apparently those who also feel that by reversing my position on Roswell I am dropping the ball and letting down the twenty thousand plus individuals who have signed the Roswell Declaration. That is anything but the case.

First, with regard to reversing my stance, it is important to remember that the objective of the Roswell Initiative has been to find the truth, not define it. Unfortunately, the truth turned out to be different from what I thought it might be, or hoped it would be. However, now that I am absolutely certain that the debris recovered from Roswell was not that from an extraterrestrial craft, I feel an obligation to get that information out as well. Not to do so would be less than forthright and less than honest.

Secondly, as for the Roswell Declarations, the plan is to deliver them to the White House, along with a cover letter to the President, during the week of the 50th anniversary of the Roswell event this July. Whether or not the government has any substantive information on UFOs, from a public relations standpoint, the situation has not been handled well. The government's quasi-official policy over the last few decades of ignoring the UFO issue has led to a definite suspicion on the part of its citizenry. A 1996 Gallup pole revealed that 71 percent of the American public believes that "the U.S. Government knows more about UFOs than they are telling us."

Although the Roswell Declaration was inspired by the 1947 Roswell event, it is by no means tied to it. The Declaration requests "an Executive Order declassifying any information regarding the existence of UFOs or extraterrestrial intelligence." Such an assurance would still be timely, appropriate, and beneficial to both the U.S. government and its people.

As is stated in the Declaration, if no information is being withheld, such an action would, nonetheless, have the positive effect of setting the record straight and clearing up years of suspicion and controversy. On the other hand, if information is actually being withheld, it would represent knowledge of profound importance to which we are all entitled, and its release would be acknowledged as an historic act of honesty and goodwill.

Jeffrey's assurances did not convince everyone. His cover letter with the 20,000 petitions suggested that there was nothing to the Roswell crash other than the recovery of a Mogul balloon, but that an executive order ending UFO secrecy was a good idea. The petitions were delivered in July 1997.

On December 9, 1997, there was a response from the Department of the Air Force and the Office of the Secretary of the Air Force. It certainly was not what anyone connected with the Roswell Declaration expected. The letter said:

On behalf of President Clinton, thank you for your letter regarding an executive order to declassify information regarding the existence of unidentified flying objects (UFOs) and extraterrestrial intelligence. Due to the large number of requests for personal intervention received by the President each week, he has asked the departments and agencies of the Federal Government to reply on his behalf in those instances where they have special knowledge or authority under the law. For this reason, your correspondence came to the Department of the Air Force for response.

Executive Order 12958, Classified National Security Information, signed by President Clinton on April 17, 1995, directs that all government records of historical value and twenty-five years old or older be reviewed and declassified, unless meeting one of nine narrowly-defined exemptions. These records must be reviewed, or exempted from declassification by April 2000.

The Air Force has identified approximately seventy-five million pages of material for review under Executive Order 12958. As of December 1, we have reviewed approximately 26.5 million pages of the material. The Air Force expects to fulfill all the requirements of the Executive Order prior to the April 2000 deadline. Therefore, since the declassification process for government records is already underway, an executive order for specific categories is unnecessary.

We trust you find this information helpful.

The letter was signed by Patricia M. Fornes, Lieutenant Colonel, USAF, of the Congressional Inquiry Division, Office of Legislative Liaison.

There were UFO researchers who realized that the answer was, more or less, a nonanswer. It did not address the specific issue of the Roswell case, but only that the Air Force, among other governmental agencies, had been ordered to declassify all material except that which fit into narrow categories. The Roswell information could easily be fit into one of those narrow categories, and no one outside the Air Force would know the difference.

That was not the end of the initiative, however. Joachim Koch, in Berlin, Germany, noted he and Hans-Juergen Kyborg had continued their work. As of December 1, 1998, they had collected more declarations, many of them in Germany. Koch and his colleagues plan to deliver more declarations to the American Embassy in Berlin once it is built and occupied in the summer of 2000.

International UFO Museum and Research Center On September 27, 1991, the International UFO Museum and Research Center's corporation was officially founded. It was housed at that time in a suite of offices on the seventh floor of the Sunwest Bank building in Roswell, rent-free. It contained little in the way of research materials and had no exhibits. It was more of a dream than an organization.

On October 24, 1992, the museum moved to 400 North Main Street, again into an area provided rent-free. At that time, they began assembling exhibits and gathering UFO-related materials. Several prominent UFO researchers who had already contributed to the creation of the museum as Founding Members donated spare books, magazines, and duplicate research files.

On January 1, 1997, the museum moved to its current location at 114 North Main Street. A year later, the leaders of the museum found even this new, expanded space inadequate because of a lack of parking, no room to establish a children's section, and no accommodations for other "educational" facilities. They developed a site plan and took an option on twenty-five acres to the west of Roswell. The multimillion-dollar site included room for bus, RV, and car parking, and several different areas for varied displays. It is a dream of what could happen in the future.

Although the facility was originally planned as both a museum and research center where all views about UFOs, pro and con, would be presented, the research aspect has fallen by the way. Several major collections of UFO-related material have been donated to the library, making it one of the largest repositories in the country, trailing behind those at CUFOS and the Fund for UFO Research. Unfortunately there are no accommodations made for researchers to use the material, nor has it been properly cataloged or inventoried.

The museum hasn't been without its problems. Walter Haut, its first president, resigned in 1996, suggesting publicly that he had grown tired of all the work without any monetary compensation. Privately, he suggested that he quit before he was forced out by other members of the board of directors. But in December 1997, he was again on the board, though Glenn Dennis was now president.

There had once been two UFO museums in Roswell, the first being John Price's UFO Enigma Museum, which had started in one room of his video rental store. Price claimed that he had incorporated his museum first and had begun to display his artifacts first, so he was, in fact, the first of the Roswell museums. He eventually quit the video business, expanding the UFO Enigma Museum into the whole building. Price was assisted by others in Roswell such as Cliff Stone and Ralph Heick, both of whom were knowledgeable about, and had studied, the UFO phenomenon.

Price, however, frequently complained that he was getting no help from the city, as was the other competing museum. He complained that those at the other museum didn't know anything about UFOs and didn't care about them. He thought their advantages were unfair and told those who walked through his doors what he thought. He was vocal in the local arena, complaining at city council meetings and in letters to the editor of the *Roswell Daily Record*.

There was no love lost between the two competing museums, and during the fiftieth anniversary celebration, both offered speakers and programs. Even visitors, including the journalists who covered the event, found an undercurrent of hostility between the two museums. Visitors to the International UFO Museum were told not to bother driving to the other end of town because Price had been forced to close, despite the fact that the programming by the Enigma Museum was listed on the city's activity schedule.

Price did close his doors in August 1997, because the building occupied by his museum had been sold. Other tenants who would pay a higher rent had been found. By that time, Price said that he was tired of fighting with everyone in Roswell. They had worn him down.

Problems continued at the International UFO Museum because there were few, if any, people among the various volunteers and officers who knew anything about UFOs. This lack of expertise has been demonstrated time and again. For example, in March 1996, an unidentified man entered the museum with a small bit of metallic debris that he claimed had come from the crash site in 1947. The story he told was that the metal came from a man who had been stationed at the base during the summer of 1947 and had been part of the cleanup crew. He had been able to slip a bit of the debris into his pocket when none of the supervising officers was looking.

The debris seemed to be mysterious. Max Littell related that he knew the name of the man who had brought it in, but he and his family wanted no publicity. Littell, respecting the request, did not reveal who it was. However, without the name of the man who owned the debris, and without the name of the man who had allegedly picked the material from the debris field in 1947, the chain of custody was broken. There was no link to the 1947 events.

Three days later, the story of the strange metallic debris was on the front page of the *Roswell Daily Record* and that evening and the next Max Littell was interviewed by Albuquerque television. Littell told them that he had contacted the New Mexico Bureau of Mines and Mineral Resources in Socorro to arrange for a scientific analysis of the debris.

Littell and the Roswell chief of police, Ray Mounts, headed across the New Mexican desert and drove to Socorro, about 150 miles away. The analysis was performed with everyone keeping an eye on the metallic debris. Charles Moore, of Project Mogul fame and a Socorro resident, participated in the analysis. He said that the debris, whatever it was, had not been part of the balloon experiments conducted during Mogul.

The link between the debris and the Roswell UFO crash would never be established. Rumors had been circulating in Roswell that the debris was from a jeweler who lived in the St. George, Utah, area. He used a mix of copper and silver, not unlike that in the debris, to fashion jewelry using an ancient Japanese technique. Eventually the rumor was confirmed and the jeweler identified the debris as scrap. What had been turned in as alien debris was nothing more than a piece of scrap material from a jewelry-making process.

The episode demonstrated the lack of understanding of the UFO phenomenon by those in the museum. The one notable exception to this lack of UFO knowledge was Dennis Balthaser, who claimed to have been interested in UFOs for a quarter century. Here was a man who, though opinionated, knew who to ask if he didn't have an answer. He wasn't willing to accept all aspects of the UFO phenomenon as real, but maintained a healthy skepticism when reviewing the materials and listening to the stories told by visitors to the museum.

Balthaser, a former highway engineer from El Paso, Texas, had moved to Roswell and then volunteered at the museum. He was put on the board of directors. He became the operations manager at the museum, and their UFO investigator. Part of his responsibility, at least as he saw it, was to try to teach the volunteers something about the UFO phenomenon. He noted that some of the volunteers had not bothered to walk through the museum and disseminated information that was totally false.

Then, on October 28, 1998, Balthaser sent out a blanket e-mail to sixty or so UFO researchers. He said that the president of the museum, Glenn Dennis, had told him to sever all "relationships" with the museum and that he, Balthaser, was not to be affiliated with it any longer.

In the same letter, Balthaser wrote, "Laura Stephey, who was hired in January 1998 to work in the library, was also fired." Balthaser noted: "Having a collection of 45,000 items in the library, fills up bookcases and shelves, but is of no value as long as the people in charge have no knowledge of ufology and present the attitude that discourages serious researchers from becoming involved." Stephey had been hired in an attempt to put order into the chaos of the library. She was also informed that she was being fired for "medical reasons."

Balthaser, in other communications, suggested that all had not been well at the museum for a long time. He wrote: "I . . . have to . . . admit being as closely affiliated with the people in charge I was limited, and several times as much as I hate to admit it said a lot of things there were not true."

Balthaser, who at one time seemed to be a supporter of the Jim Ragsdale tale, reported: "I felt pressure from Max to support the Ragsdale site . . . As much as I hate to say it, he would not listen to anyone that contradicted the Ragsdale story."

He also said, "I seriously question the Corn [impact site], Frank Kaufmann, Frankie Rowe and other things, but with different leadership in the Museum those items could be worked on and information presented that is factual."

But Balthaser and Stephey weren't the only ones who left the museum. Deon Crosby, who had been hired as the director, quit, some thought suddenly, in the summer of 1998, to take another job in Lubbock, Texas. Strained relationships at the museum might have contributed to her departure. She had not spoken to Glenn Dennis, nor he with her, in the four months prior to her resignation except when forced to do so at staff meetings or in meetings with the board of directors.

Another of the former board members, Miller Johnson, who had participated in the attempts to analyze the debris Littell had been given, also quit. Johnson had painted one of the huge murals on display in the museum. More important, he, along with Kent Jeffrey, created a model of the "alien I-beam" seen by Jesse Marcel Jr. That model of a small I-beam, about half an inch tall, an eighth of an inch wide, and nearly eighteen inches long, covered with strange purple symbols, is also still on display in the museum.

Johnson, a dedicated UFO researcher in New Mexico, finally informed other investigators, "I am thoroughly disgusted with the circus atmosphere at the UFO Museum in Roswell . . ."

The strained relationships seemed to percolate through the museum. Walter Haut, who had resigned as president and come back as a member of the board of directors, was supposed to appear on a program with Glenn Dennis and Littell in December 1998, yet at the last minute he declined, forcing the cancellation of the December lecture. The story was that Haut had not learned of the lecture until he read about it in the Roswell newspaper. He had already made other plans and refused to cancel them.

Haut, however, had long been a critic of the "commercialization" of the museum. His original idea, when he had discussed forming the museum with other witnesses living in the Roswell area, had been to create a true research center. He wanted all points of view, whether critical or supportive, to have a forum for debate. He did not envision the museum as a tourist attraction, but as a true working research center that would include an office for visiting investigators to use.

Those visiting investigators, even when they had important, specialized knowledge, were ignored. Wendy Connors visited the museum in July 1998. She came armed with a letter of introduction from George Fawcett so that she could investigate the material that he and Elmer Robert Sabo had donated. Although well treated by Crosby, Stephey, and Balthaser, all suggestions she made about the collection were ignored by Glenn Dennis.

Connors also noted that Glenn Dennis had asked her questions about the museum's research library, including the organization of the materials it contained, but didn't take the ideas to the board of directors. When Connors brought Michael Hall, a professional historian and museum director in Indiana, to the attention of the board, he was insulted by Glenn Dennis. Hall had years of experience in writing grants and grant proposals, which could have been of great benefit to the museum.

The vision of a true research center slipped away as the museum began to seriously count visitors and keep track of the numbers. Their desire for big numbers was no more evident than in July 1997, when the volunteers on the front door counted everyone walking in whether he or she had been in three minutes earlier, was

part of the group of journalists in town to cover the celebration, or
was another volunteer who had stepped out for a moment.

Littell added to that by mentioning that the New Mexico
tourist board has now recognized that Roswell is a tourist attraction.
The proximity of Roswell to the Carlsbad Caverns and Lincoln
County, where Billy the Kid created problems in the 1880s, has
been a detriment to Roswell's establishing a reputation of its own.
Now Roswell is listed as a stop for the tourist, rather than a hub
through which traffic passes on its way to other destinations.

The point, however, is that the vision is lost. Glenn Dennis is
proud of the fact that he "has never read a book or seen a video
about UFOs." Littell has been pushing the Ragsdale story as if it has
been proven beyond a doubt, and the majority of the volunteers,
who are hardworking and loyal, unfortunately know little or nothing about UFOs. It changes the research center into a tourist attraction, and for many that is enough. For others, it is a shame.

Japanese Balloon Bombs John Keel, a researcher of paranormal phenomena, said that he believed that he had come up with an explanation for the Roswell events more than twenty years ago and published it in his column in *Fate* ("The Fugo Balloons," March 1990). In his attempt to explain Roswell with the mundane, he didn't even review the current state of the investigation except to quote from Whitley Strieber's *Majestic*, a work of fiction.

Keel's theory is that Mack Brazel came across a rice paper Japanese balloon bomb some two years after the war had ended. He concluded that the object lay hidden on a remote part of the ranch until freakish winds during a thunderstorm uncovered it, and that government embarrassment about the Japanese project kept the officers of the 509th Bomb Group from revealing the real nature of Brazel's find. Keel suggested that Army Air Forces officers at Eighth Air Force headquarters then substituted a regular weather balloon for the balloon bomb to keep the myth of American invulnerability alive.

To make this theory work, it must be accepted that in postwar America, there was a reason to keep such a secret. In *Japan's World War II Balloon Bomb Attacks on North America* by Robert C. Mikesh, published by the Smithsonian Institution in 1973, the author wrote, "On January 4, 1945, the Office of Censorship asked newspaper editors and radio broadcasters to give no publicity whatsoever to the balloon incidents. This voluntary censorship was adhered to from coast to coast, a remarkable self-restraint in a free-press-conscious country . . ."

That same publication, however, noted the reason for the request. The government feared that spies for the Japanese would read those newspaper stories and report to their headquarters that the balloon bombs were reaching American territory. Documents secured after the war told of Japanese plans to use biological warfare, including the deadly anthrax bacteria, against the United States if the bombing was successful. But the Japanese abandoned the plan when they could confirm no reports of any of their balloons reaching the North American continent. They assumed, falsely, that all the balloon bombs had fallen harmlessly into the ocean.

The plan of censorship was abandoned in the summer of 1945 when six picnickers were killed by a balloon bomb in Oregon. According to the Reverend Archie Mitchell, he was in the mountains with his wife and several children. While he was parking the car, his wife and the kids found the balloon in the woods. While tugging on it, they triggered one of the bombs, causing an explosion that killed Elsie Mitchell, Jay Gifford, Eddie Engen, Sherman Shoemaker, Joan Patzke, and Dick Patzke.

These six deaths were the only casualties recorded in the continental United States resulting from enemy action during World War II. In 1949, a Senate committee approved a House bill to pay $20,000 to the families of those killed.

The deaths caused one other immediate action. The War Department began a "whispering campaign" to alert the general public about the dangers from the balloon bombs. Programs were presented in schools, in public halls, and through various civilian agencies so that the public would be aware of the danger. *Smilin' Jack,* a popular comic strip, carried a warning about the balloon bombs on August 7 and 8, 1945, about a month before the formal end of the war. The War Department thought that a well-planned, well-coordinated, low-profile program could inform the public of the danger without letting the Japanese know the balloons were reaching the United States.

On January 2, 1945, the *New York Herald-Tribune* printed a story headlined BALLOON BOMB IN ALASKA. That might be the story that caused the Office of Censorship to issue their request to many other print media to hold their stories until the end of the war. However, on August 16, 1945, the *New York Times* reported BOMB-LADEN BALLOONS FIZZLE. On January 16, 1946, the *Washington Post* carried a report headlined NINE THOUSAND BALLOON BOMBS WERE USED AGAINST THE UNITED STATES. The *New York Times* of February 9, 1946, reported RAIDS BY JAPANESE BALLOONS. In fact, the *New York Times* ran a series of articles about the bombs in 1947, including PICCARD FLIES JAPANESE PAPER BALLOON on February 17 and BALLOONS . . . BUT JAPAN NEVER KNEW THE OUTCOME on May 29.

These, plus other stories carried in local newspapers, told the public about the balloon bombs. The secrecy imposed was only for the duration of the war and did not extend beyond the signing of the Japanese surrender in 1945. After the war was won, there was no reason for secrecy, no reason to deny that the bombs had been launched and had reached the United States, and more important, no evidence that the topic was still classified.

Keel claimed that Brazel had found a pile of rice paper in his pasture, which was in keeping with his balloon bomb theory, and that "the myth goes marching on." But Keel never bothered with descriptions of the material or the crash site. He dismissed the testimony of more than three dozen witnesses who were there and handled the material.

According to Marcel, the debris was spread over an area that was more than a million square feet in size. That was too much debris for one balloon bomb, which was about thirty-three feet in diameter. In fact, in the very beginning of Mikesh's Japanese balloon bomb report, there is a picture of about a dozen military and government officials inspecting one of the balloons. It did not come apart, it did not scatter debris over a large area, and it is easily identifiable as a balloon.

Marcel did mention the parchment that Keel seized upon, but then, as so often happens, Keel ignored the rest of Marcel's descriptions. Marcel said he tried to burn some of the parchment but it wouldn't burn. This is a critical piece of evidence that is virtually ignored because it is not conventionally explainable, and for Keel's theory to work, he must explain all the facts as mundane.

Sheridan Cavitt, who would later claim that a Project Mogul balloon was responsible for the wreckage found, responded to very pointed questions about the possibility that the wreckage was the result of a balloon bomb. He said, "No way."

Bill Brazel's descriptions of the material he handled do not match those of a balloon bomb. He talked of wires that resembled fiber optics, foil that when wadded into a ball would straighten itself, and a small piece of metal so strong that he couldn't cut it or scratch it with his knife. Nothing about it resembled the debris that would have been found with a balloon bomb.

Keel, unaware of this, or ignoring it, made much of the flower-like drawings described on some of the wreckage, and claimed that Japanese schoolchildren, whom Keel thought were responsible for assembling the balloons, decorated them with such symbols. But according to Mikesh, who wrote the definitive study on the balloon bombs, the whole project was carried out under the strictest of security precautions. "While Japanese markings and stamps would normally be used to facilitate assembly of components, alphabetical letters and figures were used instead. No trace of the origin of the balloon was to be allowed and inspectors were reprimanded on any infringement of this rule. Fear of disclosing the manufacturing location or launch site which would result in reprisal attacks by B-29s were responsible for these harsh measures."

Although the facts of the construction of the balloons and the level of secrecy seemed to have ruled them out as a source of the debris, it was necessary to search further. For example, Art McQuiddy, editor of the *Roswell Morning Dispatch* in 1947, when asked if he'd ever heard the rumor, story, or explanation that Brazel had found a Japanese balloon bomb, said, "Never, ever, ever. It's not even a theory. If anyone had suggested it, I would have heard it."

Jud Roberts was the minority owner of station KGFL in Roswell. When asked if the find could have been a balloon bomb, he said, "No. This is the first time I've ever heard it."

Mikesh's balloon bomb book, part of the Smithsonian *Annals of Flight,* contained a listing of nearly three hundred balloon bomb–related incidents. It gave the locations where the bombs were recovered. The farthest east was Michigan, the farthest north was Alaska and Canada, and the farthest south was Mexico City. There were no listed recoveries in New Mexico.

Because of the fear that Mikesh might have missed something in his research, a search was conducted at the Museum of New Mexico in Santa Fe. The staff was asked if there were any documents, records, or stories of any balloon bomb recoveries in New Mexico. Charles Bennett, a museum staff member, said that he knew of "no records or indications of any balloon bomb attacks." In fact, Bennett said that he looked for that sort of thing and that he'd never seen anything like it.

Bennett did say, however, that he might have missed something and suggested that Robert Torres, also with the museum, might be helpful. Torres said, "I've never seen anything like that. No indication that any [balloon bombs] did [reach New Mexico]." Torres said that he would check the various indices, records, and charts to see if anything had been found. He never found anything that would indicate that a balloon bomb was responsible.

But the Museum of New Mexico in Santa Fe, with all its state records, files, and documents, might have missed a single story of a balloon bomb in Chaves or Lincoln Counties. David Orr at the Chaves County Historical Museum said he'd never heard of anything like it. "Not that I know of. Maybe it's too wide open here so no one found anything. I have heard of them on the west coast."

Keel said that he'd talked to a local historian in Roswell who told him it was a balloon bomb. Keel expects his readers to accept this pronouncement, even though no one else claimed to have heard such a story.

And Keel offers no documentation for his claims. He ignored the Unit History prepared by the 509th Bomb Group. These were detailed accounts of the unit's activities in 1947. While flying saucers are mentioned, the recovery of Keel's balloon bomb is not. Since the unit histories were originally classified secret, there is no reason for the recovery of a balloon bomb not to be mentioned if that is what it was. In fact, not a single document has surfaced to support the theory that Brazel discovered a balloon bomb.

It is interesting that in Keel's list of articles about the balloon bombs there is nothing earlier than 1953. In addition to the newspaper and journal articles that predated the July 1947 find by Brazel, there is a *Reader's Digest* article from August 1950 and Lincoln LaPaz's article from *Collier's* on January 17, 1953. There are also unpublished histories of several military units from 1945, 1946, and 1947 that make reference to the balloon bombs.

Keel claims that in 1947, the Army covered up the recovery of a balloon bomb because the military and the government wanted to maintain the myth of invulnerability. He offers no proof that this was the case.

A wide range of documentation, however, proves that the balloon bombs were not a secret in 1947. There were dozens of articles published about them. Keel himself admits this in the January 1991 issue of *Fate*, where he writes, "Actually there were hundreds of articles published between 1946 and 1970, particularly in regional journals and local newspapers." And that is the whole point. By 1947, there was no secrecy surrounding the balloon bombs and no reason not to tell the truth if a balloon bomb had been the culprit.

The July 9, 1947, *Roswell Daily Record* may end this aspect of the controversy once and for all. In a story on page six, a weather-man in the Albuquerque bureau is quoted: "He said that the radio-sondes periodically create excitement across the country and that two years ago they started a Japanese balloon scare."

Keel reported on rice paper and strings and ignored all the descriptions of the metal found at Roswell. He rejected the testi-mony of the witnesses, dismissing it by writing, "I suppose by 1999 there will be thousands of Roswell witnesses from that long-gone era." Unfortunately, this prediction has proven to be all too true.

Keel ignored what he couldn't explain, belittled what he couldn't ignore, and offered nothing to prove what he said. He pro-vided no documents, no names of witnesses for verification, no proof at all. His theory broke down under objective research. If it had been a balloon bomb, why are there no witnesses to it? If it was a balloon bomb, why is there no documentation for it? Can Keel offer a single newspaper article, a single report, or a single statement from the historical societies and museums in New Mexico support-ing his claims?

Jeffrey, Kent (1944–) Kent Jeffrey was born in Southern California to a military family. He grew up in various locations but considered the San Francisco area his home. He attended the University of California at Santa Barbara and graduated with a degree in physical geography. He has been an airline pilot since 1970 and is currently a 767 captain.

Jeffrey said that he has had a lifelong interest in science and astronomy and became interested in the Roswell case after learning that his father had known Butch Blanchard. In consultation with UFO researchers in Germany, he created a one-page document that became the Roswell Declaration. After the Declaration was pub-lished in a variety of magazines, Jeffrey collected more than 20,000 signatures asking for an end to the UFO secrecy in general and the Roswell case in particular.

Jeffrey was among the first to see the *Alien Autopsy* footage and to declare it a hoax. His article about it, "Santilli's Controversial Autopsy Movie (SCAM)," has been published in a number of forums and was reprinted in whole or in part in a dozen countries. *Sightings* produced a segment based on Jeffrey's article.

At one time Jeffrey was one of the most outspoken believers in the Roswell case. He conducted his own investigation into the case, but eventually began to doubt its authenticity. In the year leading to the fiftieth anniversary celebration, he came to what he described as a disappointing but inescapable conclusion that the Roswell case did not involve an alien craft, but was probably explainable as a Project Mogul balloon array. In June 1997, his article explaining his beliefs was published, first in *The MUFON Journal* and later in other magazines.

In great detail (though abbreviated here because of space limitations) he explained his reasons as follows:

> Many of the books and documentaries about Roswell imply that it is highly probable, if not certain, that the recovered debris was from a crashed flying saucer. Some of that information, however, is misleading or incorrect. It ranges from fabricated stories on the part of seemingly credible witnesses to exaggeration and selective presentation of fact.
>
> In some instances, it is probably more a case of overzealousness on the part of authors than intentional deception. In other instances, credibility is stretched beyond limits. For example, after the conclusion of the story in the movie *Roswell*, statements of purported fact just prior to the credits inform us that Jesse Marcel, Sr., died in 1986 and that "since then over 350 witnesses to the event have agreed to talk." In actuality, because so few people ever saw the debris, it is doubtful whether even one tenth that number of witnesses could ever be produced.

In retrospect, there is much about Roswell that I wish I had questioned more thoroughly, early on . . . Even before the advent of recent negative developments in the Roswell case, I have always felt that a UFO would never crash. However, because of the impressive witness testimony about which I was told, I suspended judgment and allowed for the possibility that Roswell might be an exception—some kind of one-in-a-quintillion fluke. That was, in retrospect, a mistake.

The problem with the concept of a UFO crashing is that as technology advances, so does reliability. Be it with cars, airplanes, televisions, or wristwatches, the reliability of today's technology far exceeds that of the technology of just a few decades ago. For example, because of the high reliability of their engines, long-range, twin-engine commercial jetliners are now authorized to fly nonstop across the North Atlantic. A few decades ago, that would have been unthinkable. (The positive correlation between advancing technology and reliability applies to "proven" technology, not experimental state-of-the-art machines still in the developmental phase such as experimental aircraft or space vehicles.)

With today's industry-average engine-failure rate of less than one failure per 100,000 flight hours, the chances of both engines of a two-engine jetliner failing during a given hour of flight are less than one out of 10 billion. Figuring 50,000 aircraft-ocean crossings per year, and factoring in such variables as average time over the water and average distance from land, the odds are less than fifty-fifty of a double-engine failure and consequent ditching in the North Atlantic of even one such aircraft over the next 10,000 years.

This incredible degree of reliability is found with a

technology that would be primitive compared with a UFO. Even with today's relatively "primitive" technology, our commercial aircraft have very efficient collision avoidance systems, as well as excellent radar systems for avoiding thunderstorms and their associated hail and lightning (phenomena, incidentally, that are surely not unique to this planet).

If we assume that UFOs are extraterrestrial spacecraft and that some of the many reported UFO sightings are genuine UFOs, we are dealing with machines apparently capable of high-speed right-angle turns, incredible accelerations and speeds, and wingless flight—not to mention of traveling light-years through the void of empty space in, presumably, a relatively short period of time. Such capability would require a technology totally beyond our present understanding of physics—a technology the sophistication of which we cannot even begin to imagine.

Because of the positive correlation between technology and reliability, such incredibly advanced technology would most certainly mean a correspondingly high degree of reliability. Common sense dictates that the chances of such machines crashing, breaking down, or colliding would be all but zero. It certainly would be many orders of magnitude less than the already infinitesimally small chance of one of today's twin-engine jetliners having a double-engine failure.

For me, the beginning of the end for the Roswell UFO case came last spring, when I first saw one of a number of previously classified military documents dealing with unidentified flying objects. The 289-page document was released under the Freedom of Information Act (FOIA) in March 1996 in response to a FOIA request by researcher William LaParl. It contained the minutes of the Air Force Scientific Advisory Board Conference at the Pentagon on March 17 and 18, 1948. Buried in the document was a very interesting statement by a Colonel Howard McCoy which referred to a number of unpublished UFO reports. The last sentence of McCoy's statement, however, is devastating to the Roswell case.

"We have a new project—Project SIGN—which may surprise you as a development from the so-called mass hysteria of the past Summer when we had all the unidentified flying objects or discs. This can't be laughed off. We have over 300 reports which haven't been publicized in the papers from very competent personnel, in many instances—men as capable as Dr. K. D. Wood, and practically all Air Force, Airline people with broad experience. We are running down every report. I can't even tell you how much we would give to have one of those crash in an area so that we could recover whatever they are."

My first reaction to this statement was one of disbelief. Thoughts came to mind like "This can't be correct, there must be some mistake, this guy didn't know," etc. We are probably all somewhat prone to such initial reactions of denial when confronted with facts that conflict with our preconceived notions of reality or our established beliefs. Most of the time, however, common sense, logic, and rationality prevail. On the other hand, there is sometimes an invariable refusal to give up a particular contention or belief, no matter how strong the evidence to the contrary. The result of such refusal is often illogical speculation and far-fetched scenarios, concocted in an effort to rationalize away the facts. It is a pitfall into which even credible researchers sometimes tumble.

The statement at the Scientific Advisory Board
Conference lamenting the fact that the Air Force did not
have a crashed UFO was made by Colonel Howard
McCoy, the Chief of Intelligence for Air Material
Command at Wright Patterson AFB. Wright Patterson is
where the Air Force's technical and intelligence experts are
concentrated, even today. It is where recovered wreckage
from a foreign craft of any kind with the potential for
invading our skies would be taken for technical analysis—
be it a MIG 29 or a Klingon battle cruiser. If there had
been a crashed flying saucer recovered outside of Roswell,
New Mexico, in July 1947, this is where it would have
been taken. As Chief of Intelligence, Colonel Howard
McCoy would have known about it.

In addition to the minutes of the Air Force Scientific
Advisory Board meeting, there are other military docu-
ments indicating just as unequivocally that the Air
Force was not in possession of any physical evidence
with regard to UFOs. Among these documents is a
series of communiqués dealing with "flying object incidents in the United States" between Colonel McCoy at
Wright Patterson and Major General C. P. Cabell, the
Director of Intelligence for the Air Force at the
Pentagon. In one of these communiqués, a letter dated
November 8, 1948, McCoy made three separate references to the fact that there was no physical or tangible
evidence from a flying saucer crash. Cabell used the
information from McCoy's letter for preparation of a
memorandum dated November 30, 1948, for Secretary
of Defense James Forrestal.

The lack of physical evidence is also mentioned in a
September 23, 1947, letter from Lieutenant General
Nathan Twining, Commander of the Air Materiel
Command at Wright Field, to Brigadier General George

Schulgen, a top intelligence official at the Pentagon. The Twining letter was written less than three months after the Roswell incident. The letter is also significant because it makes reference to the cooperation between the Engineering Division and the Intelligence Division at the Wright Patterson complex. This cooperation is mentioned specifically in regard to assessing the nature of the mysterious "flying objects" about which there had been so many credible reports.

The cooperation between the intelligence and engineering branches at Wright Patterson is further corroborated by a "top secret" memorandum for the Chief, Air Intelligence Division, dated October 11, 1948, signed by a Colonel Brooke Allen, Chief, of the Air Estimates Branch at Wright Patterson. The stated subject of the memorandum is "Analysis of Flying Object Incidents in the U.S." This memorandum is important because, along with the Twining letter, it confirms what is dictated by common sense—that if the engineering department possessed a crashed saucer, the intelligence department would not only be aware of it, they would also be integrally involved with its analysis and the assessment of any potential threat posed to national security.

The 1947 and 1948 military documents are definitive. They cannot be simply or smugly characterized as "absence of evidence." They are evidence. They state definitively that there was no crashed saucer.

If instead of the above documents, researchers had uncovered definitive and authentic documentation indicating the existence of a crashed saucer, such documentation would have undoubtedly been acknowledged by all and characterized as a "smoking gun." Victory would have been declared, and congressional investigations would have been all but certain.

Predictably, some in the UFO field are reacting to the 1947 and 1948 military documents with an attitude reminiscent of the platitude, "don't bother me with the facts, my mind's made up." Ironically, this is the same type of mentality of which they are so quick to accuse their detractors. Narrow-mindedness, however, can exist on either side of the fence. The facts are now clear. We can't simply refuse to acknowledge them because we don't like them. The Roswell crash didn't happen. It is time to face the music, and the band isn't playing our tune.

The 509th Bomb Group was based at Roswell in 1947. In September 1996, I had the privilege of attending the reunion of the 509th Bomb Group in Tucson, Arizona, as a guest of General Bob Scott and his wife Terry. I have known the Scotts for a couple of years. By coincidence, Bob's son is a pilot for the same airline for which I work.

At the time of the 509th reunion, I had not yet seen all the pertinent 1948 military documents and still held an inkling of hope that there might be something to the Roswell event. Prior to the reunion, I had sent out over 700 mailings to members of the reunion group in the hope of finding additional witnesses to the mysterious debris. The result was a disappointment—only two calls, neither of which was of any real help. Both of the men who called were former 509th flight engineers. One had had a very interesting UFO sighting from the ramp at Kirtland Air Force Base. The other recalled seeing a lot of extra activity around one of the hangars at Roswell near the time of the 1947 incident.

At the reunion in Tucson, I was introduced to several of the pilots who were at Roswell in 1947 and who promptly told me, in no uncertain terms, that the crashed-saucer event never occurred, period. I did not get the impression at the time, nor have I ever since, that any of these men are engaged in some kind of incredible 50-year-long massive coverup or that they were putting on an act or facade to throw me off track. Anyone who believes that to be the case is out of touch with the reality of this issue. Like every other person with whom I have ever discussed this subject, these men were in total agreement that anything as important and profound as the knowledge of other intelligent life in the universe is information that should not be censored or suppressed and to which everyone should be entitled. These men risked their lives in World War II to save the world from the kind of totalitarian governments that, among their many other crimes against humanity, unjustifiably suppressed information from their people.

The men who were at Roswell during July 1947 feel very strongly that absolutely nothing out of the ordinary happened and that the whole matter is patently ridiculous. The 509th was the only atomic bomb group in the world in 1947 and was composed of a very elite group of individuals, most of whom still feel a definite sense of pride in their former outfit. To them, the crashed-saucer nonsense, along with all the hullabaloo and conspiracy theories surrounding it, makes a mockery of and is an insult to the 509th Bomb Group and its men.

One of the 509th pilots I met at the reunion, Jack Ingham, has since become a friend and has helped me considerably in contacting additional members of the group who were stationed at Roswell during the time of the incident. When I first met Jack in Tucson, he spared no punches in letting me know exactly what he thought about the crashed-flying saucer matter. Others at the

reunion told me that if something like the crash of a
UFO had really happened at Roswell, Jack Ingham
would have known. Jack spent a total of 16 years with
the 509th Bomb Group—February 1946 to July 1962.
He retired from the Air Force as a lieutenant colonel in
January 1971.

Since last September, I have spoken with a total of 15
B-29 pilots and 2 B-29 navigators, all of whom were
stationed at Roswell Army Air Field in July 1947. Most
of them heard nothing about the supposed crashed-
saucer incident until years later, after all the publicity
started. The few men who did recall hearing something
about the incident at the time of its occurrence said that
the inside word was that the debris was from a downed
balloon of some kind and that there was no more than
"one wheelbarrow full." Not one single man had any
direct knowledge of a crashed saucer or of any kind of
unusual material. Even more significantly, in all of their
collective years with the 509th Bomb Group, not one of
these men had ever encountered any other individual
who had such knowledge.

As Jack Ingham and others pointed out, the 509th
was a very close-knit group and there was no way an
event as spectacular as the recovery of a crashed-alien
spaceship from another world could have happened at
their base without their having known about it. Despite
the fact that they, individually, may not have been
directly involved with the recovery operation, and
despite the pervasiveness of the "need to know" philosophy in the military, these men maintained that there
was absolutely no way that something of such magnitude and so earthshaking would not have been commu-
nicated among the members of the group—especially
within the inner circle of the upper echelon of B-29

pilots and navigators—all of whom had top-secret security clearances. Furthermore, unlike the atomic weapons secrets with which they were all entrusted, the existence of a crashed alien spaceship would have been much more of a social and scientific issue than a national security issue. Additionally, word was already out—the story had been published in afternoon newspapers all over the Western United States.

Most of the men of the 509th Bomb Group were primarily WWII veterans in their mid- to late twenties. (Colonel Blanchard, the commander of the group, was, himself, only 31.) Military regulations notwithstanding, human nature and common sense have to be factored into the equation. Such an occurrence—the most significant and dramatic event in recorded history—would surely have been discussed by these men, at least among themselves. . . .

The central focus of the Roswell story has been the recovery of the unusual debris from the Foster Ranch in July 1947. This is where it all started. The most important living witness to that debris is Jesse Marcel, Jr., MD, the son of Major Jesse Marcel, Sr., the intelligence officer of the 509th Bomb Group. After being out at the site, Major Marcel stopped by his house on the way back to the base and laid the debris out on his kitchen floor to show his wife and son. As a result, Jesse Marcel, Jr., got a good look at the unusual material. Potentially, the key to the whole Roswell UFO case lies in Jesse Marcel, Jr.'s memory. He saw the debris. Either it was extraterrestrial or it was not.

Despite the recent overwhelmingly negative developments in the Roswell case, I did not want to leave any stone unturned. I therefore arranged to have Jesse Marcel, Jr. fly to Washington, D.C., for a thorough debriefing session to see if we could get a better picture of the exact nature of the unusual debris that precipitated the Roswell story.

Being fully aware of the pitfalls in the use of hypnosis for memory retrieval, I decided that it still might be an avenue worth pursuing. In addition to its (controversial) use in retrieving repressed subconscious memories, hypnosis can be an effective tool in enhancing conscious memory. Law enforcement agencies sometimes use hypnosis in this manner to help a witness better remember a face or a license plate number, for example.

Because I considered our effort such an important endeavor, I wanted to find the best in the field. I also wanted someone who had maximum credibility and who was not associated with the UFO community. There was a reason for this. In the event that anything significantly positive came out of the hypnotic session, there would be a greater chance of it being taken seriously by the mainstream public.

My search led me to Neil Hibler, PhD, a clinical psychologist with an office in the Washington, D.C., area. Dr. Hibler is one of the world's leading experts in the use of hypnotic regression for forensic purposes. Law enforcement agencies all over the world have retained him for important cases. Among the agencies that have called on him are the Federal Bureau of Investigation, the National Security Agency, the Defense Intelligence Agency, and the intelligence agencies of all three armed services. Dr. Hibler has worked with subjects from all walks of life, including diplomats and generals.

On the evening of January 10, 1997, four of us met in Dr. Hibler's office for the first of three sessions. The other two sessions took place over the next two days. Jesse Marcel, Jr., who is one of the most honest and sincere persons I have ever met, cooperated completely, despite the potential controversy of any significant outcome. Dr. Hibler had suggested that everything be recorded on videotape. This was done by Denise Marcel, Jesse, Jr.'s 33-year-old daughter, who flew in from Los Angeles. Denise was especially interested in our endeavor because she has studied hypnosis formally and is a licensed hypnotherapist in California. A professional illustrator from the Washington, D.C., area, Kimberly Moeller, was also present during the second and third sessions.

Dr. Hibler's approach was to have Jesse go through the entire story twice, without the aid of hypnosis. Hypnosis was then administered for each subsequent recounting of the story. According to Denise, her father is not an easy hypnotic subject, but was definitely in a mild to medium trance by the end of the last session. The hypnosis did not, however, bring out anything new that was of significance. For that reason, confabulation (false memory syndrome) was definitely not a concern. In Jesse's words, the hypnosis simply helped "fine tune" his conscious memory. For example, by the end of the last session, he was able to recall several details about which he had previously been uncertain—the debris' already having been laid out on the floor when he first saw it, the fact that his father was in uniform, and his accompanying his father out to the car, where he saw additional debris in the trunk.

The most significant thing about the sessions in Washington is not so much what came out of them, but what didn't come out of them. There were no descriptions or memories of any kind of exotic debris or wreckage. There is a very good reason for that—there simply was no such exotic debris or wreckage for Jesse to remember. If there had been, in all probability, he would have remembered it consciously. Nonetheless, because of the extreme importance of the debris to the Roswell case, the effort was worth a try—just in case. There was no risk of a negative effect on what Jesse remembered. Hypnosis can elicit memories of things that didn't happen, but it can't take away memories of things that did happen.

Unfortunately, instead of providing any renewed hope or encouragement, the outcome of the hypnosis sessions in Washington, D.C., was, for me, the final nail in the coffin of the Roswell crashed-saucer scenario. The sessions made it absolutely clear that the material recovered from the Foster ranch northwest of Roswell in 1947 was anything but unique or exotic. As it turned out, it was extremely mundane.

According to Jesse's best recollection, the material laid out on his kitchen floor, which was representative of that at the site, consisted primarily of pieces of metallic foil, a short beam or "stick," and a few pieces of a plastic or Bakelite-like substance. Certainly, such mundane debris would not constitute the wreckage from any kind of sophisticated vehicle or craft, much less one capable of interstellar travel.

There was nothing to indicate form or structure. There was nothing to indicate some kind of ultra-advanced technology. There were no technological artifacts of any type—no remnants of anything resembling motors, servos, electronic components, instruments, a guidance system, a control system, a propulsion system, etc.—nothing. The crash of a Sopwith Camel would have left more complex and sophisticated debris. Even the debris from a two-thousand-year-old Roman chariot would have been more interesting and varied than the debris that was laid out on the Marcel kitchen floor. At least with the chariot there would have been some technological remnants such as parts of the axles and wheels.

While we have no idea what the debris from a crashed spaceship would look like, it is reasonable to assume that it would reflect a level of complexity and technological advancement beyond imagination. Postulating that a few pieces of foil, plastic-like material, and short beams constitute the remains of a machine of such capability and complexity is more than just a quantum leap, it is completely baseless and totally illogical.

In addition to being mundane, the material recovered from the Foster ranch is definitely reconcilable with the debris from an ML-307 radar reflector—the length and cross-sectional size of the beams or sticks, the pieces of foil, and the plastic-like material (now thought to be part of one of the plastic ballast cases that contained sand). Even the color of the symbols that Jesse, Jr., remembers is almost identical to the color of the flower patterns on the balsa stick that Irving Newton remembers seeing in Ramey's office.

The crashed saucer scenario requires an implausible occurrence. A flying saucer crashes northwest of Roswell, New Mexico, and leaves debris in the form of small pieces of foil, short beams that have a maximum length of about three feet, and pieces of Bakelite-like material. Amazingly, by incredible coincidence, a balloon array that disappeared in the same general area four weeks earlier carried three radar reflectors constructed from reflective foil, short beams that have a maximum length of about three feet, and pieces of Bakelite-like material.

Obviously, the idea of any such coincidence ever

happening is absurd. The debris recovered from the Foster ranch was that of an ML-307 radar reflector.

It is not hard to imagine how the apparent misidentification probably came about. During the previous two weeks, there had been a wave of sightings of flying saucers or "disks" throughout the United States and Canada. The sightings were something that were in the news daily and were on almost everyone's mind—an "unknown" in the sky. At the same time, balloon arrays under a secret project known as "Mogul" were being launched from the Alamogordo area, just under 100 miles to the west of Roswell. These balloon arrays carried ML-307 radar reflectors, which would have been totally unfamiliar to Butch Blanchard, Jesse Marcel, and the other men at Roswell AAF. The debris from one of these reflectors scattered over the desert would likewise have been something unfamiliar to them—an "unknown" on the ground.

It is understandable that the unknown debris found northwest of Roswell would have been assumed to be related to the unknown objects that had been so frequently reported flying around in the sky, the flying "disks." Such a connection, although with the benefit of hindsight, incorrect, would have been very logical and understandable for the men at Roswell to make. This is almost certainly how the Roswell story began.

In the last few months, as part of my effort to reconstruct what happened at Roswell, I have had a number of conversations with Irving Newton, the weather officer at Fort Worth Army Air Field who was called in by General Ramey to identify the unusual debris. The debris was already suspected to be part of some type of balloon device. Newton told me that he immediately recognized it as being from an ML-307 radar reflector.

An ML-307 was a box kite-like device covered with a tough, paper-backed foil that was suspended below balloons or balloon arrays to facilitate radar tracking. According to Newton, most weather officers, much less the men at Roswell or Fort Worth, would not have been familiar with such a device. Newton had worked with the reflectors a couple of years earlier during the invasion of Okinawa in the Pacific. The devices were suspended below balloons, released to gather wind data for use in helping direct heavy naval artillery fire.

In one of my conversations with Newton, quite by chance, a new and important revelation came to light. He was describing the color of the symbols on one of the balsa sticks and mentioned how it was faint and had somewhat of a mottled appearance because of "the way that the dye had bled through onto the surface of the stick." This was a very important piece of information. The symbols that Newton saw on the debris in Ramey's office were on the surface of the stick, not on tape! The tape had apparently peeled away, probably because of several weeks' exposure to sunlight while it lay out in the desert. This serendipitous revelation immediately cleared up one of the biggest questions in my mind about the Roswell case—how could Jesse Marcel, Sr., or Jesse Marcel, Jr., for that matter, not have recognized flower patterns on tape? The answer is now crystal clear. The symbols they saw were not on tape. What they saw were images of the original symbols from the dye that had bled through before the tape had peeled away. Jesse, Jr.'s testimony about the symbols definitely not being on tape was absolutely correct.

During the sessions in Washington, D.C., the professional illustrator who was present drew a very accurate depiction of what Jesse, Jr., remembered—the "I-beam-

like" member with the symbols on it. After learning
what a good recollection of the symbols Newton had, I
arranged for him to work with the same illustrator so
that we might have side-by-side sketches from the same
perspective for comparison.

As it turned out, the resemblance between the two
sketches was remarkable.

Even the artist commented that "it sure seemed like
these two men were describing the same thing."
Probably most amazing was the closeness of the color
that the two men remembered. Other than Newton's
color being more faded, the colors are nearly identical.

The most significant discrepancy was the way the
slight ridges on the upper and lower edges gave Jesse's
beam the appearance of an I-beam-like cross section.
This was probably due to a slight error in Jesse's recollection. His father, for example, remembered the small
members as having a rectangular cross section. In a
1979 interview with journalist Bob Pratt, Jesse Marcel,
Sr., stated, ". . . it was a solid member, rectangular
members, just like you get with a square stick." It is
entirely possible, however, that the particular member
that Jesse, Jr., held, could have had a ridge on its edges
for some unknown reason.

The only other really significant discrepancy was in
the color of the member. Jesse remembered it being
about the same color as that of the foil-like material,
while Irving Newton remembered it being almost
white. Judging from the pictures taken in Ramey's
office, however, the white that Newton recalled was
probably accurate. According to Charles Moore, the
project engineer for "Project Mogul," the sticks were
covered with glue or glue-like substance. This would
probably have given them a different color than that of

raw wood, as well as a different feel or texture—probably to the degree that someone who didn't know what they were, might not recognize them as wood. The only other discrepancies were minor, such as differences in the size and spacing of the symbols.

For anyone who suspects that Irving Newton is participating in a 50-year coverup and making up the story about the symbols or flower patterns, all he needs to do is check out the July 9, 1947, *Roswell Daily Record*. Rancher Mac [*sic*] Brazel is quoted as talking about sticks, foil, and tape with flower patterns on it.

Most of us have seen the now-famous pictures of the debris from Roswell taken in General Roger Ramey's office at Fort Worth Army Air Field. General Ramey, Colonel Thomas DuBose, Major Jesse Marcel, and Warrant Officer Irving Newton appear in the pictures, posing with the debris. The debris is clearly visible in all seven existing pictures. There is absolutely no question that this is the debris from an ML-307 radar reflector. If this is the same debris that was recovered from the Foster ranch, then the Roswell case is closed, period. It's over, end of subject.

In the January 1991 issue of the *MUFON UFO Journal,* there is an article by Jaime Shandera titled "New Revelations About the Roswell Wreckage: A General Speaks Up." The article included an extensive two-part interview with General Thomas DuBose, who was a colonel and General Ramey's chief of staff in 1947. DuBose met the plane carrying the material picked up outside of Roswell and personally took it to Ramey's office. During the first of the two interviews, Shandera realized that General DuBose was not familiar with and had not seen the pictures taken of the debris in Ramey's office. Shandera then sent DuBose a set of the pictures, prior to conducting the second interview.

Throughout the two interviews, Shandera questioned DuBose with the doggedness of a district attorney, asking him nine times in nine different ways whether the debris had been switched. Nine times, General DuBose made it emphatically clear that the debris had not been switched. Among DuBose's responses were "We never switched anything ... We were West Pointers—we would never have done that ... I have damn good eyesight ... I had charge of that material, and it was never switched." When shown the pictures from Ramey's office and asked if he recognized the material, he replied, "Oh yes. That's the material that Marcel brought in to Ft. Worth from Roswell."

In William Moore's book *The Roswell Incident,* Jesse Marcel, Sr., was interviewed about the debris. His responses were somewhat puzzling in that he indicated that the photos of him were of the actual debris, but that the later photos (without him) contained substituted material. Later photos with substituted debris (even if they existed) wouldn't really matter. If the debris in the photo with Major Marcel was the actual material, it was from an ML-307 radar reflector. Again, end of story.

Among Marcel's responses were "They took one picture of me on the floor holding up some of the less-interesting metallic debris. . . . The stuff in that one photo was pieces of the actual stuff we had found. It was not a staged photo."

During one of my interviews with Irving Newton, he mentioned how in Ramey's office, Marcel had pointed out the symbols and indicated that he (Marcel) thought they might be some form of alien writing. When I asked him if he was sure that it was Marcel who did that,

Newton was emphatic that it was the man who "had collected the debris from the ranch." This is, of course, one further indication that the debris in Ramey's office was the debris from the Foster ranch. There was no substitution. The debris in the pictures was the same debris collected by Major Marcel at the Foster Ranch. It was the debris from an ML-307 radar reflector.

There is also an interesting quote in Moore's book from Marcel about the so-called indestructibility of the material. It sounds like this now-legendary indestructibility was actually more the kind of indestructibility that you would find in material from something like a tough, paper-backed foil. Marcel stated, "It was possible to flex this stuff back and forth, even wrinkle it, but you could not put a crease in it that would stay, nor could you dent it at all. I would almost have to describe it as metal with plastic properties."

One could also lay tough, paper-backed foil on the ground and pound away with a sledgehammer and quite possibly not dent it. Interestingly, the sledgehammer test was only hearsay, anyway. One of the airmen allegedly performed the test and told Marcel about it afterwards. This is possibly a good example of how rumors and myth begin. Besides, if this material was so indestructible, why did it break up into hundreds or thousands of little pieces? The real answer is, of course, that it was not so indestructible because it was from an ML-307 radar reflector that was apparently dragged across the ground as the balloon array descended.

The testimony of the late Jesse Marcel, Sr., is probably the most important, as well as the most controversial, of the whole Roswell story. In essence, it forms the foundation around which the rest of the case is built. However, because the debris he recovered was not extraterrestrial, it could not have been what he said it was. That does not mean, however, that he did not believe it was extraterrestrial. In my opinion, it is very possible, if not highly probable, that he sincerely believed until the day he died that the material was something, as he once put it, "not of this earth." A less-than-perfect memory of events so long ago, in combination with the suspicion on his part of a coverup above his level of security or outside his need to know, makes such a scenario entirely plausible.

Unfortunately, because of minor, almost trivial, inconsistencies in some of the things Jesse Marcel, Sr., said, or is believed to have said, some have made caustic personal attacks against a man no longer around to defend himself—and who was, in all probability, telling the truth as he recalled it. I have now spoken with a number of men from the 509th Bomb Group who knew Major Marcel. All had nothing but the highest regard and respect for him.

Some of these attacks have been extended to Jesse Marcel, Jr., which I find astounding. As I have already mentioned, he is as sincere and honest as anyone I have ever known. Like his father before him, he served his country during time of war. Few people know it, but he was seriously injured during the Vietnam War when his helicopter was shot down, killing everyone else on board. Like all of us, Jesse might not have 100 percent perfect recall of every past event, but I would never question his word.

In a way, because the debris recovered outside of Roswell in 1947 was not extraterrestrial, none of the other witness testimony really matters. If the story of a highly unusual and totally unprecedented event is killed at the source, subsequent corroborating testimony goes out the window. For example, in the summer of 1993, a man from Seattle, Washington, made the unprecedented claim that he had found a hypodermic syringe inside a sealed can of Pepsi Cola. The story was picked up by the media, and within days there were copycat claims against the Pepsi Cola Corporation all over the country. Unfortunately for those who jumped on the bandwagon, the original claim turned out to be false. Where did that leave the subsequent claimants? Out on a limb that had been cut off, and, in this particular case, facing up to $250,000 in fines and five years in jail.

The testimony of some of the other Roswell witnesses has been all but validated in the public eye because of repeated media coverage. For this reason I will address a couple of cases.

Former mortician Glenn Dennis and the elusive nurse, Naomi Self, who supposedly witnessed alien autopsies at the base hospital is one of the best-known elements of the 1947 Roswell event. Although I know and like Glenn Dennis on a personal level, I have to say that his story has lost all credibility. Glenn, incidentally, has been fully aware of the fact that researchers have been spending time and resources in an effort to locate a "Naomi Self."

There was already significant circumstantial evidence to indicate that no such nurse ever existed, when a diligent young researcher from Arizona, Vic Golubic, all but confirmed the fact. He located the records of the Cadet Nurse Corps, where all nurses for the military were trained during the mid-1940s. When Golubic checked with Dennis about the correct spelling of "Self" and informed him about the Cadet Nurse Corps records, Dennis changed his story, telling Golubic that Self was not really the correct last name after all. Dennis, without giving a good reason for not doing so, also refused to tell Golubic the "real" last name. Sorry, Glenn, end of story.

Both my father and I got to know Frank Kaufmann very well and consider him a friend. However, as with Dennis, I have to say that in view of what we now know, there is no way that Kaufman's [*sic*] fantastic tale of a crashed spaceship with alien bodies could have any basis in reality. According to Kaufmann's story, he was one of nine military men at the top-secret recovery operation 35 miles north of town. Other than Kaufman [*sic*], the only other living member of the "original nine" was a General Robert Thomas.

The last time my father and I were in Roswell, Kaufman showed us some of his pictures, including one with him standing next to a brigadier general. My father asked Kaufman [*sic*] if that was Thomas, to which Kaufman [*sic*] replied in the affirmative. Unfortunately, my father, who spent 30 years in the Air Force, was unable to recognize the general. I later checked at the Air Force records center and learned that not only was there no living General Robert Thomas, but there never was a General Robert Thomas. On being confronted with this, Kaufman [*sic*] informed me that Thomas was really just a "code name."

The final witness testimony that I will address is that concerning Oliver W. (Pappy) Henderson. Millions have seen the "Unsolved Mysteries" broadcast about Roswell with the scene of Pappy Henderson in his flight suit, leaning over and inspecting one of several alien bodies laid out on a hangar floor just prior to their being flown to Wright Patterson. Henderson, who died in 1986, on seeing a tabloid headline and story about Roswell, apparently told his wife that the story was true and that he had flown the wreckage and bodies to Wright Patterson. My best guess is that the testimony of

Henderson's family years later was a case of memories of things read, or possibly seen in tabloid pictures, being blended or confused with memories of what Henderson may have actually said.

During my extensive conversations with pilots from the 509th, I spoke with several who knew Henderson and remembered his having discussed the incident. Apparently Henderson, a C-54 transport pilot at the time, did fly some of the debris out of Roswell, possibly to Wright Patterson. Jesse Mitchell, one of the 509th pilots at the time and a retired lieutenant colonel, told me that Henderson told him that he never saw the debris and he had no idea what it was. Mitchell was a good friend of Henderson's and almost decided to go into the roofing business with him in Roswell after Henderson left the service. Another former member of the 509th, Sam McIlhaney, also a retired lieutenant colonel who knew Henderson well, told me that they used to talk about the incident occasionally while sitting around in the hangar. According to McIlhaney, Henderson considered the whole matter a big joke and used to kid about it.

Researching Roswell is somewhat akin to prospecting, in that most of the time you spend countless hours and come up with nothing. Occasionally, however, you might hit pay dirt and come up with a real find. That happened with me during my polling of the pilots and navigators of the 509th, when I contacted Walter Klinikowski.

Klinikowski is one of the most interesting individuals with whom I have spoken during this entire Roswell endeavor. After my first conversation with Klinikowski, I soon learned from other members of the 509th Bomb Group that his piano playing was almost legendary. He told me that while in high school at age 15, unbeknown to his parents, he took his first professional job. The musician's union set him up in the pit band of a local burlesque theater, where he soon became acquainted with none other than the famous Gypsy Rose Lee.

As if his piano talent was not enough, Klinikowski later was sponsored by the Philadelphia Athletic Club as a potential member of the 1940 U.S Olympic team. The war came along, however, and the games were never held. During World War II, he was a navigator on a B-17—one of highest risk jobs in the war. Following the war, after a couple of years of civilian life, Klinikowski was recalled to the service, where he joined the 509th Bomb Group at Roswell in May 1947. He stayed with the 509th until February 1953.

What makes Walter Klinikowski so important to the investigation of the Roswell case is not his time with the 509th, but what he did afterward. For 14 years, from 1960 until 1974, when he retired from the Air Force as a colonel, Walter Klinikowski was with the Foreign Technology Division (FTD) of the Air Materiel Command (AMC), based out of Wright Patterson Air Force Base. From 1960 to 1964, he was "Deputy Director of Intelligence Collections," and then later, after spending some time abroad as a liaison officer for the FTD, he returned to Wright Patterson as "Director of Foreign Activities" from "1970 until 1974."

The fact that wreckage of a crashed UFO would have been taken to the Foreign Technology Division of AMC at Wright Patterson Air Force Base for analysis is disputed by no one, to my knowledge. If that had been case, Klinikowski would have known about it, but he didn't. Walter unequivocally assured me that there was no wreckage of a crashed flying saucer from Roswell or anywhere else at Wright Patterson. The rumors of the secret hangar and alien bodies are just that—rumors.

Klinikowski was kind enough to put me in touch with his former boss at the Foreign Technology Division, Walter Vatunac. Vatunac, who had actually been stationed at Roswell in the late 1940s, was the Director of Intelligence Collections at the Foreign Technology Division from 1957 until 1962. Like Klinikowski, Vatunac found the matter of alien bodies and a crashed spaceship very humorous and was incredulous that so many people actually believe it.

After my conversations with Klinikowski and Vatunac, Harry Cordes, a former 509th pilot and a retired brigadier general, suggested I call a former acquaintance of his, George Weinbrenner, who had also been at the FTD. I contacted Weinbrenner, who was more than accommodating, especially when he found out that I knew Walter Klinikowski. Weinbrenner told me pretty much what I had already learned from Klinikowski and Vatunac, but it was interesting talking to him, nonetheless. With respect to the crashed UFO subject, he also found it humorous and stated that "if something like that had happened, I would have known about it." He certainly would have. George Weinbrenner was the commander of the Foreign Technology Division for six years (1968 until 1974).

I cannot state strongly enough that I have absolutely no doubt that these three men were telling me the truth. I repeat, no doubt. Those who want to rationalize away the facts by suggesting that these men are still participating in some super-long-term, massive coverup might give some thought to the following. If there had been a crashed UFO, and for some reason it was still being kept secret, why on earth would these men waste inordinate amounts of their own time playing a ridiculous game of charades with me? They wouldn't. There would be absolutely no reason for doing so. All they would have had to do, would have been to politely tell me they didn't know anything, and leave it at that.

Klinikowski, Vatunac, and Weinbrenner are all retired colonels. They all held important positions at the Foreign Technology Division at Wright Patterson. As such, they represent the ultimate source of information with regard to the crashed UFO question. This is the word "right from the horse's mouth," the incontrovertible, irrefutable truth, the final confirmation—no alien bodies, no secret hangar, and no UFO crash at Roswell. Case closed.

In essence, the 1947 Roswell case has turned out to be a red herring, diverting time and resources away from research into the real UFO phenomenon. Despite overwhelming facts to the contrary, there are those, however, who will fight to keep the myth alive at all cost. Roswell is a sacred cow for some, and a cash cow for others. Inevitably, there will be fierce opposition to much of what has been said in this article. I would be the last, however, to discourage rational and thoughtful response, for healthy debate and a free exchange of ideas are part of what makes our democratic system work.

Any complete and reasonable response by those who still contend that a UFO crashed at Roswell in 1947 will need to directly address the points below, each of which would have to be a true statement if such a crash occurred:

• A machine with unimaginable technological sophistication and consequent incredible reliability would have simply broken down and crashed.

• The only known wreckage from this sophisticated vehicle, capable of interstellar travel, would have consisted solely of a few short beams, pieces of foil-like material, and small pieces of thin plastic-like material.

• By incredible coincidence, the material from the crashed spaceship would have very closely resembled the material left by the radar reflectors from a balloon array that went down in the same general area a few weeks earlier.

• Despite the fact that this would have been the most spectacular event in recorded history, and despite the fact that word was already out that something had happened (because of Lt. Haut's press release), there was absolutely no contemporary discussion or talk about such an earthshaking event among the pilots and navigators of the close-knit 509th Bomb Group.

• West Point graduate and retired general Thomas DuBose would have to have lied nine times in an interview when he stated that the debris (definitely that from an ML-307 radar reflector) shown in the pictures in Ramey's office was not substituted material and was the "real debris" recovered from the ranch northwest of Roswell.

• Major General C. P. Cabell, Director of Intelligence for the Air Force at the Pentagon, who prepared a report on the unidentified flying object situation for the Secretary of Defense, astoundingly, would have been preparing the report totally ignorant of the fact that the Air Force was in possession of a crashed flying saucer.

• Three retired Air Force colonels, all former top officials at the Foreign Technology Division at Wright Patterson Air Force base, would have been lying to me—unnecessarily wasting inordinate amounts of their own personal time in a protracted game of charades.

We have now gotten to the heart of the story and established that the debris recovered from the Foster ranch and laid out on the Marcel kitchen floor was, except for some unusual symbols, of a very mundane nature. The following should then be asked of those still arguing the issue: How do you get a crashed alien spaceship out of such ordinary debris? What basis is there now for postulating the existence of a crashed UFO?

While we don't yet have tangible evidence that alien spacecraft exist, there have been many intriguing sightings by credible people that seem to defy conventional explanation. Like the few brief tantalizing signals that have been picked up by the SETI program, the evidence for UFOs has not yet qualified as solid proof in the eyes of the scientific community.

If such confirmation does come, it would represent one of the most remarkable events in human history. The long-contemplated philosophical and scientific question of whether we are alone in the universe would be answered once and for all with absolute finality. Perhaps most important of all, the knowledge that it is possible for a civilization to survive the growing pains of becoming technologically advanced, without completely destroying itself and its environment in the process, would provide a renewed hope for the future of life here on earth.

Jeffrey, in his own words, tells why he now believes that the Roswell crash was of something of terrestrial manufacture rather than something built on another planet. Of those researching UFOs, Jeffrey is one of the few who has demonstrated that he is willing to look at the evidence pro and con. He has made his own decisions based on what he believes to be the best evidence available today.

See also *Roswell Myth*

Johnson, J. Bond (1926–) J. Bond Johnson is the man who took six photographs in Brigadier Roger Ramey's office on July 8, 1947. At the time he was a twenty-one-year-old photographer and reporter working for the *Fort Worth Star-Telegram*. When he took the pictures he was a college student who would eventually become a psychologist, licensed by California as a clinical psychologist. He has been a Methodist minister for fifty years and retired as a colonel from the U.S. Army Reserve.

All that leaves little doubt that Dr. Johnson has had a number of distinguished careers, and that he is well educated and well respected. However, his sudden claims that he was "The Roswell Photographer" and that he saw, photographed, and handled the "real" debris from the Roswell UFO crash calls these impressions into serious question.

J. Bond Johnson first appeared in connection with the Roswell UFO case in 1989. Photographs of material claimed to be debris from the crash site had been taken in the office of Brigadier General Roger M. Ramey on July 8, 1947. Research indicated that many of the *Fort Worth Star-Telegram*'s photographs had been donated to the Special Collections housed at the University of Texas at Arlington library.

Betsy Hudon, who was in charge of that collection, told UFO researcher Kevin Randle that they had four photographs taken of Roger Ramey with a rawin target device on July 8. Hudon mentioned to Randle that another fellow had recently called about those same pictures and said that he was the man who had taken them. If that was true, here was a witness who had been in General Ramey's office at the critical time on July 8. He might be able to provide some valuable insight into the events that transpired there. Here was a man to whom Randle had to speak.

But Hudon didn't think it was right to give out his name. Randle asked her if she would forward a letter to him from Randle, and that way he could contact Randle if he wanted. She said that would be fine. Randle wrote the letter, sent it, and she forwarded it to the then-unidentified photographer.

Within days Randle heard from J. Bond Johnson. He wanted

to talk about the events in Ramey's office. Randle called him back on February 27, 1989, and they spoke for about forty minutes. Randle, with Johnson's permission, recorded the conversation, so a record of it exists.

Randle has said about that first interview, "Looking at the transcripts of that interview now, I see where my enthusiasm has overwhelmed me. Listening to the tapes, I can hear where I should have spent more time listening to what Johnson had to say and a little less time talking about the case. From some of my comments I can see where the criticism that I was coaching the witness might originate. Well, not really, but then, a sharing of information before I have fully questioned the witness is not the best interrogation technique. I should have been quiet."

For example, according to the audiotapes, Johnson said, "I took the picture of General Ramey and the wreckage. General Ramey was the commander of the Twentieth Air Force at that time. Or maybe not the Twentieth, maybe the Fifteenth."

Randle said that he thought it was actually the Eighth Air Force, but Johnson said, "I think that's not right." Of course it was right, but it could be suggested from that little exchange that Randle was coaching the witness when all he was doing was correcting a minor factual error that means nothing in the overall picture.

After that, Johnson said, in a fairly disjointed way, "The *Star-Telegram*. The interesting things that you get into, that you may know about . . . oh, those pictures have been used on a couple of TV shows. One was *Star Trek*. No, *Star . . . In Search Of*, which Leonard Nimoy was the host of. And I was sitting watching the TV and it popped up and showed this picture and oh, there's my picture. That kind of thing . . ."

Johnson then brought Marcel into the story, saying that Alan Lansbury, the producer of *In Search Of*, had hosted a party to which Johnson was invited. He said, "This major was going to be there, the one from Roswell."

Randle asked, naturally, "Marcel?" Again it might be seen as coaching the witness, though Johnson already knew the name. He just couldn't think of it at that moment.

"Is he the one that got the . . ."

Randle interrupted to say, "He was the one that went out and picked up the material."

"From the rancher, yes. He heard about it in a bar and the guy says, 'Oh, I got one of those out at the place.' "

Randle said again, filling in detail, "Wait a minute. The problem is that Mack Brazel found the thing on his ranch and he contacted the folks at Roswell. There was a subsequent story. His son, Bill Brazel, came down to take care of the ranch because his dad was being held at Roswell and undergoing tests or something like that. Bill Brazel picked up some of the material. He found some scrap of it and he was in the bar talking about it and the Air Force came out the next day and picked it up. The fellow who came out was a fellow named Armstrong."

"That wasn't the major there?"

"No."

"The major was the intelligence officer or something like that."

Randle said, "Okay. Marcel was the intelligence officer. He was the one who went back to the ranch and picked it all up. So you met Major Marcel."

"Marcel, yes. He has a son. I saw the son interviewed on TV recently."

"Yeah," Randle said. "That is exactly right. I was hoping that you have found Armstrong by mistake."

"The son said interesting things. That the father came home and told us about the bodies and so forth. And then said that we can't talk about it or don't tell anybody and so forth."

This confused the issue because Randle hadn't heard anything about Marcel and bodies. He asked, "Marcel mentioned bodies?"

"No, the son."

The next question was, quite naturally, "Marcel says that his father mentioned bodies."

Johnson replied, "Came home and told us about it."

But the truth is, Jesse Marcel Jr. has claimed all along that his father never mentioned bodies at all. In fact, this has become one of the stumbling points of the Roswell case. If there had been a crash, the intelligence officer at the 509th should have been brought in on all aspects of the investigation and recovery from the very beginning. That would mean he knew about the bodies, yet he never mentioned a word about them, with only a single exception, contrary to what Johnson believed.

Having finished with that, Johnson finally said, "My interesting part of this, having taken the picture and now going back and looking at the picture because I didn't have a copy of it [meaning, I suppose, that he didn't have an original print but did have a copy of the photograph as it had appeared in the newspaper in 1947] . . . is that I don't know whether the Air Force was pulling a hoax or not. It looks like a kite . . ."

Johnson and Randle discussed the sequence of events, and how Johnson ended up in Ramey's office late that afternoon. Johnson then said, "Right. That was a hoax, I think. That's when they called and what I saw. I think I was duped."

Randle agreed with his assessment. He said, "Yes. You and all the rest of the reporters were duped."

"That we saw . . . that they came up with this weather balloon thing as an added . . . that's my feeling. I *never saw the real stuff* [emphasis added]." Again this was a spontaneous comment by Johnson. Randle was trying to figure out how everything had happened and Johnson was throwing in comments about it with no help or coaching from anywhere. Johnson would later complain that Randle had been "coaching" him, searching for specific facts, but the truth is that Randle was just asking questions and trying to sort out the new information being supplied by Johnson.

Johnson continued, "Then they came out with that story almost simultaneously afterward that the weather balloon thing . . ."

At this point in the investigation, having just started, Randle made a basic assumption. He was aware of a quote attributed to Marcel (by William Moore in *The Roswell Incident*) that suggested that if he was in the photograph, it showed the real crash debris, but if it was anyone else pictured, then it was not the real thing. Since Marcel had talked of reporters being present, and since Colonel Thomas DuBose, Ramey's chief of staff in 1947, had mentioned three or four reporters present, and since Johnson was saying that there had been no other reporters in Ramey's office when he was there, Randle concluded that Ramey had met with the press twice. Johnson noted that he did not attend a press conference, but had just met Ramey in his office to take his photographs. Johnson, in fact, now objects to the suggestion that Ramey actually spoke with other members of the press. Johnson is attempting to preserve the idea that he was the only reporter to interview Ramey on July 8.

There were a number of press accounts written after interviews with military officers. The *Dallas Morning News* noted that their reporter had interviewed Major Kirton of the Eighth Air Force intelligence office and was told that the debris was a weather balloon. But other newspapers, such as the *San Francisco Examiner,* claimed that their reporters had talked to Ramey personally about the debris in his office. When informed of this, Johnson suggested that the reporter had actually talked to the Public Information Officer when the story clearly said it was General Ramey who was interviewed.

Johnson said originally that he took two pictures, one of Ramey and one of Ramey and DuBose. He didn't know who had taken the pictures of Marcel and seemed to be surprised that there were pictures of Marcel in the files at the University of Texas. It was clear from all the pictures that Marcel was near the same debris that Johnson had photographed with Ramey and DuBose. In other words, and contrary to the suggestions by William Moore that Marcel was photographed with the "real stuff," there were no photographs of the real debris with Marcel in them, only the weather balloon spread out on the floor in General Ramey's office.

Johnson told Randle, "I took two pictures and then they said, but that time they said, 'Oh, we've found out what it is and you know, it's a weather balloon and so forth.' No big deal. I didn't press it. I accepted that. I was rather naive. I accepted that."

After they discussed the mechanics of transmitting stories over the AP wire in 1947, Randle said, "You went back to . . ." Johnson interrupted to say, "The *Star-Telegram* and gave them the wet prints of the thing. They wanted them right out. I went in and developed them and gave them wet prints. And I wrote . . ."

Interrupted by Randle then, he later said, "Seven-nine [July 9] is my story on the front page that was earlier in the day. That's when they debunked it."

Later he would suggest that what he meant was that his photograph had accompanied an article written by another reporter. However, still later he said, "Okay, this is the article I wrote that was on the front page on seven-nine . . . I went ahead and got the facts and came back and there wasn't any other reporter who wrote it for the *Star-Telegram*. I wrote it that night."

What all of this demonstrates is that, contrary to what Johnson is claiming today, in 1947 he was told by General Ramey that the debris on the office floor was a weather balloon and that he wrote an article for his newspaper about it. These are two of the things that Johnson would later claim Randle got wrong and that he, Randle, refused to change.

About a month after the first interview, Randle again talked to Johnson. Randle had had the chance to digest the materials that had flooded in and had a better feeling for what the situation was in Fort Worth in July 1947. Randle had been able to eliminate some of the material that was obviously in error. To get a better picture, Randle asked Johnson simply, "Could you just sort of tell me what you did . . . What transpired when your editor gave you the assignment to go out to the base?"

The story he told was essentially the same as it had been during that first conversation. Johnson told Randle how the assignment had been made, and how he had driven out to the base. Then he said, "I posed General Ramey with this debris piled in the middle of his rather large and plush office. It seemed incongruous to have this smelly garbage piled up on the floor . . ."

Next Johnson made the statement that he now claims he never made and that Randle has somehow misquoted, even though the quotes are on tape. He said, "I posed General Ramey with this debris. At that time I was briefed on the idea that it was not a flying disk as first reported but in fact was a weather balloon that had crashed." Ramey told Johnson, there in the office, that the debris was nothing more than a weather balloon.

Johnson has also claimed that he didn't write the July 9, 1947, article. This is important because of what the article contains. If General Ramey didn't know what the debris was, as Johnson has recently been suggesting, it would have been reflected in the article. The last paragraph of the article, however, said, "After his first look, Ramey declared all it was was a weather balloon. The weather officer verified his view." This is, of course, in direct conflict with what Johnson claims today.

In today's environment, the disagreement between Johnson and Randle has begun to take on more importance than it deserves. Johnson has claimed that he tried, without success, to get Randle to correct some of the inaccurate quotations Randle has attributed to him. However, the problem is not with Randle's quotes, but with Johnson's new version of the events.

Randle sent Johnson a tape so he could hear what he had said and understand that he, Johnson, would say those sorts of things because he had said those sorts of things before. He provided no answer to Randle except to suggest that if he had said some of those things, he had spoken in error when he and Randle talked.

Here is a man who claims to have never written speculative articles about Roswell. He claims he has nothing to sell to a public eager to buy almost anything Roswell-related. Yet he bills himself as the Roswell Photographer as he attempts to pull the spotlight in his direction. He is, in reality, the Fort Worth photographer who took several pictures of a weather balloon in General Ramey's office.

The sad thing here is that if Johnson had left well enough alone, if he had just told his tale consistently through the years, he would have something valuable to contribute to the Roswell case. It would be valuable to hear about his interaction with General Ramey, even if during that interaction he learned that the material was a balloon. But for Johnson, that isn't good enough. Now he must claim that Randle misquoted him so that he can boost his importance. Unfortunately for him, the tapes exist. Even sadder, he has copies of them but apparently won't listen to what he had to say.

Johnson, Jesse B. (1920–1988) Jesse B. Johnson was born in Temple, Texas, and lived there most of his life. In 1945, he graduated from the medical school at the University of Texas. He was a resident at the Scott and White Hospital in Temple from 1945 to 1946, when he was apparently drafted into the Army.

During 1947, First Lieutenant Jesse Johnson was assigned to

the base hospital at the Roswell Army Air Field. There is no evidence that he played any role in the alleged autopsies of alien beings found near there in July 1947, though his name has been connected to them.

Information published suggested that Johnson was a pathologist in 1947 and was called upon to perform or assist in the performance of preliminary autopsies conducted at the base hospital. That information was based on two flawed tales. One

Jesse B. Johnson. (*Photo courtesy of Walter Haut*)

of them was by Glenn Dennis, who claimed that he had known a nurse assigned to the base in 1947 who told him about the autopsies.

The other assumption was that in 1947, Johnson was a pathologist. The *ABMS Compendium of Medical Specialists* reveals that in 1947, Johnson had just completed his medical training. He had no training as a pathologist in 1947, so there was no reason to suspect that he would have been brought in to assist in the autopsies.

In fact, the information available suggests that Johnson did eventually train as a pathologist at the University of Texas Medical Branch in Galveston from 1948 to 1949. In other words, he did not have the training in 1947 but completed it after his military service.

Johnson wasn't finished with his medical education. He trained next as a radiologist in 1950 and 1951. That was apparently the specialty that he practiced for the rest of his medical career.

An interview conducted with his wife in the early 1990s revealed nothing to suggest that Johnson was ever involved in the recovery of alien bodies or their autopsy. She had no knowledge of any connection between her husband and the U.S. government. The fact that he had once trained as a pathologist seems to have confused the issue. Dr. Johnson died in 1988.

Joyce, Frank Frank Joyce might have been the first newsman to learn of the crash. In 1947, Joyce was one of the few employees of radio station KGFL. During his Sunday afternoon radio show, he would play the records, read the commercials, and operate as the engineer. More than once he had to repair the "board" to keep the station on the air.

According to Joyce, on Sunday, July 6, he called Sheriff Wilcox and asked if there was anything going on of interest. Wilcox said that he had something and handed the phone to Brazel. Joyce, as he continued to spin records, listened to Brazel tell of finding the strange metallic debris in one of his pastures.

Joyce said, "I'm not going to tell you he and I were buddies

because we weren't . . . And he starts telling me a lot of stuff that I
didn't want to hear because I thought he was crazy."

Today Joyce says little about what Brazel told him during that first
interview because he doesn't want to put words in Brazel's mouth. He
makes it clear that the story Brazel told him on Sunday afternoon was
significantly different from the one told just a few days later.

Joyce, who had been reading stories about flying saucers from
the AP newswire, added a short comment about the find Brazel had
made on his ranch north of Roswell. That was on the evening of
July 6.

On July 8, Walter Haut arrived with a press release claiming that
the Army had found a flying saucer. According to Joyce, Haut said
that he would give them an hour before he provided copies of the
release to the other radio station and the two Roswell newspapers.

It wasn't long before the teletype was filled with information
about the crash near Roswell. One of the stories stated, "The
Intelligence office reports that it gained possession of the 'Dis:' [sic]
through the cooperation of a Roswell rancher and Sheriff George
Wilson [sic] of Roswell.

"The disc landed on a ranch near Roswell sometime last week.
Not having phone facilities, the rancher, whose name has not yet
been obtained, stored the disc until such time as he was able to contact the Roswell sheriff's office.

"The sheriff's office in turn notified a major of the 509th
Intelligence Office.

"Action was taken immediately and the disc was picked up at
the rancher's home and taken to the Roswell Air Base. Following
examination, the disc was flown by intelligence officers in a super-
fortress (B-29) to an undisclosed 'Higher Headquarters.'

"The air base has refused to give details of construction of the
disc or its appearance.

"Residents near the ranch on which the disc was found reported
seeing a strange blue light several days ago about three o'clock in the
morning."

It wasn't long before there was a follow-up story on the news wire. "Sheriff's officers in Roswell said that Brizell [*sic*] told them he saw it lying on the ranch, and that he picked it up and intended to keep it. They said that he did not give a complete description of the object, other than to say it appeared somewhat like tinfoil and was large—about the size of the safe in the sheriff's office.

"Sheriff's officers said that Brizell told them he planned to keep the object, but then heard reports of flying discs and decided to drive to Roswell and report his finding to the sheriff's office."

That was followed by the cryptic message:

95

   FRR

      WAS TT [*SIC*] SAME RANCH MENTIONED LAST WEKK [*SIC*] IN FLYING DISC HULLABALOO?

      DX

         CX336P 7/8

According to Joyce, the release "made the phones go crazy." Joyce remembered that he received a call from a man who identified himself as Colonel Johnson. The colonel was screaming at Joyce, demanding to know who the hell had told him to issue the press release. Joyce explained that he was a civilian and that there was nothing that Johnson or anyone else at the Pentagon could do to him. Johnson responded, "I'll show you what I can do to you."

The colonel's anger was probably fueled by an Associated Press "add" transmitted at 5:09 P.M. Eastern Standard Time that said the story had been broken by a radio reporter.

After all this transpired, Joyce decided that he'd better find the press release and teletype messages as they came in so that he could prove to his boss that he hadn't invented the story. He searched the station until he found all the material and hid it. Unfortunately, according to Joyce, someone searched the station, found some of the hidden material, and took it.

Although Joyce didn't know it at that time, the cover story was beginning to kick in. The teletype continued to print out requests for more information. Joyce was able to save some of them:

FRR
   DID ARMY CALL IT A "FLYING DISC" OR WHAT?
   DXR.

NAJ DXR
   FYI, ROSWELL REPORTS TT [*SIC*] MAJOR JESSE A. MARCEL, INTELLIGENCE OFFICER FOR 509TH BOMBER GROUP AT ROSWELL ARMY AIR BASE [*SIC*], IS IN FORT WORTH TEX., AT 8TH ARMY HEAD-QUARTERS [*SIC*], "IF HE HANT [*SIC*] ALREADY STARTED BACK FOR ROWELL [*SIC*]." SUGG U GET DA IN ON IT FASTEST. TT MITE BE WHERE DISC WAS FLOWN.
   FRR V7/8

FRR
   DA ALREADY ALERTED. HOW RE ARMY TERMINOL-OGY—"FLYING DISC" OR WHAT PLS?
   DXR

DXR
   OUR S5&4 CALLED IT "FLYING DISC." WE UNABLE GET QUOTES FROM -4.6 OURSELVES -S 635. WE AFTER IT FASTEST. S5&4 SAID "FLYING DISC."
   FRR V7/8

JD/FRR
> **LETS HAVE TEST ARMY ANNOUNCEMENT FASTEST.**
> **JUST PUT ON AS TEST AND LET ROLL IN QUOTES.**
> **DX NJ317P7/8**

NJ DXR
> **ARMY GAVE VERBAL ANNCMENT. NO TEXT.**
> **FRR V7/8**

After that teletype exchange and the note that the Army gave a verbal announcement, which referred to a press conference being held at the Fort Worth Army Air Field on July 8, Brigadier General Roger M. Ramey showed a weather balloon. He allowed reporters to photograph it, telling them that the excitement had been generated because the officers at the 509th had failed to recognize a fairly standard weather balloon with a radar reflecting dish on it.

The teletype printed the following change to the story:

FRR 8
> **EEDITORS [*SIC*]: PLEASE SUB FOR 5TH PGH AND**
> **REMAINDER OF FRRE8**
> **-0-**

HOWEVER, OFFICERS AT THE ROSWELL ARMY AIR BASE HERE NOTIFIED IMMEDIATELY BY THE SHERIFF'S OFFICE. MAJOR JESSE A. MARCEL—INTELLIGENCE OFFICER OT [*SIC*] THE ROSWELL BASE—AND AN EN-LISTED MAN THEN CHECKED WITH THE SHERIFF.
> **SHERIFF WILCOX QUOTED BRIZELL [*SIC*] AS SAYING**

THAT "IT MORE OR LESS SEEMED LIKE TINFOIL."
WILCOX SAID THAT BRIZELL RELATED THAT THE DISC
WAS BROKEN SOMEWHAT—APPARENTLY FROM THE
FALL. THE SHERIFF SAID THAT BRIZELL DESCRIBED
THE OBJECT ABOUT AS LARGE AS A SAFE IN THE SHER-
IFF'S OFFICE. HE ADDED THAT THE SAFE WAS ABOUT
ONE-HALF [SIC] BY FOUR FEET.

BRIZELL DID NOT BRING THE OBJECT TO THE SHER-
IFF'S OFFICE, BUT MERELY DROVE THE 75 MILES FROM
THE RANCH TO ROSWELL TO REPORT HIS FINDING.
SHERIFF WILCOX SAID THAT MAJOR MARCEL LEFT
SHORTLY AFTER RECEIVING THE REPORT FOR THE
AREA WHERE THE DISC WAS FOUND.

MEANWHILE, A REPORT FROM CARRIZOZO, NEW
MEXICO, SAID THAT A DISC WAS FOUND 35 MILES
SOUTHEAST OF CORONA. THE REPORT—WHICH
WAS NOT SUBSTANTIATED—MERELY SAID THAT IT
WAS "A RUBBER SUBSTANCE AND TINFOIL EN-
CASED." HOWEVER, IT WAS PRESUMED TO BE THE
SAME AS THE ONE REPORTED TO ROSWELL.

REPORTS FROM THE ROSWELL BASE SAID THAT
MAJOR MARCEL WAS AT EIGHTH ARMY HEAD-
QUARTERS IN FORT WORTH, TEXAS, BUT THAT
"HE MIGHT BE ON HIS WAY BACK TO ROSWELL BY
PLANE NOW." HOWEVER, OFFICIALS AT THE
ROSWELL BASE SAY THEY KNOW NOTHING ABOUT
THE DISC OR ITS DESCRIPTIONG [SIC], OR WHERE
THE "HIGHER HEADQUARTERS" WHERE IT WAS
TAKEN ARE LOCATED.

V342P7/8

By July 9, the Army was claiming they had identified the debris
as part of a weather balloon and a radar target. The staged press

conference in Fort Worth, including pictures of Marcel with the balloon wreckage, had convinced everyone that nothing unusual had been found in Roswell. The story, for most of the world, was over.

But for Joyce it was not over. While working on the evening of July 9, after Mack Brazel had talked to reporters at the *Roswell Daily Record,* he was brought to the offices of KGFL.

"I remember him coming in," said Joyce, "and changing his story." Brazel crouched down about three feet from where Joyce sat at the control board and looked at the floor as he spoke. Joyce could tell that he was saying things he didn't believe.

". . . he's an old cowboy and I told him, what you're saying is not what you were saying the other night. And then he turned around and admitted that he was . . . that he had been told to come in or else . . . We had some other discussions that would curl your hair."

Joyce went on, saying, "He and I were really spooked that night he came into the station. And I told him, I said, 'Look . . .' He told me what they were going to do to us and I said, 'They're not going to do anything to us.' I yelled at him. I was really getting mad. He was worrying about somebody I don't even know was there. I knew they were there but I didn't know who they were. And . . . he didn't know either. He was really scared.

". . . he came in and asked me, 'You're not going to tell them anything, are you?' And I was mad by then and I say, 'I'm not going to tell them anything.' He and I were both in a fog by then. Him more than me because I think he had other influences, other than the people he was dealing with."

As the discussion continued, Brazel told Joyce that he couldn't do anything else. He had to tell the new story. If he didn't, it would go hard on him. He was admitting to Joyce that he was now lying but that he could do nothing else. The story of the balloon, the object he found that was "about as large as a safe in the sheriff's office," was not the truth. And Brazel knew that Joyce knew it, too.

Joyce knew the weather balloon was a quickly manufactured cover story. When his second interview with Brazel ended, the rancher walked to the door and said, "Frank, you know how they talk of little green men? . . . They weren't green." Brazel then opened the door and left with his military escort.

Kaufmann, Frank Frank Kaufmann has been under assault almost from the moment his testimony was first presented in a public environment. Most of those attacking him are doing so because Kaufmann's testimony damages their core beliefs about UFOs, MJ-12, or the Roswell case. For example, if what Kaufmann says is accurate, then the Project Mogul and New York University balloon explanations are eliminated because his testimony is incompatible with any weather balloon recovery. More precisely, if Kaufmann's testimony is accurate, then clearly all mundane explanations fail because of the extraordinary nature of what he says.

It is also true that if his testimony was to stand alone, meaning there was no independent corroboration for it, his tale would be severely weakened. However, it must be remembered he claims firsthand knowledge of the events outside of Roswell and that portions of what he says have been corroborated by others independently. In other words, his testimony does not stand alone. It is because of that documentation and corroboration that the testimony of Frank Kaufmann takes on added significance.

The original problem with the Kaufmann tales was that they seemed to defy what was known and believed about the Roswell crash. It was as if Kaufmann, without bothering to review the literature, had decided to invent a tale about the UFO crash. Kaufmann, for exam-

Frank Kaufmann on the Impact Site.
(*Photo courtesy of Kevin Randle*)

ple, suggested that the crash took place on the evening of July 4, when UFO researchers had originally claimed it was July 2.

It was on July 2, however, that Frank Kaufmann, a civilian employed at Roswell, received a call from Brigadier General Martin F. Scanlon of the Air Defense Command, ordering him to report to the radar sites at White Sands. Kaufmann was to monitor an unidentified object that had been spotted over southern New Mexico and report on its movements directly to Scanlon. Kaufmann was ordered not to leave the scope unattended for even the shortest of times. Once he had his watch established, he set up a mirror on the wall that could be seen from the outside so that the radar operator, using a flashlight, could alert him if anything changed significantly.

According to Kaufmann, he stayed at his post for twenty-four hours straight, but nothing changed. The object appeared periodically over southern New Mexico, usually just "flitting from one location to another." When Kaufmann reported that the situation had remained static during his twenty-four-hour watch, Scanlon decided to end Kaufmann's part of the operation. Although Kaufmann was ordered back to Roswell, the operators at White Sands were told to continue monitoring the object.

According to Kaufmann, he was in contact with Robert Thomas, an officer stationed in Washington, D.C., all during this time. Thomas asked Kaufmann on several occasions if he should head out to New Mexico, but Kaufmann told him not to bother for the time being. The situation was still fluid and he didn't know what would happen. At two or three in the morning on July 4, however, Thomas called to inform Kaufmann he was on the way, explaining that he wanted to be on the scene in case something happened.

Thomas's special flight from Washington, D.C., arrived early on the afternoon of July 4. He had requested some special equipment and arranged for transportation for himself and the small party of experts he had brought with him. He held a quick briefing with the men stationed at Roswell and then settled in to wait.

That evening, the situation changed radically. The object, as displayed on the radar, seemed to pulsate, the blip growing larger and brightening before shrinking to its original size and dimming. This activity kept up for a short time and then the object blossomed into a sunburst and disappeared from the screen at about 11:20 P.M. Because there were three sites tracking the object, the Army technicians were able to plot, within vague parameters, the location of the crash or landing. But the radar coverage in that section of New Mexico was not as complete as the military would have liked. The Capitan Mountains sit between the impact site and the radar sets of White Sands and Alamogordo. Other mountains rest between Albuquerque and Roswell. Coverage in some places did not extend below eight or nine thousand feet. That meant that the Army, based on what it had learned while tracking the object, knew that the object was down north of town, but didn't have a precise location.

At the Roswell Army Air Field, Kaufmann and the special Washington team received word that they had to get out to the crash site immediately. According to Kaufmann, they headed out before dawn. They drove along Highway 285, which in 1947 was a twenty-foot-wide paved road. According to Kaufmann, "We went in three jeeps [and] then four trucks, one truck with a crane. [There were] MPs, but I don't know how many trucks were with them."

Once they left the main road, they "cut across country . . . we cut straight across. We cut some fences. We went over some terrain . . .

rocks, cactus, everything." They continued straight ahead until "we came to the top [of a ridgeline] . . . and saw the damned ravine dropped off and we backed off and circled around. As we were coming down that ravine . . . we could see the glisten from the metal and we knew right away where we were. This was the area."

Complete access to the impact site, the immediate area where the object had crashed, was restricted to those with the highest clearance and a real need to know. There were nine such men, at least three of whom (Thomas, Howard Fletcher, and a man identified only as Lucas) had come from Washington, D.C. Other men, including Adair (not to be confused with AP reporter Robin Adair) and Harris, came in from the West Coast. A few assigned to the 509th Bomb Group in Roswell, including William Blanchard, Easley, and W. O. "Pappy" Henderson, were also heavily involved. Blanchard's involvement would be particularly significant in the next few days.

The main group, the nine men with the highest clearances, according to Kaufmann, covered the center of what Kaufmann called the impact site. According to Kaufmann, when they first saw the craft, they were stunned. They stood transfixed, staring at the object, momentarily unable to move. Because they had watched it on radar, they knew that something strange had crashed, but they were not prepared for what they saw. In the first moments, as the MPs scattered across the fields, taking up positions on the top of the cliff, at the access points to the area, and along the roads, the men stood staring at the ship.

The trucks and jeeps were pulled up closer and parked, setting a partial screen around the impact site. No one approached at first. One man, dressed in a protective suit and carrying a Geiger counter, advanced, checking the area for signs of radiation. Kaufmann said, "He went in there and made a number of tests. It took about fifteen minutes . . . We were all smoking cigarettes and talking about how in the hell we were going to handle this thing. We were all concerned and a little scared."

When the preliminary examination was finished, the men moved over to the site. Easley ordered the MPs to face away from the ship and to watch the surrounding terrain. No one was to approach without being identified and properly cleared.

The main part of the craft, about twenty-five to thirty feet long and twelve to fifteen feet wide, had forcibly crashed into an arroyo at the base of a tall cliff. The nine men approached it, but the others were held back, used as guards to screen the impact site. The nine made a careful examination of the ground around the point of impact, searching for additional debris.

Kaufmann said there was a major, in from Washington with the special group, who took care of the remains. He had ordered in the man in the special suit and rubber gloves and he was the one to order lead-lined body bags.

The bodies, five in number and obviously not human, were not all inside the ship. The ship's crew were small, about five feet tall, slender, and had heads that were too big for their bodies. The eyes were only slightly larger than human eyes, and they had pupils.

Two of them were found outside the craft, one sprawled on the ground and the other sitting next to a cliff. Both were dead. Looking through the hole in the fuselage, Kaufmann saw another inside the craft. It was in a chair, slumped to one side. He could see the legs of a fourth. The fifth, inside the craft, was not immediately visible. It was later that Kaufmann learned about it.

Kaufmann's attention was drawn to the being sitting near the cliff. "That's the one that I cannot forget. It had that damned serene look on its face . . . like it was at peace with the world . . . I [was] amazed at that."

The trucks were pulled forward so that they were aimed at the craft. Military jeeps, used as the command posts, were parked outside the perimeter. MPs were stationed around, facing away from the craft. These men were rotated frequently, sent back into Roswell so that no one group would get a good long look at what was happening.

"We had a special group come in who were well covered," explained Kaufmann. "[They wore] rubber gloves . . . [they] put them in body bags." These were ordered by the major, then placed in the rear of old box-type ambulances to be driven into the base hospital.

The bodies were taken into Roswell and kept in a hangar overnight. "Everything in the hangar was cleared out," according to Kaufmann, "and a single box was placed in the middle of the hangar which had a great big double door. Guards were placed all the way around it. [They] were armed with carbines. You couldn't get near the place."

Kaufmann said, "There was nothing unusual about the crate itself . . . it was maybe twenty by six . . . a large crate." Kaufmann said that he knew what was in the crate: the bodies recovered at the impact site.

Kaufmann mentioned that a photographer from Roswell, Jack Rodden (father of current Roswell resident Jack Rodden), was also deeply involved. According to Kaufmann, Rodden was brought into the hangar to photograph some of the strange debris stored inside. An enlisted man with Rodden handed him the photographic plate, let him expose it, and then took the plate back. When Rodden finished, they made a complete inventory of the photographic plates to ensure that nothing had disappeared. The photographer was then escorted to a car and driven home. He was, of course, sworn to secrecy.

When Rodden was gone, everyone except the guards was ordered from the hangar. The crate was left in the center, illuminated by a spotlight shining down on it. Although there was a full complement of guards on the outside, MPs were stationed around the interior of the hangar to watch the crate. No could enter the hangar or approach the crate without the proper clearances. According to Kaufmann, the guards had orders to shoot anyone who approached without authority.

Interestingly, Kaufmann said that the crate was shipped to

Andrews Army Air Field and then on to Patterson Army Air Field. It left Roswell at two or three in the morning. Other flights were ordered and then diverted, destinations changed in flight, while others had their paper records altered later. Kaufmann had never seen such a concerted effort to create diversions evidently intended to cover the trail just in case anyone ever tried to follow it.

Kaufmann was sure of the destination of the crate with the bodies because he, along with Thomas, was aboard the aircraft, a C-54. Pappy Henderson, one of the most trusted members of the 1st Air Transport Unit, was the pilot in command. The crate, kept in Hangar 84 on the eastern side of the flight line, was loaded onto the aircraft under conditions of maximum security at night. All the lights around the hangar area had been extinguished during the loading. The guards, along with the crews, used flashlights to see.

The airplane flew from Roswell to Andrews, where the crate was unloaded, again under the cover of darkness. For a short period, maybe as much as twenty-four or thirty-six hours, it sat in a guarded hangar at Andrews, apparently so that Army Chief of Staff Dwight Eisenhower and Secretary of War Robert P. Patterson would have an opportunity to see at least one of the bodies.

According to Kaufmann, all the bodies were not on that flight. They were split between two aircraft to ensure that the evidence would not be lost if one of the planes crashed. The second flight followed the first by about thirty minutes.

In the wake of all these events, according to Kaufmann, files were altered. So were personnel records, along with assignments and various codings and code words. By changing serial numbers, those searching later would not be able to locate those who were involved in the recovery. The trail was being carefully altered.

Kaufmann was later warned not to talk about or respond to any rumors he might hear. A lot of rumors and wild stories were sure to follow, but he should "let them fly. If they get close, keep your mouth shut . . . don't start a conversation, don't ask them how they knew. Just play dumb." Thomas said that if he tried to learn where someone heard a rumor, the very act would lend the rumor a degree of credibility.

Kaufmann also knew of individuals brought into Roswell from Alamogordo, Albuquerque, and Los Alamos. The MPs were a special unit composed of military police elements from Kirtland, Alamogordo, and Roswell. The reason was to help keep the secret. If the men didn't know one another or were separated after the event, they would be unable to compare notes and that would make the secret easier to keep.

Kaufmann's story, as it unfolded and as noted earlier, had not conformed to the conventional wisdom. When Kaufmann first began to reveal what he knew, it seemed that he was standing alone. That all changed with the appearance of William Woody. Woody said that he and his father were surprised when the wall of their house suddenly lit up one night in early July 1947. Turning, they saw a bright light moving quickly through the sky on a downward arc. He said the light was so bright that they couldn't look directly at it, comparing it to the flame of a welding torch.

Woody said that he and his father drove out a day or two later to search for the object. They drove north of Roswell, on Highway 285, but weren't allowed to turn off the main highway onto any of the dirt roads to the west because the military was there. Woody believed they made the trip on the weekend, but couldn't be sure.

Witnesses at two other locations also saw the object in the sky. Corporal E. L. Pyles, stationed at one of the satellite facilities attached to the 509th, was walking across the parade ground on the main base. He saw the bright object and believed that it was late at night, that it might be close to the weekend, and that it came down north of Roswell. Later, when he heard the balloon explanation, he didn't believe it. What this does is establish Pyles's sighting in the proper time frame prior to the press release on July 8, 1947.

There is one new piece of evidence. In July 1947, Leo B. Spear was an MP with the 1395th MP Company in Roswell. Although he didn't see anything himself, he did say that he remembered other

MPs returning from the crash site talking about the flying saucer. Spear said that he believed the story to be "BS" until he read about it in the paper a day or two later. What this does is confirm, from still another source, that the military was involved prior to July 8. It corroborates aspects of the story told by Pyles and Woody. But more important, it confirms the version of the story told by Kaufmann, which had originally defied the conventional wisdom.

The conventional wisdom has also suggested that the crashed object was a domed disc, the classic flying saucer. Gerald Anderson, whose testimony has been thoroughly discredited, talked of a domed disc. Jim Ragsdale, in the second version of his tale, described a domed disc. Other sources, primarily secondhand, suggested that it had been a disc-shaped object.

Frank Kaufmann was the first to suggest the object was not disc-shaped but was, in reality, heel-shaped. Although the idea hadn't been suggested in relation to the Roswell case prior to Kaufmann, it wasn't completely new. Kenneth Arnold didn't see a flying saucer, but something that was, according to his original testimony, heel-shaped. In the official Project Blue Book files, the illustration Arnold drew is of a heel-shaped craft. Project Blue Book files contain another heel-shaped object, this one photographed on July 7, 1947, as it flew over Phoenix, Arizona.

The corroboration for Kaufmann's story extends beyond that. Kaufmann spoke of a crash site north of Roswell, about thirty-five miles from the base. He said the military used Highway 285 and then drove cross-county to arrive at the impact site.

The location of the crash, north of town, has also been mentioned by Lewis Rickett, Dr. W. Curry Holden, and Major Edwin Easley. Holden confirmed that he had been at the site of the flying saucer crash and that he was north of Roswell, not far from Highway 285. Easley provided notes indicating that the crash site was north of Roswell, but not northwest, near Corona.

There is still another firsthand source who wishes to remain anonymous who has also corroborated the exact site as given by

220   KEVIN D. RANDLE

Kaufmann. He used the book *Roads of New Mexico* to pinpoint the location, since it was impossible to take him out there. Granted, such testimony does nothing for those who aren't privy to it, but it added more corroboration for the crash site location described by Kaufmann. He had no knowledge of what Kaufmann had said.

Dr. C. Bertrand Schultz said that while traveling north out of Roswell on Highway 285 he saw the military cordon. The soldiers were stationed to the west of the highway, but since Schultz had no desire to drive in that direction, he didn't care. Later, after Holden told him what he had seen, Schultz realized the importance of his observations. He shared it with his daughters while they were growing up in the 1950s and early 1960s and eventually told Kevin Randle about them.

The location close to Roswell was also corroborated by Dr. George Agogino, who corroborated the testimony of the "anonymous archaeologist" who spoke to Randle on the telephone. The archaeologist said that they had been working the area north of the Capitan Mountains in central New Mexico. That fits with what has been reported by others.

Frankie Rowe's father, Dan Dwyer, gave her general information about the location. He suggested that it was north of Roswell, but closer to the city than the conventional wisdom suggested. Barbara Dugger, whose grandfather was Sheriff George Wilcox, agreed with that. It was her impression that the crash site was in Chaves County, near Roswell, not far away in Lincoln County near Corona.

More critical information was supplied by Brigadier General Arthur Exon, who reported that he had flown over both sites. He mentioned tire tracks on them and reported the gouge that corroborated the tale told by Bill Brazel and suggested by Jesse Marcel Sr.

Robin Adair, a technician for the Associated Press in July 1947, said that he had been required by the AP to rent an airplane in El Paso, Texas, to fly to Roswell. He'd flown over two sites and saw soldiers at both of them. Neither site was near the Plains, but both were north and northwest of Roswell.

It must be remembered that Holden's testimony about his observations does not stand in isolation. His involvement is corroborated by other anthropologists—George Schultz, Agogino, and Frankforter. All of this is important because it corroborates what Kaufmann had said. More important, Kaufmann was saying it before these other sources had been identified and added the weight of their statements to the pile.

The point of all this is to demonstrate that there were a number of interviews conducted, that the majority of them are on either audio or videotape (audiotapes at CUFOS, videotapes at FUFOR), and that some of the interviews were witnessed by other investigators. Many of the witnesses, such as Frank Kaufmann, have been interviewed by many people. Family members, friends, and former military companions verify parts of the stories. There is a wide variety of corroboration for these tales.

What is learned is that Kaufmann, who seemed to have no knowledge of the conventional wisdom of the Roswell tale, began telling investigators about the crash site north of town. He added details to his claims that had not been discussed in the Roswell literature, mentioned on the various television shows, or published in magazines. He was the first to add some of the details, which were then confirmed as other witnesses were identified.

If the Kaufmann testimonies were eliminated, there would still be talk of an impact site north of town. It would be a little more difficult to put the whole picture together, but it could be done. For example, that location could be pinpointed based on the interviews conducted with Easley, Holden, John McBoyle (a newsman with radio station KSWS in Roswell in 1947), Woody and Schultz (talking about a military cordon off Highway 285), and Exon and Adair. What this does is underscore the importance of what Kaufmann has said.

If the Kaufmann testimony was eliminated, would there still be solid testimony about the shape of the craft? Rickett provided us with a very good description, as did McBoyle, Easley, and the anonymous archaeologist.

Although there have been a large number of reports about bodies, from Edwin Easley's firsthand comment about "Oh, the creatures" to the various secondhand testimonies, Kaufmann provided the first solid description.

What this demonstrates is that there is a large body of corroboration for Kaufmann's testimony. There are important additional firsthand sources who saw a great deal, who were heavily involved in the case, and who have reported it. There are secondhand sources who add detail to that knowledge. This new testimony shows that Kaufmann is not alone in what he saw and reported. His stories have been verified and corroborated by the testimonies of many other sources. Some of that corroboration is very subtle, such as the story told by Leo Spear. All it does is suggest a military involvement prior to Marcel reporting back to the base on July 8, and that corroborates one small detail—the date of the crash—supplied by Kaufmann.

The question that must be asked is, Why is this testimony being rejected when single eyewitness reports have been accepted in the past? Why is this testimony being rejected in favor of secondhand reports? Why is it being attacked when there is so much supporting evidence for it? Why is that supporting testimony ignored? Is there another agenda at operation here? And if so, why?

It seems that the rejection of Kaufmann's testimony is the result of friction inside the UFO community. One prominent UFO researcher, when he learned of Kaufmann, demanded to know, "Why is he talking to you?" That same man rejects Kaufmann's story, even though he has accepted others based on virtually no independent evidence. He doesn't see the incredible double standard he is imposing on the data.

Others have attacked Kaufmann based on what some of the Roswell reporters have said about his testimony. For example, much was made of the Kaufmann claim that they had erected a series of mirrors in the radar room and down the hallway so that the radar operator, using a flashlight, could signal Kaufmann and the others sent to White Sands if something appeared. The truth is that Kaufmann had talked of a single mirror erected on a wall so that those standing outside smoking could be alerted if something was seen. Kaufmann's testimony should not be rejected because one of his statements was misreported by someone else.

Kaufmann had also suggested that when the craft came apart, there was a flash on the radar screen, a sunburst display that told them something had gone wrong. Critics assumed that the radio wave sent out by the set was responsible for that burst of brightness, and have therefore rejected Kaufmann. In reality, it is possible that the destruction of the alien craft, if there had been one, might have been accompanied by a burst of electromagnetic radiation across a broad spectrum. If such was the case, then the "rain" of debris was not responsible for the "sunburst," but electromagnetic radiation was. In other words, the scope showed a burst of radio waves on the proper frequency, rather than detecting the debris from the breakup of the craft.

Kaufmann's testimony continues to be controversial. He has, in some instances, embellished his role, forcing himself more to the center than he might have been in 1947. That year he was stationed at Roswell in a civilian capacity. Much of the controversy is the result of personal agendas of some researchers, mistakes made in the reporting of others, and a desire to discredit any witness who claims bold, firsthand knowledge. Kaufmann's story remains strong, but it lacks forceful supporting corroboration.

Kellahin, Jason Jason Kellahin was an AP reporter in the summer of 1947 based in Albuquerque, New Mexico. He received a call from the New York office of the Associated Press telling him that he needed to get down to Roswell as quickly as possible. According to Kellahin, "We [Kellahin and Robin Adair] were informed of the discovery down there . . . the bureau chief sent me and a teletype operator from the Albuquerque office."

Kellahin, interviewed in his home more than forty years later, said,

"It must have been in the morning because we went down there in the daytime. It would take a couple of hours to get down there . . ."

Kellahin continued, "We went down to Vaughn. Just south of Vaughn is where they found the material."

The ranch, according to him, wasn't very far from the main highway (Highway 285) from Vaughn to Roswell. They turned from that highway just south of Vaughn, onto the Corona road. They were driving to the west and saw "a lot of cars and went over. We assumed that [this] was the place. There were officers from the air base. They were there before we got there."

Kellahin described military cars, civilian cars, and even police vehicles parked along the side of the road. In one of the fields adjacent to the road, at the far end of it, were a number of military officers, not more than five or six of them. Kellahin left his vehicle and entered the field, where he saw the scattered debris.

"This man from Albuquerque with me [Adair], he had a camera. He took some pictures of the stuff lying on the ground and of the rancher who was there . . . Brazel was there and he [the photographer] took his picture."

Kellahin asked Brazel a few questions, interviewing him there in the field. "I talked to him. He told me his name [Brazel] and we had been told it was on his ranch."

Kellahin didn't remember much about what Brazel had said. "About the only thing he said was he walked out there and found this stuff and he told a neighbor about it and the neighbor said you ought to tell the sheriff . . . it was the next day [he] went down to Roswell."

Standing there in the field, near the debris, Kellahin had the chance to examine it closely. "It wasn't much of anything. Just some silver-colored fabric and very light wood . . . a light wood like you'd make a kite with . . . I didn't pick it up. In fact, they [the military] asked us not to pick up anything . . . You couldn't pick it up and have identified it. You have to have known [what it was]. But it was a balloon. It looked more like a kite than anything else."

The debris covered a small area, not more than half an acre. The military men were standing close by as Kellahin interviewed Brazel but didn't try to interfere. "They weren't paying much attention. They didn't interfere with me. I went wherever I wanted to go. They didn't keep me off the place at all. Me or the photographer." Kellahin tried to talk to the military people, but they didn't give him any information. "They were being very, very cautious because they didn't know."

He didn't have much time for the interview because the military officers came over and told him they were finished and were going to take Brazel into Roswell. With Brazel gone and the cleanup of the debris finished, there wasn't much reason for the AP reporters to remain. Kellahin and Adair continued their trip to Roswell, arriving before dark.

Kellahin confirmed some of this, saying that "We went down to the *Roswell Daily Record* and I wrote a story and we sent it out on the AP wire . . . Adair developed his pictures and set up the wire photo equipment and sent it out."

The published story ended, "Adair and Kellahin were ordered to Roswell for the special assignment by the headquarters bureau of AP in New York."

Kellahin, when he left the ranch, had expected to see Brazel in Roswell the next day, but said, "I don't recall that I did. I think the military was talking to him and wouldn't let him talk to anyone else to my recollection . . . I saw him there but . . . there were some military people with him."

Following the story as far as he could, Kellahin talked to Sheriff Wilcox. "When we got down there to the newspaper, he was there. I saw him there or at his office . . . By that time the military had gotten into it. He was being very cautious.

"It was a weather balloon," said Kellahin. "In my opinion that's what it was. That's what we saw. We didn't see anything else to indicate it was anything else."

Once they finished in the office, Kellahin returned to Albuquerque and Adair was ordered to return to El Paso to finish his job there. By the time Kellahin returned to Albuquerque, there was a new story for him that had nothing to do with flying saucers, another assignment that was just as important as his last.

There are some points that must be made. The raw testimony from Kellahin must be put into context with that provided by others, including Adair. Both Kellahin and Adair were trying to answer the questions as honestly as they could, attempting to recall the situation as it existed in July 1947. However, they are at odds with one another. There clearly is no way for Adair to be both in El Paso, as he claimed during his interview, and in Albuquerque, as suggested by Kellahin.

Given the circumstances, there are some things that can be established. A number of newspaper articles about the events written in 1947 have been reviewed. Although many of them had no byline, they did carry an AP slug and identify the location as Roswell. Since Kellahin was the only AP reporter there, assigned by the bureau chief in Albuquerque at the request of the AP headquarters in New York, it is clear that he wrote the articles.

The first problem encountered is Kellahin's memory of getting the call early in the morning. That simply doesn't track with the evidence. Walter Haut's press release was not issued until about noon on July 8. That means there would be no reason for the AP to assign a reporter on the morning of July 8. There was no story until that afternoon. And by the morning of July 9, the story was dead—there was no reason to send anyone to Roswell because photos had already been taken of the debris in Fort Worth and the information already released. Besides, the story in the July 9 issue of the *Roswell Daily Record* makes it clear that Kellahin and Adair had already arrived in Roswell, coming down on July 8.

Second is the story that Kellahin saw the weather balloon on the Brazel ranch. His description of the location, south of Vaughn but just off the main highway to Roswell, is inaccurate. The debris field, as identified by Bill Brazel and Bud Payne, is not close to the Vaughn–Roswell highway. In fact, the field where the debris was discovered is not visible from the road around it. It is a cross-country drive.

More important, by the time Kellahin could have gotten to that field, the balloon should have been removed. In fact, according to Marcel and the newspaper articles, the balloon was already in Fort Worth if we believe what has been reported. After all, a balloon wouldn't have taken long to collect, and Marcel had done that the day before.

Kellahin's testimony of seeing a balloon out in the field is intriguing, not because he is an eyewitness to the balloon on the crash site, but because of what it suggests. If there was a balloon, it would mean that the Army had to bring one in. In other words, they were salting the area, and that, in and of itself, would be important. It would suggest that the Army had something to hide, if they were planting evidence.

Given the sequence of events, based on the newspaper accounts and other testimony, the earliest that Kellahin could have been in the field was late on July 8. However, by that time Marcel and the special flight from Roswell were already in Fort Worth. If the balloon explanation is accurate, then the evidence had long since been collected and there would have been nothing for Kellahin to see.

Kellahin also said there had been photographs taken while on that field. These photos, according to Kellahin, had been transmitted from Roswell. The photo of Brazel transmitted, however, was one that had been taken, not in the field, but in the newspaper offices. If there were pictures taken in the field, they have never been printed. Had they existed, even if of poor quality, they would have been printed. After all, what could be better than pictures of Mack Brazel with the debris in the field?

By contrast, the seven pictures taken in Ramey's office were printed throughout the country. All seven have been located. Even the fairly rare picture of Irving Newton was printed in Texas newspapers and was used by the editors of *Look* when they printed their

Flying Saucers special in 1966. But those that Kellahin claimed had been taken of Brazel on his ranch with the debris clearly displayed have never been found. That suggests that Kellahin's memory is flawed.

The best available evidence is that Kellahin did not stop at the ranch on his way down. He is mistaken about that. The lack of the photographs and the evidence about the location of Brazel on the afternoon of July 8 suggest it. The location that Kellahin gives is in error. The ranch was not close to Vaughn, and the debris field is not close to any road.

By the time Kellahin and Adair arrived in Roswell and were ready to begin reporting, some of the pressure was off. Ramey, in Fort Worth, explained that the material found in Roswell was nothing extraordinary. No longer was New York demanding pictures. In fact, several pictures had already been taken in Fort Worth.

The interview with Brazel occurred on the evening of July 8, according to the newspaper article in the July 9 edition of the *Roswell Daily Record*. Brazel was brought in by the owner of KGFL, Walt Whitmore Sr. Brazel was then interviewed by Kellahin, as well as by a reporter for the *Daily Record*. The pictures transmitted, those of Brazel and George Wilcox, are ones that had been taken in the office for that purpose. Kellahin then wrote his story, which appeared in the newspapers the next day.

With the story dead, Kellahin was ordered to return to what he had been doing. He left Roswell. Kellahin believed that nothing extraordinary had been found, and there was no reason for the events to stick in his mind.

The Majestic Twelve (MJ-12) The Majestic Twelve committee, according to documents that have leaked to the UFO community, was a distinguished group of scientists, military officers and political leaders. It was formed by President Truman to exploit, study, examine, and investigate the strange craft and alien bodies recovered outside Roswell in 1947.

The Majestic Twelve (MJ-12) Documents According to nearly every UFO investigator, the MJ-12 documents first appeared when a mysterious package arrived at the home of film producer and sometime UFO researcher Jaime Shandera on December 11, 1984. It was in a standard plain brown wrapper with no return address, but it had apparently been mailed from Albuquerque, New Mexico, on December 8. Inside was an envelope that contained another envelope that contained a black plastic canister that contained exposed but undeveloped film. The film, when developed, held the first of the MJ-12 documents, a briefing paper allegedly prepared for then President-elect Dwight Eisenhower about the crash of an extraterrestrial craft near Roswell, New Mexico, and a memo from President Harry Truman authorizing the creation of the oversight committee to study the recovered object as detailed in the briefing.

A point that is virtually overlooked in discussions of MJ-12 is that the original documents themselves are not available for proper scientific analysis. In fact, no one knows where they came from or why Shandera of all the "UFO researchers" available was selected to receive them, and after all the years of research, there has been nothing provided that proves the documents authentic. To most of the researchers, the question of provenance is difficult to overcome. Without a solid source available, there is no reason to believe the documents authentic and genuine. To trace their history, it is possible to follow them only to Shandera and William L. Moore, who authored *The Roswell Incident* with Charles Berlitz.

These documents contain what many consider fatal flaws. For example, the Eisenhower Briefing was supposedly written by Admiral Roscoe Hillenkoetter. The problem, according to opponents, is that in September 1947, when the document and the memo attached to it were created, Hillenkoetter wasn't an admiral as indicated by MJ-12, but a rear admiral, a lower and different rank. His name and rank appear twice in the document, first in a list of those who have been appointed to the MJ-12 investigative committee and then alone as the briefing officer for President-elect Eisenhower. Some of the proponents of MJ-12 such as Stan Friedman have argued that such a mistake, the incorrect rank in this case, is of little consequence.

This is on a document that, according to all the parties now involved in the debate, was created by Hillenkoetter. This is not a question of a mixed list of names, but a notation at the top of the document in which Hillenkoetter had been singled out. Hillenkoetter, knowing that Eisenhower, one of the handful of men to reach five-star rank, would be seeing this document, would not allow it to go forward with the wrong rank on it. As a military officer, aware of the importance attached to such things, especially at such a high level, Hillenkoetter would have changed the rank to reflect his true grade.

But this isn't the only problem with the MJ-12 documents. The Truman memo, attached to the Eisenhower Briefing, has been called a Special Executive Order. It seems to function as an executive order, but there is a real problem with it, one that Friedman and other proponents seem to ignore. Instead, Friedman attacks the opponents of MJ-12 for what he sees as their failures in providing proper information to inform the reader. He writes, "He [Kevin Randle] does not mention that the date on the memo was typed by two typewriters, and the period after the date points to Van Bush's office as the place where it was typed. In addition, he refers to the order as an Executive Order or EO at least 15 times, using the initials SCEO only once, which implies that there is no difference between an Executive Order and a Special Classified Executive Order."

Friedman is outraged that one source quoted in opposition to MJ-12 is Joe Nickell of the Committee for the Scientific Investigation of Claims of the Paranormal (CSICOP), but seems to have missed the fact that another source of criticism is Barry Greenwood, formerly of Citizens Against UFO Secrecy, who has made many of the same arguments as Nickell. In fact, Greenwood, former editor of *Just Cause*, wrote: "Page 2 of the Briefing Paper refers to the formation of MJ-12 'by special classified executive order of President Truman on 24 September, 1947 . . . We have checked the Truman Library's listing of executive orders and found that no orders were issued on 9/24. Executive order numbers 9891–9896 were issued respectively on 9/15, two on 9/20, 9/23, 9/30 and 10/2/47, none even closely resembling the MJ-12 subject. There is no gap in the number sequence for these dates so none are missing. Further, the number quoted in Attachment 'A' of the Briefing Paper, #092447 . . . is not an executive order number but the date of President Truman's memo, 9/24/47. Executive orders are not numbered by date but are numbered sequentially, and at the time the numbers were only four digits."

Friedman had a rationalization for this, suggesting that it had only been designated an executive order five years after it was written. In a letter to Nickell, Friedman wrote, "[We] don't have any definition of what is meant by a 'special executive order.'"

Friedman also raises the argument that this was a special classified executive order—it wouldn't be with the unclassified documents. It would require special handling because of its high classification. That seems to be logical thinking on his part.

However, had MJ-12 been a legitimate executive order, it would have fallen into the numerical sequence, even if it was highly classified. A report prepared by government employees entitled, "Congressional Research Service, The Library of Congress on Government Operations, March 17, 1987," states: "During the past 70 years, some 40 confidential or security executive orders have been occasionally issued. These were not published, but they were accounted for in the numbering system."

What this means, quite simply, is that if MJ-12 was legitimate and highly classified, it would have been in the numbering sequence, but not readily available because of its elevated security classification. The document might not be available, but the number used for it would have been in the sequence of executive orders.

But there is a real problem here. The Eisenhower Briefing had a listing of the attachments, only one of which was forwarded, or has been seen by researchers. Attachment A contains, according to the briefing itself, "Special Classified Executive Order #092447."

So once again there is something that does not match the proper format or regulations that were in force in 1947. It could be suggested, and has been, that this was a unique event, so the paperwork surrounding it would be unique, but that doesn't wash. Even for an event of this magnitude, the simple regulations surrounding the creation of executive orders, or special classified executive orders, would have been followed. They all seem to have been ignored in this case.

What this indicates is that the Eisenhower Briefing and the Truman memo are documents that do not conform to the styles used in the proper time frames. There are a number of problems, from Hillenkoetter's rank being wrong to the very technical details for issuing an executive order that are wrong. All this is suggestive of mistakes incompatible with authenticity and that the documents are, therefore, frauds.

Majestic Twelve Operations Manual One of the documents that surfaced among the Majestic Twelve Project documents was called "Extraterrestrial Entities and Technology Recovery and Disposal." This is, according to the front cover, the "Majestic Twelve Group Special Operations Manual."

Once again, a document about the alleged MJ-12 committee has come, ultimately, from an unidentified source. It is a document that has been circulating in the UFO community for a number of years and is now part of the Majestic Twelve Project.

A study of the manual reveals that a great deal of work went into its construction. This was no simple, quick-and-dirty job. It suggests someone who is familiar with the military style manuals that have been produced for decades. The cover is impressive, looks authentic, and even includes a seal to add to the visual impact. Unfortunately, it is the seal of the Department of War, an organization that ceased to exist some seven years before the manual was supposedly printed.

The manual itself is short, with the table of contents showing Appendix III beginning on page 31. That appendix, according to the manual, contains photographs. No copy in the hands of UFO researchers contains any photographs, and in fact, most copies of the manual end on page 23.

Again, as with the other MJ-12 documents, the manual is classified as "Top Secret/Majic Eyes Only." Those inside the government and the military report that an "Eyes Only" classification mark is contradictory here. "Eyes Only" documents are created for a specific person, to brief that person on a highly classified subject. A document might be created for the "Eyes Only" of the president, but this designation would not apply to a manual. Once the "Eyes Only" recipient has read the document, it is to be destroyed. There would be only a single copy of it because it was created for the

"Eyes Only" of a specific person. This would defeat the purpose of a manual.

A real mistake seems to be a classification of "Restricted." According to Herbert L. Pankratz of the Eisenhower Library, "The classification markings on the alleged MJ-12 document are not consistent with federal regulations for the marking of classified materials as of April 1954 [the date on the manual]. The 'Restricted' classification category was terminated by executive order in November 1953 and would not have been used on a document in April 1954. Federal regulations also require that the cover page reflect the highest level of classification for any material in the document. Since 'Top Secret' is a higher category than 'Restricted,' only 'Top Secret' should have appeared on the cover of the document."

In other words, the cover of the document violated the federal regulations in effect in April 1954. If the document is authentic, it should conform to those regulations. This document, like all the other MJ-12 documents, seems to be at variance with the proper government regulations. Proponents will claim that these regulations weren't ironclad and that variations do exist. However, documents created at this level would be closely monitored and would adhere to the proper regulations, especially since those regulations had just been changed. The classifications on the manual, like those on the other MJ-12 documents, are wrong, and there is no reason for them to be. It smacks of hoax.

Pankratz continued in his letter of February 6, 1995, saying, "In addition, we have no evidence in our files that a security classification referred to as 'MAJIC EYES ONLY' ever existed. Executive Order 10501 was signed by President Eisenhower on November 5, 1953. It set up three classification categories: 'Top Secret,' 'Secret,' and 'Confidential.' A fourth category, 'Restricted Data' (not the same as 'restricted'), was established by the Atomic Energy Act of 1954; and it is used only with regard to nuclear weapons." The manual, then, contains an obsolete classification mark. That is a second major mistake made by the creator of the document.

As with the rest of the Majestic Twelve Project papers, the manual contains many anachronisms. On page 4, for example, the manual instructs the retrieval units on how to keep the press and the public from learning about the alien craft. They suggest explaining the sightings and crashes as "meteors, downed satellites, weather balloons . . ." But when the manual was supposedly issued, April 1954, there were no satellites in orbit, and a suggestion by military officials that one had been recovered would have generated more press interest, not less.

It is clear that someone with a great deal of time, an intimate knowledge of the UFO phenomenon, and a computer with good word processing and graphics programs created the MJ-12 manual. That person, however, had not worked with classified material, nor did he or she understand the system. That explains why the mixed classifications are found on the front cover of the manual. It also explains why an obsolete term, "Restricted," was used. That was an attempt to conform to genuine documents.

The opinion that the manual is a fake is shared by a number of researchers. In March 1999, a coalition of UFO researchers from the Center for UFO Studies, Project 1947, and the Fund for UFO Research issued a joint statement about the Operations Manual. The joint statement said, in part, "We believe this document to be a hoax; a deliberate fake designed to mislead the public and to plant false information in the UFO research community by person or persons whose motives are unknown."

Those who signed the joint statement included Don Berliner, an aviation writer and historian, who had been singled out by the perpetrators of the Operations Manual hoax. Jan L. Aldrich, a retired Army master sergeant who had been an intelligence NCO (sergeant), a classified document custodian, and a top secret control officer, also signed. Thomas P. Deuley, a retired naval officer who had been a cryptologic officer and a Communications Security (COMSEC) custodian, was another of those who signed the statement. They were joined by Dick Hall, former chairman of FUFOR, and Mark Rodeghier, the current director of CUFOS.

Each brought an expertise to the table, and each reviewed the Operations Manual in light of their expertise. All concluded that the document was a fake. This was a cross section of the UFO community and included the man who had originally received the manual. Their conclusion that the manual was a hoax was not qualified in any fashion.

There is no doubt that the MJ-12 Operations Manual is nothing more than a fake. It does not conform to the regulations, it contains inaccurate and anachronistic information, and it is incomplete. The manual should be rejected as the fake it is.

Majestic Twelve Project When it began to seem that the last had been heard of MJ-12, that all the documents that had been published contained some fatal flaw that led to the conclusion that MJ-12 was a hoax, a new round was started. More documents were found, more documents were identified and published, and new questions were asked.

Although there had been rumors that a new package of documents had surfaced, it wasn't until October 11, 1998, that Dr. Robert Wood and his adult son, Ryan, announced that they had received a large package that contained dozens of such documents. The new group of about forty documents contained about 125 pages of information about MJ-12 and its alleged operations, but it also contained a few documents that had already made the rounds.

Like all the others, this group of documents surfaced without a provenance. Wood told researchers at the Omega Communications conference hosted by John White that he had received them from a California-based researcher named Timothy Cooper who had become an "expert" on using the Freedom of Information Act to acquire UFO-related material. While that was interesting, according to Cooper, he had received most of the new documents from a third party identified only as Cantwheel. It was not explained exactly who Cantwheel was or how he had acquired so much MJ-12 material. Cantwheel has, of course, since died.

According to the documents, Field Order 862 was issued by President Truman's Office of Assistant Chief of Staff and ordered the Interplanetary Phenomenon Unit (IPU) to head to New Mexico. A seven-page document dated July 9, 1947, subtitled "Extraordinary recovery of fallen objects in New Mexico," provides descriptions of the debris recovered and where the various pieces of debris were sent.

That same document describes the deaths of some of the men involved in the retrieval operation. Four technicians who were on the site became extremely sick during the recovery, and three of them died of heavy bleeding. One of the military policemen on the scene later committed suicide.

Another of the documents suggested that Nathan Twining investigated the crash. In a three-page report, Twining suggested that the craft was powered by "atomic engines" and that it was doughnut-shaped and about thirty-five feet in diameter.

The longest of the new documents is the MJ-12 Operations Manual. The Woods investigation uncovered nothing new about the Operations Manual. They do argue, however, that the anachronistic use of "Area 51" might be appropriate. According to them, Area 51 referred to a map location that could well have been in use prior to 1954, when the manual was allegedly written. They don't explain how the material would be sent to a base that hadn't been built in 1954.

One of the most interesting documents is dated September 24, 1947, which might be part of the Eisenhower Briefing that was not included in the first leaks of that document. It identifies a new acronym for the UFOs, referring to them as "unidentified lenticular aerodyne technology," or ULAT. Clearly ULAT means alien spacecraft.

According to that document, ULAT-1 had been recovered at a location southeast of Socorro, New Mexico. That seems to imply that part of the Barney Barnett story is accurate, though the crash was not far to the west on the Plains of San Agustin, but rather closer to Socorro. This could be seen as a thin corroboration of the Santilli autopsy film.

Those who believe in the authenticity of MJ-12, and Robert
Wood is numbered among them, have found what they believe to
be proofs of the authenticity of these new documents. The Woods
noticed that in some of the documents there was a raised "z," that
is, every "z" is slightly above the position it should be on the printed
line. A number of authenticated documents printed by the
Government Printing Office (GPO) in that same year exhibited the
"flying z." To some, this suggested the documents are authentic.

But problems suggesting fraud have also appeared. First and
foremost are the claims that no one knows where the documents
originated. There is no way to use the Freedom of Information Act
to acquire authentic copies of the documents. There is no government agency that will admit being the source of the documents, or
that copies of the documents are stored in their offices. The trail
runs from the Woods to Cooper to the dead Cantwheel and then
no farther.

In a similar circumstance, UFO researchers learned of a project
code-named Moon Dust. Part of the Moon Dust mission was investigation of foreign UFO sightings. There were documents, but Air
Force officers denied that such a project ever existed. The difference, however, is there is a provenance for some of the Moon Dust
documents. They came from the Department of State, and other
researchers, using FOIA requests, were able to obtain them. On
many, in the block for the "subject," were the code words "Moon
Dust." It was clear that there had been a secret project with that
code name and that Air Force denials about it were erroneous.

No one, however, has been able to verify the code name
Majestic Twelve or MJ-12. The documents keep surfacing inside
the UFO community, with neither the provenance nor the pedigree
needed to be convincing.

As with the Operations Manual, there are anachronisms in this
batch of documents. First, in a document entitled "1st Annual
Report of the MAJESTIC TWELVE PROJECT," there is a mention of a "retro-virus" (with a hyphen). This term in a document

dated 1952 caught the eyes of a number of researchers. All wondered about when "retrovirus" had entered the language.

UFO researchers began a quick survey of the relevant scientific literature and realized that the term *retrovirus* (a group of viruses that, unlike all other viruses and cellular material, carry their genetic fingerprint in the RNA) didn't exist in 1952. The mechanism of the retrovirus was discovered by Howard Temin, who began work on the problem in 1960. Apparently another scientist, David Baltimore, working at MIT, had independently duplicated Temin's work and they published a joint article on June 27, 1970, in *Nature*. It was after this article appeared that the term *retrovirus* entered the lexicon. The question to be asked was the same question that had been asked in the past: How could a paper produced in 1952 make reference to a term that did not exist in 1952?

Those wishing to believe in the MJ-12 documents found what they believed to be a logical explanation for this problem. The Woods, in searching for a possible alternative use of the term, including the hyphenated "retro-virus," prior to 1970, found a number of scientific articles that mentioned retrograde organisms that predated the 1952 Annual Report. The Woods wrote that Robert Green, as early as 1935, had suggested that all viruses were retrograde organisms. The Woods found other references to that term.

The Woods wrote, "One reasonable scenario is that the writer of this section of the 1st Annual Report of the MAJESTIC TWELVE PROJECT, perhaps being obsessed with jargonizing, may have simply shortened the then 'retrograde virus' to 'retro-virus.'"

Others didn't find the suggestion reasonable. To them, the use of *retrovirus*, with or without the hyphen, suggested a document that had not been created in 1952 but much later and was, therefore, fraudulent.

Another of the anachronisms was the position of Hoyt S. Vandenberg in 1952. The First Annual Report, because of what it mentions, had to be written in either late 1951 or in 1952. The cover page lists one of the members, General Hoyt Vandenberg, as the "vice chief of staff, United States Air Force." The problem was that Vandenberg was Vice Chief of Staff in 1947 when MJ-12 was allegedly created, but by the summer of 1948, he had been promoted to the Chief of Staff of the Air Force. There is no way that he would have been listed on any official document created in 1951 or later as a Vice Chief of Staff.

Still another anachronism is found in a document dated "February 1948." In the lower left corner of the memo, there is a list of agencies that are to receive the document. Listed among those is "USAFOSI." The problem is that in February 1948, the Air Force Office of Special Investigation, designated as AFOSI, did not exist. Worse for the creator of the document, it was never called the USAFOSI.

There are those who have argued that "poison pills" have been built into the MJ-12 documents to "destroy" them if they should leak. What these researchers are suggesting is that some information, hopelessly out of place or inaccurate, was included in each of the MJ-12 documents. When they were leaked into the public arena, these "poison pills" would be found and that would suggest to skeptics and disbelievers that the documents were fraudulent. The tactic, according to the researchers, is well known in intelligence circles that routinely create disinformation.

The problem with this thinking is that it is slightly off-kilter. Disinformation is not created to self-destruct. It is created to take the enemy, whoever that enemy might be, in the wrong direction. For it to self-destruct would be to defeat its propose.

However, if a leak is found that does compromise true classified information, then bad information is often pumped into that leak with the hope that all information retrieved from that source will be discredited. But that is not the same as disinformation. If MJ-12 was disinformation, as some have suggested, the effort would be made to make sure that nothing was found to suggest that it was fraudulent because that would defeat the purpose.

The Majestic Twelve Project, with its huge release of documents, should be taken for what it is. Without a proper provenance, with the anachronisms that dot it, with the information that seems to embrace almost every aspect of the Roswell case, it simply must be considered at best dubious and at worst another hoax.

Marcel Sr., Major (later Lieutenant Colonel) Jesse (1910–1986) In recent years there has been a great deal of discussion about Jesse Marcel Sr., his service record, and allegations that he lied about his career and education to various UFO researchers to inflate his importance in the Roswell case. There are those who believe that discrepancies between Marcel's military record and the statements he made to *National Enquirer* reporter Bob Pratt have proved Marcel to be a liar, and therefore his statements about the Roswell UFO crash can be rejected. In fact, Karl Pflock, in an open letter to Stan Friedman, made just this allegation.

Major Jesse A. Marcel Sr.
(*Photo courtesy of Walter Haut*)

But the situation has been muddied by those who wish to believe the worst about a man who is dead and can no longer defend himself. They have assumed that Marcel's military record is 100 percent complete and accurate, and that the transcript Pratt made of his interview, as provided to various UFO researchers and as published by UFO researcher Karl Pflock, is one hundred percent accurate and complete.

It has been suggested by many debunkers that few of Marcel's claims about his background have stood up to scrutiny. Author Peter Brooksmith, in one of his most recent UFO books, for example, suggested that Marcel had no real combat experience, that he was nothing more than a passenger on combat flights in the South Pacific during World War II. Reporters for a San Francisco television station, in a multipart story, suggested much the same thing. Although such an allegation certainly calls Marcel's record into question, it is a ridiculous statement with no evidence to support it. No one flies into combat as a passenger.

In fact, in the two citations for the Air Medal in Marcel's military file, it was written: "For meritorious achievement while participating in sustained operational flight missions . . . in the Southwest Pacific area during which hostile contact was probable and expected. These operations consisted of bombing missions against enemy airdromes and installations and attacks on enemy naval vessels and shipping. The courage and devotion to duty displayed during these flights are worthy of commendation."

In other words, Marcel was on the missions as part of his job as intelligence officer for various units in the Southwest Pacific during the war. Passengers on such flights, if there ever were any, were not routinely handed medals for "riding" along. Marcel was doing his job, and to suggest that "his combat flying was limited to a passenger's job," as Brooksmith claims, is an attempt to belittle a man's reputation without evidence to support the allegation.

Brooksmith continued in this same vein when he suggested that Marcel's promotion to lieutenant colonel was in the reserve and that he never wore the rank during his active duty service. This is designed to suggest that it was improper to address him as "colonel," and to suggest that he was attempting to claim a higher rank than he was authorized for the purpose of self-aggrandizement. The record shows that Marcel was, in fact, promoted to lieutenant colonel in the reserve and never claimed to have worn the rank on active duty.

There was a great deal of correspondence in Marcel's file addressed to Lieutenant Colonel Jesse A. Marcel. Marcel *was* a lieutenant colonel, and he *never* said that he had been anything more than a major on active duty.

Brooksmith, apparently searching for anything to destroy Marcel's reputation, continued in this same vein when he wrote that Marcel claimed to be the sole survivor of an aircraft accident during the war. Like the other allegation, this simply isn't true and seems to be the result of a misreading of Pflock's re-creation of the transcript of the Pratt interview.

In his conversation with Pratt, Marcel mentioned that he had been shot down on his third mission. Pratt had then asked Marcel, "Did everyone survive?"

Marcel said, "All but one crashed into the mountain." It seems to be quite clear that Marcel is saying that everyone survived except for one crewman, who died when he crashed into the mountain.

Here is where one of the problems with the transcript arises. Pflock, in his attempt to make the transcript clear, changed it. According to Pflock, Pratt asked, "How many missions did you go on?"

Marcel: "I had a total of 468 hours of combat time . . . was intelligence officer for bomb wing, flew as pilot, waist gunner and bombardier at different times . . . I got shot down one time, my third mission, out of Port Moresby."

Pratt: "Did everyone survive?"

Marcel: "All but one crashed into a mountain."

What the transcript actually says is: "A—I had a total of 468 hours of combat time . . . was intelligence officer for bomb wing, flew as pilot, waist gunner and bombardier at different times . . . I got shot down one time, my third mission, out of Port Moresby (everyone survive) all but one crashed into a mountain [reproduced exactly as is appears in the Pratt transcript, ellipses and all]."

One interpretation of that statement could be that Marcel was saying that everyone survived, except for a single crewman who crashed into a mountain. All we have to do is add a comma to make it clear.

Pratt asked, "Did everyone survive?"

Marcel answered, "All, but one crashed into a mountain."

It could also be interpreted to mean that all but one of them crashed into a mountain and were killed. But that still doesn't make Marcel the sole survivor, as Brooksmith claimed, because there is that one other man who lived. No matter how you slice it, Brooksmith's interpretation of the comment is flawed. Marcel made no claim of being a sole survivor of that combat mission, but Brooksmith is quick to smear his name by suggesting that he did.

There are, in fact, other, similar interpretation problems with the Pflock version of the Pratt transcript. Those attacking Marcel note that he claimed to have a bachelor's degree from George Washington University, but repeated requests to that institution have failed to produce positive results.

According to Pflock, Pratt asked, "You were all hand-picked officers."

Marcel: "Right. [I've been] around the world five times, been in sixty-eight countries. [I have] a degree in nuclear physics, bachelor's, at—completed work at George Washington University in Washington[, D.C.] . . ."

The Pratt transcript actually says, ". . . AF intelligence office for A bomb tests in South Pacific . . . Kwajalein (all hand picked group of officers) right . . . around the world 5 times, been in 68 countries . . . degree in nuclear physics (bachelor's) at completed work at GW Univ in Wash."

This interview with Pratt is apparently the only place where it is claimed that Marcel said that he had any sort of college degree. Most of those who interviewed Marcel before his death in 1986 never heard him claim to any more college education than the one and a half years shown in his military record.

It can shown that Marcel did attend classes at other universities. These seem to be military schools that were taught by civilian instructors at those universities. These classes would not have been part of the normal university curriculum, that is, not open to civilian students. These sorts of courses would not normally be recorded by the university but should be noted in Marcel's record. There is some indication of that.

According to Marcel's record, he was scheduled to attend a course at the University of Maryland, a fact the debunkers seem to have missed. To be fair, there is no indication in Marcel's record that he did attend the class. It seems that his orders were changed so that he attended an intelligence school in Pennsylvania instead.

This, in fact, provides a couple of clues about Marcel's early military career. Those wishing to destroy Marcel's reputation note that Marcel told Pratt that he had been an aide to General Hap Arnold and that it was Arnold who suggested that he attend the intelligence school. The skeptics and debunkers have said that there is nothing in Marcel's record to support this. They point out that Marcel entered the service from Houston and that he already had a school assignment at the time he entered the service. To them this proves that there was no time for him to be an aide to General Arnold, and nothing to suggest that Arnold was responsible for him going to the intelligence school.

But the record simply isn't that clear. While it is certainly true that Marcel entered the service from Houston and that he had a school assignment when he entered the service as noted earlier, he did not attend that school. There is a period of several months when he was in Washington, D.C. He had no specified assignment during that period.

Researchers have speculated about that assignment, but it is speculation based on solid information. Marcel was in Washington, D.C., and had no military assignment. Arnold was in Washington, D.C. As a general officer he was authorized an aide. Actually, he might have been authorized more than one, given his position. Often officers who are awaiting assignment or school dates are pressed into temporary duty as aides to generals. It is possible, in fact likely, that Marcel was pressed into duty assisting those assisting General Arnold. Arnold, recognizing a valuable asset, suggested a change of assignment and secured for Marcel the intelligence school assignment in Pennsylvania.

What is seen in Marcel's record is a gap of several weeks. There is nothing in his record to rule out the possibility he served as Arnold's aide, and that is the key. Those attempting to assassinate Marcel's credibility and character make much of that fact, never realizing, or not caring, that Marcel's record is incomplete.

Can it be proved that his record is incomplete? Marcel, according to a notation in the record, received the Bronze Star for meritorious service on May 8, 1945. There is no citation in his file for the award of the Bronze Star. That means the record is incomplete.

The citation for the Bronze Star was included in the unit history of the bomb group to which Marcel had been assigned in 1945. That proves there was a citation, which should have been included in his file. The citation suggests the award was made on May 3, 1945. In other words, the file is wrong on that point. Yes, it is a minor mistake and could easily be the result of carelessness in transcribing the records. But, that isn't the point here. Debunkers are attacking Marcel because his record does not agree with what he said, but that record is incomplete and inaccurate.

In fact, this sort of inaccuracy confounds other aspects of this controversy. Debunkers and skeptics are attributing actions to Marcel for which he is not the blame. The press release made on July 8, 1947, about the capture of the flying saucer is a prime example of this. The debunkers have all suggested that Marcel made the press release under his own authority. Marcel didn't have the authority to make a press release. It could only be authorized by Colonel William Blanchard, the commanding officer of the 509th Bomb Group.

But to make a case against Roswell, they must create the idea that the press release was a blunder made by Marcel. The fact is that it did not affect Marcel's career, and it certainly didn't harm Blanchard. Both men were promoted after the press release was issued. Blanchard climbed to four stars and might have been named

Chief of Staff of the Air Force had he not died of a heart attack prematurely.

Marcel is now blamed for an action that could have only come from the commanding officer of the 509th Bomb Group. Only Blanchard could order the public relations officer to issue the press release. Had Marcel wanted it done, either he or the public relations officer would have had to get approval for it from Colonel Blanchard. Walter Haut, the public relations officer in 1947, has said repeatedly that Colonel Blanchard ordered the press release. Haut says now that he can't remember if the text was dictated to him by Blanchard, or if he was merely given the facts. In either case, Blanchard was the authorizing authority, not Marcel. So Marcel didn't create the press release to thrust himself into the public eye, as been alleged by Brooksmith and others.

Finally, in a controversy that should be embarrassing to the skeptics and the debunkers, they claim that Marcel said he was a pilot on active duty. That is not what the Pratt transcript or the Pflock version of it said. What Marcel told Pratt was that he had flown *as* a pilot, bombardier, and waist gunner during his service in the South Pacific. That is quite clear on the transcript and is a real difference.

The real problem might be Marcel's claim of three thousand hours of pilot time and eight thousand total flight hours. That seems to be what he said to Pratt. But searches of FAA records show no pilot's certificate for Marcel, and when he was filling out his forms to join the service, he made no claim of such extensive flight experience prior to entering the Army.

Clearly some of that experience was gained in the Army Air Force. As an intelligence officer in aviation units, he would be expected to fly on a number of occasions. In a unit that had strategic bombers as its main equipment, there would certainly be a number of long, high-hour flights. For someone with nine or ten years of active service, it is not unreasonable to expect him to have several thousand hours of flight time as a crewman.

The real question comes down to his claim of three thousand hours of pilot flight time and no record for it. Marcel, in the Pratt interview, claimed that he began flying in 1928, the same year that the FAA was formed. In the beginning the licensing requirements were much looser and more difficult to enforce. It is easy to believe that in the late 1920s and the 1930s, someone would fly without the benefit of a government license to do so.

Marcel worked for Shell Oil Company as a mapmaker and he used aerial photographs in his work, according to his military file. Records from that time at Shell Oil are hard to locate, and the specific aviation records have long been lost. If they could be found, the records might shed some light on Marcel's claim that he began flying in 1928. It could be that as part of his cartographer's duties, he was required to fly. It could be that he acted as co-pilot on those flights. If true, it explains quite a bit.

When his record is examined there are some conclusions to be drawn. First, Marcel didn't claim to be a rated military pilot. Anyone who reads the transcript carefully realizes that Marcel never said that he was a pilot, only that he had flown as one. It's not the same thing, and it is more than likely that what Marcel said was true.

Second, to believe that Marcel was a liar, his military record must be accepted as 100 percent accurate. This is not true. The missing citation for the Bronze Star demonstrates that. If that is missing, what else can be missing?

There is nothing in the Marcel record, at this point, to allow us to brand Marcel a liar. There are disagreements between what he allegedly said to Pratt, how Pflock interpreted those comments, and what is in the record. There are even discrepancies between what is in Marcel's personnel file and other records in which he is mentioned. But none of these discrepancies are of much consequence and can be explained as simple mistakes in Pratt's transcript or the military record or even Marcel's memory.

The skeptics and the debunkers seem to believe that if they can destroy Marcel's reputation, then the whole Roswell case collapses.

But they do not report that Marcel was held in high esteem by the officers appointed above him. His ratings by Blanchard and those at Eighth Air Force are all excellent. Even in the months that followed the Roswell crash, Marcel was rated as an excellent officer.

The only negative to be found is a suggestion that he tended to overreact to some situations. Debunkers have used this to suggest that Marcel invented the Roswell crash because of this overreaction. Of course, they always neglect to report that Marcel was a perfectionist, and this caused him to micromanage some aspects of his job. This is certainly not a major criticism and is of little real consequence in the overall picture.

What is seen, in the end, is a man, Major Jesse A. Marcel Sr., who was promoted to lieutenant colonel shortly after the Roswell crash, who served his country with distinction and valor, and who was just who he said he was in July 1947. That is, he was the air intelligence officer of the only nuclear strike force in the world at the time.

This was a man whose military record does not reflect what he told a single reporter some thirty years later. The points of discrepancy are little more than trivia. They simply are not relevant given the nature of the interview, the military record, and Marcel's otherwise exemplary career and character.

The Roswell case does not rise or fall on Marcel because he isn't the only man who told tales of the alien spacecraft. Others on Blanchard's staff, including Provost Marshal Major Edwin Easley and Adjutant Major Patrick Saunders, confirmed the alien nature of the craft recovered. So even if what the skeptics report about Marcel was true, it would mean little in the overall scheme of things. It's a shame that the memory of a fine officer and World War II veteran has to be attacked because there are those who can't handle the truth. Jesse Marcel deserved better from everyone.

McKnight Affidavit In an attempt to bolster the sagging Jim Ragsdale story, and to cast doubt on the impact site identified north of Roswell, the International UFO Museum and Research Center tracked down the relatives of those who had owned the ranch in 1947. Although the impact site identified by Randle and Schmitt is currently on a ranch owned by Hub Corn, in 1947 it belonged to the McKnights. A McKnight relative was found in Iowa who said that nothing happened near there in 1947.

According to an affidavit signed on February 2, 1997, Jim McKnight said that his family had owned the property now owned by Corn for three generations. McKnight said that in the 1950s he rode the whole area on horseback. He was quite familiar with the land, and there were no good places to cross the dry Macho River bed except five miles north of the ranch, or near the corrals by the ranch house. He said that Ragsdale would have never camped near there because people didn't go there to camp, but instead went to the mountains to the west of Roswell. He said that all the ranchers and the laborers who lived and worked the area talked to one another and that he had heard nothing to suggest a crash on what is called the impact sight. Had there been such an incident, he would have heard about it.

Macho River area. (*Photo courtesy of Kevin Randle*)

The only problem with the McKnight affidavit is that it contains no hard facts. He doesn't believe there was a crash because no one mentioned it to him. He doesn't believe anyone would camp out there because no one has, as far as he knows. He doesn't believe in the crash because there were no good places to cross the dry riverbed except five miles north of the ranch house, or in view of the ranch house. It is all opinion and speculation designed to suggest that the new Ragsdale story, of being in the mountains fifty or sixty miles from Roswell, will be more acceptable.

Missing Nurse, Part I See *Self, Naomi*

Missing Nurse, Part II Entertaining the notion that Naomi Self, or one of the other variations, was not the nurse to whom Glenn Dennis referred even though he had given researchers that name, was it possible that another of the nurses at Roswell would fit the profile offered? While some researchers pursued that notion with varying degrees of success, according to them word came that the nurse had been found. A woman had come forward saying that she believed her mother might have been the missing nurse.

The woman said her mother, dead for about twenty years, had told of a mysterious flight into, she believed, New Mexico. Her mother said that the aliens were very small and that the ship was also very small. The nurse, according to the daughter, was "very hush-hush," and she said that her mother was frightened that she would slip and say too much.

The problem here is that the daughter has acknowledged her mother was not stationed at Roswell at any time, and no searches have provided any documentation to suggest that she had been brought in because of special expertise. There is no way to take the tale any further, and the daughter suggested that she was very young when she heard the details. The most likely explanation here is that the daughter half remembers a conversation from decades earlier and has plugged it into the Roswell case. Little of real benefit has emerged from this investigation.

Mogul See *Project Mogul*

Moore, Charles B. Charles B. Moore has been billed as the man who launched the Roswell incident. In June and July 1947, Moore was in New Mexico working with Dr. Albert Crary on the then-classified Project Mogul. In the course of those experiments, they launched a balloon that Moore is convinced fell on the Brazel ranch near Corona, sparking the beginning of the Roswell story. Moore is an atmospheric physicist who finished his teaching career in New Mexico. He is a Professor Emeritus of Atmospheric Physics at the New Mexico Institute of Mining and Technology.

Moore, however, has not approached the situation as a disbeliever in UFOs. He is one of the few people to have made more than one UFO report to the Air Force who hasn't been labeled as having "psychological" problems. Moore, along with a crew from General Mills, were launching balloons near Arrey, New Mexico. On April 24, 1949, they had "released a 350 gram balloon about 1020 MST and were following it with a standard ML-47 David White Theodolite." Moore made a reading at 1030 and then took over at the theodolite.

According to Moore's report, made to the Air Force's UFO investigation Project Grudge, he had looked up to acquire the balloon with the naked eye and spotted what he thought was the balloon. Moore wrote: "When the distance between the theodolite and the supposed balloon became apparent, I took over the theodolite and found the true balloon still there, whereupon I abandoned it and picked up the object after it came out of the sun. The object was moving too fast to crank the theodolite around; therefore, one of the men pointed the theodolite and I looked. The object was ellipsoid . . . white in color except for a light yellow of one side as thought it were in shadow.

"The object," according to Moore, "was not a balloon and was some distance away. Assuming escape velocity, a track is enclosed which figures elevation above the station of about 300,000 feet over the observed period. If this is true, the flight would have probably gone over the White Sands Proving Ground [later White Sands Missile Range], Holloman Air Force Base, and Los Alamos."

They lost sight of the object in the distance after watching it for about sixty seconds. They had made measurements using their equipment and a stopwatch but took no photographs. Air Force investigators labeled the sighting as "unidentified."

Clete Roberts, a radio reporter for a Los Angeles station, reported on the flying disk sightings near Arrey, New Mexico, and was interviewed by the AFOSI. Roberts was the man who reported that photographs had been taken. When he asked a naval officer about the pictures, he was told, "They didn't turn out."

Interestingly, as the AFOSI tried to find the source of the leak about the flying saucer sightings at White Sands, C. B. Moore's (misidentified as C. D. Moore) name was mentioned. The result of the investigation was that none of the reporters had talked to him. The leak, then, came not from the civilians working at the base, but from high-ranking naval officers who made offhand remarks in the presence of reporters. The reporters, always looking for a good story, had followed up on those remarks, publishing or broadcasting the results of their investigation.

In the Project Blue Book files, there is no real record of those other sightings. There is only the mention of them in the newspaper articles, and the investigation into who leaked what. The index from Project Blue Book for "20–30 April [1949]" sightings lists only the Arrey, New Mexico, report from Professor Moore.

Moore, William L. (1943–) Bill Moore has been a high school French and English teacher, a playwright, and an investigator of unexplained phenomena. He has published two books, *The Roswell Incident* and *The Philadelphia Experiment*. In the 1980s, he emerged as one of the most controversial figures in the UFO field with his claims that he had been working with AFOSI and providing information about other UFO researchers to the Air Force.

In 1989, at the MUFON Symposium held in Las Vegas, Nevada, Moore, in a controversial speech, suggested that he had been working with AFOSI, providing them with information about research being conducted by civilian and private UFO organizations. In later communications with various UFO researchers, Moore confirmed that even as a member of the board of directors of the Aerial Phenomena Research Organization, he was supplying information to the Air Force.

Moore made two other statements relevant to understanding the Roswell case. According to Friedman, among others, Moore had suggested as early as 1982 that he wanted to create some kind of a Roswell document, thinking that it might open doors that were closed. And in the April 1991 issue of *Fate*, Moore said that the disclosures he and Jaime Shandera planned to make to the assembled reporters were with the express permission of the government agents with whom they worked. These disclosures would contain both good information and disinformation because that was how the government worked.

What Moore was saying was that he had been working with the government and that he was passing disinformation along to other researchers. The question becomes, then, was MJ-12 disinformation from those government sources, or was it something of Moore's own design?

Others had thought the same thing. Jacques Vallee, in *Revelations*, wrote: "Skeptics like Philip Klass went so far as to suggest that Bill Moore had manufactured the documents [MJ-12] and mailed them to his friend."

It wasn't the only time that such questions had been raised about Moore. Richard Hall of the Fund for UFO Research was able to shed some light on this aspect of the controversy. He reported in a letter dated April 3, 1983, "The AFOSI document [which mentioned MJ-12] is not authentic in the sense of not being an original; Moore has retyped it and done a cut and paste job, as he acknowledged in answer to my direct questioning when he attended our meeting three weeks ago."

Hall followed this with another letter, dated May 16, 1989, clarifying his meaning in the earlier letter. "The situation is described in the letter [of] Moore attending . . . [a meeting] of the Fund for UFO Research Executive Committee and acknowledging to those present (including Maccabee) that he retyped (rewrote is not quite accurate) the Aquarius document [which mentioned MJ-12] and pasted the various markings onto the retyped copy. My understanding is that he did so only because the original was not sharp enough to reproduce clearly. I don't condone his doing this without saying so, but I did not then nor do I now think he faked or fabricated anything."

Moore later denied that he had done any such thing. Responding to questions raised by T. Scott Crain Jr., Moore wrote, "I did not retype the document, nor do I know who did . . . I know the version I was handed was a retype, because I had seen the original earlier on. The reconstructed version which appears in *Focus* [a publication edited and published by Moore] is the combined product of both my and Rick Doty's memory."

Later, in July 1989, Moore suggested that the whole Aquarius Telex was the result of a disinformation campaign that might have been mounted to discredit the researcher who released it. But the important fact is that everyone agrees that the Aquarius Telex is a hoax.

But Moore's comments on MJ-12 and other aspects of the Roswell case were not completed. In the December 1, 1998, issue of *Saucer Smear*, a newsletter edited by Jim Mosely, Moore suggested the names of others who might have created the MJ-12 documents. He wrote: "If they are fabrications, I did not fabricate them, nor do I have any particular opinion about who might have—except as set forth herein."

Moore then went on, writing, "Assuming, FOR THE SAKE OF DISCUSSION, that the original MJ-12 documents are fabrications, and with respect to Dr. Posner's comment about whether Phil Klass should be considered as a possible suspect in the production thereof, I would like to say that I have never seriously considered such an intriguing possibility until now."

Moore seemed to be saying that he didn't accept the possibility, but was giving it lip service. He seemed to be rejecting the idea with the tone of his letter, but at the same time he was throwing the allegation out into the public arena.

Moore also outraged parts of the UFO community with a public statement made in 1998 about his new explanation for the Roswell case which, ironically, he helped bring to the forefront of UFO research. In the November 1, 1998, issue of *Saucer Smear*, Moore wrote: "As for Roswell, you wouldn't believe how many people got mad at me when I dared to opine that perhaps the extraterrestrial explanation might not be the best anymore. No one, however—not one of them—took note of the fact that: (a) it had always been my position from the very beginning that the UFO explanation was the best one based upon the evidence available to us at the time, and that (b) If new evidence ever came to hand which caused me to rethink my position, I would say so publicly—which is exactly what I did. To clarify further, I still think the ET explanation remains valid as one of several possible explanations and that it is still worthy of further investigation and consideration. It's just that, in light of the large body of new evidence now in hand, I no longer think it is necessarily the best of those several possible explanations."

Moore dropped out of sight in 1991, resurfacing only periodically to offer his opinions on the UFO situation. He suggested that those seeking the truth about UFOs "stay away from the circus. It will only take up your time and distract your attention . . . I've been assiduously following my own advice these past several years."

N-1M An early version of the Northrop flying wing. See *Flying Wing*

N-9M A twin-engineered, propeller-driven early version of the Northrop flying wing. It last flew in May 1946. See *Flying Wing*

Newton, Irving Warrant Officer Irving Newton, one of the weather officers attached to the Eighth Air Force, was sitting alone in his office when a colonel on General Ramey's staff called. Newton was ordered to report to the headquarters building, but Newton refused, explaining that he couldn't leave the office vacant. Ramey then called him, ordering Newton to "Get your ass over here now. Use a car and if you have to, take the first one with keys in it."

When Newton arrived, a colonel briefed him quickly in the hallway, away from the reporters waiting in General Ramey's office. Newton couldn't remember who it had been, but did say the message had been clear: "These officers from Roswell think they found a flying saucer, but the general thinks it's a weather balloon. He wants you to take a look at it."

Inside Ramey's office, Newton saw the balloon lying on the floor. According to Newton, there was no question about what he was seeing. It was a rawin radar target and a small pile of black material that was the remains of a neoprene balloon.

Five or six reporters were in the room, according to Newton. They were standing back out of the way, listening to what was happening in front of them. Ramey, a couple of colonels, and the major who was supposed to be the one who had flown up from Roswell were also there.

According to Newton, the reporters didn't ask questions, and Major Jesse Marcel, who had brought the material from Roswell, later told investigators that he was not allowed to speak with the reporters. But according to Newton, "The major kept pointing to portions of the balloon to ask if I thought it would be found on a regular balloon." Newton said he had the impression the major was trying to save face and not appear to be a fool who couldn't tell the difference between a normal balloon and something from outer space.

It is not clear if this major was Marcel or Major Charles Cashon, the Public Information Officer (PIO). Newton knew neither man. Cashon, as part of his job, might have been trying to sell the balloon explanation to the press. Marcel, as an officer trained in radar operations and the group air intelligence officer, should have been able to identify a balloon, even one as ripped up as the one in Ramey's office. In fact, forty years after the report, weathercasters at various television stations were able to identify the wreckage of the balloon from the photos taken in Ramey's office.

Newton, interviewed by newspapers in the hours that followed the announcement in Ramey's office, added few details. Newton said, "We use them because they go much higher than the eye can see."

Newton said that when rigged up, the instrument "looks like a six-pointed star, is silvery in appearance and rises in the air like a kite." He also said, "Some eighty weather stations in the U.S. were using that type of balloon and that it could have come from any of them."

He said he had sent up identical balloons during the invasion of Okinawa to determine ballistics information for heavy guns. Newton was saying that there was nothing special about the balloons and targets and that the military had been using them for years.

However, as the controversy about the Roswell crash continued to grow, he began to alter his story slightly. In February 1995, Newton suggested that the balloons and targets were not as common as he had suggested. According to him, "The rawin target and balloon in question was only used at limited locations, and to my knowledge, not at Ft. Worth, not even all weather personnel were familiar with them, but we used them at 'Tinker Field' (Okla City) during training for atomic tests, and at the tests, as well as on Okinawa, during World War II. So I had no doubt in identifying it. I have no idea where one might be found today, if at all."

See also *Johnson, J. Bond; Marcel, Jesse;* **Roswell Daily Record;** *Project Mogul*

The *Penthouse* Alien Photograph Bob Guccione, publisher of *Penthouse,* claimed that he found, maybe bought, photographs that came from the real alien autopsy film, and not the fake attributed to Ray Santilli. According to *Penthouse's* Guccione, "three extraordinary images published here may well be the most important pictures in the history of photography."

To make the event seem even more important, Guccione speculated that had the government or military known about the pictures, they would have prevented their publication. The whole thing, Guccione speculates, would have been classified as top secret. The pictures would never have seen the light of day.

Keith Farrell of *Penthouse* continued in that vein, writing in the September 1996 issue: "As editor of *Omni* for the past six years I had the opportunity to work with Guccione on the development of Project Open Book, *Omni's* attempt to, simply, open the books on the government's investigation of extraterrestrial visitors to our planet. We sought to treat the subject seriously and scientifically, to deal with issues and incidents in the matter that was, above all, rational, that addressed the questions of U.F.O. believers and U.F.O. skeptics."

As Farrell praised himself and the efforts of the now-defunct *Omni,* he also noted that "your favorite magazine doesn't give up." Farrell speculated that the photographs "came into Bob's possession precisely because he doesn't get scared, and won't back off when his convictions are aroused."

According to the story, as published in *Penthouse*, the photographs had been received from a woman who claimed her father was a German scientist working in New Mexico in 1947. He had been part of the team that was assembled to exploit and investigate the crash at Roswell, but had in the past worked on the "infamous Philadelphia Experiment." She had been entrusted with a small segment of the film that her father had somehow secured. She was told never to reveal what was on it, or even its existence, to anyone.

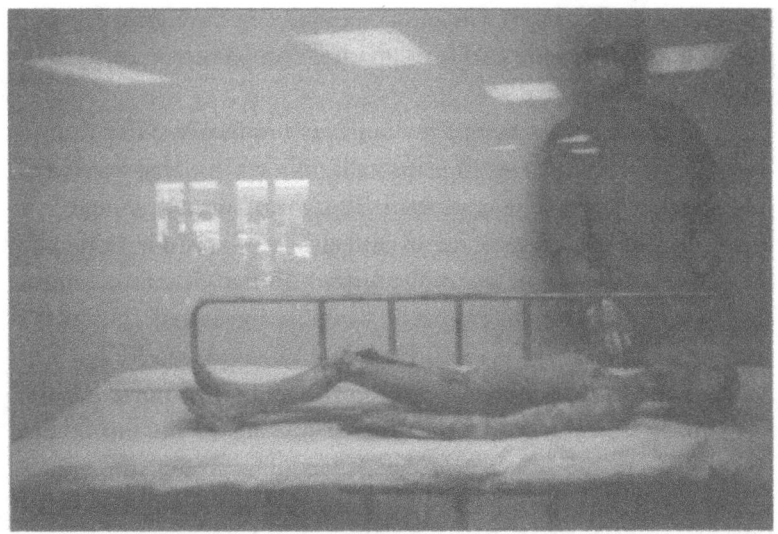

Alien from the Showtime movie *Roswell,* which appeared in *Penthouse* as the real thing. (*Photo courtesy of Paul Davids*)

Of course, the unidentified woman was told by her father that she would know the right time to reveal the existence of the film. So her father, after telling her that the possession of the film could threaten her life and that she must not reveal its existence, also told her to publicize the film when the time was right. Guccione and Farrell have no trouble accepting this contradictory information.

Guccione was quoted in a wire service story as saying "I am absolutely 100 percent convinced" of their authenticity. In late 1996, he appeared on cable television's CNBC to show the magazine and the pictures, telling the audience there was no doubt that he had the real thing. Guccione is a hero who found the photographs that every UFO researcher had wanted to find, and he was publishing them to end the government secrecy.

In fact, to demonstrate the credibility of the photographs, Guccione noted that *Omni* had a team of highly qualified experts who had been studying UFOs. Guccione implied that they had inspected the pictures and that all were impressed with them. According to *Penthouse,* "It is that unique combination of heart, mind, and irrepressible curiosity that led Bob Guccione to publish this image . . ."

The photographs themselves look very impressive. They show a badly injured being about four feet tall, thin, with a large head and, it seems, large eyes. The creature is clearly not human, though it is humanoid. If the pictures are as authentic as Guccione claims, he has broken the story of the millennium. All that Guccione said in the hype to promote the magazine would be vindicated, but only if the photographs are of the real thing.

But anyone who has seen the Showtime original movie *Roswell* has already seen this particular alien. It was one of the four or five special effects models created by Steve Johnson for the movie. Guccione, during the CNBC program, was asked about that possibility, but said that he believed the filmmakers had access to some of the same pictures that he was now publishing. They modeled their special effects creation after the real thing. He implied that the models were so accurate because, through other sources, the model makers had seen the same photographs.

Paul Davids, the executive producer of the film, has said repeatedly that he is 100 percent sure the photographs are of one of the special effects models. Asked if they could have used the real thing as a model, he said, "Absolutely not."

In fact, this is not the first time these pictures have surfaced with claims of authenticity. In June 1995, the Internet had pictures that someone posted suggesting they were of the Roswell aliens. Clearly these pictures were of the movie's alien. And in Japan in 1995, these same pictures, or very similar ones, were circulated with the same claims. The story coming from Japan even included the tales of the German scientist who had somehow gotten his hands on a few frames from an autopsy of the dead alien.

On August 8, 1996, Kevin Randle had an opportunity to speak with Guccione during a live radio debate about the authenticity of the pictures. Of course, Guccione insisted that the pictures showed the real thing. He insisted that he had paid nothing for them, but believed in their authenticity. He also said that he had seen the movie *Roswell* and that he didn't believe the creatures in the film looked anything like the alien in his photographs. The neck, according to him, was much longer on the aliens in the movie.

Of course, he was speaking of the model that had been created to give the impression of a living being. When the special effects bellows and air ducts and tubes and wires were removed, the creature, in its inanimate state, looked remarkably like the one in the photographs. Of course, it isn't the *same* one, and that might be what confused Guccione.

Other members of Steve Johnson's special effects team that created the models examined the pictures and said they were of one of their models. Johnson, when shown a fax of the color photographs from the magazine, said something to the effect that the alien didn't look like his creation. This apparent discrepancy was a problem borne of color photographs that had been photocopied into black and white and then faxed. The process darkened them to the point where they were nearly black.

Don Ecker of *UFO* magazine was able to take the story farther. According to him, he spoke to the man who delivered the pictures to Guccione. He had received them from a woman who had found them on sale at a UFO convention in Mesa, Arizona. According to

Ecker, he had the documentation to prove that the man and the woman both existed. The story of the German scientist was apparently the same that had circulated in Japan in the summer of 1995. It is certainly a better story than some woman buying authentic photographs of dead aliens at a UFO convention.

Guccione has been fooled by someone who has misrepresented the pictures, convincing the magazine publisher that they show the real thing. From the pictures that Guccione published, it is clear that they were taken in the International UFO Museum and Research Center in Roswell, in the small display they have set up using one of the movie's models. It is clear from the injuries on the head that this is the model that has been photographed. There is no doubt about the identity of these pictures.

Pflock, Karl (1943–) According to Pflock himself, he is the author of numerous works of fiction and nonfiction. He has ghostwritten nonfiction books and has been a consulting senior acquisitions and book editor for Arlington House Publishers, editor of *Libertarian Review,* a senior editor at the American Enterprise Institute, contributing editor to *Reason,* and science columnist for *Eternity Science Fiction.*

Pflock's interest in UFOs is virtually lifelong, and his "years of investigation have left no doubt in his mind UFOs are real and some almost certainly are vehicles from another planet." He was at one time the chairman of the Nation Capital Area Subcommittee of the National Investigations Committee on Aerial Phenomena (NICAP). When NICAP disintegrated, Pflock independently continued his investigations into various aspects of the UFO phenomenon, including occupant sightings, cattle mutilations, and claims of alien contact.

Pflock has an extensive background in government service. He was a senior staff member with then Congressman Jack Kemp from 1981 to 1983. He was also a Deputy Assistant Secretary of Defense (Deputy Director) for Operational Test and Evaluation from 1985 to 1989. He guided the development and implementation of

Department of Defense policy governing weapons systems and equipment testing. He also managed congressional, media, and public affairs for the Operational and Test Evaluation Office and was awarded the Defense Outstanding Public Service Medal and the Defense Superior Achievement Award.

Prior to that, he attended San Jose State University and was graduated cum laude in philosophy and political science. He served in the reserve components of the Marine Corps and Air Force from 1960 to 1966 and with the Central Intelligence Agency from 1966 to 1972.

Karl T. Pflock. (*Photo courtesy of Gildas Bourdais*)

In 1992, Pflock "returned to full-time writing and independent research after 11 years of public service." He investigated the Roswell UFO crash with a grant from the Fund for UFO Research and wrote *Roswell in Perspective,* which was published by the Fund. With Jim Moseley of *Saucer Smear* he co-authored *Shockingly Close to the Truth!* published by Galde Press, about the early years and first researchers in the UFO field.

Like so many of the UFO researchers, Pflock's background is not without controversy. In the early 1980s Daniel Kagan and Ian Summers began an objective investigation into the cattle mutilations that seemed to be plaguing the country which was eventually published in their book, *Mute Evidence.* In Colorado Springs they were introduced to Pflock and told his name was Kurt Peters. "That's Kurt with a K."

Pflock provided an explanation for this harmless deception in a 1993 article in *UFO* magazine. He wrote that he had moved from Washington, D.C., to Colorado Springs because he had realized that a writer could live anywhere. Now all he had to do was find a project that would be both interesting and would make a little money on the side. He had learned that George Erianne, a private detective, claimed to have uncovered an explanation for the cattle mutilations that involved a "gang of rogue germ warfare researchers."

The idea sounded good to Pflock because Erianne needed a writer and Pflock needed a project. Pflock wrote a proposal and sent it off to New York. Not long after that, he learned that Kagan and Summers were coming to Colorado Springs to interview Erianne for a book on cattle mutilations they were writing. According to Pflock, "Rivals! . . . I suggested it might be useful for me to be at the meeting. However, there was a chance Kagan and Summers might recognize me by name as a writer and put two and two together. Erianne suggested I use a pseudonym and say I was a researcher who sometimes helped him on his cases. Thus was the misbegotten 'Kurt Peters' born."

When Kagan and Summers learned the truth, they confirmed it with Pflock. Erianne, however, provided a slightly different take, according to Kagan and Summers. He said that he barely knew Pflock and that Pflock had been following him around for about a year trying to learn more about the mutilations. Whatever the real story, Pflock admitted that Peters had been a mistake.

Pflock returned to Washington, D.C., from Colorado Springs, and in the mid-1990s Pflock moved from Washington, D.C., to New Mexico. He began his investigation into the Roswell UFO crash, finally convincing himself that it was the result of hysteria and a balloon array from Project Mogul. He continues to investigate significant UFO sightings, lecture on the topic, and write articles for various magazines.

Press Release On July 8, 1947, the 509th Bomb Group created a worldwide sensation when they announced they had captured a flying saucer. Walter Haut, the Public Information Officer, wrote the following press release:

> The many rumors regarding the flying disc became a reality yesterday when the intelligence office of the 509th Bomb Group of the Eighth Air Force, Roswell Army Air Field, was fortunate enough to gain possession of a disc through the co-operation of one of the local ranchers and the Sheriff's office of Chaves County.
>
> The flying object landed on a ranch near Roswell sometime last week. Not having phone facilities, the rancher stored the disc until such time as he was able to contact the Sheriff's office, who in turn notified Major Jesse A. Marcel, of the 509th Bomb Group Intelligence office.
>
> Action was immediately taken and the disc was picked up at the rancher's home. It was inspected at the Roswell Army Air Field and subsequently loaned by Major Marcel to higher headquarters.

Project Mogul After forty-seven years of claiming that the artifacts found at Roswell, New Mexico, were nothing more spectacular than the remains of a neoprene weather balloon with a radar reflector, the United States Air Force finally identified the material. It was a . . . weather balloon. Not an ordinary weather balloon, but a special cluster of balloons and array train assigned to the then top secret Project Mogul. In a twenty-three-page report issued on September 8, 1994, the Air Force laid out the evidence for its conclusion.

At the beginning of their research, Air Force investigators decided that they were not going to attempt to interview all the various witnesses who have been identified by UFO researchers. Given the numbers, this isn't surprising. What is disturbing, however, is that they only interviewed five people: three retired military officers, and two civilians who were involved with Project Mogul.

One of the most important of those retired officers is Lieutenant Colonel Sheridan Cavitt. According to Jesse A. Marcel Sr., Cavitt accompanied him out to the debris field reported by W. W. "Mack" Brazel.

Kevin Randle and Don Schmitt first interviewed him in January 1990 while Cavitt wintered in Sierra Vista, Arizona. During that visit he told them that he had not been in Roswell in July 1947 and that he had not participated in any recoveries of a flying saucer, V-2 rocket, or any type of balloon.

In March 1993, Schmitt and Randle visited Cavitt at his home in Washington State. During that interview he displayed copies of his orders from 1947. According to Special Order No. 121, dated 11 June 1947, Cavitt was assigned to the counterintelligence office at Roswell and he had five days to report, meaning he had to be at

Sheridan Cavitt (*left*) and Jim Ragsdale (*right*). (*Photos courtesy of Kevin Randle*)

the base by June 16. Once he arrived, he claimed that he was given a leave, so while he had been assigned to Roswell, he was not physically present in early July 1947. Because of that, Cavitt said that he was not involved in any of the events now known as the Roswell Incident.

Interviewed again in June 1994, he mentioned that earlier he had been visited by a Pentagon colonel, Richard Weaver, but he wasn't any more candid about the events in Roswell. In fact, when asked why both Marcel and Lewis Rickett, the former master sergeant who had served under Cavitt, had identified him as the officer at Roswell, Cavitt said that he didn't know. Although he had told Weaver he was there, had recovered a balloon, and had, in fact, taken Rickett out to one of the sites, Cavitt still insisted that he had no role in those events.

Now, according to the Air Force report and the supporting documentation, including a transcript of Weaver's interview with Cavitt, things were not as he had suggested. Cavitt said to Weaver, "So, I went out and I do not recall whether Marcel went with Rickett and me, I had Rickett with me. We went out to this site. There were no, as I understand, check points or anything like that (going through guards and that sort of garbage); we went out there and we found it. It was a small amount of, as I recall, bamboo sticks, reflective sort of material that would, well at first glance, you would probably think it was aluminum foil, something of that type. And we gathered up some of it. I don't know whether we even tried to get all of it. It wasn't scattered, well, what I call, you know, extensively. Like, it didn't go along the ground and splatter off some here and some there. We gathered some of it and took it back to the base and I remember I had turned it over to Marcel. As I say, I do not remember whether Marcel was there or not on the site. He could have been. We took it back to the intelligence room . . . in the CIC office."

Cavitt told Weaver that he recognized the debris as the remains of a balloon immediately. He didn't explain why he had not bothered to communicate this rather vital piece of intelligence to Marcel, nor did Weaver ask him. Instead Cavitt kept this secret, so Marcel apparently misidentified the debris as extraterrestrial and Colonel (later General) William Blanchard ordered the announcement that the Army had recovered one of the flying saucers.

Although Cavitt identified Rickett as the man he had taken to the site, the Air Force investigators never tried to learn what Rickett had had to say. Rickett died before the Air Force officers began their investigation, but he left both an audio- and videotaped record of what he had seen and done.

Rickett provided testimony refuting some of Cavitt's claims, which might be the reason Weaver and others didn't attempt to learn what he had to say. During a recorded interview conducted on October 29, 1989, Don Schmitt asked, "The roads were blocked?" Rickett said, "Yeah, they had . . . on the road we drove on . . . MPs standing there."

Rickett also described material that he had seen. He said that he didn't think it was metal but that "it was damn hard." Describing it, he said, "It wasn't bright and shiny on one side like foil is but it wouldn't wrinkle." Clearly Rickett is discussing something tougher than the foil that would have been used on the radar targets attached to the Project Mogul balloons. Had Air Force investigators asked, copies of both the audio- and videotapes of the Rickett interviews could have been provided for them—but they never asked.

In the course of his interview with Cavitt, Weaver asked if he had been sworn to secrecy. Weaver writes, "Lt. Col. Cavitt also stated that he had never taken any oath or signed any agreement not to talk about this incident and had never been threatened by anyone in the government because of it."

In July 1947, Major Edwin Easley was the Provost Marshal at Roswell. On January 11, 1990, he was interviewed. I told him who I was and verified that he was the Provost Marshal at the base in July 1947. When he confirmed it, I asked if he was familiar with the story of the flying saucer crash. He said, "I've heard about it."

When asked, "Do you have any firsthand knowledge of it?" Easley said, "I can't talk about it." When asked again, Easley repeated, "I can't talk about it."

When finally asked, "Can you tell me if you were at the crash site?" Easley repeated, "I can't talk about it. I told you that . . . I've been sworn to secrecy. I can't tell you that."

Weaver, in his report, mentioned that he had reviewed *The Roswell Events*, created by Fred Whiting of the Fund for UFO Research. Included in it is a complete transcript of that interview with Easley, but Weaver never mentioned it. He didn't ask for a copy of the tape, available from the Fund, nor did he ask the original investigator for one. Instead he writes that Cavitt had not been sworn to secrecy, suggesting that no one had been. Easley's taped statements suggest that military officers were, in fact, sworn to secrecy about these events.

Not only did government officials attempt to keep military officers from talking, they also shut down radio reports. George "Jud" Roberts was the minority owner of radio station KGFL in 1947. Majority owner Walt Whitmore Sr. had interviewed Mack Brazel and planned to broadcast that report. Instead, according to Roberts, representatives of the FCC and New Mexico's congressional delegation called the station, ordering them not to broadcast the Brazel interview. If they did, Roberts reports he was told, they would lose their license the next day. There was no talk of hearings, just a threat to prevent the broadcast of the Brazel interview. Roberts has been interviewed on both audio- and videotape, and had Weaver asked, we certainly could have put him in contact with Roberts.

What this demonstrates is that there is a body of firsthand testimony suggesting that both military officers and civilians were sworn to secrecy and that the material recovered was not consistent with that from a Project Mogul balloon array. Weaver had access to all this data but refused to review it. While it is understandable that Weaver didn't want to interview everyone various UFO investigators had, it would seem that he would be interested in what retired high-ranking Air Force officers would have to say. He wouldn't have to rely on the interpretations of those interviews as filtered through the investigators, but could review them on both audio- and video-tape. Certainly this would not be as satisfactory as meeting the witnesses in person, but a way of determining if, as Weaver suggested, those statements had been twisted, misrepresented, or taken out of context. There is no indication that Weaver made any attempt to review this material. He rejected it out of hand because it would show the weakness of the Project Mogul explanation.

In examining the evidence for Project Mogul, it becomes clear that the case is not nearly as strong as the Air Force believed. The links to Mogul are very weak, and the Air Force investigators were unable to discover any documents that would prove their point. In the end, it is speculation based on a limited review of the evidence available.

For the Project Mogul explanation to work, it must be believed that Major Jesse Marcel was unable to identify a common type of balloon and the rawin target. It must be accepted that Cavitt did recognize the balloon but said nothing to either Marcel or Blanchard or anyone else at the Roswell base. The Air Force theory that there was something special about the Mogul balloon arrays that would have prevented easy identification by some, but obvious identification by others, including Mack Brazel's daughter, Bessie, would have to be accepted.

There are two important facts that impact on these assumptions. One is that Marcel, as the intelligence officer, was involved in Operation Crossroads, the atomic tests held at Bikini in 1946. According to Irving Newton, rawin targets were used in atomic testing. Marcel was involved in this atomic test and, because he was the intelligence officer, might have had an opportunity to see that particular equipment.

But more important is a discovery made near Circleville, Ohio, at the beginning of July 1947. Sherman Campbell, a farmer, found a balloon and rawin target on his farm. He recognized what it was immediately, but believed that because of the shiny foil, it might account for some of the flying disk reports. He took it to the sheriff, who recognized it immediately for what it was. Campbell then took it to the local newspaper office, where it was displayed for several weeks. The newspaper actually received another rawin found by another farmer who also recognized it for what it was. This demonstrates that those unfamiliar with the balloons and rawins were able to identify them as mundane rather than leaping to the conclusion that they were extraterrestrial.

Weaver then used several of the affidavits published in Whiting's report to reinforce his theory, but never uses all the information available. While the Project Mogul material resembles, in a gross sense, that found by Mack Brazel, it is not an exact match. This is demonstrated by a number of statements made by those who saw and handled the debris.

When Jesse Marcel Sr. was shown two of the photographs of the alleged debris taken of him in Brigadier General Roger Ramey's office, he said to Johnny Mann, a reporter at TV station WWL in New Orleans, "That's not the stuff I found." He recognized it as a balloon immediately from the photographs. Why, then, couldn't he recognize that same material on the Brazel ranch if that was, in fact, what he had seen in 1947?

Marcel told reporters in various interviews, "I was amazed by what I saw . . . It wasn't anything I was acquainted with . . . I could not identify [it], even tried to burn it . . . [It] looked like balsa wood but [there was] no scorch an any material we found . . . Looked like balsa wood but certainly wasn't."

Jesse Marcel Jr., when he saw the pictures taken in General Ramey's office, said that it did, in fact, resemble what he had seen, in a very gross sense. The pictures were of foil and sticks, but were not of the debris he'd seen in 1947. He described many of the strange properties others had noticed. He also said that the symbols he saw on one of the small I-beams were purple, not pinkish, and that they were about three-eighths of an inch high. Professor C. B.

Moore, a project engineer on Mogul, said the symbols on the tape used to reinforce the balsa sticks of part of the Mogul array were pink and as much as three inches high. Again, a very gross resemblance, but not an exact match.

Sallye Tadolini is quoted by Weaver. He wrote that in her affidavit dated September 27, 1993, and supplied to the FUND, she said, "What Bill [Brazel] showed us was a piece of what I still think of as fabric. It was something like aluminum foil, something like satin, something like well-tanned leather in its toughness, yet was not precisely like any one of those materials . . . It was about the thickness of very fine kidskin glove leather and a dull metallic grayish silver, one side slightly darker than the other. I do not remember it having any design or embossing on it . . ."

Weaver didn't bother with the next paragraph in the affidavit because it would create too many questions. Tadolini had continued: "Bill passed it around, and we all felt of it. I did a lot of sewing, so the feel made a great impression on me. It felt like no fabric I have touched before or since. It was very silky or satiny, with the same texture on both sides. Yet when I crumpled it in my hands, the feel was like that you notice when you crumble a leather glove in your hand. When it was released, it sprang back into its original shape, quickly flattening out with no wrinkles . . . "

Bill Brazel had found some material on the debris field. When he showed it to his father, Mack said that it looked like "part of that contraption I found." Bill said, "The only reason I noticed the tin foil . . . [I] took it out [of my pocket] and put it in the box and I noticed that when I put the piece of foil in that box . . . the damned thing just started unfolding. Just flattened out."

What all this demonstrates is that the situation in New Mexico in 1947 isn't as Weaver and the other Air Force investigators believed. There were military officers sworn to secrecy, as demonstrated by Major Easley's audiotaped statements, and there was suppression of the news media, as demonstrated by Jud Roberts's taped statements. Clearly the debris recovered at the Brazel ranch site was not the remains of a neoprene balloon and rawin target device. All this opens the door for questions, but it doesn't completely elimi-nate Project Mogul as the culprit in the events. It seems to suggest that something other than a Project Mogul balloon array was recov-ered on the Brazel ranch, and there is additional information that underscores that fact, Air Force opinion to the contrary.

First, it must be remembered that the Air Force claimed that Launch No. 4, made on June 4, 1947, is responsible for the debris. They imply in their report that these balloons were something special. In fact, polyethylene, a material that was developed for constant level balloons, might have fooled some of the less sophis-ticated witnesses because of its very nature, but the descriptions provided by the eyewitnesses suggests it was not polyethylene. However, the records show that the first of the polyethylene balloons were not launched until July 3, 1947, and therefore couldn't have been responsible for the material found on the Brazel ranch.

Balloon Launch No. 4, according to the diary kept by Dr. Albert Crary, Project Mogul leader, was made of a cluster of regular meteorological balloons made of neoprene. It did contain a "sonobuoy" or microphone, but no "official" record was kept because no data of scientific importance were recovered. Charles Moore said that he believed they had lost track of Launch No. 4 near Arabela, New Mexico, which is twenty or thirty miles south of the Brazel ranch site. Unfortunately, there is no documentation to support this claim.

The other important point, though the Air Force doesn't make it clear, is that there was nothing special about the balloons in Launch No. 4. There was nothing on it that would fool anyone. They were standard balloons, about fifteen feet in diameter, and made of neoprene. Neoprene, after exposure to sunlight, would turn from tan to black, but the color wouldn't be uniform. The portions directly exposed to sunlight would blacken faster than those in shadow. The point is that the rubber reacted to the heat

and light from the sun. Attempts to cut it or burn it would have
been successful. And surely someone, if not Marcel himself, would
have recognized the material as having come from a neoprene
weather balloon.

But what is important here is that the only documented record
for Flight No. 4 mentions exactly what it was, and there were no
rawin targets on it to create the metallic debris. Dr. Crary's diary
suggests that the first flight containing an entire array wasn't made
until the next day, June 5, and that debris was recovered east of
Roswell.

The Air Force maintains that the balloon lay in the field for
more than a month. The *Roswell Daily Record,* on July 9, suggests
that Brazel found the balloon first on June 14, ten days after the
launch, but left it there for another three weeks. What the Air Force
failed to mention is that in another article published on the same
day, in the same newspaper, it was suggested that "The weather balloon was found several days ago near the center of New Mexico by
Rancher W. W. Brazel."

A second problem here is that Bessie Brazel Schrieber reported
that she, with her father, collected all the debris, stuffing it into four
burlap bags. If that is true, then there was nothing for Marcel or
Cavitt to see later. Marcel told reporters, "We picked up what we
could but most of it was left behind." There certainly was more
material than would be accounted for by a Mogul balloon and array
train.

The Air Force also implied that the reason there was a cover-up
was to protect Project Mogul. While the project itself was highly
classified, the balloons, rawin targets, and other equipment were
not classified. There was little of intelligence value to be recovered
by Soviet agents if they knew that balloons were being launched
from the Alamogordo Army Air Field.

In fact, there was so little of importance attached to the balloons that a story about them was published in the *Alamogordo
News.* If Soviet agents were interested in Mogul and balloon

launches, that article provided more than enough clues for them. There are photos of the balloon clusters, but more important, Watson Laboratories and some of the men involved in those launches were mentioned.

Had what Brazel found been nothing more than an experimental balloon, there would have been no reason for the elaborate events that took place around it. Brazel would have recognized it and disposed of it without having to consult the local sheriff or the military at the Roswell base.

If it was only a balloon, as Sheridan Cavitt now claims, why didn't he mention it to anyone, saving the 509th from the embarrassment of announcing they had a flying saucer, only to have that statement challenged by the officers at the Eighth Air Force?

There is one other piece of evidence. Brigadier General Arthur Exon reported that in 1947 he had the opportunity to fly over the impact site and debris field. He said, "It was probably part of the same accident but there were two distinct sites. One, assuming that the thing, as I understand it, as I remember flying the area later, that the damage to the vehicle seemed to be coming from the southeast to the northwest but it could have been going in the opposite direction, but it doesn't seem likely. So the farther northwest pieces found on the ranch, those were mostly metal."

His testimony corroborates two sites and the orientation of those sites, and effectively eliminates Project Mogul. There was no way for Project Mogul to create two distinct sites that are part of a single event. Nor was there any way for Project Mogul to create the gouges mentioned by General Exon in other conversations. Weaver ignored Exon's testimony because of the damage it does to the Project Mogul theory.

In fact, the GAO, in their review of the situation for Congressman Steven Schiff, examined the Air Force position and found it inadequate. The GAO report said, "The Air Force report concluded that there was no dispute that something happened near Roswell in July 1947 and that all available official materials indicated the most likely source of the wreckage recovered was one of the project MOGUL balloon trains."

It must be noted that the GAO did not endorse the conclusion, merely reported on it. In other circumstances, when GAO investigations have corroborated information, they have commented on it positively. In this case, there were no such positive comments.

Ragsdale, James On January 26, 1993, Jim Ragsdale told UFO researchers for the first time, in some detail, how he had witnessed the crash of an alien spacecraft in July 1947, how he had watched the military begin the recovery operation, and how he, with a female companion, originally identified as Trudy Truelove, had picked up pieces of the strange metallic debris.

Don Schmitt had arranged to meet with Ragsdale and his wife at their home to discuss the story, and he recorded the interview on audiotape. Schmitt sat down with Ragsdale, who at the time was on oxygen due to his poor health. Schmitt had brought maps and photographs, hoping that Ragsdale would be able to locate the crash site and confirm some of the information that had been developed over the previous several months.

After an inquiry about Ragsdale's health, and after Ragsdale had said, "Let me see what you've got there," Schmitt asked him, "Do you remember the name of the ranch it [the crashed saucer] was on?"

Ragsdale said, "It was on . . . [the] Fisher . . ."

"Was it north of here?"

"Yes . . ." He then, with no prompting, changed the name of the ranch, saying, "It was Foster."

Schmitt had been to the impact site north of town during the trip, so he had photographs of it. Trying to make sure that Ragsdale was describing the same place, Schmitt showed Ragsdale pictures of the terrain. Looking at the photographs of the site north of Roswell, Ragsdale said, "That right there looks like the place right there."

Schmitt asked him the names of some of the ranchers and he said, "It seemed to me that place belonged to them. Either Foster or Fisher, but it sold to somebody else . . . somebody else bought the ranch after that. See, I was living in Carlsbad working the old field down there . . . worked in the old field down there. And then this girl was out there messing around with another man's wife. That how come they out in that area. And we was out there. And she's dead, the guys I shows the stuff to is all dead."

After discussing the book *UFO Crash at Roswell,* for a moment, Schmitt came back to the pictures and, showing Ragsdale the one he had picked, asked, "Do you think this looks like . . ."

Ragsdale interrupted, saying, "That looks more like it . . ."

Schmitt wanted to pin down the site, but Ragsdale just said, "We were camped out there . . . I am sure that lightning did hit him. All that weren't there. It was only about I would say high above it. Just high up above. Hell, when it came down you couldn't really tell what it was . . . what you could still see, where it hit. I think it was two spaceships flying together and one of them came down and the other one picked up what they could and got out of there."

Ragsdale then said, "But what I figure, I figure there's two spaceships and when one came down they just picked up what they could and just left the rest of them. But it was either dummies or bodies or something there. They looked like bodies. They weren't very long . . . over four or five foot long at most. We didn't see their faces or nothing like that there, but we had just got to the site and we heard the Army, the sirens and stuff all coming and we got into the damn jeep and taking off. We had to hold a fence up and go up under the damn fence onto another ranch to come out from there."

Schmitt asked, "How far would you say this is from outside of town here?"

Ragsdale replied, "Oh hell, what? Forty miles . . . It's a good thirty to forty miles."

"A good forty miles? In a northwesterly direction?"

Ragsdale, looking at the pictures, said, "Right back up here."

Still looking at the pictures, Vennie Ragsdale, Ragsdale's wife at the time, mentioned the house that was a very few miles from the impact site. Schmitt said that it was on the McKnight/Corn property line and Ragsdale said, "Yeah. I know where all that is." His wife said that she recognized the house.

Looking at more of the photographs, Ragsdale said, "There's a picture right here that looks like about where a tree . . . here's mountains and stuff here."

Then, using the map and the photographs, they discussed direction from various locations, but on audiotape, it is impossible to determine which direction was which. The discussion was "In what direction were you coming from . . . ," with Ragsdale saying, "Up this way," and Schmitt asking, "Going in this direction?" and Ragsdale saying, "In this direction right here."

Schmitt finally asked him, "The object, the craft, what was left of it. In these photos, where was the object?"

"It was laying right along back here. Right along in here. It looked about half round because around the edges, I have got a piece outside; that's what they stole when they got the car. I got two great big pieces and we had some in a box here and some other stuff, and you could take that stuff and wad it up and it would straighten itself out. I never seen anything like it. Looked something like between a plastic, it looked like carbon paper, it's what it looked . . . that's right."

Ragsdale and his female companion returned to the impact site the next morning. They heard the military arriving on the scene. He said, "Oh . . . it must have been . . . it was two or three six by six Army trucks, a wrecker and everything . . . and leading the pack was a '47 Ford car with guys in it . . . MPs and stuff . . ."

Schmitt said, "So you watched for a while."

"Yeah. Sure did . . . They cleaned everything all up. I mean cleaned it. They raked the ground and everything . . . I would say it was six or eight big trucks besides the pickup, weapons carriers and stuff like that."

Later, in the interview, Ragsdale said that he had tried to return to the site, but the place was guarded. He said, "Me and another fellow went out there and you couldn't get . . . they had the roads sealed off."

Ragsdale also described how he had shown debris to friends but unfortunately, everyone who could have corroborated the story was dead. The debris that he had taken from the site, the metal with the strange properties, had been stolen during a break-in sometime in the early 1950s. Ragsdale said that the thief knew exactly what he wanted and broke into the room where it had been hidden.

As one listens to the tape and reading the transcript, there is a feeling of conspiracy about it. The traffic accident near Clovis, New Mexico, in which Ragsdale was so badly injured might not have been an accident but an assassination attempt. Other family members and friends seemed to die under mysterious circumstances. There were break-ins and chases and feelings of spies everywhere.

The interview was hard to follow because it seemed to be all over the map. A direct question about some aspect of the UFO crash was twisted until the talk was of something else. Ragsdale and his wife seemed to have their own agenda and attempted to direct the flow of the conversation. Only occasionally was it brought back to the UFO crash.

On April 24, 1993, Randle, who had spoken to Ragsdale briefly in November 1992, spoke to Ragsdale again because there were some points that needed to be clarified. For example, if he had witnessed the crash of what Ragsdale thought, at first, was some kind of government experimental craft, why hadn't he reported it to the sheriff or the military that night? Lives could be at stake.

Ragsdale said he had been drinking that night, and that he was out in the desert with another man's wife. Neither of them were supposed to be where they were. Besides, they couldn't see much that night. The flashlight he had, according to him, had weak batteries. It wasn't until daylight that he had enough light to see the craft and the bodies. It wasn't until daylight that he knew something had actually been wrecked.

There were, according to Ragsdale, "Small people there. Three or four bodies."

He also said his companion was Trudy Truelove. According to him, she was killed in a car accident about a month after the event. Ragsdale, however, was mistaken about the name. Trudy Truelove was not killed in a car accident, and was not involved, according to her. Truelove said that it all happened to her sister.

Dr. Mark Rodeghier, scientific director of the J. Allen Hynek Center for UFO Studies in Chicago, Illinois, in June 1993 had the opportunity to interview one of Ragsdale's sons. The story, as related by him, was essentially the same as that originally told by his father.

Again in July 1993, Schmitt and Randle met with Ragsdale with the hope of a videotaped interview. Ragsdale didn't want to sit down for it, but did discuss the case again. He reinforced what he had said in the first and third interviews with Randle, and what he told Schmitt during the second, audiotaped interview. He added few new details and reinforced some of those that he had given earlier.

In September 1994, the Ragsdale story took a new turn. Max Littell of the International UFO Museum and Research Center in Roswell had been keeping in close contact with Ragsdale since he was introduced to the Ragsdale family by Schmitt. Now the tale told by Ragsdale was beginning to shift significantly. In a letter to Ragsdale dated September 10, 1994, Littell wrote:

> This letter constitutes a letter of understanding as relates to the International UFO Museum and Research Center and the information prepared by the Museum staff after a series of interviews that have occured [sic]

during the past few weeks. You have verified the total information being put into print as being totally yours, and not from any secondary source.

From this date, any net proceeds realized by the Museum will be divided with you, for your lifetime, on the basis of 25% of any gross amount to Jim Ragsdale, and 75% to the Museum.

In exchange the Museum will own the rights to do this on a permanent basis and any designation of the impact site, and all material relating thereto will be designated as "The Jim Ragsdale" incident [with incident crossed out] and site. As evidence of good faith of the Museum an initial check is attached hereto as an advance against proceeds.

Along with that was another document that told Ragsdale's story. But now it had changed radically. According to it, the object passed through the trees to impact less than a hundred yards from where his truck had been parked. Ragsdale and his friend took flashlights and walked over, spending "considerable time looking around."

Now, rather than seeing bodies or dummies in the distance, Ragsdale was close enough to touch them. They were dressed in silver uniforms and wore tight helmets. Ragsdale now claimed that he tried to remove one of the helmets but couldn't. The eyes, according to Ragsdale, were large and oval and didn't resemble anything human. Later still he would suggest that the skin of the dead alien beings was gray.

The craft, according to Ragsdale, was about twenty feet in diameter, and had a dome in the middle. The description given here is not consistent with those provided by other firsthand civilian and military witnesses, including Curry Holden and former radio newsman Johnny McBoyle.

In this interview, Ragsdale said that it wasn't too long before they heard what they believed were trucks and heavy equipment coming. "We left and were not there when whatever it was arrived." This is, of course, in direct conflict with the detailed descriptions of the convoy offered by Ragsdale in earlier interviews.

Describing how to find the impact site, Ragsdale now said, "A sign post on the Pine Lodge Road indicates 'fifty-three miles to Roswell.' Near this sign is a road going south toward Pine Lodge . . . and the turn off to Arabela leads east and south. Two or three miles down this road towards Arabela is the site of our pickup that night and nearby is the impact site."

The discrepancies that have appeared are more than the minor changes expected as someone tries to remember events in the distant past. Researchers expect a story to shift with each telling simply because of the mechanism of memory, but these changes go beyond that. Ragsdale first reported seeing the bodies in the distance and then, in his second, more dramatic version claimed he tried to pull a helmet off one. He originally provided a vague description of the aliens and then gave one that seems to match those given by people claiming to be abducted by aliens. Ragsdale said he watched the arrival of the military and described the convoy and later claimed to have left before the trucks were in view. Originally he said the crash site was thirty to forty miles north of Roswell, then he claimed it was sixty or seventy miles away.

The changes in the tale told by Ragsdale were detailed in *The Jim Ragsdale Story*, written by Max Littell. Littell told how he learned of Jim Ragsdale. "In 1993 . . . we did have an investigator/author visiting us, and when his partner took the car on another errand, he needed a ride to his motel. I offered, and the individual said, 'Great, but I need to go by and see a party on the way, if it's all right.' This turned out to be Jim Ragsdale."

Littell continued, "Getting into the car, the writer said, 'I hope Ragsdale lives until morning.' . . . The investigator had apparently recorded the interview, or had taken enough notes that he could prepare a statement from Ragsdale. He asked if I could get the statement signed and notarized . . . I said that this could easily be accomplished."

Littell wrote, "Within a few days, the instrument arrived, and I met Ragsdale for the first time. The instrument was read to him, he signed it, the document was notarized, and I mailed it back to the investigator. Notaries do not make copies of the instrument, so I do not remember any of the statements made."

This is where the statements made by Littell concerning that aspect of the episode diverge from established fact. Ragsdale was interviewed by Schmitt on January 26, 1993, and the affidavit was signed on January 27. Mark Chesney, who had waited in the car with Littell and who had listened to the tape, suggested an affidavit be made. Chesney prepared a handwritten version. He discussed it with Littell and the two of them, in Littell's office, made a few changes. Then Littell, who could type much faster than Chesney, typed it up. In other words, the instrument was not sent to Littell. He had a hand in preparing it, as well as in getting Ragsdale's signature on it.

The statement made on January 27, 1993, read:

> On a night during July, 1947, I, James Ragsdale, was in the company of a woman in an area approximately forty (40) miles northwest of Roswell, New Mexico during a severe lightning storm. I and my companion observed a bright flash and what appeared to be a bright light source moving to the southeast. Later, at sunrise, driving in that direction, I and my companion came upon a ravine near a bluff that was covered with pieces of unusual wreckage, remains of a damaged craft and a number of smaller bodied beings outside the craft. While observing the scene, I and my companion watched as a military convoy arrived and secured the scene. As a result of the convoy's appearance we quickly fled the area. I hereby swear the aforementioned account is accurate and true to the best of my knowledge and recollection.

Ragsdale signed it and Littell notarized it. He sent the original to Randle, but kept copies in the files of the International UFO Museum, which was in the process of acquiring files about the Roswell case.

After that, Littell began talking with Ragsdale frequently. It was important that Ragsdale identify the exact location of the crash, and Littell said he would drive him out. In the "Max Littell Meets Jim Ragsdale" chapter of *The Jim Ragsdale Story*, he is quoted as saying:

> Believing the alleged impact site to be only 30 miles from Roswell, I offered to take a doctor and nurse, along with oxygen. Since the site was only 30 miles from Roswell, I thought we could be out and back in two hours.
>
> At this point, Ragsdale told me, "It is not 30 miles to the site because it is 53 miles to the turn-off." I replied, "Fifty-three miles out on Highway 285 to Albuquerque would put you two thirds of the way to Vaughn." Ragsdale responded, "It's not 285 but Highway 48, Pine Lodge Road."

The question remains how Ragsdale—who had spoken to Randle several times about the case, and who was recorded by Schmitt—got from a site thirty to forty miles north of town to one where the turn-off is more than fifty. When they interviewed him, why did he insist the site was much closer to town? And why did he identify it from photographs that look nothing like the terrain around Pine Lodge that he was now describing to Littell?

This is a major change in the story. Littell has suggested that both Randle and Schmitt made a mistake when talking to Ragsdale originally. He, Littell, was able to iron out the problems, resolving the question with the "true" site, now nearly seventy miles away.

But the problem comes back to Ragsdale. Not only had he identified the site from photographs shown to him by Schmitt, but he also used a map. In fact, and according to Schmitt, in an attempt to help locate the site today, he mentioned that it was close to the El Paso Natural Gas Pipeline, which runs north of town. That is not to suggest that he was working on that line, or that it existed in 1947. It was a landmark used by Ragsdale in 1993 to help situate the impact site on the map.

The problem with Ragsdale's identification of the Pine Lodge site are the statements made by those who lived in the Pine Lodge area in 1947. Of those interviewed not a single one talked about this event. In fact, in June 1996 Littell suggested that a reporter for the *Roswell Daily Record* should check to see if anyone out in the Pine Lodge area remembered anything. That research failed to produce any corroboration.

There is one other aspect that should be discussed. Littell insists that there is physical evidence of the crash near the Pine Lodge. He pointed to a path that seems to be broken through the trees, rocks that seem to have been adversely affected by heat, and other such evidence. However, Vennie Scott, the former Mrs. Jim Ragsdale, tells a slightly different tale about the damage done in that area.

According to William P. Barrett, for a story about the Roswell crash sites written for an Albuquerque newspaper, *Crosswinds:* "Vennie Scott scoffed at the claim that damaged trees around Site No. 5 [the Ragsdale site]—where her family did in fact camp and hunt deer for decades—was evidence of a UFO crash in 1947. The trees were injured, she insisted, in 1969 or 1970 by a fire she witnessed that was caused by nearby inebriated campers. 'These drunks let their fire get away from them,' she said. 'That fire just burnt a circle and quit. And that's the place he's saying he saw the spaceship land . . . That burnt spot is not what the spaceship made, because I was about 400 feet from where the drunks set the fire . . . We helped them put the fire out.'"

But Littell wasn't done. Littell, according to Barnett, "freely acknowledged that Ragsdale Productions, Inc. [headed up by Littell's son-in-law] never tried to find or talk to any of these people [residents of the Pine Lodge area]. 'As far as we were concerned, this story of Ragsdale is valid,' said Littell. 'What am I trying to prove he's lying for? We're not going to do that. You go ahead and prove he's lying. I'm just telling you what the man said.'"

Littell did secure a second notarized statement from Ragsdale. That would mean that there were now two sworn statements available that seemed to contradict one another.

Barrett, in an attempt to be as thorough as possible, checked all this out. He noticed that the longer, second notarized first-person statement contained a significant number of different details. Besides changing the site to near the Pine Lodge, Ragsdale was talking of a nocturnal visit to the crashed craft when he even tried to pull a helmet off one of the bodies.

But the important point, according to Barrett, was, "In addition to the varying detail, Ragsdale's second statement had another problem. The document carried the seal of notary Kathy Weaver of Logan County, Oklahoma—home of Ragsdale's daughter, Judy Lott—along with Weaver's written declaration that the two-page document was 'subscribed and sworn to before me this 15th day of April, 1995.' Weaver admitted to *Crosswinds* [that is, Barrett] last month that Ragsdale didn't actually sign the statement in her presence. 'I swear to God he did not,' she said."

Apparently what happened, according to Barrett's story, is that Weaver added her signature and embossed notarial seal after Judy Lott, a co-employee of the same firm where Weaver worked, brought the document, already signed, to Weaver's office. Because she knew Lott, she notarized the statement. Weaver agreed, again according to Barrett's story, that it's "bad practice for notaries to attest to a signature not written while they're watching but that 'we do it all the time.'"

This procedure, under legal precedent, invalidates the force of the notarization. According to Barrett, "All that remains is an unsworn statement—a mere piece of paper, really—without the added credibility that it has been rendered in the presence of

Almighty God subject to the laws of false swearing and even per-
jury."

Judy Lott denied that Ragsdale had signed the statement without a notary present. She told Barrett, "We had the notary come to
our home because Dad was too ill and couldn't leave the house."
But then, confronted with the information that the notary had
denied ever meeting her father and hadn't witnessed the signature,
Lott acknowledged that her father had not signed it in front of the
notary. In fact, according to other information, Ragsdale might not
have even been in Oklahoma when the affidavit was signed.

With the second statement invalidated, it meant that the only
affidavit left was the one that was based on Schmitt's tape-recorded
interview and had been created by Chesney and Littell in January
1994. In an ironic twist, it was Max Littell who was the notary on
the first statement. It meant that he was the witness to the Ragsdale
signature on the only valid affidavit.

To bolster the Ragsdale testimony, Stanton Friedman was interviewed about his opinion of the Ragsdale tale. He said, "I could not
imagine any reason for his lying knowing full well that he was
dying. Obviously I would like backup testimony, but the woman is
also dead."

Littell wrote, in *The Jim Ragsdale Story:* "Even Stanton Friedman
who has interviewed hundreds of people said, of the video interview:
'The man was completely lucid, positive in his actions and statements, and I would equate this to a death bed confession.'"

But there are even problems with the idea that the video statement was made about five days before Ragsdale died. Vennie Scott,
the former Mrs. Ragsdale, told a number of people that she found it
difficult to believe that Jim Ragsdale was saying anything to anyone
five days before his death. She maintains that Ragsdale was in and
out of a coma during the last several weeks of his life, so that he
wouldn't have been able to provide any statements. The timing of
the deathbed statement seems to be a matter of dispute.

Of course, this isn't the end of the tale. In 1998, James Houran and Stephen Porter reviewed the Ragsdale story using a technique known as statement validity analysis (SVA). Using the statements made by Ragsdale, specifically those made in the second affidavit and in the text of *The Jim Ragsdale Story*, they analyzed the information using both SVA and fact pattern analysis.

Under the criterion for the SVA, it was concluded, "The results of this statement analysis indicate that the Ragsdale accounts were *not credible* [emphasis in original] according to known features of memories for true events."

The same conclusion was reached when the fact pattern analysis was applied to the Ragsdale tale. It was noted, "The results of this fact pattern analysis indicate that the Ragsdale accounts are *not credible* [emphasis in original] in that they exhibit major factual inconsistencies and, independent of the nature of the event itself, include potential implausible information."

In their final conclusions, Houran and Porter wrote, "SAV and fact pattern analysis by the second author [Porter] suggested that 'The Jim Ragsdale Story' is not credible. We argue, therefore, that the story represents either a deliberate fabrication or false memories of imagined experience."

Given the circumstances, that is, the change from Ragsdale's original tale to his second, and the analysis by disinterested third parties, it would seem that the Ragsdale testimony could be eliminated. It could be argued, however, that the interference of Max Littell and the attempts by the IUFOMRC to obtain an "exclusive" story were the cause of the alteration. The first tale, told under no inducement, might be closer to the truth. Houran and Porter thought that an analysis of the first tales might provide an insight into the Ragsdale story.

Houran received a copy of the first affidavit and a copy of the Schmitt interview with Ragsdale for analysis. Using the same techniques, they reviewed the material. In the "Results and Discussion" section of their report, Houran and Porter wrote that "a free recall account is requisite followed by a series of follow-up questions to do a competent assessment. . . . According to S.P., the problem with Ragsdale's 1993 testimony is that it is completely non-focused, disjointed, and with no free recall account. . . . Consequently, conducting SVA on the present materials would not be productive or meaningful. . . ."

That wasn't the end, however. Houran and Porter wrote, "Having said this, S.P. noted one glaring sign of non-credibility in this account, namely the complete lack of description of any interactions between Ragsdale and his companion. It is reasonable to expect that this would constitute a major part of his narrative, given the novelty and bizarreness of the shared experience. In our opinion, there is also a clear 'conspiratorial' air about the interview. . . . Given our careful scrutiny of Ragsdale's testimony from both 1993 and 1995, we conclude that there is no evidence for its validity in a *forensic* sense, and we recommend therefore that serious researchers discard it."

See also *International UFO Museum and Research Center; Statement Validity Analysis*

Ramey, Brigadier General Roger Maxwell (1903–1963) Roger Ramey was born in Sulphur Springs, Texas, grew up in the area, and attended the United States Military Academy at West Point. He was commissioned as a second lieutenant in the cavalry in June 1928. He transferred to the Air Corps in November 1929 after he had completed flight training at the Air Corps Primary Flying School, Brooks Field, Texas, and the Air Corps Advanced Flying School, Kelly Field, Texas, in September 1929.

During World War II, he held a number of important positions in bomb groups in the Pacific Theater. He was promoted rapidly, finally obtaining the rank of brigadier general on July 1, 1943. In January 1944, he returned to the United States, where he assumed command of the 38th Flying Training Wing at Kirtland Flying Field in New Mexico. In November he was named the chief of staff of the XXI Bomber Command, based on Saipan in the

Pacific, and in January 1945 assumed command of the XX Bomber Command in the China-Burma-India Theater. In April 1945, he became the commanding officer of the 58th Bomber Wing, based in the Marianas Islands, and in November 1945, after the end of the war, returned with that unit to March Field near Riverside, California.

In July 1947, Ramey was the commanding officer of the Eighth Air Force, a unit that was considerably smaller than it had been at the height of the war. One of its major components was the 509th Bomb Group, the only nuclear strike force in the world in 1947. When the story of the crashed flying saucer was reported by Colonel William Blanchard in Roswell, Ramey was quick to identify the material as having come from an ordinary weather balloon. Pictures of Ramey and his chief of staff, Colonel Thomas DuBose, appeared in newspapers around the country in the days that followed.

Ramey was eventually promoted and in July 1952 was a major general and the Deputy Chief of Staff for Operations of the Air Force. His last promotion was to lieutenant general, and he retired in 1957. Roger Ramey died in 1963.

Ramey Message During the photograph session in General Ramey's office of the weather balloon supposedly brought to Texas from Roswell on July 8, 1947, a shot was made of Ramey crouched by some of the scattered debris from the rawin target. In that photograph, Ramey is holding a piece of paper that, while not facing the camera straight on, was photographed so that it appeared that words could be seen.

In photographs ordered from the Special Collections at the University of Texas at Arlington Library, a slight discoloration appeared on the paper Ramey was holding, suggesting that something might be read. In 1991, Don Schmitt sent a copy of that photograph to Dr. Richard Haines, a former NASA research scientist, asking if he could read anything on the paper. Haines, using a microscope, scanned the message and reported that he could see vague words but could not make out the individual letters of those words. In a few cases, he could identify a random letter, but that was no help in understanding what might be printed on the paper. Haines thought that a better quality photograph, or an enlargement of the letter area, might reveal more of the message, but didn't seem to think it would be of much real use.

That was where the matter rested until 1998, when J. Bond Johnson, who had taken six of the seven photographs in General Ramey's office, decided to investigate further. Johnson put

together a team to inspect the photographs that included Ron Regehr, a space and satellite engineer. Using a huge blowup of the photograph, a computer, and a variety of software and camera equipment, Johnson's team was able to see more of the message that Ramey held. Or rather, they claimed that they could read it with some degree of certainty.

In the upper left-hand corner, they saw what they believed to be the image of a telephone and concluded that Ramey was holding a "telephone message sheet" because of this "telephone logo." They then claimed to have "positively identified a number of words in the message. There were, quite naturally, gaps in what they could see, and they noted that the message had been typed in all capital letters.

Their interpretation of the message was:

Brigadier General Roger M. Ramey.
(*Photo courtesy of USAF*)

AS THE ... 4 HRS THE VICTIMS OF THE ... AT FORT WORTH, TEX ... THE "CRASH" STORY ... FOR 0984 ACKNOWLEDGES ... EMERGENCY POWERS ARE NEEDED SITE TWO SW OF MAGDALENA, NMEX ... SAFE TALK ... FOR MEANING OF STORY AND MISSION ... WEATHER BALLOONS SENT ON THE ... AND LAND ... rOVER CREWS ... [SIGNED] ... TEMPLE.

If what they found was accurate, and others could corroborate what they had seen, then it was a breakthrough on the Roswell case. Here was a document with an indisputable provenance. General Ramey was holding it in his hand, and copies of the photograph put out over the INP soundphoto wire provided a time and a date. According to a copy of the photograph that came from the Bettmann Photo Archives in New York City, J. Bond Johnson had taken the picture on July 8, 1947, and it had been transmitted at 11:59 P.M., or one minute before midnight.

There were gaps in what they could read, and some of the phrases they spotted made little sense in the context of what else could be seen. However, the reference to victims,

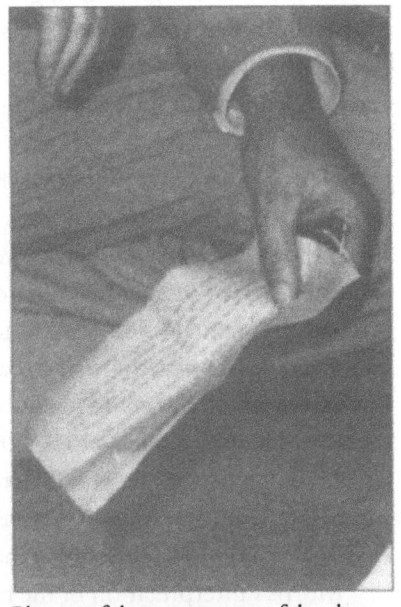

Blowup of the message part of the photograph taken by J. Bond Johnson on July 8, 1947. (*Photo courtesy of* Fort Worth Star-Telegram, *Photo Collection, The University of Texas at Arlington Libraries*)

to weather balloons, and to Magdalena, New Mexico, were important clues. These words seemed to tie the message to the Roswell events, and suggested that some kind of a quick response was required by the military, either at Eighth Air Force headquarters in Fort Worth or by the 509th Bomb Group in Roswell.

Others began to request copies of the pictures from the Special Collections in Texas. They brought their expertise to bear on the message in Ramey's hand. To the delight of many, they could also see letters, words, and images as suggested by Johnson and his team. The problem was that many of those doing the work were not seeing the same things as Johnson and his team.

For example, the telephone logo that Johnson's team reported looked more like a gray smudge on the paper than anything else. One well-known UFO researcher said that the telephone resembled the Liberty Bell as seen on the back of a Franklin half-dollar rather than a telephone. It was, as Russ Estes would later describe it, "faces in the clouds."

Neil Morris, a technician who works for the University of Manchester in England and part of the Johnson "Roswell Photo Interpretation Team," began to work on the message as well. His interpretation of the symbols did not agree exactly with that made by other components of Johnson's team. He did do one thing that was beneficial to all researchers, and that was to break down the message line by line so that it would be easy to follow his interpretation of the message. He used capital letters to represent the parts of the message of which he was sure, lowercase letters to represent his best guess at some letters, an asterisk to denote a letter he couldn't decipher, and a dash where there was little more than a smudge on the message.

Morris's interpretation of the message was:

(1)————————-***ARY WERE—————————AS
(2)————————fxs 4 rsevl VICTIMS OF THE WR eck and CONVAY ON TO
(3)—————————*** AT FORT WORTH, Txe.
(4)—————————***S** smi Ths *ELSE* ***** unus-d**e T&E A3ea96 L******

(5)————SO ught CRASHE s pOw*** *** N*****
SITEOne IS reMotely *****
(6)————***D* bAsE ToLd ***a* for we**ous BY
STORY are 8*****
(7)————lly thry even PUT FOR BY WEATHER
BALLOONS n*d** were
(8)————**** **la** I***denver*****
(9)
(10)   Temple

It was not an exact match for what Johnson had released and in fact went off in a couple of new directions. In the new version, while the word *victims* remained, as did *Fort Worth, Texas,* nearly everything else was different. One of the major points in the Johnson version was the wording that suggested, "Emergency Powers are needed Site Two SW of Magdalena, NMex." It suggested that those interpreting the message were seeing, to some extent, what they wanted to see, as Estes had said.

John Kirby, a researcher who is interested in the Roswell case and who works for a huge company in the computer field, also looked at the message. Using his expertise and equipment, he was unable to see much of anything. He did agree that the third line contained the words, "At Fort Worth, Tex." The second line, which many consider the critical line, said, according to Kirby "are the remains of the material you commanded we fly." If the word *victims* is changed to *remains,* the nature of the entire message is altered. *Victims* implied someone killed in the accident, but *remains* could refer to anything, including the remnants of a weather balloon also visible in the photograph of Ramey holding the message.

In still a different version, David Rudiak, another careful researcher who is interested in the Roswell case, suggested only a little of what others had seen. According to him, and using the same mix of capitals for what he was sure of and lowercase for what he

suspected, and brackets to suggest alternative words and phrases, he
reported the message read:

(1)——————————— officer

(2)———(jul)y 4th the VictIMs of tHE weECK you
fOrWArdEd TO The

(3) ————EaM At FORT WORTH, TEX.

(4)————5 pM THE "DISC" they will ship [swap?] FOR
A3 8th Arrived.

(5)———or 58t(h) bom(be)r sq(?) Assit [Assess] offices?
AT ROSwe(II) AS for

(6)——54th SAID MIStaken————[meaning? weather?
balloon?] of [is] story And said

(7) news [clip, chat, dirt] out is OF WEATHER BAL-
LOONS which were

(8)———— Add[And, Ask] land d————[dirt cover?]
crews.

(9)

(10)   rAMEy

Those weren't, of course, the only alternative interpretations
that were offered. Russ Estes, using a 16-by-20 print made by the
University of Texas Library, applied his expertise to the examination. Estes, a professional documentarian, was able to use a professional quality $50,000 video camera with a $7,500 macro lens to
capture the image. Then, using his huge, $80,000 computer and a
variety of technically complex and professional quality software
programs, he examined the message every way he could think of,
including a with jeweler's loupe, magnifying glass, and microscope.
He even scanned it at 9,000 dpi so that it created a file that was 1.7
gigabits in size and could be manipulated and enlarged even further.
He said that he could seen nothing that he would be willing to
swear to in court. He said there was simply nothing there to see.

Pressed on the point, because others were seing all sorts of words and phrases, Estes did say that he could make a "best guess" about the images on the message. Looking at an 8-by-10 photographic blowup of just the message area, using the same techniques and equipment, he could see, with a limited amount of confidence, "Fort Work, Tex." On the line below that where one group saw "Disk" and another saw "ELSE," Estes believed he saw "ELA*." He did say that it made no sense to him, just that that was what the ambiguous smudges that everyone was attempting to make into words looked like to him.

As for the signature block, he could see nothing that resembled either of the claims. At best, there might have been an "M" in the middle of the word and the possibility of an "LE" at the end. That gave the nod to "Temple," but Estes said it was more "faces in the clouds."

That wasn't, of course, the end of it. Schmitt, working with Tom Carey from Pennsylvania and Don Burleson of Roswell, came up with their own interpretation of the message—at least according to Burleson. Burleson, writing in the January 7, 2000 issue of *Vision,* a monthly magazine published by the *Roswell Daily Record,* noted: "A number of attempts have been made to read the Ramey letter. Quite frankly, most of these attempts are amateurish, and even some UFOlogists have concluded that there is nothing in the Ramey image that advances the case for the Roswell incident. They are MISTAKEN."

Burleson wrote that he had spent a year working on deciphering the letter. He said that he had the advantage of being the director of a computer lab and that he had a background in cryptanalysis. According to him, "I'm quite used to reading things that I wasn't meant to read." Of course, the problem for Burleson, as well as the others, is that this is not an encrypted message, but a plain text message. Cryptanalysis has little of real importance to say in trying to read what is printed on the paper.

Burleson wrote that he had been using several excellent computer image enhancement software packages, "including LUCIS, the most advanced software used today in such fields as

microscopy." Burleson was suggesting that he used very expensive
equipment and very advanced software. To hear Burleson tell it, his
was the most sophisticated analysis attempted to date and his results
were spectacular.

Burleson, who didn't provide a line-by-line breakdown, wrote,
"Here is my reading, so far . . . [Indeterminate parts of words are
indicated by hyphens, and missing words are indicated by parenthe-
ses.] A few spots are a bit tentative, but essentially the letter reads":

**RECO-OPERATION WITH ROSWELL DISK 074MJ-AT
THE ()() THE VICTIMS OF THE WRECK YOU FORWARDED
TO THE TEAM AT FORT WORTH, TEX () ON THE "DISK"
MUST HAVE SENT LOS ALAMOS ADVANCED () URGENT.
POWERS ARE NEEDED SITE TWO AT CARLSBAD, NMEX.
() SAFE TALK NEWSPAPER MEANING OF STORY AND ()
() () ONLY SHOW () () BY WEATHER BALLOONS () WAVE
() () AND LAND L-DENVER CREWS. [signed] TEMPLE.**

In keeping with the tradition started by Morris, an attempt to
give the message as determined by Burleson a line-by-line reading
was made. Remember, this is not necessarily how Burleson would
have broken it down by line, but it does provide a way of comparing Burleson's reading of the message with that supplied by so many
others.

> **(1) RECO-OPERATION WITH ROSWELL DISK 074
>   MJ-**
> **(2) -AT THE () () THE VICTIMS OF THE WRECK YOU
>   FORWARDED TO THE**
> **(3) TEAM AT FORT WORTH, TEX**
> **(4) () ON THE "DISK" MUST HAVE SENT LOS
>   ALAMOS ADVANCED ()**
> **(5) URGENT. POWERS ARE NEEDED SITE TWO AT
>   CARLSBAD, NMEX.**

**(6) () SAFE TALK NEWSPAPER MEANING OF
STORY AND**

**(7) ONLY SHOW () () BY WEATHER BALLOONS ()
WAVE () ()**

(8) L-DENVER CREWS

(9)

(10)   TEMPLE

Interestingly, the interpretation of the message, as given by Burleson and credited to Schmitt and Carey, doesn't even agree with what Carey is now suggesting. In a publicly posted e-mail dated March 29, 2000, Carey suggested first that the "take" on the Ramey memo is that of Carey and Schmitt and not "Burlson [*sic*] or anyone else . . . All of us continue to work on the memo as best we can, so there will no doubt be more to say in the future."

Carey's breakdown of the message, again based on an attempt to put it into a line-by-line reading for easy comparison, is:

(1) RECO . . . OPERATION . . . AT THE

**(2) JULY 4ᵀᴴ THE VICTIMS OF THE WRECK YOU
FORWARDED TO THE**

(3) . . . AT FORT WORTH

**(4) SSOR ON THE "DISK" MUST THUS SAVE FOR
THE ATOMIC LABORATORY**

**(5) URGENT POWERS ARE NEEDED SITE TWO NW
ROSWELL, NMEX**

**(6) SAFE TALK WANTED FOR MEANING OF STORY
AND**

**(7) MISSION [OR OBJECTIVE] NEXT CREW OUT
TODAY WEATHER BALLOONS**

(8) 509 HAS LAND SURVEYOR CREWS

(9)

(10)   R RAMEY

Given Carey's objection to what Burleson had written in the *Roswell Daily Record,* and given that Burleson seemed to believe that his interpretation was the only one to make sense while the others were "amateurish," what does this say about the credibility of these attempts to read the document held by Ramey? Estes's suggestion of faces in the clouds begins to look more like the right answer as those who have a specific agenda are seeing, in the memo, exactly what they wish to see.

That opinion has been expressed by some of the others who are attempting to understand the Roswell case. UFO researcher Stan Friedman contacted Rob Belyea, the owner of ProLab, asking him to examine high-resolution scans made of the negative. Friedman had actually paid someone in Fort Worth to hand-carry the original negatives from the Special Collections to a computer lab to have these scans made. The results were then sent on to Friedman, who supplied them to Belyea. Belyea said that he couldn't spend hours examining the message but that he could rule out or confirm the interpretations made by others by using his software to decide on character count and combinations of letters. It was not at all unlike the work being done by Russ Estes in California, though Estes was actually trying to read the message rather than just confirm interpretations.

While Friedman stood on the sidelines watching and not commenting on the research, Belyea did say specifically that he could not see "Magdalena" in the text as the Johnson team had suggested. Belyea did say, "They're pulling off all sorts of [readings], but they're making some of it up."

Remember, Estes had said much the same thing but much more eloquently when he suggested it was all "faces in the clouds." Estes had then added, "Sorry, but I just can't see any of these things."

Estes pointed out, as did others, that the message was a teletype rather than something from a typewriter. Given that, the message would have had to be in all capital letters, and nearly everyone agreed, because the teletype machines had no capability for lower-case letters. That was an important point in trying to understand and to interpret what was on the paper held by Ramey.

There is an additional problem, only partially addressed in the search of the message. This was a military message sent from one military installation to another, which means there should have been some military jargon in it. The attempts at reading it have failed to account for any military jargon. The closest is Rudiak's attempt to place military unit designations in the message. He noted in one place where he thought 58 or 58th Bomber Squadron might have been indicated. He also located a second place where 54th SAID could indicate some kind of a military unit, although no one has yet located a unit with that designation.

Rudiak also noted that what he thought as "5 PM" made no sense because the military would have used the twenty-four-hour clock and it would have said, "1700 Hrs" rather than "5 PM." That is a valid point.

This leads to another point that has not been covered. In the vast majority of message traffic on teletypes from that era I have reviewed in the last six months, much of it contained no punctuation marks. Instead, they were abbreviated as words. For example, rather than use a comma, the term CMA was used. A period was PD. None of the interpretations account for these sorts of things, and that could be complicating the interpretations of the message. In none of the various interpretations of the message has anyone suggested that some of the words might actually be the abbreviations for punctuation marks.

And there is an even more important point. If this is a message that deals with the Roswell case, and all of us agree that such message traffic would be classified, it is interesting that no one had suggested that classification markings are missing from the document. Whether Ramey received it or transmitted it, there should be a classification stamp at the top and bottom of the sheet. Messages are not allowed out of the communications center without the proper markings on them. If those markings are not present, it means that the document is not classified, and therefore is not very important.

Further, if this is Ramey's draft of the message to be transmitted, the classification markings should still be there. But, more important, that message would have been created on a regular typewriter and not a teletype machine. If that is the case, then there is no reason for it to be typed in all capital letters, so the interpretations are suddenly changed.

In fact, it seems strange that Ramey, a general officer who had handled classified material long before this event, would be so cavalier in handling this message. Before crouching by the wrecked weather balloon and radar target in his office, had he held a classified message, he would have given it to his aide, he would have set it in his desk drawer, or he would have had it locked in the safe by his secretary. That is the proper way to handle classified material, and Ramey wouldn't make such an elementary mistake, especially with a camera and a reporter in his office.

What it boils down to is that there is no consensus on what the message says, the best way to review it, or what to do next. One researcher, a champion of the Roswell case, said that it had to be assumed that the message had something to do with the Roswell case because Ramey is holding it while Johnson is taking his picture. There really is no reason to make that assumption. The message could be about almost anything and the words and images being seen might be a reflection of what the researcher wants to see rather than what is actually there.

Another researcher suggested that the word "victims" as it appears in the message is the critical word. To him, it "jumped off the page." The problem is that those looking at the message don't see it as a universal. One man said that he thought it was "remains." Estes noted that it seemed to be a mix of upper- and lowercase letters, with those doing the viewing seeing what they wanted to see. To Estes the first letter looked more like a "P" than a "V." He noted that there seemed to be a lowercase "I" in the word, and that the last letter looked more like an italic "5" than it did an "S."

Those researchers who suggest that "victims" is the critical word are corrrect. There is little in the way of interpretation that can be made if "victims" is in the message. However, if the word is, in fact, "remains," then the tone of the message changes and suddenly it is not the smoking gun that some of the Roswell researchers have suggested. This might be a message that describes the remains of a weather balloon located elsewhere, as an alternative explanation.

However, the question then becomes, Are they seeing that word because they believed it was there based on their communications with other researchers also attempting to read the message? A short, informal experiment was conducted in an attempt to answer that question. The photograph showing only the message was provided to a small number of computer experts, scientists, and forensic experts. They were told nothing about the possible contents of the message, if anyone had been able to determine some, part, or all of the message, or the circumstances under which the picture was taken. In other words, they were given the message without any sort of bias attached to it.

Of those independent researchers, only one believed that he could see the critical word "victims." Others couldn't resolve it with any degree of certainty, and two thought it might be "remains." The rest of the message, as interpreted by those researchers, was as mixed as that given by the UFO investigators.

In the end, this is an attempt to read letters and words that are sometimes vague to the point of being little more than gray smudges on the paper. The message was read in the light of interpretation of the person doing the reading and his or her belief of what it should say. None of the various teams attempting these interpretations have been able to read much with any degree of certainty. All the teams and the individuals have put their own spin on the message, while often suggesting that others are making mistakes. While all of this has been an interesting exercise, it added nothing of consequence to the knowledge pool of the Roswell case to this point.

Randle, Kevin D. (1949–) Kevin Randle began writing about UFOs while still serving in the United States Army as a helicopter pilot. He had entered the Army right out of high school, entered the warrant officer flight program, and was graduated in the summer of 1968. Within weeks of that graduation ceremony, he was in Vietnam flying with the 116th Assault Helicopter Company based at Cu Chi. In March 1969, Randle was transferred to the 187th Assault Helicopter Company at Tay Ninh. During those assignments, he flew missions in three of the four tactical zones in Vietnam.

Upon discharge from the Army, Randle attended the University of Iowa and joined the Air Force ROTC program, believing that he would eventually be called to active duty and trained as a fighter pilot. Although Randle was a distinguished military graduate, the Air Force was reducing its force, taking only academy graduates and distinguished ROTC graduates into flight training. The problem for Randle was that no slot would be found for more than two years. Rather than place his life on hold, he opted for a limited tour of active duty.

While in the Air Force, both on active duty and in the reserve, Randle was a public affairs officer, a general's aide, and an intelligence officer. He was promoted several times and completed his active reserve duty as a captain and the director of intelligence for an airlift group.

Randle attended a variety of graduate schools, first as a journalism major at the University of Iowa and later in psychology at California Coast University. He received a master's degree in psychology, as well as a doctorate from California Coast and a second master's degree in military studies from the American Military University.

Randle began his study of UFOs while still a high school student. In 1972, he published his first article about UFOs in *Saga's Annual UFO Report.* Throughout the 1970s, he published a number of articles concerning a variety of UFO sightings, including tales of alien abduction, photographic cases, and those involving some sort of physical evidence. In 1975, he was asked by Jim Lorenzen to investigate the wave of cattle mutilations that were sweeping the Midwest and West.

Kevin D. Randle. (*Photo courtesy of Kevin Randle*)

In the early 1980s, Randle was disillusioned by the UFO field. Hundreds of thousands of reports had been collected, but all seemed to be the same as those collected before. Another investigation of a light in the night sky or a disc seen during the day was not going to advance knowledge of the phenomenon.

In 1988, after a debate about the reality of UFOs held at a science fiction convention in Wisconsin, Randle was asked by Don Schmitt, a man he had met at the convention, to assist in the Center for UFO Studies' planned Roswell investigation. It was believed that his military background would be beneficial because many of the witnesses were former military officers.

In February 1989, Randle and Schmitt made their first trip to New Mexico. Although the trip started unpropitiously, the final interview was with Bill Brazel Jr. in Carizozo. Brazel described the metallic debris he had seen, his run-in with military officers, and how his father reluctantly told him bits and pieces of the story.

Randle and Schmitt made a number of additional trips to New

Mexico, meeting in Albuquerque and then driving on down to
Roswell. The investigation uncovered new information, convincing
Randle that not only had something extraordinary happened, but
that there was enough new information that a book could be written about it.

During the investigation, Randle interviewed a large number of
former officers of the 509th Bomb Group, finding a surprising
number of them who suggested the crash was real. He also learned
that whatever had happened, it had been highly unusual, based on
the reaction to the events by the officers and men stationed at
Roswell. These interviews, with men who had nothing to gain and
who had no desire for the spotlight, were persuasive.

In July 1991, *UFO Crash at Roswell* was published. It was followed by *The Truth About the UFO Crash at Roswell* in 1994. The
information included in the books was used as a basis for the
Showtime original movie *Roswell*.

Randle also published, in 1989, *The UFO Casebook*, which was
a review of the history of the UFO field to that point, covering
some of the better-known UFO cases. He has also published *A
History of UFO Crashes* (1995), *Conspiracy of Silence* (1997), *Project
Blue Book—Exposed* (1997), *Project Moon Dust* (1998), *The Randle
Report* (1997), and *Scientific Ufology* (1999). With Russ Estes, he
has published *Faces of the Visitors* (1997) and *Spaceships of the
Visitors* (2000).

With Estes and Dr. William P. Cone, Randle wrote *The Abduction Enigma* (1999), which examined the case for alien abduction.
Randle's other abduction book, *The October Scenario*, had been published in 1988 and took a radically different view of the abduction
phenomenon, suggesting that some accounts of abduction were real.

During the 1990s, Randle clashed with a number of other
UFO researchers, most notably Stan Friedman. Randle had found
little to support the idea of a second "Roswell" crash on the Plains
of San Agustin, a theory endorsed and supported by Friedman.
Although Randle was the first to speak to Gerald Anderson, a man

who claimed firsthand knowledge of the events on the Plains, it was Friedman who spent the most time investigating Anderson's story. The Anderson tale collapsed in 1995 when it was proven that Anderson had created a fake telephone bill to make Randle look bad and had lied about other aspects of his story.

Randle and Friedman clashed again over the MJ-12 documents, which Friedman believed to be authentic and Randle was convinced were a hoax. Randle found a questioned document expert in New York who had examined the Eisenhower Briefing and the Truman memo at the request of Friedman, and who had concluded both were faked. Although it had been Friedman who had provided the documents to the examiner, Friedman failed to report on the negative results.

The biggest point of controversy was the split in the Randle and Schmitt team in 1995. Although they had worked together on the Roswell investigation, they lived in communities that were about 350 miles apart. The time together was devoted to the investigation, though there was discussion of personal histories and background. Schmitt told Randle that he was a medical illustrator by trade and a UFO investigator by choice.

Milwaukee magazine did a story on Don Schmitt early in 1995 in which it was alleged that Schmitt was not a medical illustrator and that he did not have the educational or employment background he had claimed. Randle and Schmitt devised a strategy to combat the negative, and what Randle believed to be false, allegations made against Schmitt.

Part of the strategy was a video production planned by Russ Estes and eventually produced as *Roswell Remembered,* in which he would document the investigation by Randle and Schmitt. Sitting in front of the video camera, Schmitt explained his background and his interests. In the course of the interview, out of necessity considering the rumors that had been spreading, Estes asked Schmitt if he worked at the post office as had been alleged. Schmitt looked into the camera and said, "No."

Within hours the truth was learned. Schmitt did, in fact, work at the post office. Even with the negative developments, Randle remained friendly with Schmitt, learning later that Schmitt had been telling others that he, Schmitt, believed that Randle was a government agent. That became the last straw for Randle. Schmitt had betrayed their friendship by spreading the tale that Randle was a spy planted on him.

Randle continues to study the UFO phenomenon but has realized that the number of sightings of UFOs that might be considered alien spacecraft is much lower than originally thought. Visitation, while taking place, does not happen with the regularity that some have thought. Randle, through his writings, has made it clear that he believes, based on the evidence and testimony, that what fell at Roswell was a craft built on another world. To him, the evidence for that is overwhelming.

See also *Friedman, Stanton T.; Majestic Twelve (MJ-12); Schmitt, Donald R.*

The Real Roswell Crashed-Saucer Coverup by Philip J. Klass

This book is filled with small but often critical mistakes. Yes, there are times when the author hasn't made these errors, and there are editors, copyeditors, typesetters, and a dozen others who make them for the writer. But there comes a point when these errors can't be blamed on someone else and reveal a lack of concern for detail and an inaccuracy in reporting.

For example, Klass, when writing about the first Jim Ragsdale affidavit, which was based on Don Schmitt's January 29, 1993, interview, claimed that Schmitt had typed it. Nowhere, in any of the various books or articles that have been written on this case, has it ever been suggested that Schmitt typed the affidavit. Instead, Mark Chesney, a former NASA engineer and CUFOS investigator, after hearing the tape of the Ragsdale interview and learning that Ragsdale's health was not very good, suggested an affidavit. Chesney drafted it, and Max Littell typed it for signature.

Klass suggests that J. Bond Johnson, the reporter-photographer for the *Fort Worth Star-Telegram* in 1947, had taken seven pictures in General Roger Ramey's office on July 8, 1947. Johnson had originally said that he had taken two, but when the pictures were examined, it was clear that he had taken six. The seventh was clearly taken by someone else.

Of course, these are all minor points, but they do suggest the general sloppiness with which the book was thrown together. There are, however, much larger issues with this work. Clearly, the intent of some of it was to convince the public that those who suggest a saucer crashed near Roswell have been less than candid in the presentation of the evidence. But it seems that Klass is the one who is less than candid.

Take, for example, his discussion of the top secret document dated 10 December 1948. It is Air Intelligence Report No. 100-203-79, "Analysis of Flying Object Incidents in the U.S." It would seem logical that the officers creating the document would have access to all the classified information needed to accurately assess the situation. In fact, Klass makes just that argument: The officers writing the report would not lie about the state of the situation to their superiors. They would tell their superiors everything they knew. And if Roswell was the crash of an alien spacecraft, it should be mentioned in this report, claims Klass.

The report included an important paragraph about the origins of the objects. It reads, "THE ORIGIN of the devices is not ascertainable. There are two reasonable possibilities: (1) The objects are domestic devices, and if so, their identification or origin can be established by a survey of the launchings of airborne devices . . . (2) Objects are foreign, and if so, it would seem most logical to consider that they are from a Soviet source . . ."

What this document demonstrates is not the all-knowing access to every classified report that Klass has suggested. Instead, the authors are speculating that the flying objects might be a domestic project, making it imperative that any such project be revealed to the Air Force because of its responsibility for air defense. In other words, the authors of the top secret report did NOT have complete access to everything. And that leaves the door wide open for a Roswell UFO crash, a fact that Klass conveniently overlooks or forgets to mention.

Klass also makes much of the letter written by Lieutenant General Nathan F. Twining, which begins by telling us that the phenomenon was real and not an illusion. Klass is very impressed with page three, in which Twining suggests that there is a lack of recovered crash debris that would prove the case. Klass believes that the fact there was no mention of the Roswell crash in the letter, dated September 23, 1947, proves conclusively that there was no Roswell crash.

What he doesn't tell the reader is that the letter was written in response to a request from Brigadier General George Schulgen, who had sent sixteen to eighteen cases to Air Materiel Command headquarters to be analyzed. Twining's letter is in response to that request, and since there was nothing of a crashed saucer nature in the items supplied, there was no mention of it in the response. Instead, there is a mention of a *lack* of recovered crash debris, which in and of itself is means little in relation to the Roswell case.

And what of Brigadier General Arthur Exon, who supplied some very dramatic testimony about the Roswell crash? Exon's role is reduced to a single footnote in which Klass quotes Karl Pflock, who claims that Exon told Pflock he was "speculating" about what would happen had there been a crash.

Klass had the transcripts of the interviews with Exon that Don Schmitt and Kevin Randle had conducted. He knew what Exon said, and knew that it was all on tape. He knew that Exon hadn't been "speculating" when he spoke about those events. He was describing the events that he had witnessed in 1947, and describing what others had told him about their examination of the debris found at Roswell.

In arguing away the evidence, a major problem for Klass, with

Exon's statements, is his acknowledgment of a gouge in the terrain. Klass is, naturally, pushing the Project Mogul explanation for Roswell. He trots out the *Roswell Daily Record* article from July 9 to prove that what Mack Brazel found was parts of a balloon array train. Although it is on the same page of the *Roswell Daily Record,* Klass has never mentioned the article that suggested the debris was found only days earlier.

He mentions that William Moore interviewed Charles Moore (no relation) when Moore was researching his book. Bill Moore described the situation on the Brazel ranch to Charles and asked if it could have been one of their balloons. Charles said that it couldn't.

But Klass suggests that Bill Moore hadn't been fair in his description of Mogul material, and in fact, when shown the *Daily Record* article, Charles Moore said that Mogul could explain the debris field. That is, if the description in the newspaper was accurate. But based on the testimony of Exon, Bill Brazel, and Bud Payne, there is evidence that there was a gouge in that field. Each of the men described that gouge, but Klass does not acknowledge that. The testimony of Exon, Brazel, and Payne is credible and devastating to the Mogul explanation. A flimsy balloon can't make a gouge in hard dirt.

Klass is not above misleading readers when it suits his purpose. On page 119 he writes, "Further, that this train of balloons, radar targets, and instruments *had been tracked by ground and later airborne radar to within 17 miles of the Brazel ranch* [emphasis in original] before radar contact was lost."

That statement is based solely on the memory of Charles Moore, who didn't say that it had been tracked by radar, but that it was his memory that Flight No. 4 had been lost near Arabela, New Mexico, which is twenty to thirty miles south of the Brazel ranch. There is no documentation to corroborate Klass's statement, and in fact, the single bit of documentation that does exist suggests there were no radar targets and no array train attached to Flight No. 4.

Klass's claim of both airborne and ground radar is wrong. The diary by Mogul leader Dr. Albert Crary refers not to radar, but to radio transmissions from the sonobuoy. It makes no mention of the rawin targets, and if there were no targets, then there was no metallic debris to be scattered, and the whole Mogul explanation is eliminated.

The next entry in the diary noted: "Whole assembly of constant balloons sent up at 0500." Crary explicitly notes for this next flight that the "whole assembly" was launched. It is thus reasonable to conclude that had the whole assembly been launched the day before on Flight No. 4, Crary would have mentioned it in his diary, another piece of evidence Klass overlooks. Accordingly, the very crucial claim made by Klass suggesting documentation and radar confirmation of a Mogul flight near the Brazel ranch turns out to be erroneous and based on conjecture and the nearly fifty-year-old memories of Charles Moore.

It almost seemed that Klass didn't want to write this book. He went through the motions, but didn't have his heart in it. His past investigations had often turned up new information, and his arguments made some sense. But here there is only conjecture heaped on speculation and underscored by invention. There is nothing in the book that hasn't been said before, and much that has been disproved. There is just too much wrong with this work for anyone to take it seriously. In some respects, it is worse than the earlier debunking book published by Prometheus Books because so much more was expected from Klass.

There is nothing in this book that proves Roswell was not a crash of an alien spacecraft. There is nothing that proves the debris found was of a wrecked Project Mogul balloon. It is just more of the same tired arguments that have been made and disproved in the past. Had Klass brought his once critical eye and pointed sense of humor to this work, it could have contributed so much to our understanding and knowledge.

Reluctant See **Whitmore Jr., Walt**

Report of Air Force Research Regarding the "Roswell Incident"
(1994) Apparently inspired by the Government Accounting Office
investigation of the Roswell case, the Air Force initiated their own
investigation, which some believed to be a preemptive strike.
Colonel Richard L. Weaver, Director, Security and Special Program
Oversight, concluded, "The Air Force efforts did not identify any
indication that the 'Roswell Incident' was any type of extraterrestrial event or that the Air Force has engaged in a 47 year conspiracy
or 'cover-up' of information relating to it. Therefore, it is assumed
that pro-UFO groups will strongly object to the attached report and
denounce it as either short-sighted or a continuation of the 'cover-
up' conspiracy. Nevertheless, the attached is a good faith effort and
the first time any agency of the government has positively
responded officially to the ever-escalating claims surrounding the
Roswell matter."

The problem for the Air Force was that they had to make a
good-faith effort or their report would be picked apart. They concluded, based on their investigation, that the material found by
Mack Brazel and retrieved by Jesse Marcel Sr. was the remains of the
balloon array train launched as part of Project Mogul. They implied
in their report that the Mogul balloons and array, which were classified top secret, were so unusual that it would be expected that regular line officers and ranchers would be unable to easily identify
them as such. In fact, one writer dismissing the Roswell case took
this line of thought to the extreme, suggesting that Mogul was so
unusual that it had never before been seen in the history of flight.

The reality of the situation is that the Mogul balloon arrays,
while unusual in and of themselves, were in fact off-the-shelf weather
balloons and radar targets. There was nothing in them to fool any of
the witnesses who claimed to have seen the debris. The balloons were
so commonplace that the Alamogordo newspaper printed pictures of
a Mogul array on July 10, 1947, suggesting that the mystery of the
"flying disks" had been solved at the local air base. The balloons in
the photographs were regular weather balloons.

In fact, the Air Force interviewed only five witnesses for their report, settling only on those who would tell them what they wanted to hear about Project Mogul. Rather than treading on the thin ice of having to suggest that an Air Force general, Arthur Exon for example, was badly mistaken or deluded, they ignored his testimony, which had been clearly recorded in a number of different publications.

Exon, interviewed again in 1998, reconfirmed what he had said on tape when he had been interviewed on separate occasions by Kevin Randle and Don Schmitt. He told Carey that he had no firsthand knowledge of the crash debris or the bodies of the alien flight crew being brought to Wright Field, though he had heard those things from friends and colleagues who were at the base and who would have been firsthand witnesses. In other words, those he trusted told him that recovered crash debris and bodies were being brought to the base, and had Exon said that to an "official" investigator, then that investigator would have had the ability to track down some of those witnesses. This was clearly something that Weaver didn't want to do.

More important, Exon confirmed that he had flown over the area of the debris field and the impact point. He said that there were two distinct sites, one of which had only metallic debris. Stories that he had flown over many sites in New Mexico after the events gave way to the original report of two sites in an orientation that put one near Corona and the other near Roswell.

The Air Force also ignored the testimony of Edwin Easley, the Roswell provost marshal, who had told Randle that he had been sworn to secrecy, in direct contradiction to what the Air Force had claimed. No Air Force investigator acknowledged Easley's statements, though they quoted from affidavits that appeared in the Fund for UFO Research's *The Roswell Events*. A transcript of the Easley interview in which he said he was sworn to secrecy was included in that work, though the Air Force apparently didn't read it.

The Air Force also ignored Patrick Saunders, the base adjutant, who was still alive when they conducted their investigation. It would seem that a man who had been on Blanchard's staff, who had held a position that put him in a position to know the truth, and who had retired as a full colonel would have been a valuable witness. Saunders, before his death in 1995, noted that he believed that the crash at Roswell was the result of a crash of an alien craft and not the wreckage of a weather balloon.

Instead of talking with the officers from the base at Roswell, Weaver and his investigation focused on the civilians who had been with Project Mogul. With the exception of Sheridan Cavitt, who told Weaver that he had gone out to recover a balloon, they interviewed no one from Roswell.

Weaver's report concluded: "The Air Force research did not locate or develop any information that the 'Roswell Incident' was a UFO event. . . . Additionally, it seems that there was over-reaction by Colonel Blanchard and Major Marcel, in originally reporting that a 'flying disc' had been recovered when, at that time, nobody for sure knew what that term meant since the it [sic] had only been in use for a couple of weeks."

Importantly, Weaver also wrote, "It appears that the identification of the wreckage as being part of a weather device, as reported in the newspapers at the time, was based on the fact that there was no physical difference in the radar targets and the neoprene balloons (other than the numbers and configuration) between Mogul balloons and normal weather balloons."

In other words, Weaver was suggesting that Mogul was just like normal weather balloons. There was nothing to distinguish it from those used by the weather service. As they conducted their good-faith effort, they apparently missed the comment by Mack Brazel in the July 9, 1947, issue of the *Roswell Daily Record*. He had said that he had found weather balloons on two other occasions and this was nothing like those. Had it been a Mogul balloon, it would have been exactly like that.

This report contained virtually nothing about the tales of alien bodies. Weaver noted that and explained that there were several reasons, including the fact that there were no "alien" passengers in the Mogul arrays. He noted that those who claimed to have seen bodies were often identified by "pseudonyms," suggesting that there was nothing to their stories. He also wrote, "The review of Air Force records did not locate even one piece of evidence to indicate that the Air Force has had any part in an 'alien' body recovery operation."

Weaver concluded his report: "During the course of this effort, the Air Force kept in close touch with the GAO and responded to their various queries and requests for assistance. . . . It is anticipated that they will request a copy of this report to help formulate the formal report of their efforts. It is recommended that this document serve as the final Air Force report related to the Roswell matter, for the GAO, and any other inquiries."

To Weaver's mind, and to that of most news organizations, this was the end of the matter. The Air Force had investigated, determined that they had done nothing wrong and had participated in no cover-up, and announced their results. For some reason, the media believed them this time.

Roswell Alien Photographs See *Alien Autopsy;* Penthouse *Alien Photograph*

Roswell—Case Closed In what has been described as the Air Force's second final report on the Roswell case, Air Force investigators tried to deal with the stories that alien creatures had been recovered from the wreckage of their ship. This despite the fact that Colonel Richard Weaver, in the first final report, suggested that it would be the final word on the Roswell case.

As was the case with the first final report, the second looked impressive on the surface. It is filled with affidavits from those who participated in the Air Force's high-altitude research into ejection systems and parachutes during the 1950s. There are dozens of photographs, including those of anthropomorphic dummies that were dropped from extremely high altitudes during those tests.

The theory developed in this report is that the witnesses who claimed to have seen bodies were not lying. They were mistaken. What they had seen were the results of the high-altitude experiments. They had seen the anthropomorphic dummies that had been dropped by the Air Force.

The problem with the theory was that none of the tests had begun until 1953, six years after the events outside Roswell. The first of these tests near Roswell hadn't begun until nearly a decade after the flying saucer crash. According to the Air Force, the witnesses had become confused about the time frame and compressed the events in their minds so that the dummies they had seen in 1957 were the alien bodies they reported having seen in 1947.

Of course, the photographs of the anthropomorphic dummies included in the text look exactly like what they are, anthropomorphic dummies. They are robust dummies, nearly six feet tall with obvious human facial features and human characteristics. They are not, as have been described by various witnesses of the aliens, short, thin, nearly spindly individuals with large heads and large eyes.

To make matters worse, the Air Force based their theory on the testimony of three men, Gerald Anderson, Glenn Dennis, and Jim Ragsdale. Long before the Air Force began their investigation, Gerald Anderson's story had been revealed as a hoax. Although Stan Friedman continued to stand by it, the majority of UFO researchers had rejected it because of the inconsistencies in it and the lack of corroboration.

Glenn Dennis, although once considered to be among the best of the witnesses, had never seen the alien bodies himself. His story of bodies was based on the descriptions supplied to him by a nurse who he claimed had been part of the preliminary autopsy held at the Roswell Army Air Field. If that was the case, then Dennis's testimony was useless in an attempt to verify the anthropomorphic dummies as the culprits.

But UFO researchers, including Vic Golubic, had determined that there had been no mysterious nurse giving Glenn Dennis descriptions of alien creatures. If there was no nurse, then the Dennis story of an alien autopsy at the base had to be discarded. Further, if the story was discarded as a hoax, then it certainly could provide no support to the Air Force claim of anthropomorphic dummies.

Finally the Air Force used the story told by Jim Ragsdale, because in his description of the crash site, he said, ". . . it was either dummies or bodies or something laying there. They looked like bodies." This was the clue that provided the identification of the bodies. Ragsdale had suggested they were dummies.

While it could be argued that Ragsdale, confronted with the remains of an alien creature, might think it was a dummy, that analysis isn't necessary. Ragsdale's tale of alien creatures has been rejected by most serious researchers as a hoax. He changed details in his story, shifting the site of the crash from the Corn ranch to a site about sixty miles from Roswell.

More important, though it is not mentioned in the Air Force report, Ragsdale, who suggested that he had only seen the bodies (or dummies) from a distance, began to tell people that he had gotten down close to them. In later interviews, he not only got close to them, but was pulling the helmets off the bodies. His description of the facial features now matched that given by those claiming abduction. In other words, they had teardrop faces with pointed chins and large, black, oval-shaped eyes. In no way could such a description come close to matching an anthropomorphic dummy. Apparently Air Force investigators had missed these later details.

The Air Force supported its theory with the testimony of two others, Vern Malthais and Alice Knight. Both had known Barney Barnett, and both were relating the story that Barnett had told them in the 1950s. Barnett claimed to have come across the remains of an alien ship and the bodies of the flight crew. Unfortunately, this testimony, like that of Glenn Dennis, is secondhand.

As does the first final report, this new document does nothing to increase the knowledge of what happened outside of Roswell. While it does attempt to account for the stories of alien bodies, it fails because it addresses the wrong testimony, relies on "time compression" and, like its counterpart, fails to account for the testimony of high-ranking military officers. Even Philip Klass argued that the Air Force was making a mistake with this report because it was unbelievable.

This second final report is an even worse effort than the first. That earlier report, at least, seemed plausible to those who knew little or nothing about the Roswell case. This one seemed to be plausible to no one regardless of how little or how much was known about the case. It did cause one important question to be asked: "If there is nothing to the Roswell case, why is the Air Force working so hard to prove it? Why do they care what a bunch of UFO researchers believe?"

Roswell Daily Record It was the *Roswell Daily Record* that announced on July 8, 1947, that the officers at the Roswell Army Air Field had captured a flying saucer. It was the *Roswell Daily Record* that announced on July 9 that General Ramey had emptied the Roswell saucer, and that the "Harassed Rancher" was sorry that he had told the tale. These articles have become important proof for both sides of the UFO crash argument. To believers, the articles suggest that something unusual happened outside Roswell. To the nonbelievers, those same articles suggest that what fell was nothing more than a weather balloon.

On July 8, the headline announced, RAAF CAPTURES FLYING SAUCER ON RANCH IN ROSWELL REGION. A smaller headline read, NO DETAILS OF FLYING DISK ARE REVEALED. And below that ROSWELL HARDWARE MAN AND WIFE REPORT DISK SEEN. The story read:

> The intelligence office of the 509th Bombardment group at Roswell Army Air Field announced at noon today, that the field has come into possession of a flying saucer.

According to information released by the department over the authority of Maj. J. A. Marcel, intelligence officer, the disk was discovered on a ranch in the Roswell vicinity, after an unidentified rancher had notified Sheriff Geo. Wilcox, here, that he had found the instrument on his premises.

Major Marcel and a detail from his department went to the ranch and recovered the disk, it was stated.

After the intelligence office here had inspected the instrument it was flown to "higher headquarters."

The intelligence office stated that no details of the saucer's construction or its appearance had been revealed.

The rest of the article concerns the sighting, on July 2, by Dan Wilmot and his wife while sitting on their porch. Some researchers had at one time speculated that the craft seen by the Wilmots was the same one that had crashed later that night, but there is no reason to believe that.

The next afternoon, the *Daily Record*'s headline announced GEN. RAMEY EMPTIES ROSWELL SAUCER. The smaller headline said RAMEY SAYS EXCITEMENT IS NOT JUSTIFED. The story, datelined Fort Worth, read:

An examination by the army revealed last night that mysterious objects found on a lonely New Mexico ranch was a harmless high-altitude weather balloon—not a grounded flying disk.

Excitement was high until Brig. Gen. Roger M. Ramey, commander of the Eighth air forces with headquarters here [Fort Worth], cleared up the mystery.

The bundle of tinfoil, broken wood beams and rubber remnants of a balloon were sent here yesterday by army air transport in the wake of reports that it was a flying disk.

But the general said the objects were the crashed

remains of a ray wind [*sic*] target used to determine the direction and velocity of winds at high altitudes.

Warrant Officer Irving Newton, forecaster at the army air forces weather station here, said, "We use them because they go much higher than the eye can see."

The weather balloon was found several days ago near the center of New Mexico by Rancher W. W. Brazel. He said he didn't think much about it until he went into Corona, N.M. last Saturday and heard the flying disk reports.

He returned to his ranch, 85 miles northwest of Roswell, and recovered the wreckage of the balloon, which he placed under some brush.

Then Brazel hurried back to Roswell where he reported his find to the sheriff's office.

The sheriff called the Roswell air field and Maj. Jesse A. Marcel, 509th bomb group intelligence officer, was assigned to the case.

Col. William H. Blanchard, commanding officer of the bomb group, reported the find to General Ramey and the object was flown immediately to the army air field here.

Ramey went on the air here last night to announce the New Mexico discovery was not a flying disk.

Newton said that when rigged up, the instrument "looks like a six-pointed star, is silvery in appearance and rises in the air like a kite."

In the Roswell, the discovery set off a flurry of excitement.

Sheriff George Wilcox's telephone lines were jammed. Three calls came from England, one of them from the London Daily Mail, he said.

A public relations officer here said the balloon was in his office, "and it'll probably stay right there.

"Newton, who made the examination, said some 80 weather stations in the U.S. were using that type of balloon and that it could have come from any of them."

He said he had sent up identical balloons during the invasion of Okinawa to determine ballistics information for heavy guns.

In the same issue of the newspaper there is another story. This one is told by Mack Brazel, the only public record made by him that has survived. The article's headline read, HARASSED RANCHER WHO LOCATED 'SAUCER' SORRY HE TOLD ABOUT IT. It went on to say:

W. W. Brazel, 48, Lincoln county rancher living 30 miles south east of Corona, today told his story of finding what the army at first described as a flying disk, but the publicity which attended his find caused him to add that if he ever found anything else short of a bomb he sure wasn't going to say anything about it.

Brazel was brought here late yesterday by W. E. Whitmore, of radio station KGFL, had his picture taken and gave an interview to the Record and Jason Kellahin, sent here from the Albuquerque bureau of the Associated Press to cover the story. The picture he posed for was sent out over AP telephoto wire sending machine specially set up in the Record office by R.D. Adair, AP wire chief sent here from Albuquerque for the sole purpose of getting out his picture and that of sheriff George Wilcox, to whom Brazel originally gave the information of his find.

Brazel related that on June 14 he and an 8-year-old son, Vernon were about 7 or 8 miles from the ranch house of the J.B. Foster ranch, which he operates, when they came upon a large area of bright wreckage made up on [sic] rubber strips, tinfoil, a rather tough paper and sticks.

At the time Brazel was in a hurry to get his round made and he did not pay much attention to it. But he did remark about what he had seen and on July 4 he, his wife, Vernon and a daughter Betty, age 14, went back to the spot and gathered up quite a bit of the debris.

The next day he first heard about the flying disks, and he wondered if what he had found might be remnants of one of these.

Monday he came to town to sell some wool and while here he went to see sheriff George Wilcox and "whispered kinda confidential like" that he might have found a flying disk.

Wilcox got in touch with the Roswell Army Air Field and Maj. Jesse A. Marcel and a man in plain clothes accompanied him home, where they picked up the rest of the pieces of the "disk" and went to his home to reconstruct it.

According to Brazel they simply could not reconstruct it all. They tried to make a kite out of it but could not do that and could not find any way to put it back together so that it would fit.

Then Major Marcel brought it to Roswell and that was the last he heard of it until the story broke that he had found a flying disk.

Brazel said that he did not see it fall from the sky and did not see it before it was torn up, so he did not know the size or shape it might have been, but he thought it might have been about as large as a table top. The balloon which held it up, if that was how it worked, must have been about 12 feet long, he felt measuring the distance by the size of the room in which he sat. The rubber was smoky gray in color and scattered over an area about 200 yards in diameter.

When the debris was gathered up the tinfoil, paper,

tape, and sticks made a bundle about three feet long and 7 or 8 inches thick, while the rubber made a bundle about 18 or 20 inches long and about 8 inches thick. In all, he estimated the entire lot would have weighed maybe five pounds. There was no sign of any metal in the area which might have been used for an engine and no sign of any propellers of any kind, although at least one paper fin had been glued onto some of the tinfoil.

There were no words to be found anywhere on the instrument, although there were letters on some of the parts. Considerable scotch tape and some tape with flowers printed upon it had been used in the construction.

No strings or wire were to be found but there were some eyelets in the paper to indicate that some sort of attachment may have been used.

Brazel said that he had previously found two weather observation balloons on the ranch, but that what he found this time did not in any way resemble either of these.

"I am sure what I found was not any weather observation balloon," he said. "But if I find anything else besides a bomb they are going to have a hard time getting me to say anything about it."

What is important here are the descriptions of the debris, which do match that of the Project Mogul balloons. Skeptics have pointed to those descriptions to make their case. They overlook, however, Brazel's comments that he had found other weather balloons and this was nothing like those. That, to many researchers, is the most important statement. Brazel knew what weather observation devices looked like because he had seen them before, but what he found this time was not like those.

Roswell Initiative See *International Roswell Declaration*

Roswell in Perspective The first of what became an anti-Roswell investigation was financed by a grant from the Fund for UFO Research. Karl Pflock wanted to reexamine the evidence that suggested that a spacecraft had crashed outside Roswell. He wanted to attempt to corroborate the information, much of it discovered by Kevin Randle and Donald Schmitt.

A close reading of *Roswell in Perspective* finds that there are errors in it. He condemns Frank Kaufmann, lamenting that Kaufmann had said his name had appeared in the *Congressional Record,* but that when Pflock asked to see it, Kaufmann failed to produce it. This turned out to be problem more in the nature of a semantic difference. Kaufmann has produced a "Congressional Recognition" in which his name is mentioned, along with those of some of the most important scientists and governmental leaders of the day. They were celebrating Dr. Robert Goddard in Roswell. The Congressional Recognition is not quite the same as the *Congressional Record,* but it is a fine hair to split.

Pflock also noted that Frankie Rowe's testimony is suspect because she claimed that her father, a Roswell firefighter, had made a run outside the Roswell city limits. According to Pflock, a former Roswell city councilman had told him that in those years, the fire department didn't make runs outside the city. The truth, based on the official fire department records, is that in 1947 the fire department did make runs outside the city.

Pflock rejected the idea that what crashed near Roswell was a spacecraft based on the testimony of three witnesses, whom he identified as Bessie Brazel Schrieber, Jason Kellahin, and Reluctant (Walt Whitmore Jr.). One of them, Whitmore, even claimed to have remnants of the balloon stored at his house. All he had to do was find them and then everyone would see what had been found by Mack Brazel.

A close reading of Bessie Brazel Schrieber's testimony reveals that it is in direct conflict with that provided by nearly everyone else. For example, she claimed to be at the ranch during July 1947, but Brazel's son Bill said that his father was alone and that was why Bill felt he had to travel from Albuquerque to Corona to help out. Loretta Proctor, Brazel's closest neighbor in July 1947, said that Brazel often took her son, Dee, out on the ranch because Brazel was alone that summer.

Bessie said that she, her brother Vernon, and her father cleaned up all the metallic debris, which she believed to be the remains of a weather balloon. They filled four gunnysacks and stored them under the porch. Jesse Marcel Sr. and Sheridan Cavitt both talked of seeing the debris in the field. Cavitt claimed, in his interview with Colonel Richard Weaver, that it was nothing more than the remains of a balloon, but the point was that it was still in the field after Bessie said she had picked it all up.

Bessie said that her father didn't return to Roswell after they had gone into town to tell the sheriff about the debris. She did remember military personnel coming out to the ranch, but they came to the house to collect the gunnysacks. He father, according to her, simply did not disappear for nearly a week.

Edwin Easley, of course, mentioned that Brazel had been held in the guest house at the base at the time Bessie said her father was at home. Jud Roberts talked of how Walt Whitmore Sr. and another station employee drove to Corona to collect Brazel and kept him overnight at Whitmore's house. Walt Whitmore Jr. said that he remembered Brazel getting up early and making coffee. Half a dozen others mentioned Brazel in town, escorted by military personnel. The most damaging of the contrary reports, however, is that from the newspapers showing Brazel in the offices of the *Roswell Daily Record,* where he was interviewed about his find, proving that Bessie's memories on the point are in error.

Jason Kellahin, the AP reporter, suggested that he had seen the balloon in Brazel's field, surrounded by military officers, and interviewed Brazel there. Kellahin said that pictures of the balloon and

Brazel were taken and then he, Kellahin, drove on into Roswell. Kellahin's memory of that meeting is not consistent with any other available information. At the time Kellahin was allegedly in the field talking to Brazel, other testimony suggests that Brazel was already in Roswell. The timing of the event, based on a reconstructed timeline that comes not from human memory, but from events as described in various newspapers, proves that Brazel was not in the field with military officers when Kellahin said he was.

Most damaging here is Kellahin's claim that photographs of the balloon and Brazel were taken. If those photographs had been taken in 1947, they would have been published by some newspaper somewhere. The fact that they were not suggests that they were never taken.

Robin Adair, who accompanied Kellahin on his rounds in Roswell, said that he had not driven to Roswell as Kellahin said, but had met him there. Adair was the man who supposedly took the photographs, but he denied it on several different occasions.

Finally there are the tales told by Walt Whitmore Jr. He claimed that based on the directions given to him by Brazel, he had driven up to the debris field. He told Pflock and others such as Kevin Randle that he had seen the metallic debris and picked some of it from the ground. He knew that it was interesting, but he also believed that it was parts of a balloon. For years he kept it in his safe deposit box. However, he moved it to his "junk room," and although he searched for it for two years, he was never able to find it.

But that statement, given in the 1990s, does not agree with the statement he gave to Bill Moore in the late 1970s. In his earlier interview, he said that he got to the debris field after it had been cleaned by the military. He found an area that had been cleaned, but he found no metallic debris. In other words, he had radically altered his tale.

Pflock had used these three stories as the foundation for his belief that what had crashed was a balloon array from the then-classified Project Mogul. These reports seemed to suggest that something very ordinary had fallen near Corona. It had apparently fooled Mack Brazel, but not his daughter. It fooled Bill Brazel, who found a few small fragments in the weeks that followed, but not his sister. It had fooled some members of the 509th Bomb Group, but not the rancher's child.

Because of these flaws, *Roswell in Perspective* must be read carefully. Each reader must determine what he or she is willing to accept as accurate information and what should be rejected. The quality and quantity of the witnesses should be considered, as should the entire package of eyewitness testimony.

Roswell Myth Kent Jeffrey, who developed the Roswell Declaration and once believed that an alien craft fell outside Roswell, now believes that the crash at Roswell can be explained by the wreckage of a weather balloon. Jeffrey now believes that no craft or bodies were recovered. Jeffrey, in his article, wrote that the case was now closed—there was no flying saucer.

In that article, he challenged those who believe that something crashed outside Roswell in July 1947 to prove the case to him. To do so, he suggested that seven points that he brought up at the end of his article must be explained. He raised other questions in his article that are easily answered, and he accuses the Roswell proponents of selective reporting of the data. Let's take a quick look at some of that, and then answer his seven points one at a time.

Jeffrey wrote about the men of the 509th Bomb Group: "Most of them heard nothing about the supposed crashed-saucer incident until years later, after all the publicity started. The few men who did recall hearing about the incident at the time of its occurrence said that the inside word was that the debris was from a downed balloon of some kind and that there was no more than 'one wheelbarrow full.'"

Overlooking the fact that highly classified events would not be discussed among the officers because they were, by definition, highly classified, let's look at a statement by Colonel (later Brigadier

General) Thomas DuBose. According to him, and recorded on videotape on August 10, 1990, "He [Major General Clements McMullen, deputy commander of SAC] called me and said . . . Nobody, and I must stress this, no one was to discuss this with their wives, me with Ramey, with anyone. The matter, as far as we're concerned, it was closed."

What is seen here is evidence of orders coming from the head-quarters of the Strategic Air Command that the officers of the Eighth Air Force and the 509th Bomb Group were not to discuss this matter among themselves. Those who were not involved would not be told about it because of the high classification. And those former members of the 509th who believe that had something like this happened they would have heard about it must rethink their theory. Many military units have secrets that are shared only with those who have a need to know. To suggest a sharing of classified material with those who are not cleared to hear it reveals a misunderstanding of how this works. And remember, DuBose acknowledged that an order had been given.

Jeffrey also used the testimony that was published by William L. Moore in *The Roswell Incident* and later by Moore and Jaime Shandera in their articles about the debris taken to Brigadier General Roger Ramey's office. Jeffrey, however, wrote: "Among Marcel's responses were 'They took one picture of me on the floor holding up some of the less-interesting metallic debris . . . The stuff in that one photo was pieces of the actual stuff we had found. It was not a staged photo.'"

Jeffrey does not report the rest of the quote, which tends to refute his contention that the debris on the floor was never switched. Marcel supposedly also said, "Later, they cleared out our wreckage and substituted some of their own. They then allowed more photos. Those photos were taken while the actual wreckage was on its way to Wright Field. I was not in those."

If that wasn't enough, when the record is checked, it is discovered that Moore and Shandera have published three versions of the original quote, each altered to fit the circumstances as they were developing during various investigations. Moore provided a transcript of the February 1979 interview with Marcel that now said, "General [Roger Maxwell] Ramey allowed the press in to take *two pictures* of this stuff. *I was in one, and he and Col. DuBose* were in the other. [Emphasis added to show the difference in the quote.]"

In their article "Three Hours That Shook the Press," in *Focus*, new series Vol. 5, nos. 7–9, September 30, 1990, Shandera and Moore wrote, "In his interview with Moore (*The Roswell Incident*) Maj. Marcel maintained that the debris in the *two photos of him* is the real stuff [emphasis added]."

The quotes by Moore and Shandera referring to the number of pictures taken in General Ramey's office, who was in those pictures, and the situation around them can't be trusted. In fact, Marcel himself has been quoted by a disinterested third party. Reporter Johnny Mann accompanied Marcel to Roswell in 1980 to interview him about the UFO crash. Mann found the picture of Marcel posed by the weather balloon and told him, "Jess, I gotta tell you. This looks like a weather balloon."

According to Mann, Marcel said, "That's not the stuff I found on the ranch."

In other words, the only ones to report that Marcel was photographed with the "real" debris were Moore and Shandera. All evidence to the contrary was apparently overlooked by Jeffrey as he attempted to prove that what was on the floor in Ramey's office was the material found out on the Foster ranch.

Jeffrey also wrote: "Rancher Mac [*sic*] Brazel is quoted as talking about sticks, foil, and tape with flower patterns." But Jeffrey doesn't quote the last and possibly most important part of the July 9, 1947 story. Speaking of the balloon explanation, the newspaper reported, "Brazel said, that he had previously found weather observation balloons on two other occasions . . . but that what he found this time did not in any way resemble either of these."

But if what was found was a Project Mogul balloon as alleged, or just any sort of balloon as Jeffrey suggested, then it would have been exactly like those. Project Mogul Flight No. 4, the alleged culprit in the debris field crash, was made of weather balloons and radar targets. It contained nothing to fool Brazel, Marcel, or anyone else.

Jeffrey, in the seven points he believes proves his case, wrote, "A machine with unimaginable technological sophistication and consequent incredible reliability would not have simply broken down and crashed." He was saying that he just didn't believe that flying saucers would crash.

Even if the "perfect" machine could be built, there are always the human factors (in this case the alien factor, unless you want to believe them infallible, too), and the environmental factors in this extremely weak argument. In today's world, aircraft are designed to withstand strikes by lightning. However, according to a recent *Primetime Live* on ABC, lightning was a contributing factor in the recent destruction of a commercial jet.

Yes, the mean time to failure has improved. Yes, computers, electronics, and machinery all operate much longer, but they do still break. And when they don't break on their own, there is always someone there to make a mistake causing them to break. In other words, this argument is without foundation.

Jeffrey next wrote, "The only known wreckage from this sophisticated vehicle, capable of interstellar travel, would have consisted solely of a few short beams, pieces of foil-like material, and small pieces of thin plastic-like material."

Yes, that is basically the debris as described by those who were on the Foster ranch. He didn't mention the fiber optics described by Bill Brazel Jr., but that doesn't alter Jeffrey's point. There is not the range of debris you would expect from a crashing craft.

Of course, that doesn't cover the craft and bodies found elsewhere. Jeffrey was quick to point out, angrily, that there was no craft and there were no bodies, and therefore his point remains valid. He rejects, out of hand, all reference to the craft and bodies, weakening his argument considerably. You can't reject testimony simply because you don't like it. If you can offer a reasonable motive for that rejection, then you can proceed with your case. If you reject it because it is inconvenient, then your point is not valid. Jeffrey has ignored the statements by Major (later full colonel) Edwin Easley, Major (later full colonel) Patrick Saunders, Brigadier General Arthur Exon, Dr. W. Curry Holden, reporter Johnny McBoyle, and many others. Each spoke of the second crash site in firsthand terms.

Jeffrey's next point is, "Despite the fact that this would have been the most spectacular event in recorded history, and despite the fact that word was already out that something had happened (because of Lt. Haut's press release), there was absolutely no contemporary discussion or talk about such an earthshaking event among the pilots and navigators of the close-knit 509th Bomb Group."

This is absolutely ridiculous when it is remembered that these were trained officers who were schooled in keeping their mouths shut, and that according to General DuBose, orders had been issued by the top command in Washington, D.C. When the 509th was formed, with the purpose of dropping the atomic bombs, the men were brought to the base and told that they would be involved in a special assignment. They were told to tell no one of this. As a security check, they were allowed to glimpse "special" equipment or "special" orders. They all were given a leave before having to report back for training.

Herculean efforts were made to track each of those men, engage them in conversation, and see just how much they would talk about their "special" assignments or the "special" equipment they had seen. Each who mentioned anything was dismissed from the unit and returned to his original assignment. The point is, these men knew that you didn't talk out of school to anyone who did not have "A NEED TO KNOW."

Jeffrey then wrote, "West Point graduate and retired general Thomas DuBose would have had lied nine times in an interview when he stated that the debris (definitely that from an ML-307 radar reflector) shown in the pictures in Ramey's office was not substituted material and was real debris recovered from the ranch northwest of Roswell."

This is one of the weakest arguments Jeffrey has made. First, he accepts as completely accurate Shandera's interview with DuBose, but according to DuBose and his wife, Shandera neither took notes nor made a tape recording. In other words, Jeffrey accepted Shandera's version of the events with no corroboration.

But when DuBose was asked by other researchers if he had seen the Roswell debris, he said, "Never." After the publication of Shandera's interview, he was asked again if he had ever seen the real debris and in a letter, he wrote, "NO!"

Billy Cox, a disinterested third party and a writer for *Florida Today*, interviewed DuBose for an article he wrote for the November 24, 1991, edition of that newspaper. Cox reported that DuBose told him essentially the same story as outlined in *UFO Crash at Roswell*. In a letter dated September 30, 1991, Cox wrote: "I was aware of the recent controversy generated by an interview he (DuBose) had with Jamie Shandera, during which he stated that the display debris at Fort Worth was genuine UFO wreckage and not a weather balloon, as he had previously stated. But I chose not to complicate matters by asking him to illuminate what he had told Shandera; instead, I simply asked him, without pressure, to recall events as he remembered them . . . he seemed especially adamant about his role in the Roswell case. While he stated that he didn't think the debris was extraterrestrial in nature (though he had no facts to support his opinion), he was insistent that the material that Ramey displayed for the press was in fact a weather balloon, and that he had personally transferred the real stuff in a lead-lined mail pouch to a courier going to Washington . . . I can only conclude that the Shandera interview was the end result of the confusion that might occur when someone attempts to press a narrow point of view upon a 90 year old man. I had no ambiguity in my mind that Mr. DuBose was telling me the truth."

This demonstrates that DuBose didn't lie nine times. There is a disagreement between what Shandera reported about what DuBose said, and the videotape and other reporters' notes of what DuBose actually said. The problem is not DuBose, but Shandera.

Next Jeffrey wrote, "Major General C.P. Cabell, Director of Intelligence for the Air Force at the Pentagon, who prepared a report on the unidentified flying object situation for the Secretary of Defense, astoundingly, would have been preparing the report totally ignorant of the fact that the Air Force was in possession of a crashed flying saucer."

Actually, that is not exactly true. Are there any instances in which military officers wrote to civilian representatives of the government and lied? Yes. Senator Jeff Bingaman asked the Congressional Inquiry Division, Office of Legislative Liaison about Project Moon Dust. In April 1993, Lieutenant Colonel John E. Madison wrote, "In addition there is no Project Moon Dust or Operation Blue Fly. Those missions have never existed." This is not an accurate statement.

More important, when Madison's statements were challenged, Colonel George M. Mattingley Jr. wrote that Moon Dust had existed, but was never used. Mattingley had to know that Moon Dust had been deployed. He gave Bingaman a history of Moon Dust. Therefore, Mattingley knowingly lied to a U.S. Senator, as did Madison.

This is not exactly the same situation described by Jeffrey, but it does establish a precedent. Yes, military officers have knowingly lied to civilian government representatives when they believed national security was at stake.

Finally Jeffrey wrote, "Three retired Air Force colonels, all former top officials at the Foreign Technology Division at Wright-Patterson Air Force Base, would have been lying to me—unnecessarily wasting inordinate amounts of their own personal time in a protracted game of charades."

Again, this argument is weak on the face of it. When history is carefully examined, there are many examples of military officers serving in critical positions but not in possession of complete information. During World War II the United States had broken a number of Japanese codes and were reading intercepted messages under the code name Magic. Very few knew about it. On Mac-Arthur's staff in the Southwest Pacific there were two people who were "Magic" qualified, MacArthur and MacArthur's chief of intelligence. To suggest that Magic didn't exist because other high-ranking members of MacArthur's staff had said at some point that they heard nothing about it is ridiculous. If you had interviewed those men before "Magic" was publicized, would they be lying if they said Magic didn't exist, because, to them, it didn't?

More important, Jeffrey only recently let it slip that these three colonels, all of whom had been with Foreign Technology, didn't begin their tours until 1957, ten years after the events at Roswell. By that time, if the case was of a crashed flying saucer, there would have been no need to know for these men. This weakens Jeffrey's argument considerably.

Finished with that, Jeffrey asked, "What basis is there now for postulating the existence of a crashed UFO?"

Simple. The testimony of Edwin Easley, himself a retired colonel, who told investigators the craft was extraterrestrial. The testimony of Patrick Saunders, himself a retired colonel, who wrote on the flyleaf to *The Truth About the UFO Crash at Roswell:* "Here's the truth and I still haven't told anybody anything," which he then signed. And the testimony of Arthur Exon, himself a retired brigadier general, who talked of two distinct sites, and of the people at Wright-Patterson who had examined the debris and bodies of the alien creatures.

The question that can be asked here, in sort of a reverse on what Jeffrey has written, is, Why would these men create this story if it was not true? They did not seek the spotlight, as so many others have. They did not expect a monetary reward for their information. In fact, they gained nothing by suggesting there was anything true to the story of the crashed saucer.

Jeffrey has written that the case is closed. To his mind, he has solved it with interviews he conducted and his own analysis of the situation. But such isn't the case because he dismissed too much testimony that doesn't fit with his view. As noted, you can't reject inconvenient testimony until you provide a proper framework for that rejection. He has failed to do so, and therefore his reasons for rejecting the idea of the Roswell UFO crash are less than persuasive.

See also *ATIC; DuBose, Thomas; Easely, Edwin; Exon, Arthur; Jeffrey, Kent; Johnson, J. Bond; Moore, William L.; Ramey, Roger; Saunders, Patrick*

Roswell Photo Interpretation Team See *Ramey Message*

Roswell Remembered California documentary producer Russ Estes interviewed many of the witnesses and investigators of the Roswell UFO crash in the mid-1990s with an eye to creating a video record of case. *Roswell Remembered* was the final product. *Roswell Remembered* takes an in-depth look at the whole story, the people who lived it and the researchers who reported. Included are interviews with some of the more controversial figures such as Glenn Dennis and Gerald Anderson, and some who hadn't told their stories in front of a camera until Estes convinced them to sit down. Estes himself provides some commentary about the case but the real value here is the opportunity to see the witnesses tell their own stories without the words being filtered by writers and investigators. *Roswell Remembered* adds to the general body of information about the case without seeming to take sides in the debate. It is a presentation of the material carried by the witnesses themselves.

Roswell UFO Crash: What They Don't Want You to Know by **Kal K. Korff** In a book that is packed with every negative fact that has ever been written about the Roswell crash, Korff has not been able to provide anything that is particularly new or interesting. It is a rehash of information that has been circulating throughout the UFO community for the last half decade.

As just one example, his anti–Jesse Marcel Sr. chapter seems to be the information published by Robert Todd, without much of a rewrite. Korff attacks Marcel, suggesting that he was little more than a passenger on bombing missions against Japanese targets during World War II, overlooking the fact that Marcel was commended by his superiors for his participation in those raids. As an intelligence officer, part of his job was to assess the damage inflicted by the bombers, so while not on flying status as a permanent member of a flight crew, he was assigned on a rotational basis to flight crews. The criticism leveled here is not fact, nor is it particularly accurate.

Korff also attacks Marcel for the claim that he was shot down on one of the missions. Korff notes, correctly, that there is nothing in Marcel's military record to corroborate the statement. However, such things are not routinely noted, so it wouldn't be in his record. His son, however, adds a little corroboration by reporting that his mother had a blouse made of the silk from the parachute used.

To be fair, it is important to note that Marcel did claim to have attended a number of civilian universities. He even seemed to have claimed a degree, though that statement, made to Bob Pratt, is somewhat garbled. Checks at the universities have failed to find records of Jesse Marcel, with the exception of the University of Louisiana.

As a second example, Korff reports that Frankie Rowe's testimony should be rejected because the Roswell Fire Department didn't make runs outside the city limits in 1947. Here is proof that Korff didn't bother to review facts reported by others. Had he called the fire department, he would have learned that they did make such runs in 1947, and they continue to do so today.

For those interested in the "facts" not reported in the pro-Roswell books, this is not the proper source. Karl Pflock's and Phil Klass's work, though flawed as well, have not taken only the negative to make a case. A clearer picture is seen by reading those books.

Korff's anger at the pro-Roswell reporters, the witnesses, and anyone who believes the Roswell case is the result of the crash of an alien ship is evident. That anger often clouds his view, and his book degenerates into an attack with little in the way of factual information to back it up.

See also *Marcel Sr., Major Jesse;* **Real Roswell Crashed-Saucer Coverup; Roswell in Perspective;** *Rowe, Frankie*

Rowe, Frankie In 1947, as the twelve-year-old daughter of Roswell fire fighter Lieutenant Dan Dwyer, Rowe said that she had had the opportunity to see some of the strange metallic debris recovered in the crash and that her father had told her of the strange machine and craft that he had seen. Although she initially told little of what had happened, she expanded the story until she told of threats by military officers and a living creature recovered, and included her sister in the tale. The expansion, explained as the whole story finally told, was one of the points of controversy and suggested to some of the more skeptical researchers that she was grabbing part of the spotlight for herself.

According to Rowe, her father had come home, disturbed, and told the family that there was something he had to say. He told them that he, with a number of other firefighters, had been on a run that was about thirty miles north of town and a few miles west, where he at first believed that there had been an aircraft accident. When they reached the site, they realized that it wasn't an airplane, and Rowe said her father had called it a "flying saucer or something."

Rowe did say that her father had mentioned bodies. According to her, he had said that he had seen two bodies in body bags and one survivor that was walking around. The bodies, according to the description, were of small creatures, about the size of a ten-year-old child. The face looked like a bug known as the Child of the Earth. She thought her father had said that the creatures were pinkish.

She had no other information about her father's involvement. Rowe wasn't alone in her memories, however. In a signed affidavit,

Helen Cahill, Frankie's sister, wrote that when she had been visiting her parents in 1948, he father told her that something very important had happened, but he wasn't going to give her details, telling her she was better off not knowing.

That wasn't the end of Rowe's involvement. According to her, she had been taken to the doctor's office in July 1947. She had no ride home and walked over to the fire station to wait for her father to go off duty. She was in the fire station when a New Mexico State Trooper arrived. He talked of having been involved in the security at the crash site and that he had something to show the firefighters. He pulled his hand out of his pocket, revealing a bit of metallic material.

Rowe, on videotape, told researchers, "I got to pick it up and crumple it one time . . . It didn't feel like I had anything in my hand . . . It didn't make a sound like the tinfoil that we had been peeling off gum wrappers for the war effort . . . it felt like it was even thinner. It was kind of like a pewter color . . . it wasn't like highly polished sterling silver . . . but it didn't have the shine to it."

All the firefighters felt the material and crumpled it into a ball. Rowe said that it would unfold itself with a fluid motion until it was straight and flat. She said that others tried to cut the material with their knives and failed. They tried to burn it, but it would not burn. It was stronger than anything they had seen. Rowe said that she couldn't figure out how the piece had come to be jagged, because no one could cut it.

Several days later, a military officer, along with a number of enlisted men, came to the house. They asked Rowe's mother who had been at the fire station. Once they had that information, the younger children were sent out to play while Rowe and her mother sat at the dining room table.

The officer took charge and asked the questions. He suggested to Rowe that she had seen nothing, but Rowe was only twelve and didn't know what the officer wanted. She said that she had and told him about it. Again he said that she had seen nothing. Eventually, she understood what was being said, but only after he suggested that she would be taken into the desert and the family would be separated. Once he was convinced that Rowe would not talk about the strange metal and the family would forget about the fire run outside the city, he left.

Cahill, who was already married and therefore not present in 1947, in her affidavit noted that Rowe had told her in the 1960s about what had happened. Rowe also told her sister that the material "ran like water."

It should be noted that the fire department records, while confirming that the department did make runs outside the city in 1947, do not confirm a run in early July to the north of town. They also confirm, as does the city directory, that Frankie Rowe's father was a lieutenant in the fire department. Family members who were contacted did confirm parts of the story that Frankie Rowe has told.

In the end, however, there is no incontrovertible proof that Dan Dwyer made a fire run outside the city and then found alien creatures. There is no proof that Frankie Rowe handled the strange metallic debris, nor that she was visited by members of the military who suggested she not tell her story. There are only small confirmations that suggest she was involved to a limited degree.

Saunders, Major (later Colonel) Patrick (1919–1995) Patrick
Saunders was born in Alabama and died seventy-six years later in
Florida. He attended the University of Florida and was graduated
from the University of Nebraska at Omaha and the Air War
College. During World War II he flew thirty-seven combat missions
and was awarded the Legion of Merit, the Silver Star, a Bronze Star
with Oak Leaf Cluster, the Distinguished Flying Cross, and the Air
Medal with three Oak Leaf Clusters. Patrick Saunders died in
November 1995 after a fall that put him into the hospital.

During his military service, he was the base adjutant at the
Roswell Army Air Field. It was the position he held in July 1947,
when the alleged crash took place. When asked by UFO investigators about the possibility of the UFO crash, he said that he knew
nothing about the little green bodies and that the whole thing was a
big joke. He did confirm that he had been the 509th's adjutant for
only a few weeks when the events of July 1947 transpired.

Asked if he could remember any of the rumors and which of
those might have some truth to them, he said simply, "I can't specify
anything." Saunders, it seemed, was not a witness to the story.

But later, when both *UFO Crash at Roswell* and *The Truth
About the UFO Crash at Roswell* were published, he bought copies.
In fact, he bought lots of copies, because, according to what he

wrote on the first page of *The Truth About the UFO Crash at Roswell,* that was the truth.

The quotation, in his own handwriting, on the first page of that book is "Here's the truth and I still haven't told anybody anything!"

In the months before he died, he confided in a number of close and lifelong friends that suddenly the officers of the 509th Bomb Group were confronted with a technology greater than that of Earth. "They," meaning the creatures in the flying saucers, had control of the sky. The Air Force was powerless against them. And they, the members of the U.S. Army Air Forces, had just seen the power of control of the sky. It was one of the factors that defeated the enemies in World War II.

Saunders went on, telling people that military officials had no idea what their, the pilots of the craft, intentions might be. Their technology was more advanced than that of the United States. Top military leaders didn't know if the alien beings were a threat, so the government was reluctant to release any information about them.

What's important here is that Saunders did not share this information with UFO researchers or outsiders. He kept it to himself, telling close friends and family only after the story had been told by so many others. It can't be said that he was seeking fame or fortune by creating a tale to put himself in the limelight. He told only his closest friends and family.

Saunders mentioned to those same friends and family that he planned on making a videotaped statement to be released upon his death. Unfortunately, he didn't have the time to make that tape. All that is left is the single statement he placed in the book.

Scanlon, Brigadier General Martin F. (Mike) (1889–1980) Martin F. Scanlon was born in Scranton, Pennsylvania, attended Pennsylvania and Cornell universities, and was commissioned as a second lieutenant in the regular Army in 1912. He rose through the ranks with a variety of promotions, eventually reaching the temporary rank of brigadier general on October 1, 1940. He reverted to his permanent rank of colonel on April 11, 1946, and retired from military service as a brigadier general on February 21, 1948, his last assignment apparently at Mitchell Field, New York, as a public relations officer.

Scanlon had been associated with intelligence work for part of his career. During the 1930s, Scanlon had been the air attaché to the U.S. Embassy in London. His duties included developing intelligence on various European air forces, especially those of the British and the Germans. With the establishment of the Army Air Force in June 1941, the commanding general, General Henry "Hap" Arnold, brought Scanlon back to the United States to become the first Assistant Chief of Air Staff, Intelligence (AC/AS Intelligence). Scanlon's responsibilities were to develop the intelligence needs of the Air Force. He advocated that Air Intelligence be developed with an eye on responding to the threats that would be faced by Allied flyers and the needs of aviation during the war. In other words, Scanlon, working directly for General Arnold, was determining the methods of collecting intelligence, evaluating of that intelligence in light of the needs of AAF, and seeing that intelligence was disseminated in a timely fashion.

Scanlon was connected to Roswell on two occasions. In September 1942, he became the commander of the 38th Flying Training Wing in Roswell. There was also a facility located

Brigadier General Martin F. Scanlon. (*Photo courtesy of Walter Haut*)

in Santa Ana, California. He left Roswell in August 1944, but his name was linked to the 1947 crash by Frank Kaufmann.

Scanlon, upon retirement from the military, joined Republic Aviation as director of export and vice president in 1948. He retired from Republic in 1957. In January 1980, he died of congestive heart failure at Walter Reed Hospital at the age of ninety.

See also *Kaufmann, Frank*

Schmitt, Donald R. Donald Schmitt of Hubertus, Wisconsin, is the coauthor of two books about the Roswell case, *UFO Crash at Roswell* and *The Truth About the UFO Crash at Roswell.* He was at

one time Director of Special Investigations at the Center for UFO Studies, served on their board of directors, and worked with Dr. J. Allen Hynek on various UFO investigations.

Schmitt told friends that he made his living as a medical illustrator, had worked undercover for either local authorities or the Drug Enforcement Agency, was a college graduate, and was actively pursuing his Ph.D. at Concordia University. He had become interested in UFOs as an outgrowth of his interest in the Kennedy assassination. He had seen the work done by the Warren Commission and thought that it lacked candor and reality.

Donald R. Schmitt. (*Photo courtesy of Kevin Randle*)

There was a hint of a government cover-up. It was this interest in peeking beyond the cover-up that led to his interest in UFOs.

In an interview conducted by Gillian Sender for *Milwaukee*

magazine, Schmitt said that he had attended the University of Wisconsin-Milwaukee and Marquette University, taking classes in criminology, theology, and sociology. Schmitt told Sender that he had received a master's degree from UWM and a bachelor of arts degree from Concordia College. It was the strength of that educational background, as well as his work with local police agencies, that seemed to suggest that Schmitt was one of the best-trained and most qualified of the UFO investigators.

Sender, for some reason, began to check into Schmitt's claims. She learned through Lisa Soik of the Franklin Information Group of Milwaukee, a company that specializes in checking backgrounds, that Schmitt had not attended either UWM or Marquette. He couldn't be a doctoral candidate at Concordia because the college had no doctoral programs. In 1995, when she checked, she did learn that Schmitt had been enrolled at Concordia but hadn't taken classes for about two years.

A month after the article appeared in the February 1995 issue of *Milwaukee* magazine, a letter to the editor explained Schmitt's real occupation. According to that letter, Schmitt had been working full-time at the Hartford (WI) Post Office. That meant that Schmitt had been less than candid about his real job as well as his educational background.

In March 1995, several of the leaders of the UFO field called Kevin Randle to ask him about the revelations in the magazine. Randle defended Schmitt, telling them that the article was little more than a hatchet job designed to undermine Schmitt's credibility. Randle said that Schmitt had assured him that he was a medical illustrator who had provided the drawings for a 600-page medical textbook and that he didn't work at the post office.

On March 13, 1995, Ken Eppler, the postmaster at Hartford, issued a short letter. It said, "In the letter section of the March, 1995 issue of *Milwaukee* magazine, it is implied that Donald Schmitt has worked full-time for the U S Postal Service since 1974. Not only is this untrue, but I have never made such a statement to

Milwaukee magazine or anyone else." It was signed, "Sincerely, Ken Eppler." I have reproduced this letter exactly as typed.

In April 1995, while on a research trip to Roswell, Schmitt sat down for documentarian Russ Estes to answer questions about the Roswell investigation for what would become *Roswell Remembered.* By this time, the talk in the UFO field was about Schmitt and his alleged misrepresentations. Though Estes had no real interest in the internal politics of the UFO field, the story had reached a high level. Before the camera rolled, Estes told Schmitt that he was now obligated to ask questions about Schmitt's background. It simply was too hot a topic to avoid. Schmitt said that he understood and he was ready to answer all such questions honestly.

Estes pointed out during the interview that almost everyone had had, at one time or another, "day" jobs. Nearly everyone had worked in a restaurant, carried newspapers as a kid, or worked in a grocery store bagging purchases. The majority of those who did UFO investigations had day jobs that paid the bills. No one cared what the day job was as long as the quality of the research was high and could be verified. Estes then asked, "Do you work at the post office?"

Schmitt looked into the camera, shook his head, and said, "No."

Within twenty-four hours, a postal employee in Hartford confirmed that Schmitt did in fact work at the post office, and had been a full-time employee for nearly fifteen years. According to the seniority list, Schmitt had worked there since April 2, 1983. Eppler's letter had been strictly accurate, but it hadn't been the whole truth and nothing but the truth.

That did not mark the end of the ordeal. Several researchers had suggested that his claim to have illustrated a medical textbook would end some of the controversy, if he could produce it. He said that he didn't have a copy because it was quite expensive. When asked for the name of the book, he failed to supply it.

Other researchers suggested that an honest statement describing his work at the post office would help him. If he would now admit the truth, then the controversy would end. But Schmitt went on the attack, now telling people that he did work at the post office and that he had never lied about it. He wanted to know what the problem was. Several of the prominent researchers in the UFO field were employees of the post office.

In the March/April issue of the *International UFO Reporter*, Schmitt wrote a very short "letter to the editor" that said:

> Recently several parties have raised questions concerning my educational background and place of employment. Although these matters should not, and do not, have any bearing on the Roswell investigation Kevin Randle and I have conducted, I thought it best to offer these clarifying comments.
>
> I have been an employee of the U.S. Postal Service since 1974. I worked part-time until 1983, when I became a full-time rural letter carrier. During all this period, I have been a freelance commercial artist. I will soon receive a bachelor's degree from Concordia College with a major in Liberal Arts, and I've been accepted into the newly-established graduate program in criminal justice studies at Concordia.
>
> I would like to offer my sincerest apologies for any false or misleading statements I made about my background. I regret any misunderstandings that may have sprung from this.
>
> As a consequence, I have resigned, effective April 13, 1995, as Director of Special Investigations of the Center for UFO Studies. I will continue, with the support of my colleagues, as a CUFOS board member. I want to thank all those who have offered their support and friendship to me during the past few months.

That wasn't, of course, the end of the problems. It came out that Schmitt, while working with Randle, had told a number of other investigators, as well as those in the UFO community, that he suspected Randle was a government agent. He suggested to some that they be careful with information that they provided Randle. Schmitt had no evidence of this; it was merely a suspicion that he was expressing to a few people.

Schmitt's troubles weren't over, however. He had interested *Omni* in the story of Glenn Dennis's missing nurse, Naomi Self. Schmitt had told pro-UFO reporter Paul McCarthy that he had checked for the nurse's records, and they were missing. All records of her had been expunged. Schmitt had also suggested that a search of military records had failed to find the records of a number of men who had served at Roswell in July 1947. Schmitt was suggesting that some records were missing because those individuals had been involved in some aspect of the crash retrieval.

McCarthy began his search at the Army Records Center in St. Louis. Within days he had located, with the assistance of the staff there, the records of the nurses who had not transferred to the Air Force when the services split. He could find no evidence that any of the nurses' records had disappeared, or that any records were missing. McCarthy's article turned negative, suggesting that both Schmitt and Randle had been a little free with the conclusions they drew. McCarthy suggested that a properly conducted search would have revealed the information because it hadn't taken him long to find it. To him it meant the Roswell investigation had been sloppy.

Schmitt, of course, wrote a rebuttal, suggesting that the problem was McCarthy's. Schmitt wrote in the summer of 1997: "We were pleased that he [McCarthy] corroborated absence of records in directories we suggested for nurses headquartered at Roswell Army Airfield in 1947. But all too quickly, his motives became starkly obvious. He attempts to paint an ill-conceived picture of misinformation and shoddy work on our part. With all the lackluster skill of 20/20 hindsight. Not only are his observations totally inaccurate, his misrepresentations and false characterizations are downright libelous."

Schmitt then confessed that he often used circuitous routes to find information. Rather than approaching the St. Louis Records Center directly, Schmitt noted, "Each and every inquiry to the Records Center in St. Louis was via computer records directly through DoD and VA. We learned or [sic] lesson at CUFOS not to send FOIAs to specific government agencies regarding a named individual or event for fear of tipping out [sic] hand."

The real truth was that Schmitt often failed to return telephone calls, and supplied incomplete or inaccurate information to McCarthy. He failed to supply documentation that McCarthy requested. Schmitt told Randle that he had letters and other documents showing that all avenues of inquiry have been pursued, which would prove that McCarthy's article was inaccurate. Schmitt, however, failed to produce any of those documents. The article set back serious research into the Roswell case.

It wasn't long after this that Schmitt lost his position on the board of directors of CUFOS. They failed to vote him back onto the board, replacing him with Tom Carey.

Schmitt still lectures about UFOs in general and the Roswell case in particular, frequently appearing at the International UFO Museum and Research Center in Roswell.

See also *Dennis, Glenn; International UFO Museum and Research Center; Randle, Kevin*

Schreiber, Bessie Brazel See **Roswell in Perspective**

Second Site Although Marcel opened the door to the second site in his many recorded interviews, the Air Force didn't bother to enter. Instead, they ignored all testimony that would lead in that direction, pretending that it didn't exist. If the stories of a second site were nothing more than the secondhand ramblings of family members, then the testimony might be considered very weak and unimportant. However, there is a body of additional testimony that lead's in that direction, testimony from those who were on the second site and can speak of it, the craft, and the bodies firsthand.

These witnesses have located that site just north of Roswell, about thirty-five miles from what had been the front gate of the base. Some of the references are vague, while others are very precise. All lead to the conclusion that there was a second site where the main section of the craft and bodies were located. If true, this testimony calls the Project Mogul explanation into serious question. If there were two sites, then the Mogul explanation simply doesn't work. And if there was a site where a craft and bodies were found, no conventional explanation can explain the facts.

Many people spoke of a site just north of Roswell, not far to the northwest near Corona. William Woody reported seeing something bright in the sky west of Roswell. It seemed to be dropping toward the ground. It can be argued that what Woody reported was the craft just prior to the crash. If that is the case, the question that comes to mind is what would have been burning on the cluster of balloons. They were, after all, filled with helium, an inert gas.

Woody's testimony, however, is more important because of another aspect. He, along with his father, drove north out of Roswell during the July 4 weekend, either on Saturday or Sunday. To the west, on the side roads from Highway 285, they saw soldiers blocking the way. When they tried to turn in that direction, they weren't allowed to leave the main highway. There was no reason to block those roads for the recovery of a Project Mogul balloon. In fact, there is no evidence that any roads were ever blocked when any Mogul equipment was being recovered.

The testimony of a man who was a boy in 1947 might not be considered as the most reliable. However, Dr. C. Bertrand Schultz, a vertebrate paleontologist working near Roswell, was heading north on Highway 285 that same weekend. According to him, he saw the soldiers standing along the dirt roads to the west. He didn't want to drive in that direction, so he wasn't that interested in them.

Later, he learned from a colleague, Dr. W. Curry Holden, that something had crashed. Holden, interviewed just before his death in 1993, said that he had been at the site north of town where the craft and bodies had been found. To Schultz, it was clear that the military men he saw were part of the cordon of the area.

Army counterintelligence agent Master Sergent Lewis Rickett also suggested a site close to Roswell. In a taped interview with Don Schmitt, he said, "I remember it took us about forty-five minutes. I said, 'How far are we going out here and he [Sheridan Cavitt] said, 'It's just over here . . .'"

Major Edwin Easley, who had been responsible for cordoning off the area, said that the site was closer to Roswell, north of town. He made no mention of a location far to the northwest, near Corona, probably because the Debris Field was of little importance when compared to the Impact Site, where a craft and bodies were located.

There are some secondhand witnesses who reported what fathers or grandfathers had said. Frankie Rowe, whose father was a firefighter with the Roswell department, said that he made a run outside the city limits to where the bodies had been found. She believed that it was close to town. And there is no evidence that the Roswell Fire Department ever made a run into Lincoln County to the site of the Debris Field.

Barbara Dugger said that her grandmother, Inez Wilcox, told her that her grandfather, Sheriff George Wilcox, had been to a site no more than thirty miles from Roswell where the craft and bodies had been discovered. Mack Brazel did visit the Chaves County sheriff, rather than the Lincoln County sheriff, and there is no evidence that Wilcox or his deputies made a trip outside the county.

All of this suggests a second site closer to Roswell. There is testimony of two distinct sites. Air Force investigators apparently stayed away from any testimony that would lead to the second site. They spoke to no one who would suggest that there might have been another site, including Air Force Brigadier General Arthur Exon.

During a taped interview in May 1990, Exon said, "It was probably part of the same accident, but there were two distinct sites. One, assuming that the thing, as I understand it, as I remember flying the area later, that the damage to the vehicle seemed to be coming from the southeast to the northwest, but it could have been going in the opposite direction, but it doesn't seem likely. So the farther northwest pieces found on the [Brazel] ranch, those pieces were mostly metal."

Exon was saying, based on his firsthand observations, that there were two sites and that the site farther to the northwest was mostly metal. In other words, Exon's observations corroborated the information that there was a second site, that the Brazel ranch contained mostly metal, and that there was another site closer to Roswell.

Although it is clear that the Air Force investigators had access to all these data and that they had read both the Randle and Schmitt books, they didn't bother to interview General Exon. Tapes of the interviews were available from both the researcher who conducted the interviews and UFO organizations interested in the case.

See also *Brazel, Bill; Debris Field; Easley, Major Edwin; Exon, Brigadier General Arthur; Holden, W. Curry; Impact Site; Marcel Sr., Major Jesse; Wilcox, Sheriff George A.; Wilcox, Inez*

Self, Naomi (a.k.a. Selff, Naomi Maria) It was Glenn Dennis who introduced the missing nurse concept into the Roswell case. It was only a day or so after the crash that he spoke to a nurse whom he later identified as Naomi Self for various Roswell investigators. He met her at the officers club on July 9 or July 10, based on reconstructions of the events, where she told him the tale of a preliminary autopsy of little creatures from another star system. She told him not to tell a living soul about the event, and within days she was transferred off the base, apparently sent to England. Dennis received a note from her, telling him her military address in England. The letter he wrote to her came back marked "Deceased." She had been killed in an aircraft accident that had killed five other nurses, according to the medical personnel at the base in Roswell.

One of the first things UFO researchers did was check the year-book produced in 1947 by the Information Office of the 509th Bomb Group. It contained the names and photographs of the majority of the people assigned to the base that year. Walter Haut, the editor of the book, said 10 to 20 percent of the people failed to appear in the book, so when there was no picture for a Naomi Self, that wasn't particularly significant.

Researchers next checked the *New York Times Index*. A search of every aircraft accident from July 1947 through 1955 revealed no aircraft accidents in England, Europe, or the United States that had claimed the lives of five nurses as Dennis had claimed.

Don Berliner, who was working with Stan Friedman, made a search using the *Stars and Stripes,* a newspaper printed for the military overseas. It contains military news, and if a group of Army nurses had been killed in an aircraft accident, it should have been reported there. It was not.

There was a secondary problem developing as well. There was talk, some of it from investigators, some of it from Dennis himself, that suggested that his interest in the nurse might have been more than just friendship. After all, if they weren't more than friends, why, after a short stop before going overseas, did she drop him a note with her address in it? That implied a somewhat stronger relationship. In 1947, Glenn Dennis was already married and had a young daughter. He shouldn't have been writing notes to unmarried nurses, especially since he has described her as very religious.

Searches of the various available records of the 509th Bomb Group including the very detailed Unit History for the spring and summer of 1947 provided no references to a nurse named Self. The base telephone directory, published in August 1947, listed numbers for many of the officers, including some of the nurses, but had no listing for Naomi Self. Every document checked by researchers failed to produce any corroboration for her existence. None of this was significant in and of itself because not everyone at the base had been listed in those various sources. In the aggregate, however, it was becoming quite worrisome.

With the help of a police officer, one investigator was able to identify five women named Naomi Self and spoke to four of them. Dennis had also said she had a brother named William, and more than 250 men with that name were located. The work has been duplicated simply because no one has had any luck, and these efforts were no more effective than any of the others. In other words, the nurse Dennis identified has not been found. In fact, there is no trace that she ever existed.

A number of former members of the medical team at Roswell in 1947 have been located. A nurse, Rosemary Brown, for example, said that she had no memory of a nurse who had been with the unit for a short period, as described by Dennis, or of a nurse named Naomi. A doctor said that he remembered very little of the staff at Roswell because it was so long ago.

The single exception is a man named David Wagnon, whose record does place him in Roswell at the proper time. He seems to remember the nurse, but that is based more on a description, since he was unable to remember the name himself. It is a single verbal account with no corroborative documentation to back it up, and at this time, we need to have that documentation.

In fact, there is no documentation for the existence of a nurse at Roswell named Naomi Self. A researcher in Arizona, V. G. Golubic, undertook the search for the nurse in much the same fashion that Tom Carey undertook the search for the archaeologists. He has identified about eighteen women who were assigned to the base as nurses, both military and civilian, in the correct time frame, nurses who were not part of the yearbook or the base telephone directory but whose names did surface in various documents recovered through Freedom of Information Act requests, interviews, and other sources.

Golubic has spoken to another nurse (other than Rosemary Brown) who was at Roswell in 1947, and she has no memory of

Naomi Self. According to Golubic, he has found no trace of her, except for the confirmation provided by David Wagnon. Golubic has spoken to Wagnon a number of times about it. He also points out that he has spoken to twenty to twenty-five members of the medical team at Roswell, and Naomi just doesn't surface.

Dennis told some people that he had not provided them with the nurse's real name. He had given us information that was close, but her real name was Naomi Maria Selff. He told another researcher that the nurse's real name was Naomi Sipes. But again, even with the new name, there was no documentation.

But the tale doesn't end there. When it was pointed out that no documentation, no corroboration, nothing verified the existence of the nurse, Dennis changed the tale again. He had not supplied anyone with the right name. In fact, the last name didn't even begin with an "S." He was changing the tale as he was confronted with the evidence, and such changes do not bode well for the credibility of his tale.

He also said that Naomi Self was born in Minnesota, and that she completed all her schooling in Minnesota. Not according to various authorities in Minnesota. No one has been able to find a single document or record to confirm this. Naomi Self didn't go to school anywhere in Minnesota. And remember, given her age and occupation, the search can be limited to a few specific years.

What this means is that a comprehensive search, carried out over more than five years by a dozen or more researchers, has failed to produce any evidence that a nurse, by any of the names given by Dennis, disappeared. While the story is interesting and intriguing, it is also baseless. There was no nurse at Roswell who disappeared after assisting in a preliminary autopsy of alien creatures.

See also *Dennis, Glenn*

Spaatz, General Carl (Tooey) (1891–1974) Carl Spaatz was born in Boyerstown, Pennsylvania, and attended the United States Military Academy at West Point. He graduated in 1914, commissioned as a second lieutenant of Infantry, and detailed to the Army's aviation school in San Diego, California, for flight training.

In 1916, he served under General John J. Pershing during his expedition in Mexico. Two years later, in 1918, he was again serving under Pershing, but this time with the American Expeditionary Force in France. He was a flight leader with the Thirteenth Pursuit Squadron during World War I. He shot down three German Fokker aircraft.

During World War II, Spaatz commanded units in all theaters of the war. He commanded the Eighth Air Force and later was the Commander of the Strategic Air Forces in the Pacific. He supervised the final attacks on Japan, including dropping the atomic bombs on Hiroshima and Nagasaki. He was present during the surrenders in Berlin and Tokyo.

In July 1947, Spaatz was the commanding general of the U.S. Army Air Forces, and had there been a UFO crash at Roswell, it would have been reported to him. Some of the decisions about the reporting of the incident and the recovery of the craft would have been his.

Spaatz retired in June 1948 and lived in Chevy Chase, Maryland. He was a contributing editor of *Newsweek*. He advised the Chief of Staff of the Air Force and was the chairman of the National Executive Board of the Civil Air Patrol. He also served on a variety of other boards, most of which had some connection to the military. He died in 1974 of congestive heart failure at the age of eighty-three.

Statement Validity Analysis Statement validity analysis (SVA) is an established method in forensic psychology for evaluating the credibility of witness reports. It is a systematic procedure for assessing the credibility of memory reports and has been used for decades in Germany. SVA consists of a criteria-based content analysis (CBCA). An analysis is made of the verbal report. Nineteen CBCA criteria have been proposed to reflect the qualitative and quantitative differences between credible reports and fabrications.

Tests of the CBCA have produced positive results. In a study in which forty child abuse statements were analyzed, twenty confirmed by admissions of guilt or by corroborating physical evidence and twenty considered "doubtful," CBCA differentiated between the two groups. The results of the test have been challenged by some, suggesting that the single-rater method precludes any firm conclusions about the validity. The psychological literature does provide limited support for the SVA technique in analyzing the credibility of verbal reports.

To date, the SVA and other assessment methods have been applied only to the Jim Ragsdale testimony. Specifically, the second report by Ragsdale, told to Max Littell of the International UFO Museum and Research Center, has been analyzed using SVA and fact pattern analysis. Both of the methods suggested that the Ragsdale tale was either a fabrication or the result of a false memory.

See also *Ragsdale, James*

Strickland, Marian Although she saw little concerning the Roswell case, some of the information Strickland had was extremely important. In 1947, Marian Strickland lived on a ranch not far from the one managed by Mack Brazel. He husband, Lyman, and Brazel were friends, and Brazel visited their ranch periodically. She provided some insight into the events of July 1947 and added another voice to those who suggested something unusual happened that summer.

In an interview conducted on videotape in 1990, Strickland, then living in Roswell, said, "We had a little old dinky shack that had a porch that wasn't any wider than that. My husband . . . all ranchers go out on the porch to see where it's raining . . . how much and who got some. He had to stand out there to see where it was raining and there was so much thunder and lightning that I begged him to come in the house. Finally there was this terrible thunderclap and he came in and says, 'That hit something.' "

What she had done was confirm the tale of the thunderclap that seemed out of place. She and her husband had heard it on the night of the storm. It corroborated the secondhand reports that Mack Brazel had heard something that hadn't sounded right.

Strickland also remembered seeing Mack Brazel in the days that followed his stay in Roswell. Her husband and Brazel were sitting at the table while she continued her chores and brought coffee. She said, "I heard pieces of the conversation. How nasty the officers at the air base were. The whole neighborhood was scandalized that the army would treat people like that . . . people who had good intentions. He [Brazel] made it plain he was not supposed to tell that there was any excitement about the material [found on the ranch]. He was a man who had integrity. He definitely felt insulted and misused, and disrespected. He was worse than annoyed . . . and felt that he had been kicked around. He was threatened that if he opened his mouth, he might get thrown in the back of the jail. He gave that impression."

Strickland's final piece of information was that she hadn't seen any of the strange metallic debris described by so many others, but her daughter had. According to her, Bill Brazel had brought a small piece of the foil to the ranch and let all the kids play with it.

Marian Strickland died several years ago.

See also *Brazel, Mack; Easley, Mayor Edwin*

Stringfield, Leonard H. (1920–1994) As Jerry Clark noted in his tribute to Stringfield published in the *International UFO Reporter,* had it not been for him, the discussion of crash/retrievals (Stringfield's term) would not be taking place today. In the late 1970s, Stringfield was almost the only voice suggesting that these were reports that should interest researchers. Instead, almost universally, UFO investigators rejected such claims because they simply couldn't be true.

Stringfield was born and raised in Cincinnati. He graduated from Withrow High School in 1939. He attended the University of Cincinnati's School of Journalism. His college career was interrupted by the Japanese attack on Pearl Harbor. He served with the

Fifth Air Force, first at Wright Field and later in the Pacific Theater. By the end of the war, he had moved from public relations to intelligence and counterintelligence.

When the war ended and Stringfield was discharged, he joined DuBois Chemical Company in the advertising department. He created the art department and stayed there for thirty years. He retired as the director of public relations.

Stringfield's passion, other than his stamp collecting, his tropical fish, and his birds, was UFOs. While in the Pacific, on a flight to Tokyo, he saw three UFOs. It created a lifelong interest, and some suspected it might have been the reason that he always traveled by train or bus.

In 1954, he started the *C.R.I.F.O. Newsletter* and changed it to the *C.R.I.F.O. Orbit* a year later. He published it until 1957. It was also in 1957 that he published his first book, *Inside Saucer Post . . . 3-0 Blue,* which summarized his position with the Air Defense Command from 1953 to 1957. It was a strange relationship, with Stringfield supplying them with information about UFOs in his area. The Air Force didn't employ civilians in their UFO research. He said that his code name, or special code, was *Foxtrot Kilo 3-0 Blue.* The Air Force denies that such an arrangement ever existed.

In 1977, Stringfield published his second book, *Situation Red, the UFO Siege!* It was in that book that he first tentatively began to explore the idea of crash/retrievals. Many in the UFO field thought that he had made a grave mistake, and that UFOs simply don't crash.

Shortly after that, he began to investigate some stories and was among the first to interview, and then report on, the statements made by Jesse Marcel Sr. The two had a somewhat common background because they had served on the same island in the Pacific during the war in similar capacities but had not met there.

From those interviews grew his series of monographs, or Status Reports, on crash/retrievals. Although criticized by some in the UFO community because he reported all the stories that came his way, most understood Stringfield's method. He would evaluate the stories, attempting to suggest how reliable a report might be, but he also believed that it was necessary to report as much of the information as possible. Stringfield said that he never knew when one of those reports might provide the clues that others needed to solve a small part of the UFO problem.

Stringfield was always quick to assist friends and colleagues in their searches for more information. He helped a number of them interview witnesses who had asked not to be identified. Stringfield would arrange the interview, allowing the witness to tell as little or as much as he or she wanted to. He did not violate the confidences of his witnesses.

Stringfield's contribution to the UFO field was great. In his quiet way, he sat back, provided clues for those who wanted them, and let others pursue the leads. Without Stringfield many of researchers might never have begun to look into the crash/retrievals. That could be his greatest contribution.

Threats One of the most consistent aspects of this story is the number of people reporting that they were threatened by members of the U.S. military and representatives of the U.S. government. It wasn't just a single source, but a wide variety, including women and children. It is one of the more frightening aspects of this story.

George Wilcox, as the Chaves County sheriff, was one of the first civilians involved in the case. He talked to Brazel, saw some of the debris, and may have been at the second site, where the bodies were found. He worked with the military, fielded phone calls from the press, and later tried to explain to those who asked that he wasn't involved. He did such a good job that some of the original investigators believed that he had no role in the case, other than alerting the 509th to the fact that Brazel was in town with strange debris.

But later investigations revealed that Wilcox had a major role. He had been told, according to his daughter, Phyllis McGuire, not to talk about it. The military wanted him to remain silent.

Wilcox's granddaughter, Barbara Dugger, made the extent of the threats clear. Her grandmother told her that the military police came to the jailhouse "and told George and I (that if we) ever told anything about the incident, talked about it in any way, not only would we be killed, but they would get the rest of the family."

Military officers continued to make the rounds. Frankie Rowe reported that "the military came to our house and they basically threatened us if we said anything about it. They were going to take mother away and they were going to take daddy away so we basically forgot everything we ever saw . . . we could never talk about this. As far as we were concerned, the whole incident never happened." She then repeated, "If we ever talked about it, we were threatened."

It wasn't until later that the whole story emerged. During a radio interview about the case at Roswell, Rowe, when the host asked her his first question, froze, not because of mike fright, but because of the accent of the show's host. Hearing his eastern accent filled her with dread. Rowe had suddenly remembered what he had said and it hadn't been about Orchard Park. He had said he would kill the whole family.

Helen Cahill, Rowe's sister, remembered how angry her father had been about the threats. She mentioned they had threatened all the firemen who had gone on that run out to the crash site. There were city police involved, too, and they were threatened.

A few of the civilian witnesses were only told that they weren't supposed to discuss the case with outsiders. Mack Brazel never reported that he had been threatened. He had been held by the military for over a week, and he gave his word that he wouldn't talk about it. Bill Brazel said that his father had taken an oath that he wouldn't talk about it and he didn't, other than to mention a few things to Bill. He never suggested that bodies had been found or that he'd seen them. Whenever he was questioned by Bill, he always said the same thing: He'd promised that he wouldn't tell.

Jud Roberts, the minority owner of radio station KGFL, told investigators for television programs, books, and nearly anyone else who would listen that he had been threatened by the Federal Communications Commission. According to Roberts, Walt Whitmore Sr. and one other employee had picked up Mack Brazel at his ranch and returned with him to Roswell.

Whitmore interviewed Brazel using a wire recorder, planning to broadcast the interview sometime on July 8, 1947. Before they could do that, according to Roberts, he received a number of telephone calls telling him that the interview was not to be broadcast. According to Roberts, if they did broadcast it, they could all begin looking for new jobs because they would be out of the radio business. The threat wasn't veiled in any way. If they played the interview with Brazel, they would lose their broadcast license.

The military men and women involved in the retrieval weren't immune from the threats or security oaths. Each, as they completed their assignments, was again reminded of the various oaths they had taken. In most cases, it was a gentle reminder that each had seen many things that the government considered classified and that he or she was not supposed to talk about it to those not authorized to hear.

Others provided additional information about that. Frank Kaufmann said that the men were taken into the brief-

George "Jud" Roberts. (*Photo courtesy of Kevin Randle*)

ing room in small groups so that no one man would have the names of many of the others who were involved. They were told that the retrieval was classified at the highest levels and that no one was to talk about it under any circumstances. The men were then released out one door while those waiting for the next briefing came in another. That way no one would be inclined to ask too many questions because he would never know who had been involved and who had not.

That's what makes this case different from all the other events reported over the years. The military went to extraordinary lengths to keep the information under wraps. In 1945, during the waning days of World War II, FBI agents and military officials requested that American citizens keep their knowledge of the Japanese balloon bombs to themselves. Although the Japanese were actively trying to learn if the bombs were reaching the American continent, no Americans were threatened.

At Roswell, the government went after everyone who had knowledge of the events, threatening them with prison or death. And they threatened parents by telling them that their families would be killed.

If the report had come from a single individual, a case could be made that the person had overreacted or had misunderstood a request. But there are several people, each from a different location, not knowing what was said to others. The stories are consistent.

What made the events at Roswell so different that the government felt that it had to threaten American citizens? What made this secret so important that they could not rely on the veracity and the loyalty of the citizens?

The simple truth is that Roswell represented something that had never happened before, and the government believed that it had to protect us. That was why they threatened.

Truth About the UFO Crash at Roswell, The by **Kevin D. Randle and Donald R. Schmitt** This is the second of the Roswell books written by Randle and Schmitt, and it contained a great deal of new information surrounding the alleged retrieval operation on the impact site. New witnesses such as Jim Ragsdale were revealed for the first time. The book was not about strange metallic debris, but about the craft and the bodies of the alien flight crew.

In their enthusiasm for the case, Randle and Schmitt overlooked what might have been clues about the veracity of some of those new witnesses. Ragsdale's tale, which should have been reported, should also have carried some cautionary note. A close review of his interview with Schmitt provided a few red flags. These, however, were ignored.

That is not to say that they did not report on negative information. Although they accept the tale told by Dr. W. Curry Holden, and Randle has followed up the initial interviews and data with a great deal of research, they also reported that neither Holden's wife nor daughter thought the story to be true. Both said they had never heard him mention it, and both suggested that his advanced age had confused him. He jumbled memories together, confusing times, dates, and what they believed to be events. Randle did note that Holden's story was corroborated by his colleagues, and that he, Randle, had been careful during his interview to provide Holden with no verbal cues about what he wanted Holden to say.

Even with the flaws, including their belief that the Glenn Dennis story is real, there is solid information in the book. They were able to identify the impact site, based not on a single witness, but on several who claimed to have inside knowledge. Interestingly, using maps and photographs, these witnesses selected the same location, just to the west of Highway 285 north of Roswell.

The most important contribution of the book, however, might be the analysis offered of the various explanations offered by skeptics, debunkers, and the Air Force over the last fifty years. The thorough analysis of the V-2 and missile testing, the balloons, including the Japanese balloon bombs, and the aircraft and experimental aircraft accident theories are put to rest. The research in these areas was excellent.

In the end, flaws and all, the book contributes to the overall picture of the crash near Roswell. It adds valuable new information and some keen insights into the events. Coupled with Randle's later writings, in which he examines some of the mistakes, a clearer picture of the Roswell case can be drawn.

Twining, General Nathan F. (1897–1982) Nathan F. Twining was born in Monroe, Wisconsin, at the end of the nineteenth century. He began his active military career with the 3rd Oregon Infantry, a National Guard unit, in June 1916. He entered the United States Military Academy at West Point in 1917 after having failed the entrance exam for the Naval Academy, and graduated as a second lieutenant in November 1918. He saw no service in Europe during World War I.

In 1923, he began flight training at Brooks Field, Texas, and graduated in 1924. He was assigned as an instructor pilot at Brooks and then March Field, and finally joined the 18th Pursuit Group in Hawaii, serving as commander of the 26th Attack Squadron.

For the next several years, he held a variety of assignments. In December 1941, as World War II started, Twining was a lieutenant colonel who had just been assigned to the Operations Division. In February 1942, he became the Assistant Executive in the Office of the Chief of the Air Corps.

General Nathan F. Twining. (*Photo courtesy of USAF*)

In July 1942, the newly promoted brigadier general was sent to the South Pacific as the chief of staff to Major General M. F. Harmon. The following January, Twining was named the commanding general of the 13th Air Force.

As the commander of the 13th Air Force, Twining was on board a B-17 when it crashed into the Coral Sea in 1943. Twining and fourteen other men escaped as the plane sank in less than a minute. He and the others spent five days and six nights drifting in two rubber rafts with no food and only half a canteen of water. They had the fresh water resupplied by rain. The only food was an albatross shot by Twining and eaten raw. Search planes finally rescued them.

Twining held a series of postwar commands. These included a term as the commander of the Air Materiel Command at Wright Field in 1947. Information suggests that the debris recovered at Roswell was sent on to Wright Field for examination. On September 23, 1947, Twining signed the controversial letter about the flying saucers, suggesting first that they were real, but denying there had been any proof in the form of crash-recovered exhibits.

In 1950, he was appointed the Vice Chief of Staff, and in 1953, the Chief of Staff of the Air Force. On March 26, 1957, President Eisenhower nominated him to become the Chairman of the Joint Chiefs of Staff. The nomination was approved and in August, he was sworn in as chairman.

Twining retired in 1960, but became a vice chairman of the Holt, Rinehart and Winston, Inc., publishing company. He died in March 1982 of cardiopulmonary arrest at the Wilford Hall Medical Center at Lackland Air Force Base outside of San Antonio, Texas.

The Twining Letter There are those who believe that a letter written by Lieutenant General Nathan F. Twining on September 23, 1947, proves that there was no crash at Roswell. Skeptics, citing the letter, claim that it shows the flaw in the thinking of the UFO community. They also take it further, claiming there were no secret studies, and that the Air Force quit active investigation of flying saucers in 1969.

In the aftermath of the crash at Roswell, a number of policies were established. It would be forty years before they were understood. It would be forty years before their existence, as well as the documentation supporting them, would be uncovered. But it was the discovery at Roswell that set the tone for UFO research. Had the crash not taken place so soon after the first flying saucer reports were made, and had it not happened in such a remote section of the country, the history of the phenomenon might have been radically different.

The policy of secrecy became clear when Twining wrote his response to inquiries directed to the Air Materiel Command. This letter, classified as secret in 1947, has become all things to all sides of the UFO question. To understand it and its ramifications, it is necessary to look beyond it to the reasons why it was created, what it was meant to accomplish, and the mood of those in command positions during the summer of 1947.

The letter itself was drafted in response to an inquiry from Brigadier General George F. Schulgen, who was the assistant chief of staff for air intelligence. Schulgen, among others in the military and civilian intelligence agencies, including the FBI, had noticed an apparent lack of concern by the "Topside" about the flying saucer reports. In an undated page from FBI files that apparently accompanied a U.S. Army Air Force estimate of the situation dated July 30, 1947, an officer wrote, "Lack of topside [high-ranking officers at the "top"] inquiries, when compared to the prompt and demanding inquiries that have originated topside upon former events, give more than ordinary weight to the possibility that this is a domestic project, about which the President, etc. know."

The problem here was that the conclusion wasn't valid. The FBI had consulted with Colonel L. R. Forney of the Intelligence Division of the War Department (later the Defense Intelligence Agency). Forney told FBI Special Agent S. W. Reynolds that the discs were not Army or Navy vehicles. In fact, several agencies of the U.S. government, including the Atomic Energy Commission, were denying that the discs belonged to them or that there were any secret experiments that would account for the sightings.

The silence from the top said just the opposite. It appeared that the secrecy was so tight that even the highest levels of intelligence inside the Army Air Force were kept in the dark. Reynolds, who was also in contact with Lieutenant Colonel G. D. Garrett, who served under Schulgen and should have been in a position to know the answers, concluded that the discs were probably "a very highly classified experiment of the Army or Navy."

There was historical precedent for the belief. According to Garrett, when the ghost rockets were flying over Sweden in 1946, the "high brass" of the War Department "exerted tremendous pressure on the Air Forces Intelligence to conduct research and collect information in an effort to identify these sightings." In sharp contrast, there were now sightings over the United States and the "high brass" appeared to be "totally unconcerned." This led to the conclusion that the high brass already knew the answers to the questions about the identity of the objects. They just weren't interested in sharing the answer with those in the trenches.

FBI Agent Reynolds wasn't completely satisfied with the answer and called his liaison at the War Department, Colonel L. R. Forney. Forney had inquired about classified Army projects and learned that the Army had no idea what the discs were. Further checking by Garrett, even pressing Schulgen for an answer, demonstrated that Schulgen couldn't offer an explanation. It was agreed that the inquiry should be taken to a higher level. General Curtis LeMay, head of research and development, reported that "a complete survey of research activities discloses that the Army Air Forces has no project with the characteristics similar to those which have been associated with the Flying Discs."

It seemed that the question had been answered. Still, there were those concerned about the situation, so it was decided to make a direct request for information from the commanding officer of the Air Materiel Command, headquartered at Wright Field, Ohio. Accompanying the request to General Twining was the first of the intelligence community's estimates concerning the flying saucers. Although the study contained specifics of sixteen cases, the body of the resulting report mentions eighteen. These were the best sightings since the May 17 report from Oklahoma City and included the

Kenneth Arnold sighting, ending with a case from Elmendorf Field, Alaska. Five of the cases involved military pilots, including the Maxwell Field sighting by four pilots on June 28. Six of them were made by civilian pilots, including the July 4 sighting near Emmett, Idaho, made by a United Airlines flight crew.

The estimate contained conclusions based on the information used to prepare it. It seemed that the officers did not think the flying discs were much of a mystery. They believed they were mechanical, aerial objects. They just didn't know whose, but based on the lack of concern from the top, they believed that they had to be a classified U.S. project. It was the only conclusion that made sense to them.

This, then, was the situation in late summer of 1947. And this was the information that Twining's staff used to prepare the report to be sent down to Schulgen. They used nothing other than the information supplied to them, adding nothing to the discussion at all.

The response from Twining must have surprised everyone. They had believed that the AMC would know all about the flying discs, yet Twining was telling them, essentially, that the phenomenon was real and should be investigated but that the flying disks weren't ours.

In the letter, General Twining, following the recommendations of his staff, said that an investigation of the "flying discs" should be continued. The subject of the letter was "AMC Opinion Concerning 'Flying Discs.'" It was directed back to the Commanding General, U.S. Army Air Forces, in Washington, D.C., and was marked for the attention of Brigadier General George Schulgen.

The letter said:

> 1. As requested by AC/AS-2 there is presented below the considered opinion of this Command concerning the so-called "Flying Discs". This opinion is based on interrogation report data furnished by AC/AS-2 and preliminary studies by personnel of T-2 and Aircraft Laboratory,

Engineering Division T-3. This opinion was arrived at in a conference between personnel from the Air Institute of Technology, Intelligence T-2, Office, Chief of Engineering Division, and the Aircraft, Power Plant and Propeller Laboratories of Engineering Division T-3.

2. It is the opinion that:
   a. The phenomenon reported is something real and not visionary or fictitious.
   b. There are objects probably approximating the shape of a disc, of such appreciable size as to appear to be as large as man-made aircraft.
   c. There is a possibility that some of the incidents may be caused by natural phenomena, such as meteors.
   d. The reported operating characteristics such as extreme rates of climb, maneuverability (particularly in roll), and action which must be considered evasive when sighted or contacted by friendly aircraft and radar, lend belief to the possibility that some of the objects are controlled either manually, automatically or remotely.
   e. The apparent common description of the objects is as follows:
      (1) Metallic or light reflecting surface.

Page two began with the heading "Basic Ltr fr CG, AMC WF to CO, AAF, Wash. D.C. subj 'AMC Opinion Concerning "Flying Discs"'":

      (2) Absence of trail, except in a few instances when the object apparently was operating under high performance conditions.
      (3) Circular or elliptical in shape, flat on bottom and domed on top.

(4) Several reports of well kept formation flights varying from three to nine objects.

(5) Normally no associated sound, except in three instances a substantial rumbling roar was noted.

(6) Level flight speeds normally about 300 knots are estimated.

f. It is possible within the present U.S. knowledge—provided extensive detailed development is undertaken—to construct a piloted aircraft which has the general description of the object in sub-paragraph (e) above which would be capable of an approximate range of 7000 miles at subsonic speeds.

g. Any developments in this country along the lines indicated would be extremely expensive, time consuming and at the considerable expense of current projects and therefore, if directed, should be set up independently of existing projects.

h. Due considerations must be given the following:—

(1) The possibility that these objects are of domestic origin—the product of some high security project not known to AC/AS-2 or this command.

(2) The lack of physical evidence in the shape of crash recovered exhibits which would undeniably prove the existence of these objects.

(3) The possibility that some foreign nation has a form of propulsion possibly nuclear, which is outside of our domestic knowledge.

3. It is recommended that:

a. Headquarters, Army Air Forces issue a directive assigning a priority, security classification and Code

Name for a detailed study of this matter to include the preparation of complete sets of all available and pertinent data which will then be made available to the Army, Navy, Atomic Energy Commission, JRDB, the Air Force Scientific Advisory Board Group, NACA, and the RAND and NEPA projects for comments and recommendations, with a preliminary report to be forwarded within 15 days of receipt of the data and a detailed report thereafter every 30 days as the investigation develops. A complete interchange of data should be effected.

4. Awaiting a specific directive AMC will continue the investigation within its current resources in order to more closely define the nature of the phenomenon. Detailed Essential Elements of Information will be formulated immediately for transmittal thru channels.

N. F. Twining
Lieutenant General, U.S.A.
Commanding

The problem for researchers today is that one paragraph about the "lack of physical evidence in the shape of crash recovered exhibits." Clearly Twining and the highest-ranking members of his staff would have been notified if a flying disc had crashed. The laboratories and facilities to examine and exploit such a find were at the Wright Field–Patterson Field complex in Dayton, Ohio. Reverse engineering of captured foreign rockets, aircraft, and weapons was accomplished at the Foreign Technology Division there.

The argument can be made that no mention of the crash debris from Roswell was made because it had not been included in the reports forwarded to Twining. Since it wasn't included, Twining's staff saw no reason to inform Schulgen and others of its existence, especially since they could accomplish their task without mentioning it. While those in Washington were expecting AMC to tell them that no further investigation was necessary because the answers were held at the top, Twining was telling them that such was not the case. The investigation should be continued, and in fact it was recommended that a priority, classified, code-named project be created for the collection of intelligence about the flying discs. It also pointed out that the AMC would continue to investigate "to more closely define the nature of the phenomenon."

There is another consideration here, and that is the level of classification of both Schulgen's original requests and AMC's eventual response. First, it must be remembered that the Twining letter was classified "Secret." That meant that anyone with a secret clearance would have access to the information. Nearly every officer in the military is routinely granted a secret clearance. In addition, thousands of civilians working at the Pentagon and throughout the federal government also have secret clearances.

Second, if Roswell happened and debris was picked up, it would have been classified at a higher level than secret. In fact, the accepted wisdom is that the Roswell information is one of the highest and most tightly held secrets. Clearly it was classified as top secret in 1947 when the Twining letter was written and it continues to be classified top secret today. To include the data in the report would require that the whole report be classified as top secret.

While there is no reason why the report couldn't have been classified at a higher level, the protocols for dealing with top secret material are different than those for secret. Instead of keeping it in a safe, for example, top secret requires a vault. Access to top secret is limited and requires that it be signed out. If it is to be destroyed, two officers must be present to certify that the document has been properly destroyed. A single officer can destroy material classified as secret or lower.

What develops is a dilemma. What is happening here? On the one hand, those at certain levels of the intelligence community could learn nothing about the flying disks, the lack of "topside" interest suggesting that answers already existed and those at lower levels were going to give up searching. On the other, suddenly came a directive from on high that told them it was a serious problem and that a coordinated investigation should be a priority. That meant, quite simply, that the answers didn't exist at the top.

There is a second consideration here. If the flying discs were a top secret experiment of some kind, and if it was as closely held as it appears to have been, the last thing Twining and his staff would have done is suggest that a priority investigation be initiated. They would be telling lower-level officers to begin a campaign that had the mission of exposing the secret. They would put not only the resources of Army Intelligence into revealing the secret, but also those of the FBI, because of the interest shown by the Bureau.

Instead, had the flying discs been ours, Twining would have suggested that the whole project be dropped. If inquiries continued, a quiet word in the right ears would have stopped the investigation and possible compromise.

What Twining's response proves is that Twining and his staff, although aware of the Roswell crash, wanted to gather additional intelligence about the flying discs. They made the suggestion, but then added the statement about the lack of recovered debris. In other words, Twining was telling those ranked below him not to bother with the stories of flying saucer crashes because the debris didn't exist. He was shutting off one area of investigation, suggesting that those reports, prominent in the press, were hoaxes or misidentifications, as had been reported. He didn't want anyone looking into those reports because they would lead back to Roswell.

Of course, none of this answers the question of the Twining claim that there is a lack of crash debris. All it does is show that there was concern at a high level and that conclusions that those at the highest levels knew all about the flying discs are wrong.

Once again there is proof, but the proof, in the form of the documents, leaves something to be desired. Convincing arguments can be made in both directions, but in the end, all that can be said is that this is not the final word. Something more is needed.

UFO Crash at Roswell by Kevin D. Randle and Donald R. Schmitt In the first of the two books written by Randle and Schmitt, they tell the Roswell tale following, for the most part, the conventional wisdom of the day. The book is their reinvestigation of the Roswell UFO crash, told from their points of view and providing a chronology of their investigation.

As a basic book about the Roswell case, this is the one to read. It explains how the situation developed. It provides a list of the important witnesses and who they were in 1947. Randle and Schmitt discovered a number of witnesses who had not been identified and report on them. It is clear from the text that both now believe that a UFO crashed at Roswell, and they present the eyewitness testimony to support that belief.

If there is a flaw, it is the retelling of parts of the story. True, they lay out the information in the first section and then provide the details of that investigation in the second. Such a format does provide an insight into the way the information was developed and why it was accepted, but at times the repetition becomes a distraction.

UFO Crash at Roswell: The Genesis of a Modern Myth by Charles A. Ziegler and Charles B. Moore This book was designed, apparently, to take advantage of the publicity surrounding the fiftieth anniversary of the UFO crash outside Roswell. As has become fashionable, especially in academic circles, the authors assumed that the crash was not of an alien spacecraft and that this is the one time that Air Force investigators told the truth. With the Project Mogul explanation on the table, all that remained was for the authors of the five chapters to explain why people want to believe in a myth.

Much of the book seemed to be constructed without arguments in mind. What this means, simply, is that the authors appeared to take "academic" papers and rewrite them, substituting the words *Roswell* or *UFO* in places where other words such as *religion* had originally appeared. Two of the chapters seemed more concerned with a general discussion of myth rather than a specific discussion of Roswell. In other words, myth wasn't a hot topic, but Roswell was.

The most interesting and most relevant of the chapters was written by Charles Moore, who has been identified in the skeptical and journalistic communities as the man who "launched the Roswell myth." He was a member of the New York University project that was launching the Project Mogul balloons from Alamogordo in 1947.

Moore's section, because it deals specifically with the events of 1947 told from his perspective as a graduate student working on the balloon project, provides the best information. His technical discussions of the winds aloft, the composition of the atmosphere a hundred thousand feet above the surface of the Earth, and the trajectories of the balloons is interesting and seemingly scientific. Unfortunately, part of his proof that a Mogul balloon fell on the Brazel ranch is based on his memory of what happened to Flight No. 4. He remembers that it launched on June 4, 1947, and seemed to disappear from their monitoring equipment near Arabela, New Mexico. This important piece of the puzzle is accepted unquestionably by those who believe Mogul was responsible for the debris found by Mack Brazel, but there is no documentation to substantiate it.

The only written record for the June 4, 1947, launch is the

diary kept by Dr. Albert Carry. Moore, interpreting the entry, which does document a launch on June 4, believes that it suggests a full-blown array was attached to the cluster of balloons. Other researchers have suggested that the wording suggests only balloons because it says nothing about rawin targets. If there were no targets, then there was nothing to scatter the metallic debris, and therefore the Mogul explanation fails.

The book was designed as a debunker piece, as the bibliography points out. It references nearly every anti-Roswell book or article ever written but somehow misses most of the pro-Roswell material. It offers all the anti arguments but presents nothing from the pro side. It accepts Mogul as the explanation, ignoring the important testimonies of the witnesses who were on the scene but suggested that what was found was something more unusual than a weather balloon. It is a book that will probably disappear from sight quickly.

V-2 Rockets There are those who have claimed that the debris found by Mack Brazel was nothing more than the remains of a V-2 rocket that went astray. Ron Schaffner, writing in *UFO Brigantia*, suggests that the debris was the nose cone and parachute assembly from that errant V-2.

Schaffner makes a good case for why the government, the military, or the range officers and scientists at the White Sands Proving Grounds (later the White Sands Missile Range) might have wanted to cover up an errant rocket. According to Schaffner, a V-2 with a faulty gyroscope strayed off course on May 29, 1947. The missile crashed into a cemetery about a half mile south of Juarez, Mexico.

According to the records from White Sands, this was a modified V-2 made from captured German rocket parts. It was the second in a series of rockets fired by General Electric and Army Ordnance in connection with their Hermes II missile project. The official report says, "The rocket left the launching platform normally but no program was evident after 4 seconds. Observers at the emergency cut-off station realized the rocket was moving to the south slightly but judged the angle was so steep that the rocket would fall within the limits of the proving ground. Cut-off occurred at 46 seconds and the rocket landed near the site of Juarez in the Republic of Mexico."

V-2 rocket. (*Photo courtesy of Kevin Randle*)

The result of that error was a suspension of firings until the Chief of Ordnance could be convinced that future missile firings could be controlled. If a rocket was fired in violation of those orders only to fall onto open rangeland in central New Mexico, the men involved would certainly want that information kept secret. A V-2 was tested on July 3, 1947, and if there was a mistake on the parts of a few eyewitnesses, the V-2 might account for the debris found by Mack Brazel on the morning of July 5.

An examination of the facts surrounding V-2 firings in July 1947 will shed additional light on the theory. Descriptions of the debris, descriptions of the crash sites, and the extraordinary efforts to cordon off the area suggest that the crash was not of a V-2, but something else. When all the facts are brought into play, the area for speculation about the V-2, or any of the other rockets being tested at White Sands, shrinks to nonexistent.

Marcel, among others, described a debris field that was more consistent with an aircraft accident than a rocket crash. Several rocket experts, including Dr. Gerald Brown, explained that the V-2 would leave a crater with little debris scattered over the fields, not the widespread debris described by the eyewitnesses.

Schaffner explained that the Army later released a photo of Marcel holding material that resembled tin foil. There were at least seven photos taken in Fort Worth that show the shiny, foil-covered, ripped-apart radar target and black rubber remains of a balloon.

Schaffner said that he wasn't much of a betting man, but he would be willing to bet the pot that the photos taken in Fort Worth do indicate the "chute" of a V-2. In that case, he would lose the bet. Irving Newton, the weather officer, was convinced by his first sight of the debris that it was part of a rawin target balloon.

The evidence in the photographs themselves proves that Newton was right. The remnants show the radar reflecting targets, the balsa sticks used to support the structure, and even some of the rubberized sections of the balloon. There is no doubt that the debris photographed in Ramey's office was the remains of a balloon. There is no evidence, from any of the witnesses who were in the office that day or in the photographs themselves, to support the belief that it was part of a V-2.

Marcel, when interviewed more than thirty years after the event, described the size of the debris field, which would seem to rule out the aluminum foil chutes that Schaffner was proposing. According to the descriptions of those chutes, there was a chute of aluminum foil eight feet in diameter, made of ribbons covered with metallic mesh, and a second chute about fourteen feet in diameter that was deployed to slow descent. Neither contained enough material to cover the pasture to the extent reported.

The direct testimony of the eyewitnesses seems to suggest that Schaffner's theory of a crash V-2 is incorrect. While it is certainly possible that Marcel, even as the head of the intelligence section of the 509th Bomb Group, might not have known about the experiments in New Mexico with the V-2, he certainly would have been able to identify the components as something of terrestrial manufacture.

And even if Marcel had somehow been fooled, would the other officers of the 509th, including the commander, been unable to identify the foil, the parachute, and the capsule as being something made on Earth? The important point is that they wouldn't have to know it came from an errant V-2, only that it was made of materials like those manufactured elsewhere on the planet.

Many of the men of the 509th had been in the Army during
World War II and had been stationed in England during the V-2
attacks there. In other words, they were not unfamiliar with the
wreckage of the V-2. Pappy Henderson, a pilot with the 1st Air
Transport Unit stationed at Roswell in July 1947, even had a piece
of V-2 debris that he had picked up in England during the war.
According to Sappho Henderson, her husband described the
Roswell debris as "weird. It was like nothing he'd ever seen."

Another blow to Schaffner's theory comes from Capt. Sheridan
Cavitt, who when asked if he ever participated in the recovery of
material from a crashed V-2, said, "No. After the one that almost
hit a town (Juarez) they made sure that no errant rockets got close
to the ground again." Cavitt later underscored that he had never
participated in the recovery of any rocket or missile while he was
stationed at Roswell.

Cavitt took it further by saying that the men at Roswell
wouldn't have retrieved the material Brazel had found if it had been
a V-2. It is not that far from Alamogordo and the White Sands
Proving Ground to the Brazel ranch. Had it been a V-2, the material would have been reclaimed by the officers and men at White
Sands. And those at White Sands would have known the rocket was
missing, and even though they didn't have complete radar coverage
in that area, they would have known the general area where the missile landed. They would have been out to retrieve it long before
Mack Brazel walked into the Chaves County sheriff's office.

It is possible that all these people were somehow fooled, though
it seems unlikely. But that doesn't address the major point of
Schaffner's argument, that is, that an errant V-2 would have been
kept secret because officials at White Sands had attempted the
launch in violation of the ban imposed after the crash in Juarez. He
points out, correctly, that there was an attempted launch on July 3,
and that if there was a mistake about the date, the V-2 might
account for the debris.

The problem is that the launch on July 3 was an experiment

that never got off the pad. According to an article in the *Chicago Sun*, "A faulty mechanism was blamed today (July 4, 1947) for a V-2 rocket accident in which eight persons were sprayed with acid yesterday (July 3).

"Lt. Col. Harold R. Turner, commanding officer at the White Sands Proving Grounds, said the accident occurred while the Army prepared to fire the 25th German V-2 rocket from the field."

The *Los Angeles Times* of July 4 added to the story, reporting that "Acid showering from a German V-2 rocket burned two men seriously and caused minor injuries to six others . . . The injured, all military personnel, were flown to the Army's William Beaumont General Hospital, just across the state line at El Paso, Tex."

This confirms that the officers and officials at White Sands were not trying to keep the attempted launch a secret, not when the commander was giving statements to the press about the accident at the Proving Grounds.

There are additional facts that can be brought to bear. Dr. Gerald Brown was a NASA engineer. When the debris field and the metal were described to him, he had a few explanations to offer. He pointed out that an A-9, a two-stage rocket, could have created the gouge that had been reported on the crash site. He said that Duraluminum, used in the nose cone, was extremely tough and could account for some of the debris found. He said that some of the wiring on the V-2 and A-9 was such that heat would cause the interior of the wiring to melt, leaving a hollow tube that could give the impression of fiber optics. The Germans, in labeling some of the interior structures of the rockets, used a combination of the Greek alphabet, scientific notations, numbers, and geometric symbols. And as for the dead bodies, he mentioned that there were a few experiments where animals had been launched into space, possibly as early as 1947.

Duraluminum is very strong and has very good high-temperature properties. In other words, if Marcel had found a piece of Duraluminum, he might not have been able to burn it. However, repeated blows from a sledgehammer would cause it to shatter. Marcel didn't report that the metal shattered, only that they had been unable to scratch or dent it.

Brazel's description of the monofilament fishing line does not sound like a wire that has had the center melted from it. Brown also mentioned that the wire he described would be fairly brittle. It wouldn't take much to snap it.

In fact, most of Brown's suggestions didn't fit the descriptions of the material as reported by more than a dozen independent witnesses who saw it. Brown's Duraluminum and partially melted wire resembled the material in a very gross sense but did not match it.

Jesse Marcel Jr., who described the symbols he'd seen, said that he recognized none of them. Had they been from the Greek alphabet, scientific notations, Arabic numbers, or words in German, Marcel would have recognized them as such. He might not have been able to read them, but he certainly would have been able to identify them.

June Tyree, who has lived in the Corona area all her life, also deflects the V-2 or errant rocket theory. According to her, there were no rumors of such an event among the ranchers. Even when a secret experimental plane crashed in the mountains not far from Corona during World War II, the ranchers heard about it, and many teenagers drove up to see it. But there was never a rumor of a rocket or missile from White Sands crashing so close to Corona.

Brown was left with no explanation for the bodies. Descriptions of them by the people who saw them suggested that they weren't human and that they weren't animals. Even human bodies that had been burned in an intense fire didn't match the descriptions. And those who were on the debris field or the impact site where the bodies were found were uniform in their descriptions. There had been no fire, though Frank Kaufmann had mentioned scorching on the ground away from the point of impact.

Schaffner mentioned that Rhesus monkeys were launched as part of the experiments in the early 1950s. He found no evidence that monkeys had been used in 1947. Rhesus monkeys are small animals, about the size of a large house cat, and certainly wouldn't be confused with the remains of a human pilot.

Wright-Patterson's Aeromedical Lab did conduct five biological flights using the V-2. The problem is that they began on June 11, 1948, or nearly a year after the debris had been found by Brazel. More important, those experiments were badly botched, and they contained only a single animal (including mice) and not three or four. It should be noted that they failed in each of the five attempts to recover a living specimen. Each died as a result of a parachute failure, or when the missile failed to perform as programmed. And there was no attempt to cover up any of these mistakes.

In our private discussions with Brown, he would not move away from the idea that the debris or the gouge could have been caused by a V-2 or an A-9. He did say, however, "If you gentlemen can prove that it wasn't a rocket, then I don't know what you have."

What Brown didn't know was that there was only a four-day window of opportunity for the V-2 crash. Brazel told Bill Rickett that he'd been in the field four days before and there had been no wreckage there then.

The only attempted launch of a V-2 in that time frame was the ill-fated July 3 event. It never got off the ground and was reported in the newspapers, and therefore cannot account for the debris found by Brazel. In fact, according to the records from White Sands, there was a V-2 launch on May 16, the attempt on July 3, and another on July 10. On May 29 there was the Hermes II launch, and on June 12, a WAC B was launched. There is nothing in the records that fits into the four-day window for a crash on the Brazel ranch.

What we have is speculation that what was found was the remnants of a V-2 and the suggestion that a ban on launches forced the officials at White Sands to try to cover up their blunder. The descriptions of the debris by the men and women who handled it do not match that of an aluminum and mesh parachute. The debris field is too large for a V-2, the gouge is not consistent with a V-2, and the accounts of bodies do not fit the speculation that they were animals. The photos taken in Fort Worth, which Schaffner didn't examine, clearly show the remains of a Rawin target device and a rubber balloon.

While it is true that men trying to protect their careers after an errant V-2 crash might hide the truth, it is not true that the cover-up would extend for over forty years. When those men moved on or retired, the evidence of the cover-up would have begun to surface.

But the most damaging item is the report from the *Chicago Sun* and the *Los Angeles Times*, to name two sources. There is the story of that attempted launch spread over the papers for the world to see. If there was a cover-up, it wasn't very effective in 1947. Had the debris discovered near Roswell been the results of a V-2, documents to prove it would exist, and none do. The search for the truth of what happened in Roswell no longer must address the V-2 theory. It just doesn't account for all the facts.

Whitmore Jr., Walt There is one witness, unidentified by Karl Pflock but named "Reluctant" by him, who provided the best clues to the Mogul balloon array explanation for the Roswell crash. Pflock wrote that Reluctant wanted to keep his name out of the story, and given the facts, it is not surprising. If Reluctant was identified, it would become clear that Reluctant's story, as told to Pflock, was significantly different from what he told William Moore in the late 1970s.

Reluctant is Walt Whitmore Jr., a lifelong resident of Roswell. He was in the house when his father brought Mack Brazel home, and heard the story of the debris field directly from Brazel. There is no reason not to identify Reluctant today. He died a number of years ago.

Describing the testimony of Reluctant (Whitmore), Pflock wrote, "Brazel sketched a map for me, showing which roads to take and how to find the site. I drove there alone . . . a distance of 65 or 70 miles. No one was there when I arrived, I do not remember seeing any sign that anyone had been on the site . . . I am certain I was on the site before any military personnel got there."

According to Whitmore, "The site was a short distance from a ranch road. The debris covered a fan- or roughly triangle-shaped area, which was 10 or 12 feet wide at what I thought was the top end. From there it extended about 100 to 150 feet widening out to

150 feet at the base . . . The material was very light. I could see it blowing in the wind."

Whitmore, according to Pflock, described the material as "white, linen-like cloth with reflective tinfoil attached to one side. Some pieces were glued to balsa wood sticks, and some of them had glue on the cloth side, with bits of balsa still stuck to it. Most of the pieces were no larger than four or five inches on a side, although I found one or two about the size of a sheet of typing paper. None of the sticks was more than a foot or so long."

Whitmore told Pflock, and researcher Kevin Randle, that he had collected some of the material and taken it home. Pflock reported that Whitmore told him, "It is . . . stored in a safe and secure place." He told Randle that it had been in a safe deposit box for a number of years, but that he had removed it so that it was now somewhere in his "junk room."

Those aren't the only statements made by Reluctant on the record. Although the source is less than sterling, Charles Berlitz and William Moore report in *The Roswell Incident* that Whitmore "said that while he did not see the actual crash site until after the Army Air Force had 'cleaned it up,' he did see some of the wreckage brought into town by the rancher. His description was that it consisted mostly of a very thin but extremely tough metallic foil-like substance and some small beams."

Interestingly, Berlitz and Moore also report Whitmore telling them, "Some of this material had a sort of writing on it which looked like numbers that had been either added or multiplied. He recalls that his father went out to the site in a Buick but was turned back by armed MPs who had set up a road block."

Other aspects of Whitmore's statements to Pflock are corroborated by *The Roswell Incident*. According to the book, Whitmore "ventured out to the site and found a stretch of about 175–200 yards of pasture land up-rooted in a sort of fan-like pattern with most of the damage at the narrowest part of the fan . . ."

Whitmore also provided Berlitz and Moore with a description

of the material. "[T]he largest piece of this material that he saw was about four or five inches square, and that it was very much like lead foil in appearance but could not be torn or cut at all. It was extremely light weight."

Comparing Whitmore's testimony to Berlitz and Moore with that given to Pflock, a few changes are found. In the 1990s, Whitmore described seeing the debris, but with Berlitz and Moore he only described seeing the remains of the cleanup effort. He mentioned seeing debris, but in the custody of the sheriff.

Whitmore's description of the material, as detailed in the Berlitz and Moore book, is more consistent with that provided by others such as Marcel, Brazel, and Rickett than it is in his later interviews. When Randle spoke to him, it was clear that he was describing something that sounded like the material used in balloon construction. It is also clear that his description of the material has changed over the years. What he described in the mid-1990s was not what he described about twenty years earlier.

Whitmore's story has grown since he first told it to Moore. It has changed significantly since he first was interviewed, and his description now resembles a weather balloon. And though he claimed to have bits of the debris, he was never able to produce it. Had he been able to do that, then the discussions about his testimony would be different. Without the debris to corroborate his tale, it is one that stands alone.

Wilcox, Sheriff George A. Years later George A. Wilcox, the Chaves County Sheriff in July 1947, would complain about the way the military handled the retrieval of the flying saucer. He was angry with himself for bringing the military into it because they claimed jurisdiction and completely cut him out of it. And there were the threats made by the military during the days that followed. If he'd had it to do over again, he said, he would have notified the press first, and let the reporters get to the crash site before he told the Army a thing about it.

Mack Brazel arrived at the jail sometime on the afternoon of Sunday, July 6, according to the witnesses. Deputy B. A. Clark took the initial report and then turned it over to Sheriff Wilcox. Because Brazel was an old-time cowboy, dressed in old clothes and scuffed boots, Wilcox didn't pay much attention when Brazel walked in. But Brazel not only brought a story of a crashed flying saucer, he had some of the material with him. It was material that neither Wilcox nor Clark could identify.

Wilcox decided that the best thing to do was call the military at the base. According to his daughter, Phyllis McGuire, the military arrived at the office almost as soon as the sheriff got off the phone. There had been no discussion about Brazel being crazy or whether the sheriff was sure the material was unusual. The military officers came as soon as they were notified.

McGuire doesn't remember exactly who arrived. She was chased out of the jail while the men discussed what Brazel had found. They were in a small room off the main office, with Brazel and a box of the debris that he brought with him. She did remember, however, that her father sent two of his deputies out to the ranch.

Jay Tulk, husband of Wilcox's daughter Elizabeth, arrived at the jail after the military. He asked the sheriff what was going on with all the military vehicles parked outside. Tulk and Wilcox retreated to the small room where the debris was stored and talked about it there.

The soldiers and Brazel left the office. Wilcox called the base, but no one there had any new information. With Brazel and the officers now gone, things quieted down.

On Monday, July 7, there was no further news. But on Tuesday things changed radically. Wilcox, wondering what was happening, dispatched two deputies to the ranch. McGuire and her sister, Elizabeth Tulk, thought that the sheriff might have traveled out there himself. Barbara Dugger, Elizabeth's daughter, also said that Wilcox himself had gone. She got the information from Inez

Wilcox, her grandmother. It doesn't matter now whether it was two deputies, or the sheriff and a deputy. Whoever it was, they couldn't get close. The Army had cordoned off the roads and was stopping and turning back all traffic, even deputy sheriffs.

Wilcox then tried to get more answers from the military at the base, but again, no one had much to say. Then, Walter Haut issued the famous press release. From that point the sheriff and his deputies were busy fielding phone calls from around the world. McGuire said that her father was up all night taking calls from Germany, England, France, and Italy, as well as every state in the union.

Soon afterward, on July 9 or 10, Wilcox was visited by military officers. They wanted to retrieve the box of debris that Brazel had left in the small room in the sheriff's office. The sheriff had made sure that the box was guarded. Now the military wanted it, and they ordered the sheriff to say as little as possible about the recent events, and to refer all calls to the base.

Although Wilcox was a civilian law enforcement officer, he did have a working relationship with the base. When

Sheriff George A. Wilcox. (*Photo courtesy of Paul Davids*)

one of the men at the base got into trouble in town, the sheriff would alert the provost marshal. To maintain the status quo, and because it seemed that the crash was a military matter, Wilcox felt obligated to keep the facts to himself.

McGuire wanted to know more about what had happened. She

pestered her father, asking questions about what Brazel had found, what the military had been doing there, and about the flying saucer itself. Finally her mother, Inez, knowing exactly what the military had said and that they had ordered complete silence, told McGuire to stop asking questions.

Years later, Barbara Dugger, while living with Inez, learned more about the events of July 1947. According to Dugger, Inez (known as Big Mom by the family) told her that a flying saucer had crashed near Roswell. She made Dugger promise never to tell because the military had sworn her and her husband to secrecy.

According to Dugger, the sheriff knew more about the crash than he would ever let on. Inez told her granddaughter that there had been bodies found, little men with big heads wearing gray suits that were like silk, and that there had been a burned area and metallic debris. Inez and the sheriff never discussed the crash except during that week in 1947. The military had cordoned off the area and refused to let anyone through who did not have official military business.

Dugger wanted to know more, but Inez was hesitant to talk about it. However, the story was something that she'd kept buried inside her long enough. She had to tell someone. She cautioned Dugger a number of times, telling her that she could never tell anyone what she was about to hear.

Dugger said that someone had come into the office (obviously Brazel) and told the sheriff about the incident. She said, "My grandfather went out there and when he got out there, there was a big burned area . . . they saw debris. He saw debris. I don't know if he was alone . . . It was in the evening."

Dugger asked if he'd seen little space beings and was told "there were four of them."

"What did they have on?"

"They were, like gray . . . their heads were large and the little suit they had on was like silk or something . . . like that kind of material."

Dugger wanted to know if the little men were alive or dead.

"She said I think one of them was alive. I said, 'Did granddaddy help it?' and she said, 'I don't know.' And that was that. She didn't tell me anything else."

Dugger made it clear that her grandmother had not seen this, but was repeating what the sheriff had told her after he had returned that evening. Dugger pointed out that her grandfather would never talk about it. The events were a shock to him. She said that after this he never wanted to be sheriff again. He'd had it. Inez ran for sheriff, but in the late 1940s Chaves County wasn't ready for a female sheriff, and she lost.

Dugger pointed out that the sheriff's job was one that required both her grandparents to spend days at the jail. Inez took care of the recordkeeping and the day-to-day administration. Inez knew as much about the operation of the office as the sheriff.

The discussion had taken place in the early 1970s. Dugger, who was living with her grandmother at the time, was watching one of the moon landings, and it was then that Inez told her about the flying saucer.

The thing that most impressed Dugger was the action of the military. Once the initial flap was over and they had recovered the box of debris, Wilcox was visited again. Dugger, repeating what Inez had told her, said, "When the incident happened, the military police came into the jailhouse and told George and I (that) if (we) ever told anything about this incident, talked about it in any way, not only would we be killed, but they would get the rest of the family."

Dugger asked, "Did you hear them say that, Big Mom," and she said, "Yes, I did."

Dugger said that Inez and the sheriff believed the threat. They didn't think the military officers were joking about it. According to Dugger, when the military men spoke, "she sat up and listened." She said that her grandmother was a loyal citizen and that "those men were not kidding." The military never contacted them again.

Wilcox was never told what Brazel had found. In an article written by Inez several years after the event, she said, "However, the

officer who picked up the suspicious saucer, admonished Mr.
Wilcox to tell as little as possible about it and refer all calls to
Walker Air Force Base."

Wilcox's role, which at first had seemed minor, was in fact very
important. Without his phone call, the information might have
spread farther and faster, so that the Army would have been unable
to contain it. With that phone call, Wilcox became a major player
in one of the most successful military disinformation operations of
all time.

See also *Wilcox, Inez*

Wilcox, Inez Although it was not published while she was alive,
Inez Wilcox, wife of the Roswell sheriff, wrote an article about her
"Four Years in the County Jail." She envisioned it as a story for
Reader's Digest telling about the years her husband had been the
Chaves County sheriff.

The article, written before the story of the Roswell UFO crash
returned to the national media, provides a glimpse of what was happening at the sheriff's office in the summer of 1947. Wilcox wrote:

> One day a rancher North of town brought in, what
> he called a "FLYING SAUCER", there had been many
> reports all over the United States by people who claimed
> they had seen a FLYING SAUCER. the rumors were in
> many variations, The saucer was from a different planet,
> and the people flying on it, were looking us over. The
> Germans had invented this strange contraption, a
> formible weapon. Other tales, that one had landed and
> strange looking people all seven foot tall or more walked
> from it, but quickly departed on sighting any on looker.
> All the papers played the stories up, and many people
> searched the skies at night to catch sight of one. Since
> no one had seen a flying saucer, Mr Wilcox called head-
> quarters at Walker Air Force Base, and reported the

find. Before he hung up the telephone almost, an officer walked in. He quickly loaded the object into a truck and that was the last glimpse any one had of it.

Simultaneously the telephone began to ring, long distance calls from News papers in New York, England, France Government officials, Military officials, and the calls kept up for 24 hours straight. They would speak to no one but the Sheriff. However the Officer who picked up the suspicious looking saucer, admonished Mr Wilcox to tell as little as possible about it and refer all calls to Walker Air Force Base. A secret well kept, for to this day, we never found out if this was really a flying saucer.

Although she talked to her granddaughter Barbara Dugger about the UFO sighting, she didn't mention it to others. The statement she wrote about the incident is so ambiguous that it could be claimed by all sides in the debate as proving their point. Her statements to Dugger help clarify the situation, as Dugger understood it, but Inez Wilcox did little other than prove that the sheriff had been asked not to talk about a matter that could have serious ramifications.

Willmon, Anna There are new witnesses being identified all the time. Some of them come forward with their tales, but others, such as Anna Willmon, are found through investigative work. She didn't come forward to tell her tale, but she did agree to talk to investigators once it was learned that she believed she had seen the Roswell craft and the bodies from it.

By the time investigators found her, Anna Willmon was elderly. Her mind was not as sharp as it once had been. She had vague memories of the events and tried as best she could to tell what she had seen.

She said she had been in the Capitan Mountains west of Roswell with her husband. They were returning to Roswell when her husband saw something shining and stopped to look for it. They turned to the north from the old Pine Lodge Road, twenty or so miles from Roswell. Willmon said that she thought the property now belonged to the Corns. She said that she didn't know who owned that land in 1947.

Together they worked their way toward the object, moving through the brush. They found an object that reminded her of an overturned washtub. It wasn't very large, maybe twelve or so feet long. She did see the bodies of the flight crew, "little guys," she called them. She said it looked as if one of them had gotten out of the craft, walked a short distance, then laid down. He wasn't very big.

She said that she could see little of the skin and didn't see the eyes, so she couldn't describe them. The skin looked like burnt rubber, a grayish-brownish color that was hard to define.

She said that she went back to the car so that she could search for a telephone. She called the military to let them know that they had found something. Again she said that it was on the Corn ranch, but that she didn't remember who owned it then.

Neither she nor her husband was at the craft when the military arrived. They met the truck near the road and gave them instructions. They left the scene and didn't talk to anyone about what they had seen.

Willmon kept no diary and wrote no letters, and those she had known in 1947 who might have been able to corroborate what she said in 1994 were long dead. All that she had now was a tale that fit, generally, into the scheme of things told by a number of other witnesses. There was no proof of what she told.

To be fair, the timing of her story, that they were on the scene in the late afternoon, does not fit. The location, not far off the Pine Lodge Road, is too far south of the Corn site as it is identified today. It is interesting that she brought up the Corns, but it is also possible, given the interview date of 1994, that she had heard something about the impact site location being situated on the Corn ranch. Although the Corn location was not well known in 1994, it was not secret, either.

Willmon did the best she could answering questions about what she had seen. It was clear that she was sincere, but it was also clear that she wasn't as sharp as she once had been. Shortly after the interview, she moved from Roswell to California. She died in California about a year later.

Woody, William In July 1947, William Woody was only thirteen years old and living eight to ten miles south of Roswell. While watching the night sky with his father, they saw a bright white light with red streaks in it. The light took a long time to fall, finally disappearing behind the terrain to the northwest of the farm.

Woody said that there was no shape behind the light. It was a bright glow with a red tail that seemed to brighten once or twice. It was in sight for several seconds, giving Woody and his father an opportunity to study the light. Woody said that it was larger than a meteor and so bright that it made an impression on him that has lasted all these years.

A neighbor, Jeff Hopper, also reported the light. There was no sound associated with it. It was off to the southwest and moving to the north. Hopper doesn't remember much about it now, and his advanced age might be part of the problem. He did confirm that the light he and his neighbors saw was something real and that he didn't believe it was a meteor.

Some time in the next day or two, Woody and his father tried to drive out to the area where they thought the object had come down. Given the size of the light, larger than any meteor they had ever seen, they were convinced that it had landed somewhere to the northwest of Roswell. Both believed that they could find something.

But according to Woody, the military had blocked the Vaughn Highway (Highway 285, which runs through Roswell and north to

Vaughn and eventually to Santa Fe). All the access roads that led off to the west had been blocked by military vehicles. No one was allowed into the area, and they were forced to turn around. Woody himself said that he saw the military but he hadn't gotten out of the truck. His dad said that the military wouldn't let them enter any of the side roads. They had no choice but to turn around.

Woody said that he had no doubt that the light he saw was related to the crash. He believes that because of the military roadblocks outside Roswell when they tried to find the light. Woody, his father, and Jeff Hopper are among the very few people who reported seeing something on the night of the crash.

XB-35 See *Flying Wing*

XF-95A This experimental aircraft has been suggested as a possible culprit in the Roswell crash. It was a single-seat fighter with a delta wing design. The thick fuselage as well as the delta wing design were somewhat reminiscent of the craft reported at Roswell. Research, however, showed that the first flights of the XF-95A didn't take place until September 1948. That effectively eliminates it as a candidate.

YB-49 The jet-powered version of the Northrop flying wing, first flown in October 1947.

    See also *Flying Wing*

Lightning Source UK Ltd.
Milton Keynes UK
UKHW040852300920
370788UK00001B/74

9 780380 798537